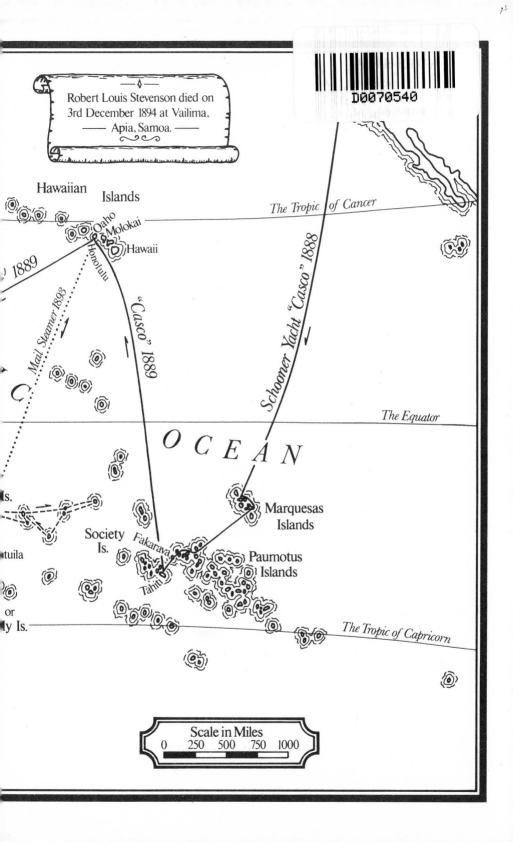

Robert Louis Stevenson died on
3rd December 1894 at Vailima,
—— Apia, Samoa. ——

D0070540

Hawaiian Islands

The Tropic of Cancer

Oaho Molokai
Honolulu Hawaii

1889

Mail Steamer 1893

"Casco" 1889

"Casco" 1889

Schooner Yacht "Casco" 1888

The Equator

O C E A N

s.

Marquesas
Islands

Society
Is. Fakarava
tuila
Paumotus
Islands

Tahiti

or
y Is.
The Tropic of Capricorn

# THE
# ROBERT LOUIS STEVENSON
# TREASURY

## Also by Alanna Knight

*Fiction*

LEGEND OF THE LOCH

THE OCTOBER WITCH

THIS OUTWARD ANGEL

CASTLE CLODHA

LAMENT FOR LOST LOVERS

THE WHITE ROSE

A STRANGER CAME BY

THE WICKED WYNSLEYS

*Historical novels*

THE PASSIONATE KINDNESS

A DRINK FOR THE BRIDGE

CASTLE OF FOXES

THE BLACK DUCHESS

COLLA'S CHILDREN

*Non-fiction*

SO YOU WANT TO WRITE

*Plays*

THE PRIVATE LIFE OF R.L.S.

GIRL ON AN EMPTY SWING

*Radio*

DON ROBERTO
(R. B. Cunninghame Graham)

ACROSS THE PLAINS
(R. L. Stevenson)

# THE
# ROBERT LOUIS STEVENSON
## TREASURY

Compiled by
ALANNA KNIGHT

**SHEPHEARD-WALWYN**

© ALANNA KNIGHT, 1985

First published in 1985 by
Shepheard-Walwyn (Publishers) Limited
26 Charing Cross Road,
London WC2H 0DH

British Library Cataloguing in Publication Data

Knight, Alanna
    Robert Louis Stevenson Treasury
    1.   Stevenson, Robert Louis—Criticism and
    interpretation
    I. Title
    828'.809      PR5496
    ISBN 0-85683-052-6

Printed in Great Britain by A. Wheaton & Co. Ltd., Exeter

To John Cairney
actor and friend

# Acknowledgments

Some 200 books have been written about Stevenson on both sides of the Atlantic, and countless articles by the famous and not so famous have contributed to his legend. In my research for this book, I have consulted as many books and articles as I could lay hands on, including the Tusitala Edition of his collected works, and exhaustive searches in the archives have revealed a great deal, but by no means all, of the literature about him. Inevitably much material has eluded the compilers of libraries and is missing from private collections of Stevensoniana. It is gratifying, however, that passing years unveil manuscripts by Stevenson himself, such as *The Cévennes Journal* and *An Old Song*.

In my research over the past ten years two works have proved outstanding: *Voyage To Windward* by J.C. Furnas (Faber & Faber, London, 1952) – for Stevenson students this remains the outstanding and definitive biography – and *The Violent Friend* by Margaret Mackay (Doubleday, New York, 1968), the story of Mrs. R.L. Stevenson. I am indebted to Mr. Furnas and to Doubleday for permission to quote from these two works.

In the compilation of any reference book, a comprehensive, up-to-date bibliography is an absolute essential; I most gratefully acknowledge the invaluable assistance of Roger G. Swearingen's *The Prose Writings of Robert Louis Stevenson* (Macmillan, London, 1980).

Many thanks also to:

Mrs. Jaqueline Kavanagh, BBC Written Archives; Elizabeth Sutter, BBC Glasgow and Janice Herwig, CBC Toronto, for dealing promptly with my written enquiries and for providing material for the Radio and Television section;

Patricia M. Howell, of Beinecke Rare Book and Manuscript Library, Yale University Library, New Haven, Connecticut, Sara S. Hodson, of the Huntington Library, San Marino, California, and Ellen Shaffer, Curator of the Silverado Museum, St. Helena, California, for furnishing details of unpublished manuscripts by Stevenson;

Charles Scribner's Sons, New York, for permission to quote from Lloyd Osbourne's *An Intimate Portrait*;

Anthony P. Shearman, City Librarian, Sheena McDougall and Margaret Mackay of the Edinburgh Room, Edinburgh Central Library, for answering numerous queries;

Michael Smethurst, University Librarian and the staff of Aberdeen University Library;

*Acknowledgments*

Dr. Konrad Hopkins, of Wilfion Books, Paisley, for so kindly adding to my collection of Stevensoniana;

Anthony Werner, Barry Shaw and Margaret Stovold from Shepheard-Walwyn (Publishers) Ltd., London, and my editor and friend, Iseabail Macleod of Edinburgh, with all of whom I have worked in the closest harmony during the producing and editing of this work.

Finally, to my husband Alistair, not only for his patience and moral support but for his assistance in ferrying books and taking copies: to him my gratitude and love are boundless.

# Contents

# List of Illustrations & Maps

# Introduction

Robert Louis Stevenson suffered the fate of one destined to be a legend in his own lifetime. News of his early death in Samoa in 1894 aged only forty-four – not from consumption but from a cerebral haemorrhage brought about by overwork – had hardly reached London and New York before its extraordinary effect became apparent. Everyone, it seemed, was rushing into print. Those who had ever been in Edinburgh's New Town were determined to write lyrically about Leerie the Lamplighter and the wan-faced child staring out of the windows of 17 Heriot Row. Every man who had bent an elbow in a Leith Walk howff had a tale to tell about 'yon Stevenson laddie; "Velvet Coat" they called him'; while every woman who had sighed at the sight of his bizarre and romantic figure striding cloaked down Princes Street, or leaning over the North Bridge, was determined to write about this marvel for the local newspaper or literary magazine. University Library shelves in the English-speaking world grew heavy with dust-covered theses by worthy Eng.Lit. students speculating on the origins of his lesser-known works and plays.

The spate continues nearly a century later. In paradise, Stevenson must smile. He entertained no such exalted ideas about his own importance as a writer. He described his adventure yarns as 'tushery'; 'No need for psychology or fine writing', he wrote to Henley of *Treasure Island*. 'It's awful fun, boys' stories; you just indulge the pleasure of your heart, that's all; no trouble, no strain . . . just drive along as the words come and the pen will scratch.'

Meeting George Saintsbury at the Savile Club one day, Stevenson opened what threatened to be a stiff converstion with the words, 'I'm told you think what I write is rot'. 'No', replied the professor, 'I think *some* of what you write is rot. Now, will you come and dine with me tonight?' Stevenson accepted and a friendship developed with respect on both sides.

Stevenson's letters reveal his self-doubts; he was constantly questioning and reviewing his own abilities. Never lulled into false attitudes when popularity came his way, he was the first to admit that his prose often fell short and that he had his good days – a precious few – and his bad days – a great many. Sometimes he did write rot. Then there were occasions when he spoke with the tongues of angels and others when he had the divine gift of prophecy. Besides possessing the magnetism of a brilliant talker, he had a splendid ear and the rare ability to use the Scots language in readable prose.

His writing life was short, but prolific; thirteen novels in twelve years. These include two unfinished ones, *St. Ives* and *Weir of Hermiston*, and two in collaboration with his stepson Lloyd Osbourne. Childless, Stevenson loved children and had a boy's sense of fun. *The Wrong Box* tickled his sense of the ridiculous: 'Nothing like a little judicious levity', remarks one of the main characters. 'Nor can any excuse be found', adds Stevenson in his preface. 'The authors' (himself and Lloyd) 'can but add that one of them is old enough to be ashamed of himself and the other young enough to learn better.'

Apart from the opium-induced *Jekyll and Hyde*, his novels were not inspired but written out of desperation; out of hunger and the need to survive. Newly-wed, with a wife and child to support, he also had the urge to gratify the *bon viveur*'s expensive tastes in wine. His doctor had recommended wine for his health, advice with which Stevenson was more than ready to comply. His health also demanded a constant and expensive search for places in the sun.

My own introduction to Robert Louis Stevenson began with *A Child's Garden of Verses* in kindergarten days, then as a schoolgirl seeing Spencer Tracy in the movie 'Dr. Jekyll and Mr. Hyde'. To this day, I can clearly remember that long walk home afterwards in a thick November fog, a terrifying experience. *Treasure Island* I read to my small sons as we sailed in a stormy Mediterranean one December, heading for the Middle East. It was not until my elder boy's English project much later that I learned the history of *Treasure Island* and discovered to my delight that Stevenson's most famous work was conceived at Braemar, a mere sixty miles from where we lived.

'My native air was more unkind than man's ingratitude; and I must consent to pass a good deal of my time between four walls . . .' The words held magic and they began my own quest for Stevenson. I saw him at 31, tubercular, full of fears for the future, thin to emaciation, fussed over by too many mothers from the cradle to the grave: Margaret Stevenson and Cummy, his nurse, later his wife Fanny and stepdaughter Belle.

'On a chill September morning, by the cheek of a brisk fire, and the rain drumming on the window . . .' these words were my personal key to unlock a world of magic. I read everything I could lay hands on – biographies, magazines features, articles. Actor John Cairney asked me to write a play for him about Stevenson. I did so, and from that sprang *The Passionate Kindness*, the story of .Stevenson's love for Fanny Osbourne. Radio talks and documentaries led to further research, and in compiling this volume, I have learned more and more about Stevenson. At every turn there is some new facet, some undreamed-of angle on the man and the writer. It seems one can never learn it all. It is as if he still lives, just a little way off, a personality constantly developing, expanding, enlightening. Every work I read leads me further on this insatiable quest. Henry James described Stevenson's life as 'a fable, more romantic than any he had written'. I hope that you, the reader, idly turning a page or following the thread of a cross-reference, will feel Stevenson's magic reaching out to touch your life in that same way, and that this moment for you will be the beginning of the great adventure of Robert Louis Stevenson.

Alanna Knight
Aberdeen
1984

# Reader's Guide

In compiling this *Treasury* my intention has been to assemble in one volume as much as possible of the material which has accumulated on the life and work of Robert Louis Stevenson. The sole restriction has been to confine the subject matter to what has appeared in the English language.

For ease of reference the material has been arranged in the eight Parts outlined below. Each has a separate alphabetical sequence and is cross-referenced internally and to other Parts.

1. **People, Places and the Printed Word**
   This, the main section of the book, is more than a bibliography, giving information on all aspects of Stevenson the man and writer. A wide variety of sources has been consulted, uncovering much that is new, including stories and anecdotes by those who loved him and those who loathed him; details of how his works came to be written; accounts of the numerous places he visited on his travels and the many interesting people he met.

   As his most popular works have been published in so many editions, bibliographical information is limited to details of first publication as well as the volume number in the Tusitala Edition. For further information readers are referred in Part 8 to existing bibliographies.

2. **Unpublished Manuscripts**
   Listed by title and with reference to the library or collection where it is kept.

3. **Fictional Characters and Places**
   An index of over 450 of the main characters, places, etc. in his novels, short stories and plays.

4. **Index of Letters from Stevenson**
   Listed under the recipient's name with a brief description of the content, date and place of writing.

5. **Index of Poems and Musical Settings**
   Poems are listed under first line and title with references to the Tusitala Edition. This is followed by a list of musical settings.

6. **Films, Television and Radio**
   A catalogue of films made in the United Kingdom and the United States, together with cast lists, producers, directors and so on. Adaptations of works by or about Stevenson from the archives of the British and Canadian Broadcasting Corporations are also included.

7. **Classified List of Stevenson's Published Works**
   This list gives title and date of first publication and, for short stories,

essays, etc., the collection in which they eventually appeared.

To it is appended a list of contents of the Tusitala Edition, which remains the most popular collection of Stevenson's works.

8. **Further Reading**

A list is provided for general interest and for more detailed bibliographical information.

# Chronology

Many of the dates concerning Robert Louis Stevenson's life and works may be more precisely fixed from his letters (see Part 4). A selection of publications has also been included to emphasise that Stevenson's writings were always prolific despite chronic ill-health and constant wanderings in search of a place where his life might be prolonged for a few more years.

1850   13 November, born 8 Howard Place, Edinburgh.
1852   Alison Cunningham (Cummy) enters the household to become his nurse.
1853   Move to 1 Inverleith Terrace, Edinburgh (now No. 9).
1857   Move to 17 Heriot Row; Stevenson's education begins at Henderson's Preparatory School, Edinburgh.
1863   Tour with his parents on the Continent.
1867   Summer, family acquire Swanston Cottage at the foot of the Pentland Hills as a country retreat.
      November, Stevenson enters Edinburgh University in the faculty in engineering.
1869   2 March, elected to Speculative Society.
1871   April, gives up engineering for law. Six essays in *Edinburgh University Magazine*, January-April.
      Autumn, entered the Edinburgh firm of W.F. Skene and Peacock for legal training.
1872   Spring, Bridge of Allan and Dunblane.
      July, visits Germany with Sir Walter Simpson.
      9 November, passes preliminary examinations for the Scottish Bar.
      December to –
1873   January, Bridge of Allan and Malvern.
      July, meets Fanny Sitwell and Sidney Colvin at Cockfield Rectory, Suffolk, home of his cousin Mrs. Maud (Balfour) Babington.
      November to – 'Roads' in *Portfolio*, December, first published essay.
1874   April, Menton, France.
      May-June, Edinburgh and Swanston; London and Hampstead to stay with Colvin; 3 June, elected to Savile Club.
      July-August, cruises the Inner Hebrides with Simpson. August, 'Notes on the Movements of Young Children', and 'On the Enjoyment of Unpleasant Places', in *Portfolio*.
      November, resumes law classes.
      December, London and Cambridge with Colvin.

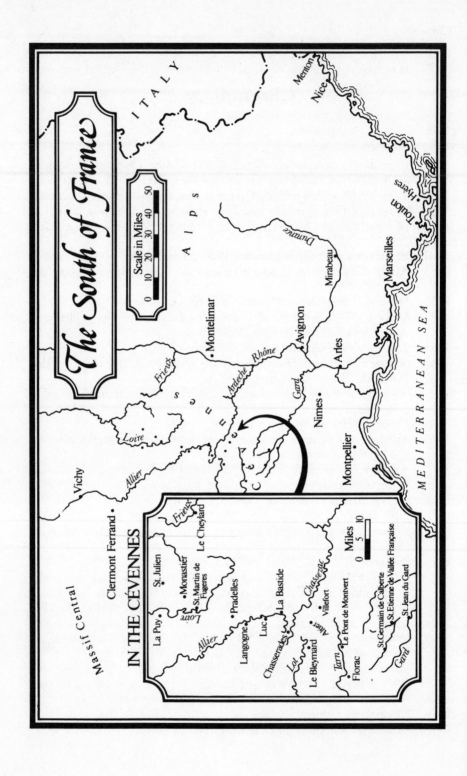

1875 February, meets W.E. Henley in Edinburgh Infirmary.
March-April, with cousin Bob Stevenson, visits artists' colonies
of France.
July, called to the Scottish Bar; returns to France.
September, returns to Edinburgh.

1876 January, walking tour in Ayrshire and Galloway.
April-May, London
Summer, canoe trip with Simpson in France; meets Fanny Osbourne
at Grez-sur-Loing.
Autumn, Grez and Barbizon.

1877 January-February, London.
Spring, Paris, at 5 rue Douay with Fanny Osbourne.
Summer-Autumn, Paris, at 5 rue Ravignan with Fanny Osbourne.
October, 'A Lodging for the Night' in *Temple Bar* (first published
short story).
December to –

1878 March, Paris with Fanny Osbourne. 'The Sire de Malétroit's
Door', in *Temple Bar*; 'Will o' the Mill', in *Cornhill*, January.
April-May, Edinburgh and Swanston. April, *An Inland Voyage*, first
book, Kegan Paul, London.
June, Paris, secretary to Professor Fleeming Jenkin at the Paris
Exposition.
August, London and Paris; Fanny Osbourne returns to California.
September-October, walking tour through the Cévennes.
October-December, London and Edinburgh, *Edinburgh: Picturesque
Notes*, Seeley, Jackson & Halliday, London, December.
December to –

1879 January, Swanston with Henley, at work on *Deacon Brodie*.
February-May, London.
June, France. *Travels with a Donkey in the Cévennes*, Kegan Paul,
London.
July, Edinburgh and London.
August, sails for New York.
September-December, Monterey, California with Fanny
Osbourne and family.
December to –

1880 May, San Francisco (Fanny living in Oakland); married 19 May,
San Francisco.
June-July, honeymoon at Silverado, Napa County.
August, sails for Liverpool with Fanny and stepson Lloyd Osbourne.
August-September, Edinburgh and Strathpeffer.
November to –

1881 April, Davos, Switzerland; meets John Addington Symonds.
*Virginibus Puerisque*, Kegan Paul, London.
May, France.

June-July, Pitlochry, Perthshire.
August-September, Braemar. Begins *Treasure Island*.
October to –
1882 April, Davos, *Familiar Studies of Men and Books*, Chatto & Windus, London, February.
April-June, London and Edinburgh.
June-July, Stobo Manse, near Peebles. *New Arabian Nights*, Chatto & Windus, July.
July-August, Kingussie.
September, in search of a home in the South of France with cousin Bob; rejoins Fanny at Marseilles.
October, move into Campagne Defli, St. Marcel, near Marseilles.
December, Marseilles and Nice.
1883 March, Chalet La Solitude, Hyères.
July-August, Royat.
November, *Treasure Island*, Cassell, London.
December to –
1884 January visited by Baxter and Henley at Hyères; excursions to Nice where Stevenson is taken ill. *Silverado Squatters*, Chatto & Windus, London.
February, returns to Hyères with Fanny.
June-July, Royat; outbreak of cholera at Hyères; returns to London.
Late summer, Wensleydale and Bonallie Towers, Bournemouth.
1885 Spring, settled at Skerryvore, Bournemouth. *A Child's Garden of Verses* and *More New Arabian Nights (The Dynamiter)*, Chatto & Windus, London.
November, *Prince Otto*, Chatto & Windus.
1886 January, *Dr. Jekyll and Mr. Hyde*, Longmans Green, London and Charles Scribner's Sons, New York.
July, *Kidnapped*, Cassell, London and Scribner's, New York.
November, London with Colvin.
1887 May, Thomas Stevenson dies in Edinburgh; returns to Skerryvore.
August, sails for New York with his mother, Fanny and Lloyd.
September, Newport, Rhode Island; settles at Saranac Lake.
November-December, *Memories and Portraits*, Chatto & Windus, London and Scribner's, New York.
1888 March, Fanny leaves for California to visit family; Henley's letter regarding plagiarism by Fanny of 'The Nixie' begins quarrel with his old friend and collaborator.
April, New York City.
May, Manasquan, New Jersey.
June, San Francisco; sets out on first South Seas voyage aboard the *Casco*. *Black Arrow*, Scribner's, New York and Cassell, London.
July-August, the Marquesas.
September, the Paumotus.

October, the Society Islands.

December, the Sandwich Islands; Honolulu.

1889　June, sets out aboard the *Equator* for the Gilbert Islands. *The Wrong Box*, with Lloyd Osbourne, Longmans Green, London and Scribner's, New York. September, *Master of Ballantrae*, Cassell, London and Scribner's, New York.

December, first sight of Samoa; purchases land in Upolu to build Vailima.

1890　February, Sydney, Australia.

April–August, third cruise aboard the *Janet Nicholl* to the Gilbert, Marshall and other islands; Stevenson stays briefly at Noumea, New Caledonia, while Fanny and Lloyd continue cruise.

August–September, Sydney.

October, settles in Samoa.

November, building of Vailima begins.

1891　January, Sydney to escort mother, newly arrived from Scotland, to Samoa.

1892　April, *Across the Plains*, Chatto & Windus, London and Scribner's, New York.

August, *A Footnote to History*, Cassell, London and Scribner's, New York.

1893　January, Vailima complete.

February, Sydney.

April, *Island Nights' Entertainments*, Cassell, London and Scribner's, New York.

August, outbreak of civil war in Samoa; defeat and banishment of Chief Mataafa.

September–October, Honolulu. *Catriona*, Cassell and Scribner's.

November to

1894　November, despite improved health, finding writing difficult; abandons *St. Ives* for *Weir of Hermiston*; Samoan chiefs build 'Road of the Loving Heart' in gratitude for his support; feast in celebration of its completion on his 44th birthday.

3 December, Vailima, dies of cerebral haemorrhage.

# Part 1
# PEOPLE, PLACES AND THE PRINTED WORD

# A

**Academy, The,** London. Stevenson contributed many reviews, etc. between 1874 and 1885. It was one of the many periodicals which remembered him with an excellent obituary.
(*See also* Part 4 (Letters))

**Across the Cévennes in the Footsteps of R. L. Stevenson and his Donkey,** (*see* **Evans, Andrew J.**)

**'Across the Plains'**, Part II of *The Amateur Emigrant*, written 1879, revised and published in *Longman's Magazine* 1883; in book form by Chatto & Windus, London and Scribner's, New York 1892; Tusitala Edition *18*.

Subtitled 'Leaves from the Notebook of an Emigrant between New York and San Francisco', it is an account of Stevenson's first travels in America when he crossed the continent in August 1879 to persuade Fanny Osbourne to divorce her husband Sam and marry him. The preface by Sidney Colvin is a 'Letter to the Author' '. . . lest any reader should find the tone of the concluding pieces less inspiriting than your wont . . . they were written under circumstances of especial gloom and sickness. "I agree with you the lights seem a little turned down", so you write to me now; "the truth is I was far through, and came none too soon to the South Seas, where I was to recover peace of body and mind. And however low the lights, the stuff is true . . ."' *Dedication* 'to Paul Bourget' (1852–1935), French novelist and critic, whom Stevenson greatly admired, 'Traveller and student and curious as you are, you will never have heard the name of Vailima, most likely not even that of Upolu, and Samoa itself may be strange to your ears. To these barbaric seats there came the other day a yellow book with your name on the title, and filled in every page with the exquisite gifts of your art. Let me take and change your own words: *"J'ai beau admirer les autres de toutes mes forces, c'est avec vous que je me complais à vivre."* R.L.S.'
(*See also* **'Monterey'**)

**Adams, Henry,** (1838-1918) eminent American historian and a friend of Henry James. *Henry Adams and his Friends: A Collection of his Unpublished Letters*, Houghton Mifflin, Boston, 1947; *Letters of Henry Adams 1858-91*, Constable, London 1930

Adams visited the Stevensons in Samoa in 1890 during the early stages of the building of Vailima which he described as '. . . . a clearing dotted

1

with burned stumps . . . a two-storey Irish shanty . . . squalor like a
railroad navvy's board hut.' Of Stevenson he wrote: 'A man so thin and
emaciated that he looked like a bundle of sticks in a bag, with dirty
striped pyjamas, the baggy legs tucked into coarse woollen stockings,
one of which was bright brown in colour, the other, a purplish dark
tone . . .'

Of Fanny Stevenson he noted: 'A woman in the usual missionary
nightgown which was no cleaner than her husband's shirt and drawers
but she omitted the stockings . . . her complexion and eyes were dark
and strong, like a half-breed Mexican . . . Though I could not forget the
dirt and squalor, I found Stevenson extremely entertaining . . .' Later he
added 'Stevenson returned our call the other day . . . He was cleaner,
and his wife was not with him.' Two weeks after this event, Adams
reported, 'Last evening Stevenson came at five o'clock and brought his
wife to dine with us. Their arrival was characteristic. He appeared first,
looking like an insane stork, very warm and restless. I was not present
and the reception fell on little Mrs. Parker . . . Presently Mrs.
Stevenson, in a reddish cotton nightgown, staggered up the steps, and
sank into a chair, gasping and unable to speak. Stevenson hurried to
explain that she was overcome by the heat and the walk. Might she lie
down? Mrs. Parker sacrificed her own bed, and gave her some cognac.
Stevenson says his wife has some disease, I know not what, of a paralytic
nature, and suffers greatly from its attacks. I know only that when I
arrived soon afterwards, I found her on the piazza chatting with Mrs.
Parker, and apparently as well and stalwart as any other Apache
squaw . . .'

Entertaining for the Stevensons at this time was a considerable strain on
their finances, as Stevenson reported in a letter to Henry James,
regarding Adams' visit, '. . . I would go oftener to see then, but I had to
swim my horse the last time I went to dinner, and have not yet returned
the clothes I had to borrow . . . a guest would simply break the
bank . . . What would you do with a guest at such narrow seasons? Eat
him? Or serve up a labour boy fricasseed?'

When the artist John La Farge accompanied Adams on a visit to Vailima
for breakfast, their food went ahead of them in a basket (at the
Stevensons' request). Adams wrote, 'We found Stevenson and his wife
just as they had appeared at our first call, except that Mrs. Stevenson did
not think herself obliged to put on slippers, and her night-gown costume
had apparently not been washed since our last visit . . . both Stevenson
and his wife were very friendly, and gave us a good breakfast – or got it
themselves, and kept up a rapid talk for four hours . . . Both La Farge
and I came round to a sort of liking for Mrs. Stevenson, who is more
human than her husband. Stevenson is *a-itu.* – uncanny . . . Their travels
have broken his wife up; she is a victim of rheumatism which is
becoming paralysis, and, I suspect, to dyspepsia; she says that their

voyages have caused it, but Stevenson gloats over discomforts . . .
Compared with their shanty a native house is a palace; but this squalor
must be somehow due to his education . . . His early associates were all
second-rate . . .'

**Adcock, A. St. J.,** (ed.) *Robert Louis Stevenson: His Work and Personality,*
Hodder & Stoughton, London 1924. Stevenson, man and author, as
portrayed through examples of his writings

**'Address to the Samoan Chiefs, October 1894',** *Bookman*, London,
February 1895; *McClure's Magazine*, July 1895

Stevenson wrote to Alison Cunningham (*Letters*, Tusitala Edition 5, p.
174): 'I helped the chiefs who were in prison; and when they were set
free, what should they do but offer to make a part of my road for me out
of gratitude? Well, I was ashamed to refuse, and the trumps dug my road
for me, and put up this inscription'. (*See* **Road of the Loving Heart**)
'We had a great feast when it was done, and I read them a kind of
lecture.'

**Address to the Samoan Students at Malua.** Upolu, January 1890,
first published in Balfour's *Life* 1901. Speech made to school run by
Rev. J. E. Newell of the London Missionary Society; Stevenson also
translated it into Samoan

**Address to the Speculative Society,** (*see* **Speculative Society, The**)

**Adirondack Mts.** (*see* **Saranac**)

**Admiral Guinea,** a Melodrama in Four Acts, written in collaboration
with W. E. Henley, privately printed, 1884; first published (with
*Deacon Brodie* and *Beau Austin*) in *Three Plays* by W. E. Henley and R. L.
Stevenson, David Nutt, London 1892; separate publication by
Heinemann, London 1897; Tusitala Edition 24; first performed 29
November 1897 at Avenue Theatre, London

The Admiral, now John Gaunt, reformed slaver-captain, is visited by
the sinister Blind Pew, who has a villainous plot to rob Gaunt with the
innocent collusion of Kit French, suitor of his daughter Arethusa. (Blind
Pew and the Admiral Benbow Inn had already appeared in *Treasure
Island*.)

The plays were written while Stevenson was living in Bournemouth.
*Admiral Guinea* carries a dedication 'With affection and esteem to
Andrew Lang,' dated 27 September 1884. Stevenson was carried along
by Henley's enthusiasm under Fanny's disapproving eye. She wrote that
the plays 'were invented and written in the fervid, boisterous fashion of
Mr Henley, whose influence predominated, except in the actual literary
form . . . it was agreed between them that did one object to what the
other had written, it should be stricken out without argument — a

procedure that I cannot but believe was damaging to the work of both.' In *An Intimate Portrait of R.L.S.*, Lloyd Osbourne comments: 'In the interval of Henley's absences' (from Bournemouth) 'Stevenson gladly returned to his own work, and had as a playwright to be resuscitated by his unshaken collaborator, who was as confident as ever.' Stevenson described *Admiral Guinea* as a 'low, black, dirty, blackguard, ragged piece: vomitable in many parts — simply vomitable . . .' (Letter to Henley, Tusitala Edition *33*, p. 43). He was however convinced that 'the theatre is a gold mine; and on that I must keep my eye.' So he informed his father who apparently had little faith in the venture, while assuring Henley in the earlier letter that 'the stage is a lottery, must not be regarded as a trade, and must never be preferred to drudgery . . . It is bad enough to have to live by an art — but to think to live by an art combined with commercial speculation — that way madness lies.'

*Adrift in the South Seas: Including Adventures with Robert Louis Stevenson* (*see* **MacCallum, Thomas Murray**)

*Adventures Among Books,* (*see* **Lang, Andrew**)

*Adventures in Criticism,* (*see* **Quiller-Couch, Sir Arthur Thomas**)

'**Adventures of Henry Shovel**', an unfinished story, first published in Tusitala Edition *16*, 1924

'**Aes Triplex**', an essay, first published in *Cornhill Magazine,* April 1878; in book form in *Virginibus Puerisque*, 1881; Tusitala Edition *25*

**Ah Fu,** Chinese cook, joined the Stevensons on voyage to Marquesas. He was devoted to Fanny, both having a flair for cooking. She described him as 'civilised just so much as we should like to have him, and a savage just so far as it is useful.' Ah Fu remained with the Stevensons for five years, but before Vailima was built in Samoa, he requested leave to return to China to visit his widowed mother. 'Just one trip, I come back quick.' The plea was irresistible and he had thriftily saved his wages, supplemented by fifty pounds from the Stevensons, which were changed into gold pieces. But Ah Fu never returned and was never heard of again.

*Alan Breac Stewart and his Associates,* (*see* **Pratt, Tinsley**)

*Alan Breck Again,* (*see* **Smith, Arthur D. Howden**)

**Aldington, Richard,** *Portrait of a Rebel, Robert Louis Stevenson.* Evans, London, 1957. Recommended for its perceptive study of Stevenson's formative and student days in Edinburgh

'*Alison Cunningham*', (*see* **Guthrie, Lord James** and **Skinner, R.T.**)

**Allen, Maryland,** 'South Sea Memories of R.L.S.', *Bookman,* New York,
   August 1916

**'Alpine Diversions',** an essay, first published in *Pall Mall Gazette,*
   26 February 1881; in book form in *Essays and Criticisms,* Herbert S.
   Turner, Edinburgh, 1903; 'Swiss Notes', *Further Memories,* Tusitala
   Edition *30*

**Amateur Emigrant, The,** brings together 'From the Clyde to Sandy
   Hook' (Part I) and 'Across the Plains' (Part II) in one volume; first
   published Edinburgh Edition 1895; Tusitala Edition *18*
   Stevenson's journey by immigrant ship and immigrant train per-
   manently damaged his health. He suffered from insomnia, fevers and
   semi-delirium, and he arrived in San Francisco in August 1879 to learn
   that Fanny Osbourne had returned to her husband and was living in
   Monterey, the old capital of California.

*Anatomy of Paradise,* (*see* **Furnas, J.C.**)

**Anderson, Doctor**
   Summoned to Vailima to attend the dying Stevenson on 3 December
   1894, he murmured 'How can anybody write books with arms like
   these?' to which Stevenson's mother replied 'He has written *all* his books
   with arms like these!'

**Anderson, Lord A. M.,** 'David Balfour, Yr., of Shaws, Advocate',
   *Juridical Review.* Vol. 33, 1921, Inaugural address to Scots Law Society,
   October 1921.

**Angus, D.,** 'Stevenson's "Lost" Home', *Scots Magazine,* August
   1979 (1 Inverleith Terrace); also his first school and Canonmills.

*'Another Glimpse of R.L.S.',* (*see* **Carrington, James B.**)

**Anstruther, Fife**
   As a student of engineering at Edinburgh University, Stevenson spent
   his first vacation studying the harbour works at Anstruther and wrote to
   his mother 'I am utterly sick of this grey, grim sea-beaten hole. I have a
   little cold in my head, which makes my eyes sore; and you can't tell how
   utterly sick I am, and how anxious to get back among trees and flowers
   and something less meaningless than this bleak fertility.' (*See also* **'Coast
   of Fife, The'**)

*'Answering R.L.S.',* (*see* **Doughty, Leonard**)

**Apemama**
   One of the Gilbert Islands (now spelt **Abemama**), it was described by
   Stevenson as 'a low island except for coconuts, is just the same as a ship

at sea . . . brackish water, no supplies and very little shelter . . . I pine
for an island with a profile'.

His stepson, Lloyd Osbourne, in the Preface to *The Wrecker* notes 'An
Apemama house of the kind corresponding to a "smart, attractive bijou
little residence" with us, is a sort of giant clothes basket of much the
same colour and wattle, with a peaked roof, and standing on stilts about
a yard high. With a dozen pairs of human legs under it, you can steer it to
any spot you like – provided it is level, – and begin your modest
housekeeping without further fuss.

'We started ours in Apemama with four such houses, forty-eight pairs
of legs, and the king, Winchester in hand, firing in the direction – but
over the head – of anyone who seemed backward . . .'
(*See also* **In the South Seas; Tembinok, 'King'**)

**Apia,** a port on the north coast of Upolu, Samoa, first sighted by Stevenson, voyaging on the trading schooner *Equator*, 7 December 1889.

They were to build Vailima at the foot of Mount Vaea and Stevenson
was to be buried on its summit almost exactly five years afterwards in
1894. Fanny too, would have her ashes laid in her husband's tomb twenty
years later, in 1914.
(*See also* **Upolu; Vailima, Samoa;** Plate 18)

**'Apology for Idlers, An',** an essay, first published in *Cornhill
Magazine,* July 1877; in book form in *Virginibus Puerisque* 1881; Tusitala
Edition 25.

**'Appeal to the Clergy of the Church of Scotland, An',** pamphlet
published by Blackwood, Edinburgh and London, 1875; Tusitala
Edition 26.

**'Appin Murder, The'** (*see* **Cameron, D.L.; Cameron, John; McKay,
D.N.**)

**'Apprenticeship of Robert Louis Stevenson',** (*see* **Crockett, Samuel
Rutherford**)

**Archer, William,** (1856-1924), critic, born Perth, educated Edinburgh
University.'R.L.S. at Skerryvore', *Critic*, 5 November 1887; 'R.L.S.:
His Style and Thought', *Time*, November 1895; 'In Memoriam
R.L.S.', *New Review*, January 1895

At their first meeting in Skerryvore, Archer was much impressed by
Stevenson's vitality and grace 'He now sits at the foot of the table rolling
a limp cigarette in his long, limp fingers, and talking eagerly all the
while, with just enough trace of a Scottish intonation to remind one that
he is the author of *Thrawn Janet* and the creator of Alan Breac Stewart.
He has still the air and manner of a young man, for illness has neither
tamed his mind nor aged his body. It has left its mark, however, in the

pallor of his long oval face, with its wide-set eyes, straight nose, and thin-lipped sensitive mouth, scarcely shaded by a light moustache, the jest and scorn of his ribald intimates. His long hair straggles with an irregular wave down his neck, a wisp of it occasionally falling over his ear, and having to be replaced with a light gesture of the hand. He is dressed in a black velvet jacket, showing at the throat the loose rolling collar of a white flannel shirt; and if it is at all cold, he has probably thrown over his shoulders an ancient maroon-coloured shawl, draped something after the fashion of Mexican poncho. When he stands up you see he is well above the middle height, and of a naturally lithe and agile figure. He still moves with freedom and grace, but the stoop of his shoulders tells a tale of suffering.' (*See also* Part 4 (Letters))

**Armour, Margaret,** *The Home and Early Haunts of Robert Louis Stevenson,* Edinburgh, 1895

**Arnold, William Harris,** 'My Stevensons', *Scribner's Magazine,* January 1922. Contains note on *Kidnapped* in Stevenson's handwriting and reference to the Journal he kept as a law clerk in Edinburgh (9 May-5 July 1872); reference is also made to other early works

*As We Were,* (*see* **Benson, E.F.**)

**Ashe, Rev. Matthew,** 'Stevenson's Catholic Leaning', *Catholic World,* November 1942. A claim largely based on Stevenson's championing of Catholic missionaries, in particular Father Damien of the Molokai Leper Colony

*Atalanta,* New York. Magazine for girls which serialised *Catriona* under its original title, *David Balfour,* December 1892-September 1893

*Athenaeum, The,* London. Contained an anonymous review entitled 'The Works of Robert Louis Stevenson', 14-21 August 1895. (*See also* Part 4 (Letters))

**Athenaeum Club, London,** 'Elected to membership, 1888': (This information was proudly displayed on Stevenson's calling card).

*Atlantic Monthly, New York.* Contained an anonymous and defamatory article entitled 'Stevenson Unwhitewashed', March 1900

*'Atween the Pentland's Muckle Knees: With Stevenson at Swanston',* (*see* **Skae, Hilda**)

*'Auld Kirk in the Glen, The: Memories of Glencorse and R.L.S.'* (*see* **Skae, Hilda**)

*Autobiography, An,* (*see* **Trudeau, Dr. E.L.**)

**'Autumn Effect, An',** an essay, first published in *The Portfolio,* April-May 1875; collected in Tusitala Edition *30*.

# B

**Babington, Rev. Churchill**

Husband of Stevenson's cousin, Maud Balfour, whom he visited in July 1873 at Cockfield Rectory, Suffolk.
(*See* **Sitwell, Fanny**; **Colvin, Sir Sydney**; Part 4 (Letters))

*Back to Treasure Island,* (*see* **Calahan, Harold Augustin**)

**'Bagster's Pilgrim's Progress'**, an essay, first published in *Magazine of Art,* February 1882; Tusitala Edition *28.*

**Baildon, H. Bellyse,** *Robert Louis Stevenson: A Life Study in Criticism,* Chatto & Windus, London, 1901. Interesting for its account of Stevenson reading to the author an early version of the play *Deacon Brodie.* Baildon and Stevenson collaborated briefly on *The Trial Magazine* (*see* Part 2); 'The Late Mr. R.L. Stevenson: A Schoolfellow Remembers', *Daily News,* 19 December, 1894; 'Some Recollections of Robert Louis Stevenson', *Temple Bar,* March, 1895; *Stevenson: Homes and Haunts of Famous Authors,* Chatto & Windus, London, 1906.
(*See* Part 4 (Letters))

**Bailey, Mrs. H. S.,** *A Note on Robert Louis Stevenson, 1850-94.* The Priory Press, London, 1913 A concise 16-page life study

**Baker, Ray Jerome,** *Honolulu Then and Now,* Baker, Honolulu, 1941. Description of Stevenson 'era' in Honolulu, c. 1889

**Bakers (of Saranac)**

In September 1887 the Stevensons went to Saranac Lake in the Adirondack Mountains where Dr. Trudeau had established a clinic for the treatment of tuberculosis. They lodged with the Bakers in a house Stevenson described as 'bald and isolated on a bluff overlooking the river . . . the kind of house that a prosperous guide would run up in his spare time with the help of a local carpenter.'
(*See* **Trudeau, Dr. E.L.**; **Saranac**)

**Balfour, Miss Amelia,** Stevenson's incognito for Lady Jersey (*see* **Jersey, Countess of,**)

**Balfour, Dr. George,** uncle who first diagnosed Stevenson's condition as tubercular

**Balfour, Graham,** *The Life of Robert Louis Stevenson,* London, 1901; *A South Seas Trader,* Macmillan, London, 1896

Stevenson's second cousin read law at Oxford and visited Vailima in' 1892 en route for Micronesia. Although none of them had seen him since boyhood, the tall, fair, handsome young man with a moustache was unmistakably a Balfour (according to Stevenson's mother). He soon adapted to Vailima standards for, on his first afternoon, observing that the family went barefoot about the house and the woods, he did likewise: 'Why, he's the same kind of fool we are,' said Stevenson delightedly. Graham had come for a month but stayed more than a year. Although much younger than his literary cousin they shared the same family background and Graham provided conversation about the world for which Stevenson still pined. He shared Lloyd Osbourne's bachelor cottage and the two men became firm friends. His interest in Samoa extended to politics and learning the language. Fanny's divorced daughter, Belle, fell in love with him and her mother made no secret that she would have been delighted by the match.

'It will be a wrench when he goes,' she wrote. 'He says he will come back, but I know what will happen; he will marry somebody and we'll hate his wife, and there'll be the end of it, for of course, if we hate his wife, he must hate us . . .' His biography, the first official one of Stevenson, is necessarily inhibited by the fact that at the time of writing Fanny Stevenson was still very much alive.

**Balfour, Jane Whyte,** 'Chief of our aunts'. Stevenson's childhood favourite aunt who ran Colinton Manse for his grandfather after his grandmother's death. She was unmarried. (*See* Part 4 (Letters))

**Balfour, Mr. and Mrs. J. Craig,** 'Robert Louis Stevenson: By Two of his Cousins', *English Illustrated News,* May 1899

**Balfour, John,** uncle. Served in India. Returned to Edinburgh dedicated to fighting cholera outbreaks.

**Balfour, Rev. Dr. Lewis,** grandfather. Minister of Colinton, 1823-1860

**Balfour, Margaret Isabella,** mother (*see* **Stevenson, Margaret Isabella**)

**Balfour, Maud,** cousin (*see* **Babington, Rev. Churchill**)

**Balfour, Michael,** son of Graham. 'How the Biography of Robert Louis Stevenson Came to be Written', *Times Literary Supplement,* 13 January 1960. Reminiscences of his father Graham and Stevenson in Samoa.

**Balfour, Rhoda,** wife of Graham

**Balfours of Pilrig**

Stevenson was proud of his connection with this adventurous and substantial family owning lands between Edinburgh and Leith. A Balfour had fought at Bothwell Brig in 1679 and another had been ruined by the Darien Disaster in 1700.

**'Ballads'**, a collection of poems first published by Chatto & Windus, 1890; Tusitala Edition *23*.

**'Ballads and Songs of Scotland, The'**, a review first published in *The Academy*, 8 August 1874; Tusitala Edition *28*

**Bamford, Doctor,** attended seriously-ill Stevenson when he arrived in California, August 1879 (*see* **Monterey; Part 4 (Letters)**)

*Bancroft's History of the United States,* Stevenson's 'Bible' in America. He carried all six volumes with him on his first journey to California. (*See* **'Across the Plains'; New York**)

**Bandmann, Dan**
Veteran actor, toured stage version of *Jekyll and Hyde* in United States. Visited Stevensons in Saranac in 1887.

**'Banker's Ward, The'**, Stevenson's first serial, which appeared in *The Sunbeam*, 1866. (For other contributions to this school magazine, *see also* Part 2 (The Sunbeam Magazine))

**Barbizon**
Although the famous 'Barbizon School' had been eclipsed by the deaths of Corot and Millet, a colony of landscape painters lingered in this village near Paris. Stevenson's cousin Bob was a lively member and here they spent the summer of 1875 together and a deep friendship with the American artist, Will Low, was also formed. (*See* **Daplyn, A.J.; Hotel Siron; Low, Will H.**)

**Barnett, David,** *A Stevenson Study: Treasure Island.* David Macdonald, Edinburgh 1924. Claims that the topography of Edinburgh seen from the Pentland Hills at Swanston inspired *Treasure Island*

**Barrie, Sir James Matthew,** (1860-1937). *An Edinburgh Eleven: Pencil Portraits from College Life,* London 1913; *Letters of James Barrie,* (ed.) Viola Meynell, London 1924; 'Scotland's Lament (for R.L.S.)', *Bookman* Extra Number, Hodder & Stoughton, London, 1913; 'Gavin Ogilvy [J.M. Barrie] on Stevenson', *British Weekly,* November 1888

The Scottish dramatist and novelist described fellow-student Stevenson, after they had crashed bodily into one another crossing Edinburgh's Princes Street: 'Glancing up I saw a velvet coat, a lean figure with long hair (going black) and stooping shoulders, the face young and rather pinched but extraordinarily mobile, the manner doggedly debonair. He apologised charmingly for what was probably my fault . . . then, taking

me by the arm, he led me away from the Humanities' (class which
Barrie attended) 'to something he assured me was more humane, a
howff called Rutherford's where we sat and talked by the solid hour.'
This convivial interlude ended with Stevenson pursuing Barrie along
the street with shouts of 'Stop, thief' and describing him to startled
passers-by as 'a man with a wooden leg and a face like a ham.'

They never met again. Correspondence in later life led to talk of a
visit to Vailima and, in April 1893, Stevenson wrote to Barrie with a
revealing pen-portrait of the family at Vailima:

'FANNY V. de G. STEVENSON: *The weird woman. Native name:
Tamatai.* This is what you will have to look out for, Mr Barrie. If you
don't get on with her, it's a pity about your visit. She runs the show.
Infinitely little, extraordinary wig of grey curls, handsome waxen
face like Napoleon's, insane black eyes, boy's hands, tiny bare feet, a
cigarette, wild blue native dress usually spotted with garden mould. In
company manners presents the appearance of a little timid and precise
old maid of the days of prunes and prisms – you look for the reticule.
Hellish energy, relieved by fortnights of entire hibernation. Can make
anything from a house to a row, all fine and large of their kind. My
uncle, after seeing her for the first time: "Yes, Louis, you have done
well. I married a besom myself and have never regretted it" . . .
Doctors everybody, will doctor you, cannot be doctored herself . . . A
violent friend, a brimstone enemy . . . Is always either loathed or
slavishly adored; indifference impossible. The natives think her uncanny
and that devils serve her. Dreams dreams, and sees visions.'

ROBERT LOUIS STEVENSON: *The tame celebrity. Native name: Tusitala.*
Exceedingly lean . . . general appearance of a blasted boy – or blighted
youth . . . Past eccentric – obscure and oh no we never mention it –
present industrious, respectable and fatuously contented. Used to be
fond of talking about Art, don't talk about it any more . . . Really
knows a good deal but has lived so long with aforesaid family and
foremast hands, that you might talk a week to him and never guess it.
Friendly grocer in Sydney: "It has been a most agreeable surprise to
meet you, Mr Stevenson. I would never have guessed you were a literary
man!" Name in family, The Tame Celebrity. Cigarettes without inter-
mission except when coughing or kissing. Hopelessly entangled in apron
strings. Drinks plenty. Curses some. Temper unstable. Manners purple
in an emergency, but liable to trances. . . . Given to explaining the
Universe – Scotch, sir, Scotch.'

BELLE [Fanny's daughter]: *Native name: Teuila.* Runs me like a baby
in a perambulator, sees I'm properly dressed, bought me silk socks, and
made me wear them, takes care of me when I'm well, from writing my
books to trimming my nails . . . manages the house and the boys who are
very fond of her. Does all the hair cutting of the family. Will cut yours

and doubtless object to the way you part it. Mine has been re-organized twice.

LLOYD [Fanny's son]: *Native name: Loia.* Six foot, blond, eye-glasses – British eye-glasses, too. Address varying from elaborate civility to a freezing haughtiness. Decidedly witty. Has seen an enormous amount of the world. Keeps nothing of youth, but some of its intolerance. Unexpected soft streak for the forlorn. When he is good he is very, very good, but when he is cross he is horrid. Of Dutch ancestry, and has spells known in the family as "cold blasts from Holland". Exacting with the boys and yet they like him. Rather stiff with his equals, but apt to be very kindly with his inferiors – the only undemonstrative member of the family which otherwise wears its heart upon both sleeves; and except for my purple patches the only mannered one.' (*See* Part 4 (Letters))

**Baxter, Charles,** (1848-1919), Edinburgh lawyer, fellow student of Stevenson's at Edinburgh University, their friendship and correspondence continued until the end of Stevenson's life. When Baxter married in 1877, he received this letter, 'I wish you a rare good time and plenty of children . . . the past looks very delightful to me; the past when you were not going to be married and I was not trying to write a novel . . . the past where we have been drunk and sober and sat outside grocers' shops on fine dark nights, and wrangled in the Speculative, and heard mysterious whistlings in Waterloo Place, and met missionaries from Aberdeen; generally the past. But the future is a fine thing also in its way; and what's more, it's all we have to come and go upon. So, let us strike up the Wedding March, and bedeck ourselves with the loose and graceful folds of the frock coat, and crown ourselves with Sunday hats as with laurel; and go, leaping and singing and praising God, and under the influence of Champagne and all the finer feelings of humanity, towards that adored edifice, or secular drawing-room, from whence you, issuing forth, shall startle mankind with the finest splendours of the wedded Chawles. Proudest moment of my life, C.B.'

In the Dedication to *Kidnapped,* published 1886, Stevenson wrote, 'My dear Charles Baxter, If you ever read this tale, you will likely ask yourself more questions than I should care to answer: as for instance how the Appin murder has come to fall in the year 1751, how the Torran rocks have crept so near to Earraid, or why the printed trial is silent as to all that touches David Balfour. These are nuts beyond my ability to crack. But if you tried me on the point of Alan's guilt or innocence, I think I could defend the reading of the text. To this day you will find the tradition of Appin clear in Alan's favour. If you inquire, you may even hear that the descendants of "the other man" who fired the shot are in the country to this day. But the other man's name, inquire as you please, you shall not hear; for the Highlander values a secret for itself and for the congenial exercise of keeping it. I might go on for long to justify one

point and own another indefensible; it is more honest to confess at once
how little I am touched by the desire for accuracy. This is no furniture
for the scholar's library, but a book for the winter evening school-room
when the tasks are over and the hour for bed draws near; and honest
Alan, who was a grim old fire-eater in his day, has in this new avatar no
more desperate purpose that to steal some young gentleman's attention
from his Ovid, carry him awhile into the Highlands and the last century,
and pack him to bed with some engaging images to mingle with his
dreams.

As for you, my dear Charles, I do not even ask you to like this tale. But
perhaps when he is older, your son will; he may then be pleased to find
his father's name on the fly-leaf; and in the meanwhile it pleases me to
set it there, in memory of many days that were happy and some (now
perhaps as pleasant to remember) that were sad. If it is strange for me to
look back from a distance both in time and space on these bygone
adventures of our youth, it must be stranger for you who tread the same
streets – who may to-morrow open the door of the old Speculative,
where we begin to rank with Scott and Robert Emmet and beloved and
inglorious Macbean – or may pass the corner of the close where that
great society, the L.J.R., held its meetings and drank its beer, sitting in
the seats of Burns and his companions. I think I see you, moving there by
plain daylight, beholding with your natural eyes those places that have
now become for your companion a part of the scenery of dreams. How,
in the intervals of present business, the past must echo in your memory!
Let it not echo often without some kind thought of your friend,

R.L.S.

Skerryvore, Bournemouth.'

*Catriona*, the sequel to *Kidnapped*, was published in 1893 with the
dedication to: '*CHARLES BAXTER*, Writer to the Signet': 'My dear
Charles: It is the fate of sequels to disappoint those who have waited for
them; and my David, having been left to kick his heels for more than a
lustre in the British Linen Company's Office, must expect his late re-
appearance to be greeted with hoots, if not with missiles. Yet, when I
remember the days of our explorations, I am not without hope. There
should be left in our native city some seed of the elect; some long-
legged, hot-headed youth must repeat to-day our dreams and
wanderings of so many years ago; he will relish the pleasure, which
should have been ours, to follow among named streets and numbered
houses the country walks of David Balfour, to identify Dean, and
Silvermills, and Broughton, and Hope Park, and Pilrig, and poor old
Lochend – if it still be standing, and the Figgate Whins – if there be any
of them left; or to push (on a long holiday) so far afield as Gillane or the
Bass. So, perhaps, his eye shall be opened to behold the series of the

generations, and he shall weigh with surprise his momentous and nugatory gift of life. You are still – as when first I saw, as when I last addressed you – in the venerable city which I must always think of as my home. And I have come so far; and the sights and thoughts of my youth pursue me; and I see like a vision the youth of my father, and of his father, and the whole stream of lives flowing down there far in the north, with the sound of laughter and tears, to cast me out in the end, as by a sudden freshet, on these ultimate islands. And I admire and bow my head before the romance of destiny.

R.L.S.

Vailima, Upolu, Samoa, 1892.'

*(See* **Edinburgh; Edinburgh University; Ferguson, De Lancey and Waingrow, Marshall; L.J.R. Club; Speculative Society, The;** Part 4 (Letters))

**Baxter, Grace,** wife of Charles

**Bay, J. Christian,** *Echoes of Robert Louis Stevenson,* Walter M. Hill, Chicago, 1920; *Unpublished Manuscripts of Robert Louis Stevenson's Record of a Family of Engineers,* London, 1929

**B.B.C.** (*see* **British Broadcasting Corporation**)

'**Beachcombers, The**', projected story to follow *The Wrecker* and *The Ebb-Tide,* which never materialised

'**Beach of Falesá, The**', a short story, first published in six weekly instalments, 2 July to 6 August 1892 in *Illustrated London News*; in book form in *Island Nights' Entertainments,* 1893; Tusitala Edition *13* (*See* Part 6 (Radio))

The story is narrated by Wiltshire, a rough-and-ready South Seas trader who takes a native wife, Uma. He becomes the target of an evil rival trader, Case, who also invokes the superstitions and taboos of the natives to gain his ends. A realistic account of life in the Pacific and one of Stevenson's best stories.

*Beach of Falesá, The,* (*see* **Thomas, Dylan**)

**Beau Austin** a play written in collaboration with W.E. Henley, privately printed by R. & R. Clark, Edinburgh, 1884; first published in *Three Plays* by W.E. Henley and R.L. Stevenson, David Nutt, London, 1892; *Plays,* Tusitala Edition *24*

Dorothy Musgrave is in love with and betrayed by George (Beau) Austin, confidant of the Duke of York. Her long-faithful suitor Fenwick pleads with Beau to offer her marriage. He does, and after considerable conflict and recrimination, she agrees and all ends happily.

First performance London's Haymarket Theatre on Monday, 3 November 1890 with H. Beerbohm Tree as Beau Austin, Fred Terry as John Fenwick and Rose Leclerq as Miss Evelina Foster, Dorothy's aunt.

**'Beggars'**, an essay, first published in *Scribner's Magazine*, March 1888; in book form in *Across the Plains*, 1892; Tusitala Edition *25*

**Beecher, Henry Ward,** (1813–87), American abolitionist preacher and Fanny's childhood neighbour in Indianapolis

**Beeching, J.,** 'The Works of Robert Louis Stevenson', *Bookman* Extra Number, London, 1913

**Beinecke Collection,** Stevenson's letters and papers acquired by Edwin J. Beinecke for Yale University, (*See also* **McKay, George L.**)

**Bennet, James,** *Robert Louis Stevenson at Buckstone*, privately printed, Edinburgh, 1967. Meetings with artist Sam Bough at Buckstone farmhouse, near Edinburgh

**Bennett, Arnold,** (1867-1931), *Journals of Arnold Bennett* (ed.) Norman Flower. Interesting for an account of his delight on reading *Weir of Hermiston*, 1932

**Benson, E.F.,** (1867–1940), English novelist. Third son of Edward White Benson (Archbishop of Canterbury). 'The Myth of Robert Louis Stevenson', *London Mercury*, July–August 1925
His book *As We Were* (Longmans Green, London 1930) contains scurrilous and inaccurate statements about Stevenson as man and writer.

**Béranger,** *see Encyclopaedia Britannica*

**Bermann, Richard A.,** *Home from the Sea: Stevenson in Samoa*, Bobbs-Merrill, New York, n.d.

**'Best Thing in Edinburgh, The',** *see* **Osbourne, Katharine Durham**

**Bibiliographies of Stevenson's Writings,** (*See* **Ellwanger, W.D,**; **McKay, George L.**; **Prideaux, Col. W.F.**; **Slater, J.H.**; **Swearingen, Roger C.**; *also* **Catalogue** (various); (Part 8)

**Bibliography of Twelve Victorian Authors,** *see* **Ehrsham, T. G. and Deily, R.H.**

**Biographical Notes on the Writings of Robert Louis Stevenson** *see* **Gosse, Sir Edmund William**

**Black and White Magazine,** London. Serialised 'In the South Seas' and 'The Bottle Imp'. 5 January 1895 issue contained an anonymous article entitled 'Robert Louis Stevenson in an English Home: Skerryvore'

**Black Arrow, The,** a novel, first published (under the title of 'The Black Arrow: A Tale of Tunstall Forest. By Captain George North') in *Young Folks*, 30 June–20 October 1883; in book form (as *The*

*Black Arrow: A Tale of Two Roses*) by Cassell, London and Scribner's,
New York, 1888; Tusitala Edition 9ᐟ

An adventure story for young readers, still popular despite its
somewhat archaic language, it is set on the Yorkist side of the Wars of
the Roses. The hero, Master Richard Shelton, assisted by loyal outlaws
from the Greenwood and by the heroine (disguised as a boy), seeks to
defeat his rascally uncle, Sir Daniel, and to support the cause of King
Richard. The Tusitala Edition has a Prefatory Note by Mrs. R. L.
Stevenson: 'The season for invalids in Hyères, where we had spent the
winter of 1883–1884, comes to an end with the spring months. My
husband was still so weak after an almost fatal illness that we were in
doubt whether he would be strong enough to join in the general exodus;
but the increasing epidemic of cholera so near as Toulon forced us to
make the attempt. Travelling by easy stages, we first tried Vichy, with
ill success. The climate proved enervating, and the meals at the hotel – at
all the hotels so far as we could judge – were apparently meant for
persons suffering from a plethoric habit, and hardly a proper diet for
visitors with sick lungs. After a couple of days' trial we shook the dust of
Vichy from our feet and moved on to Clermont-Ferrand. This was a
shade better, though we had doubts as to its sanitary condition; and the
picturesque streets, besides, were close, and likely to become more
airless as the summer advanced. However, *The Black Arrow*, begun in the
châlet in Hyères, and continued here and there at our various stopping
places, was again taken up and another chapter written, while my son
and I scoured the neighbourhood in search of a more suitable spot for the
ensuing months. *The Black Arrow* was conceived and written to fill a
serial order from Mr. Henderson for his paper, *Young Folks*, where
*Treasure Island* first saw the light. No one could accuse my husband of
showing a mercenary spirit in the sale of *The Black Arrow*, for which he
accepted Mr. Henderson's offer of about three dollars a thousand words,
just after receiving two hundred and fifty pounds from Mr. C. J.
Longman for the magazine rights of *Prince Otto* . . . Within a short
distance of Clermont my son and I came upon an enchanting little
watering-place, then comparatively unknown to the English tourists,
called Royat . . . Caesar himself had bathed in the healing water of the
Royat springs . . . In the centre of the old town, a little above the hotels,
stood an ancient cathedral, part of it in tolerable preservation and still
used for the services of the Catholic Church. Its walls were loop-holed
for purposes of defence, there were hooded projections on the towers
for sentries, or perhaps archers, and the iron-bound doors were solid
enough to withstand a battering-ram . . . Here amid these romantic,
almost theatrical surroundings, *The Black Arrow* was continued with
almost no effort, and chapter after chapter was despatched to Mr.
Henderson. The fresh air of the hills, the easy nature of his work, and the

pleasant, quiet life had a favourable effect on my husband's health. He was soon able to take long drives on the beautiful Puy de Dome road; and in the evenings he often went down to the grounds of the casino, where an excellent string band played in a little kiosk . . . Our descriptions of Royat in our letters to my husband's parents induced them to join us. They were so charmed with the place that they remained with us the rest of the summer, which gave my husband the advantage of his father's able criticism on *Black Arrow*.'

Stevenson was less complimentary about his effort which he described as 'tushery', informing Henley (*Letters*, Tusitala Edition *32*, p. 242) that he had begun it because he was fit for little else: 'The influenza has busted me up a good deal; I have no spring, and am headachy.' He wrote one and a half chapters on the first day, Saturday 26 May 1883 and by Monday had completed four chapters. By the end of June when he finished the novel he had confessed in a letter that he had 'forgotten what had last happened to several of his principal characters' and was awaiting proofs of the early instalments before he could continue. 'Nowhere do I send worse copy than to *Young Folks'* [who were serialising] for with this sort of story, I rarely rewrite; yet nowhere am I so well used.'

Others were more complimentary when the book appeared and G. M. Trevelyan, the historian, wrote 'it reproduces a real state of society in the past . . . like a good historical novel. The book reads like the outcome of an eager and imaginative study of the Paston Letters.'
*Dedication:* 'Critic on the Hearth', Saranac Lake, April 8, 1888.' (*See also* **Royat** )

**Black, Margaret Moyes,** *Robert Louis Stevenson*, 'Famous Scots' Series, Oliphant, Anderson & Ferrier, Edinburgh, 1898. Contains references to Journal kept by Stevenson during his time in an Edinburgh law firm
(*See also* **Skene, Edwards & Garson**)

**Blanch, Josephine Mildred,** *Robert Louis Stevenson and Jules Simoneau*, privately printed, 1921,the story of a friendship and reminiscences of Stevenson's Californian days

**Bland, Henry Mead,** 'Stevenson's California', *Pacific Short Story Club*, n.d.

**'Body-Snatcher, The'.** First published in the *Pall Mall Christmas 'Extra'* for 1884 and again in the *Pall Mall Gazette* 31 January and 1 February 1885; Tusitala Edition *11*

This was one of the tales of horror written at Pitlochry (Scotland) in 1881 and then, according to Stevenson (*Letters*, Tusitala Edition *32* p. 158) 'laid aside in a justifiable disgust'. It is the story of Doctor Wolfe

MacFarlane and his accomplice Fettes who rob graves in the interests of
medical science and profit, with dire results.
Stevenson received £30 for it. Men wearing sandwich-boards paraded
through the streets of London advertising it with posters so gruesome
that they were suppressed by the police, while Stevenson told Colvin
that he had 'long ago condemned the story as an offence against good
manners'. (*See also* Part 6 (Media))

**Boer Independence,** *see* **'Protest on Behalf of Boer Independence'**

**Bogue** *see* **Wogg**

*Bohemian, The,* contained an anonymous article entitled 'R.L.S.', 1893

**Bok, Edward W.,** 'The Playful Stevenson', *Scribner's Magazine,* August
1927

Sent by Scribner's to Saranac, to deliver proofs, Bok described
Stevenson as 'not a prepossessing figure . . . with his sallow skin and
black dishevelled hair, with fingernails which had been allowed to grow
very long, with fingers discoloured by tobacco . . . a general untidiness
which was all his own . . . an author whom it was better to read than to
see . . . yet his kindliness and gentleness more than offset the
unattractiveness of his physical appearance'.

**Bonifacio, Señor,** Fanny Osbourne's landlord at Monterey, California,
1879, when Stevenson arrived there from Scotland.
(*See also* **Monterey**)

**Boodle, Adelaide,** a friend of the Stevensons during their time at Skerryvore. *R.L.S. and His Sine Qua Non: Flashlights from Skerryvore by the
Gamekeeper*, John Murray, London, 1926
Adelaide Boodle described her first meeting with the Stevensons in their
'new home', 'Ushered into a carpetless room, bestrewn with packing-
cases and straw. There RLS and his wife, in happy security, were
overhauling buried treasure . . . Both were curiously clad. He had on
the velvet coat and dark red tie that were afterwards to become to so
many of us almost part of his actual personality; her garment was a
mysterious-looking overall (I believe, a painting-apron) admirably
adapted to her needs at the moment . . . How clearly it all comes back;
the radiant cordiality of their welcome. Had we been friends of long
standing we should have been fully satisfied . . . Tea was called for, and
we drank it like nectar, in an intoxication of delight. RLS at his very
best . . . As a host, in those surprising circumstances he surpassed
himself. Lightly perched on his packing-case, and emphasising his words
with a brandished teaspoon, he flowed from one anecdote to another
with a brilliance that only those who have listened to him in his inspired
moments can imagine. It was chiefly nonsense that he talked, the gay

enchanting nonsense of a perfectly happy child . . . The chief thing about his wife was the depth and tenderness that glowed in her unfathomable eyes. No other eyes were ever at all like them . . . full of yearning kindness that one's heart might draw from inexhaustibly in time of need . . . But how those glorious eyes could flash with righteous anger. The mention of cruelty in any shape would bring the smouldering fires to a blaze. I have seen her quivering with passion, alight with fury . . . like a lurid light of a volcano, a terrible glory that held one's gaze transfixed.' (*See* Part 4 (Letters); Plate 10)

**Book Buyer, The,** contained anonymous articles entitled 'Some Stevenson Pictures', June 1902; 'Stevensonia: The Trudeau Dedications', February 1895

**'Book of Joseph, The',** dictated to his mother during a visit to Colinton Manse, February-April 1857. First published in Vailima Edition, 1923; Tusitala Edition *28*

**Book of R.L.S., A,** (*see* **Brown, George E.**)

**Bookman,** (London) contained anonymous articles entitled 'R.L. Stevenson Pictures', January 1894; 'Robert Louis Stevenson', a tribute by Barrie, Crockett, McLaren and Gordon, February 1895; 'The Late Sir W. Simpson, Bart, and Robert Louis Stevenson', July 1898; 'Robert Louis Stevenson', October 1913

**Bookman Extra Number,** Hodder & Stoughton, London 1913. Issue devoted to Stevenson which contains tributes and essays from various writers (brought up to date and extended tributes in February 1895 issue)

**'Books which have Influenced Me',** an essay, first published in *British Weekly*, 13 May 1887; Tusitala Edition *28*

**Booth, Bradford A.,** 'The Vailima Letters of Robert Louis Stevenson', *Harvard Library Bulletin*, Cambridge, Mass., April 1967; *Selected Poetry and Prose of Robert Louis Stevenson,* HM Press, New York, 1968

**Boston Bibliophile Society,** (*see* **Hitherto Unpublished Prose Writings**)

**'Bottle Imp, The',** a short story, first published in four weekly instalments, 8 February to 1 March 1891 in *New York Herald*, and *Black and White*, London, 28 March and 4 April 1891; in book form in *Island Nights' Entertainments*, 1893; Tusitala Edition *13*

A traditional folk-tale of the genie in the bottle, with a Samoan setting, this story was translated into Samoan, whose readers could not conceive 'fiction' since all their legends were based on fact, however tenuous. Assuming therefore that the Stevensons' wealth came from the

The entrance hall at Vailima. *Mansell Collection*

command of just such a magic bottle, departing guests would linger in Vailima's opulent entrance hall where the bolder would whisper: 'Please, Tusitala, maybe we now see bottle?'
(*See also* Part 6 (Radio))

**Bough, Samuel,** (1822–78), Scottish landscape painter and friend of Stevenson's student days
(*See* **Edinburgh: Picturesque Notes;** and **'Late Sam Bough, R.S.A., The'**)

**Bourget, Paul,** dedicatee of **'Across the Plains'**

**Bournemouth,** The Stevensons came to this seaside resort in 1884 and lodged at 'Wensleydale' and 'Bonallie Towers' from late summer 1884 to spring 1885, when they moved to a permanent home in 'Skerryvore'. (*See* **Skerryvore**)

**Bowman, John,** *Robert Louis Stevenson*, Chantry Publications, London, 1949. A brief 32-page biography

**'Boy's Adventure with R.L.S., A',** (*see* **Paul, Sir James Balfour**)

**Braemar,** the Aberdeenshire village in Upper Deeside, the area made popular by Queen Victoria's new castle at nearby Balmoral. It was the birthplace of *Treasure Island*, conceived in the cottage of the late

Miss MacGregor, Castleton of Braemar, during August/September 1881

(*See* **Treasure Island; Skinner, R.T.; Todd, Rev. William**)

'**Brasheana**', name given to sonnet sequence of Stevenson's student days, based on a rather shady Edinburgh howff (inn) owned by a bad-tempered publican called Brash who did not care for his University clientele, roistering, drunken and poor

**Braxfield, Lord,** (1722–99), Scottish judge noted for his harsh treatment of political prisoners. Brutal, hard-living, hard-drinking prototype of Lord Weir in *Weir of Hermiston*

**Bridge of Allan,** a town near Stirling, scene of early summer holidays of Stevenson family.
(*See also* **MacCulloch, J.A.; Morrison, Alexander**)

**Brill, Barbara,** *Valiant in Velvet,* the story of Stevenson's early days in Edinburgh. Play, 1969, (photo-copy of manuscript in Edinburgh Room, Edinburgh Central Library); *Robert Louis Stevenson,* Loughborough, 1975

**British Broadcasting Corporation,** *Robert Louis Stevenson, 1850–1950,* a radio commemoration, Edinburgh, 1950, also six broadcast lessons on R.L.S. for Scottish schools, Autumn Term 1950, BBC Publications, 1950
(*See also* Part 6 (Media))

**Bronson, Creole M.,** editor of *Monterey Californian.* (*See also* **Monterey,**)

**Brown, Alice,** *Robert Louis Stevenson,* a study with prelude and postlude by L. I. Guiney. Privately printed, Boston, 1895. Dedicated to William Henley

**Brown, George,** *Pioneer Missionary and Explorer,* Hodder & Stoughton, London, 1908
Fighting Wesleyan, greatly admired by Stevenson. His autobiography describes their meetings at Vailima.

**Brown, George E.,** *A Book of R.L.S.: His Works, Travels, Friends and Commentators,* Methuen & Co., London, 1919

**Brown, Hilton,** 'On a Hill in Samoa (a visit to Robert Louis Stevenson's grave)', *Scots Magazine,* October 1950; 'The Plot in Stevenson', *Scots Magazine,* February 1950. Stevenson's sources of creative inspiration; his methods as a fiction writer.

**Brown, Robert Glasgow** (*see* **London: The Conservative Weekly Journal**)

**Brownies**

When Stevenson needed a story he often maintained that he found it in sleep (*Dr. Jekyll and Mr. Hyde* is a prime example). For convenience he called this creative device his 'Little People' or 'Brownies' and described them as ' . . . near connections of the dreamer's . . . who share in his financial worries . . . only I think I have more talent . . . can tell him a story piece by piece, like a serial, and keep him in ignorance of where they aim . . . they do one half of my work for me while I am fast asleep, and in all human likelihood, do the rest for me as well, when I am wide awake and fondly suppose I do it for myself. They have not a rudiment of a conscience.'
(*See* **'Chapter on Dreams, A'**)

**Buckland, Tin Jack,** South Seas trader ('Tin' = Mr.)

Fellow passenger on cruise of *Janet Nicholl* with the Stevensons in 1890. Flamboyant Australian described by Stevenson as 'Sydney gent and Gilbert Islands beachcomber in alternate layers'. Spent part of year in brief binge in Sydney before returning to the dull trading post. Fanny described him as 'a beautiful creature, terribly annoying at times, but with something childlike and appealing . . . that made one forgive pranks in him that would be unforgivable in others'. One of his favourite pranks was a wardrobe containing greasepaints, a false nose, a wig and whiskers. When he went ashore he would dash into a crowd wearing the disguise, terrifying the islanders and causing near-panic.

**Buckley, Jerome Hamilton,** *William Ernest Henley*, Princeton University Press, N.J. 1945. A study in the 'Counter-Decadence' of the Nineties. Contains reference to Henley's collaboration and association with Stevenson

**Buell, Lewellyn M.,** 'Eilean Earraid: the Beloved Isle of Robert Louis Stevenson', *Scribner's Magazine*, February 1922 (*See also* **Dhu Heartach**)

**Burgess, Gelett,** 'An Interview with Mrs. Robert Louis Stevenson', *Bookman*, New York, September 1898

Designer of two bronze plaques for Stevenson's tomb on Mt. Vaea (plates 24 and 25). One in Samoan bore the words, 'The Tomb of Tusitala . . . Thy people shall be my people and thy God my God, where thou diest, will I die'. This was decorated by a thistle and a hibiscus flower. On the other side was the 'Requiem'. (*See also* **Requiem**)

**Burlingame, Ed. Livermore,** (1848–1922), Editor of *Scribner's Magazine*, 1866–1914

In 1887 Stevenson wrote, 'I am now a salaried party, I am a *bourgeois* now; I am to write a weekly paper for *Scribner's*, at a scale of payment which makes my teeth ache for shame and diffidence . . . I am like to be a millionaire if this goes on, and be publicly hanged at the social revolution; well, I would prefer that to dying in my bed; and it would be a godsend to my biographer, if ever I have one'. (*See* Part 4 (Letters))

**Burlingame, Roger,** *Of Making Many Books*, Scribner's, New York, 1946. Comments on Stevenson's early relationship, confusions and misunderstandings with Scribner's and McClure

**Burlington Lodge Academy,** Spring Grove, Isleworth, Middlesex. His parents having been ordered to Menton for the sake of Margaret Stevenson's health, Stevenson was sent to boarding school for a term in the autumn of 1863. Although he wrote enthusiastically for 'The School Boys' Magazine' — four stories (three marked 'to be continued') — the measure of his homesickness can be taken from the letter begun in French (12 November 1863) and ended in English: 'hope you will find your house at Mentone nice . . . My dear papa, you told me to tell you whenever I was miserable. I do not feel well and I wish to get home. Do take me with you.'

**Burns, Robert,** (1759–1796)
The *Encyclopaedia Britannica* turned down Stevenson's article on the Scottish poet which they had commissioned at a fee of five guineas. While Stevenson exulted in Burns' brilliance as a writer he regarded him as having the morals of a tom-cat, 'Mr. Carlyle has made an inimitable bust of the poet's head of gold; may I not be forgiven if my business should have more to do with the feet, which were of clay?' Scotland was outraged by this piece of *lèse-majesté*. To his friend Edmund Gosse he had confessed difficulties in the writing, 'A kind of chronological table of Burns' various loves and lusts and have been comparatively speechless since there was something in him of the vulgar, bagman-like, professional seducer'. In 'Some Aspects of Robert Burns', he wrote, 'He sank more and more towards the professional Don Juan who plumes himself on the scandal at the birth of his first bastard'. (*See also* **'Some Aspects of Robert Burns'**)

**Burriss, Eli Edward,** 'The Classical Culture of Robert Louis Stevenson', *Classical Journal*, XX, 271. Stevenson considered as 'sedulous ape to Hazlitt, Lamb, Wordsworth, to Sir Thomas Browne, Defoe, Hawthorne, Montaigne, Baudelaire . . .'

**Bushnell, G.H.,** 'Robert Louis Stevenson and "Henderson's Weekly"'. *Scots Magazine*, November 1942. Discusses Stevenson's associations with James Henderson of *Young Folks*, etc.

**Butcher, Lady Alice Mary,** *Memories of George Meredith*, Constable,

London, 1919. Contains references to Meredith's long friendship with Stevenson

**Butts, Denis,** *Robert Louis Stevenson*, Bodley Head monograph, London, 1966. Emphasis on *Treasure Island* and *A Child's Garden of Verses*

**'Byways of Book Illustration',** an essay, first published in *Magazine of Art*, November 1882; Tusitala Edition *28*

# C

*Cadger's Creel, A,* (*See* **Douglas, Sir George**)

**Calahan, Harold Augustin,** *Back to Treasure Island,* A. & C. Black, London, 1936

**Calder, Jenni,** *R.L.S.: A Life Study,* Hamish Hamilton, London, 1980; *The Robert Louis Stevenson Companion* (ed.), Paul Harris, Edinburgh, 1980. A miscellaneous selection from Stevenson's best-loved works; *Stevenson and Victorian Scotland* (ed.) Edinburgh University Press, 1981. Original essays by David Daiches, Michael Balfour, J.C. Furnas and others

**Caldwell, Elsie Noble,** *Last Witness for Robert Louis Stevenson,* University of Oklahoma Press, 1960. Belle Strong's view of her stepfather in Samoa, which was intended as a joint project with Caldwell before Belle's death in 1953

**Calistoga, California,** (*see* **Silverado Squatters, The**)

**Calvinism**

Stevenson was reared on the stern principles of Calvinism which he inherited from Balfours and Stevensons. 'Engineer, physician, Calvinist theologian – serious Scots are known as such throughout the English-speaking world. Louis had all three of those elements smelted into his life from the moment he opened his blue eyes which, baby-fashion, quickly turned dark hazel. He could have been a standard article, lean, long-legged credit to engine room or surgical theatre, hard-headed but sentimental, not always sober on Saturday, usually at church next day. But, both emotionally and physically, he was born to trouble as the sparks fly upward'. (J. C. Furnas's *Voyage to Windward*).
(*See also* **Christianity of Stevenson; Morals**)

**Cameron, D.L.,** 'The Appin Murder; Notes on the Historical Ground-work of *Kidnapped* and *Catriona*', *Atalanta,* 1893–4

**Cameron, John,** 'The Appin Murder, a Summing up', *Scottish Historical Review,* Vol. 33, No. 116, October 1954

**Camisards, The,** French parallel to the Scottish Covenanters whose adventures fascinated Stevenson during his travels in the Cévennes.
(*See* **Travels with a Donkey in the Cévennes;** Part 2 (Colonel Jean Cavalier))

**Campagne Defli**

On the Riviera in search of a place where Stevenson could live without imminent dangers of haemorrhage, they found, in the St. Marcel suburb of Marseilles, Campagne Defli set in a large estate overlooking a valley of white cliffs and woods. At £48 per year it was ideal and Fanny wrote to her mother-in-law, 'It is a garden of paradise, and I cannot tell you how I long to have you here to enjoy things with us'. A few months later funeral bells tolled in the village and corpses were carried on coffin-lids past the house – one (claimed Fanny) was left to bloat in the sun outside their gate. She panicked, and believing it was a typhus epidemic (in actual fact it was enteric fever), insisted Stevenson leave immediately for Nice where he took ill and she rushed to his aid. However, the change of air and doctor were speeding his recovery. Returning to Campagne Defli, Fanny wrote to him, 'Don't you dare come back to this home of "pizon" until you are really better . . . deserting your family as you have done and being hunted down and caught by your wife. You are a dear creature and I love you but I am not going to say that I am lonesome lest you come flying back to this den of death.'

  'Campagne De – fli: (he wrote)
   O me!
  Campagne De – bug:
   There comes the tug!
  Campagne De – mosquito:
   It's eneuch to gar me greet, O!
  Campagne De – louse:
   O God damn the house!'

A month later Fanny had also succumbed to vague illness and depression. Stevenson wrote to his mother (*Letters*, Tusitala Edition *32*, p.219), 'I do not go back, but do not go forward – or not much. It is, in one way, miserable – for I can do no work; a very little wood-cutting, the newspapers, and a note about every two days to write, completely exhausts my surplus energy; even Patience I have to cultivate with parsimony. I see, if I could only get to work, that we could live here with comfort, almost with luxury. Even as it is, we should be able to get through a considerable time of idleness. I like the place immensely, though I have seen so little of it – I have only once been outside the gate since I was here! It puts me in mind of a summer at Prestonpans and a sickly child you once told me of.'

**Campbell, Ian,** (ed.) *Selected Short Stories of R. L. Stevenson,* Ramsay Head Press, Edinburgh, 1980

**'Canonisation of Stevenson, The'**, (*see* **Schyler, Montgomery**)

**'Cannonmills'**, an unfinished short story, first published in Vailima Edition, 1923; Tusitala Edition *16*

**Cap of Youth, The,** (*see* **Steuart, John A.**)

**Carlyle, Thomas,** (1795–1881)

The Scottish writer was considered 'an eccentric Conservative' by Stevenson, who voted against him in favour of Disraeli in the Edinburgh students' election for the Rector of the University in 1867. Carlyle won.

**Carothers, Alva,** 'The Road of Loving Hearts to Stevenson's Tomb', *St. Nicholas Magazine*, November 1926

**Carré, Jean-Marie,** *The Frail Warrior*, Noel Douglas, London, 1931. Search for the true Stevenson; dreamer, mystic and bohemian. Translated from the French by Eleanor Hard

**Carrington, James B.,** 'Another Glimpse of R.L.S.', *Scribner's Magazine*, August 1927. 'Christmas at Silverado'. *Mentor*, December 1928. Pilgrimage to Napa Valley and the old mining camp made famous by its brief association with Stevenson and Fanny during their honeymoon in 1880

**Carruthers, Mr.,** British lawyer

Carruthers and his Samoan wife were the Stevensons' nearest neighbours at Vailima. They sent them a gift of pineapples when they arrived, to which he received their thanks and reply, 'As soon as we eat them, we plant the tops'.

**Carson, Mrs.**

Stevenson's voluble and kindly landlady in San Francisco. She befriended him when he was living on seventy cents a day, supplemented by a few dollars for occasional pieces in the San Francisco *Bulletin* while he waited for Fanny's divorce to come through. Hungry, unhappy, his teeth rotting, he wrote to Gosse, (*Letter*, Tusitala Edition 32, p.100) 'Few people . . . have known each other so long or made more trials of each other's tenderness and constancy'. From Monterey he had written (*Letters*, Tusitala Edition 32, p.87), 'I am going for thirty now; and unless I can snatch a little rest, I have, I may tell you in confidence, no hope of seeing thirty-one . . . To start a pleurisy about nothing, while leading a dull, regular life in a mild climate was not my habit in the past . . . I believe I must go. It is a pity . . . for I believe the class of work I *might* yet give out is better and more real and solid than people fancy. But death is no bad friend; a few aches and gasps and we are done . . .' (*See* Part 2 ('Adventures of John Carson'))

**Carson, Robbie**

Stevenson's philosophy of death was small consolation when Mrs. Carson's younger son Robbie almost died of pneumonia. To help his landlady, he helped to nurse the boy day and night to the detriment of his

own health. Heartbroken, he wrote to Colvin (*Letters* Tusitala Edition
*32*, p.109), 'Never, never any family for me! . . . I did all I could to help;
but all seems little, to the point of crime, when one of these poor
innocents lies in such misery.'
(*See also* **Children**)

'**Cart-Horses and the Saddle-Horse, The**', a fable, Tusitala Edition
   *5* (*see also* **Fables**)

*Casco*, schooner-yacht in which the Stevensons set forth from San
   Francisco on 28 June 1888 bound for the South Seas

*Cassell's Family Papers,* favourite reading matter of Stevenson's nurse,
   Cummy. His childhood was livened by having its serials read out by
   Cummy and their weekly visit to the 'shop around the corner' to
   collect the next weekly instalment was an eagerly-awaited event.
   (*See* Plate 8)

'**Castaways of Soledad, The**', an incomplete story, privately printed
   for Thomas B. Lockwood, Buffalo, N.Y., 1928

*Catalogue (1)* (sale) of an almost unparalleled collection of unpublished
   Stevensonian letters from the library of Mrs. William B. Hayden of
   New York City, New York, 1924

*Catalogue (2)* (sale) of autograph letters, original manuscripts, books,
   portraits and curios from the library of the late R.L.S., consigned by
   the present owner, Mrs. Isobel Strong, to Anderson Auction
   Company, New York, 1914–16

*Catalogue (3)* of important unpublished autograph letters of R.L.S., and
   the manuscripts of his then unpublished play *Monmouth*; sold by
   Christie, Manson & Woods, London, 11 July 1922

*Catalogue (4)* of valuable books and manuscripts, rare and important
   Stevensoniana, the property of Lloyd Osbourne; sold by Sotheby,
   Wilkinson & Hodge, London, 5–7 February 1923

*Catalogue (5)* of books from the library of R.L.S. at Vailima, sold by
   order of Mrs. W.E. Safford of Washington, D.C.; New York, 1926

**Catalogue of the Books and Manuscripts of Robert Louis Stevenson
   in the Library of the Late H. E. Widener, A,** with a memoir by
   A. S. W. Rosenbach, Philadelphia, 1913

**Catalogue of the Stevenson Collection** 1950 and 1978, available in Edinburgh
   Room, Edinburgh Central Library.

**catalogues**; *see also* **Colgate, H.A.; McKay, George L.; New York
State University; Trinity Academy**

**Catriona,** a novel first serialised under the title *'David Balfour, Memoirs of his Adventures at Home and Abroad'* in *Atalanta*, New York, December 1892 to September 1893. After publication it was found that many persons were confused by the two titles, as both books told of the adventures of the same hero. For that reason in Britain the name of the sequel was changed to *Catriona.* In book form, Cassell, London, Scribner's, New York, 1893; Tusitala Edition 7
 'A sequel to "KIDNAPPED". Being memoirs of the further adventures of DAVID BALFOUR at home and abroad in which are set forth his misfortunes anent the Appin murder; his troubles with Lord Advocate Grant; captivity on the Bass Rock; journey into Holland and France; and singular relations with James More Drummond or Macgregor, a son of the notorious Rob Roy, and his daughter Catriona. Written by himself and now set forth by ROBERT LOUIS STEVENSON.'
 The novel was written with Stevenson's usual rare turn of speed, begun on 13 February 1892. On 13 March he wrote 'I have this day triumphantly completed 15 chapters, 100 pages — being exactly half.' With sundry interruptions, proofs and visitors, he completed the work in seven and a half months and wrote on 30 September: *'David Balfour* done and its author along with it, or nearly so.' (Letter to Colvin, Tusitala Edition *34* , p. 244). He was pleased with the story declared it 'nearer what I mean than anything I have done: nearer what I mean by fiction . . . tempted to think of it as my best work; . . . I shall never do a better book . . . my high-water mark . . .'
 (*See* **Baxter, Charles**)

**Catriona and Kidnapped,**(*see* **Curry, George**)

*'Centenary of Robert Louis Stevenson',* (*see* **Hayes-McCoy, G.A.**)

*Century Magazine,* New York
 Bought Stevenson's collection of short stories *New Arabian Nights* in 1882, shortly after publication in London. Fanny wrote to her mother-in-law (Margaret Mackay, *The Violent Friend*): 'I am so pleased that it was in the Century, for every friend and relation I have in the world will read it. I suppose you are even prouder of Louis than I am, for he is only mine accidentally, and he is yours by birth and blood. Two or three times last night I woke up just from pure pleasure to think of all the people I know reading about Louis.'

**Cévennes Journal, The, Notes on a Journey through the French Highlands,** Mainstream Publishing, Edinburgh and Taplinger Publishing, New York, 1978. Stevenson's personal notebook, some of which was subsequently published as *Travels with a Donkey.* The remainder, including several of his drawings of the region, appear in print for the first time in this volume.

**'Cévennes Link with R.L.S., A'** (*see* **Skinner, R.T.**)

**Chalet La Solitude,** (*see* **La Solitude**)

**Chalmers, Rev. James,** martyr hero and New Guinea missionary whom
Stevenson described as 'one of the greatest personalities' he had ever
known

**Chalmers, Stephen,** *The Penny Piper of Saranac, An Episode in Stevenson's
Life,* with Preface by Lord Guthrie, Houghton Mifflin, New York,
1916; 'The Man in Portsmouth Square', *Overland Monthly*, January 1930.
The first public monument to Stevenson is in Portsmouth Square, San
Francisco, where he often wrote in the sunshine during his stay at 608
Bush Street, December 1879-May 1880. (*See* Plate 16)

*Chambers Journal,* contained anonymous articles entitled 'Robert Louis
Stevenson: the Hills of Home', 2 February 1901; 'The Popularity of
Robert Louis Stevenson', October 1905

**Chapman, John Jay,** *Emerson and Other Essays,* Moffat, New York,
1909
Chapman accuses Stevenson of being 'the most extraordinary mimic that
has ever appeared in literature'

**'Chapter on Dreams, A',** an essay, first published in *Scribner's
Magazine,* January 1888; in book form in *Across the Plains,* 1892;
Tusitala Edition *30*

**'Character, A',** an essay, first published in the Edinburgh Edition 1896;
Tusitala Edition *30*

**'Character of Dogs, The',** an essay, first published in *English
Illustrated Magazine,* February 1884; in book form *Memories and Portraits,*
1887; Tusitala Edition *29*

**Charity Bazaar, The,** a play, first published in Edinburgh Edition
1898; Tusitala Edition *5*
This 'allegorical dialogue', as it was sub-titled, was written and privately
printed in 1868, 'a boyish skit on the occasion of a charity bazaar held at 17
Heriot Row, Edinburgh' — the Stevenson home.

**'Charles of Orleans',** an essay, first published in *Cornhill Magazine,*
December 1876; in book form in *Familiar Studies of Men and Books,*1882;
Tusitala Edition *27*

**Charteris, Evan,** *John Sargent,* Heinemann, London, 1927. Refers to
the artist's friendship with, and portrait of, Stevenson; *Life and Letters
of Edmund Gosse.* Heinemann, London, 1931. Refers to projects of
Stevenson on Benjamin Franklin and Hazlitt.

**Chase, J.S.,** 'Stevenson and Monterey: Thirty Years After', *Chambers Journal*, March 1912

**Chesterton, Gilbert Keith,** (1874–1936), *Robert Louis Stevenson*, Hodder & Stoughton, London, 1927

'I believe that the lesson of his life will only be seen after time has revealed the full meaning of all our present tendencies. I believe it will be seen from afar like a vast plan or maze traced out on a hillside, perhaps traced by one who did not even see the plan while he was making the tracks . . . Stevenson will win, not because he has friends or admirers or the approval of the public or the assent of the aesthetics. He will win because he is *right* – a word of great practical import which needs to be re-discovered. He may or may not be eclipsed for a time; it would be a truer way of putting it to say that the public may or may not be eclipsed for a time . . . The idea that a great literary man who has said something novel and important to mankind can vanish suddenly and finally is ridiculous. The pessimists who believe it are people who could believe that the sun is destroyed for ever each time it sinks in the west. Nothing is lost in the magnificent economy of existence; the sun returns, the flowers return, the literary fashions return.'

**Chevillon's** (*see* **Hotel Chevillon**)

**childhood notes,** autobiographical fragments dated May 1873. First published in Graham Balfour's *Life* 1901. (*See* **'Memoirs of Himself'**; **'Rosa Quo Locorum'**.)

**Children**

Stevenson was always aware of the child who lurked within him, whom he had never outgrown. For this reason perhaps he had considerable rapport with children, Lloyd Osbourne, Nelitchka Zassetsky, etc. He suffered agonies for his friends bereaved of their children.

Why he and Fanny remained childless has been the subject of fascinated speculation by many biographers, as to whether it was planned because of Stevenson's illness and the age difference since Fanny, at forty, was middle-aged biologically when they married. There was, however, one alarm recorded from Hyères. In March 1884 Stevenson wrote to Walter Simpson, 'I must tell you a joke. A month or two ago, there was an alarm; it looked like family. Prostration: I saw myself financially ruined. I saw the child born sickly, etc. Then, said I, I must look at this thing on the good side; proceeded to do so studiously; and with such result that when the alarm passed off – I was inconsolable.'

He also was aware of the fragile nature of the parent-child relationship and during his own difficult years at Heriot Row wrote, 'The love of parents for their children is, of all natural affections, the most ill-starred. It is not a love for the person, since it begins before the person has come

into the world, and founds on an imaginary character and looks . . . and
because the parent either looks for too much, or at least for something
inappropriate, at his offspring's hands, it is too often insufficiently
repaid . . . What do we owe our parents? No man can *owe* love; none can
*owe* obedience. We owe, I think, chiefly pity; for we are the pledge of
their dear and joyful union . . . the solicitude of their days and the anxiety
of their nights . . . They have all been like the duck and hatched swan's
eggs, or the other way about; yet they tell themselves with miserable
penitence that the blame lies with them; and had they sat more closely, the
swan would have been a duck and home-keeping, in spite of all.' (From
'Reflections and Remarks on Human Life').

(*See also* **Stevenson, Thomas** (Stevenson's relations with his father);
**Carson, Robbie; Henley, William Ernest; Sitwell, Bertie;
Osbourne, Lloyd**)

**Child's Garden of Verses, A,** a collection of poems, first published by
Chatto & Windus, 1885; Tusitala Edition *22*

*Dedicated*    'To Alison Cunningham' (his nurse Cummy), 'From Her Boy':
For the long nights you lay awake
And watched for my unworthy sake:
For your most comfortable hand
That led me through the uneven land:
For all the story-books you read:
For all the pains you comforted:
For all you pitied, all you bore,
In sad and happy days of yore: –
My second Mother, my first Wife,
The angel of my infant life –
From the sick child, now well and old,
Take, nurse, the little book you hold!'

(*See* Part 6 (Radio))

**'Child's Play',** an essay first published in *Cornhill Magazine*,
September 1878; in book form in *Virginibus Puerisque*, 1881; Tusitala
Edition *25*

*Christianity Confirmed by Jewish and Heathen Testimony,* (*See* **Stevenson,
Thomas**)

**Christianity of Stevenson**
Reared to a rigorous Calvinism, Stevenson toyed with agnosticism and
atheism at University, especially under the influence of his cousin Bob
Stevenson. His parents remained in ignorance until one day in 1873,
Thomas Stevenson read the somewhat blasphemous aims of the 'L.J.R.'
The scene that followed was described in a letter to Charles Baxter, 'My
dear papa was in a devil of a taking . . . The thunderbolt has fallen with a

vengeance now. . . . You know the aspect of a house in which somebody
is still awaiting burial; the quiet steps, the hushed voices and rare
conversation, the religious literature that holds a temporary monopoly,
the grim, wretched faces; all is here reproduced in this family circle in
honour of my (what is it?) atheism or blasphemy . . . My father put me
one or two questions as to beliefs, which I candidly answered. I really
hate all lying so much now – a new-found honesty that has somehow
come out of my late illness – that I could not so much as hesitate at the
time; but if I had foreseen the real hell of everything since, I think I
should have lied, as I have done so often before. I so far thought of my
father, but I had forgotten my mother. And now! they are both ill, both
silent, both as down in the mouth as – as I can find no simile . . . If it
were not too late, I think I could almost find it in my heart to retract
but . . . am I to live my whole life as one falsehood? Of course, it is
rougher than hell upon my father, but can I help it? They don't see either
that my game is not the light-hearted scoffer; that I am not (as they call
me) a careless infidel . . . I am, I think, as honest as they can be in what I
hold. I have not come hastily to my views. I reserve (as I told them)
many points until I acquire further information, and do not think I am
thus justly to be called "horrible atheist" . . . father's purpose of
praying down continuous afflictions upon my head . . . What a curse I
am to my parents! . . . O Lord, what a pleasant thing it is to have just
*damned* the happiness of (probably) the only two people who care a damn
about you in the world . . . Here is a good heavy cross with a vengeance,
and all rough with rusty nails that tear your fingers, only it is not that I
have to carry it alone; I hold the light end, but the heavy burden falls on
these two.' His proposed speech on the Duke of Argyll delivered before
the Speculative Society (*see* Part 2 'Law and Free Will') did nothing to
help the worsening situation, as he wrote to Mrs. Sitwell (22 September
1873, Letters, National Library of Scotland, Edinburgh), 'He [Thomas
Stevenson] said tonight he wished he had never survived . . . "A poor
end," he said, "for all my tenderness." And what was there to answer?
"I have made all my life to suit you – I have worked for you and gone out
of my way for you – and the end of it is that I find you in opposition to
the Lord Jesus Christ. I find everything gone. I would ten times sooner
see you lying in your grave than that you should be shaking the faith of
other young men and bringing ruin on other houses as you have brought
it upon this . . . I thought," he said "to have had some one to help me
when I was old." '
A year later he was to write to her again (Letters, National Library of
Scotland, Edinburgh), '. . . How dark and foolish are the ways in which
people once walked, thinking them lit up with eternal sunlight, and
what we now see to be so much gauze and cardboard, imperishable
masonry! . . . God help us all, amen. For I do cling a little to God, as I
have lost all hold on right and wrong. You cannot think things both right

and wrong, you know; the human mind cannot do it, although I daresay
it would be devilish clever if you could; and when you come to a stone
wall in morals, you give them up and be damned to them. I beg your
pardon, but that's the only English idiom which explains my meaning.
So I say, I cling to God; to a nice immoral old gentleman who knows a bit
more about it all than I do, and may, sometime or other, in the course of
the ages, explain matters to his creature over a pipe of tobacco; nay, and
he may be something more than this, and give one that sense of finish and
perspective that can only be had one way in the world. I daresay it's all a
lie; but if it please me to imagine it —'

Many years later, Lloyd Osbourne was to write in *An Intimate Portrait*,
'Tolstoy had a profound influence over him and did much to formulate
his vague and sometimes contradictory views. Tolstoy virtually
rediscovered Christianity as a stupendous force in the world; not the
Christianity of dogma, supernaturalism, hell, and heaven, but as a
sublime ethical formula that alone could redeem society. Stevenson in
this sense was an ardent Christian. It was characteristic of him to say,
"Christ was always such a great gentleman; you can always count on
His doing the right thing," and he used to instance the marriage-feast at
Cana with a special pleasure. "What a charming courtesy to these poor
people – to help their entertainment with a better wine!"

'Yet in the accepted religious meaning Stevenson was wholly an
unbeliever. He wanted "no pass-book to heaven with the items entered
regularly by an administrative angel". Certain phases of emotional
Christianity struck him, indeed, as abominably egotistical and selfish.
"Think a little more of other people's souls and less of your own," he
said once to an anxiously confiding lady. "I am sure Christ never
intended you to concentrate all your thoughts on yourself."

Stevenson's Christianity exposed him to many charges of contradiction.
The unbeliever, who in Samoa went to church, taught in a Sunday
school and had prayers daily in his household, could not escape some
caustic criticism; nor could the essayist, who by implication, at least,
seemed at times almost conventionally religious. The truth was he
thought the multitude unable to grasp his own lofty faith; thought that it
needed supernaturalism, ritual, and sensuous impression to stir the little
ideality it possessed. As opposed to materialism, Stevenson infinitely
preferred denominational religion so long as it retained the least spark of
sincerity. In a half-civilised country like Samoa whose people were just
beginning to emerge from primitive superstition, it seemed to him
essential to support the native churches – Congregational, Wesleyan,
and Roman Catholic – by an active concurrence; and in this connection
it must be confessed that Stevenson had an illogical sort of inherited love
for religious forms and ceremonies. He could roll out the word "God"
with an indescribable conviction, and nothing pleased him more than to
read his own prayers aloud and endow them with the glamour of his

extraordinarily affective voice. He liked too – best of all, I think – the beautiful and touchingly patriarchal aspect of family devotions; the gathering of the big, hushed household preparatory to the work of the day, and the feeling of unity and fellowship thus engendered. It was certainly a picturesque assembly – Stevenson in imposing state at the head of the table, I at his right with the Samoan Bible before me, ready to follow him with a chapter in the native language, the rest of the family about us, and in front the long row of half-naked Samoans, with their proud free air and glistening bodies. We were the *Sa Tusitalá*, the Clan of Stevenson, and this was the daily enunciation of our solidarity.' (*See also* **Kelman John; Prayers Written for Family Use at Vailima; Morals**)

*'Christmas at Silverado'*, (*see* **Carrington, James B.**)

**'Christmas Sermon, A'**, an essay, first published in *Scribner's Magazine*, December 1888; in book form in *Across the Plains*, 1892; Tusitala Edition 26

*Chronicle of Friendships, A,* (*see* **Low, Will H.**)

**Chuchu,**

The sentimental setter-crossed-with-spaniel who accompanied the Stevensons on their Silverado honeymoon was, according to Stevenson, 'the most unsuited for a rough life. He had been nurtured tenderly in the society of ladies; his heart was large and soft; he regarded the sofa cushion as a bed-rock necessary of existence. Though about the size of a sheep, he loved to sit in ladies' laps; he never said a bad word in all his blameless days; and if he had ever seen a flute, I am sure he could have played upon it by nature. It may seem hard to say of a dog, but Chuchu was a tame cat.'

**Churchill, William,** 'Stevenson in the South Seas', *McClure's Magazine*, December 1921

**'Citizen and the Traveller, The'**, a fable, Tusitala Edition 5 (*see also* **Fables**)

*City of Chester,* Inman Road Mail Steamer on which the newly-wed Stevensons sailed to Liverpool from New York in August 1880, for reconciliation with his parents

**'Claire',** the story of an Edinburgh prostitute, based on Stevenson's early love for Kate Drummond

Rumour (emanating from Gosse) after Stevenson's death declared that Stevenson had half-finished the manuscript of 'Claire' which Fanny forced him to burn. (*See* **Drummond, Kate; 'Travelling Companion, The'; Steuart, John A.**)

**Claire, Maurice,** *A Day with Robert Louis Stevenson,* Hodder & Stoughton, London, n.d. An illustrated book of 44 pages on Vailima, Samoa

**Clark, Sir Andrew,** eminent physician whom the young Stevenson was urged to consult in London

Dr Clark told the elder Stevenson, who came promptly to London for his verdict, that although he feared consumption in view of the patient's weak chest and family history, 'lesions' might exist but there were no overt symptoms present of tuberculosis. He added firmly that until their son was in sturdier health (he weighed a mere 118 pounds) exams, further study of law or any other taxing activity might only quicken his decline. Rest, food and sunshine were recommended. Mrs. Stevenson timidly suggested accompanying her son to Torquay, but Dr Clark, ahead of his time in assessing the dangers of the parent-child relationship, shrewdly recommended the Riviera – alone. Small wonder Stevenson wrote to Mrs. Sitwell en route for joyous exile, 'Clark is a trump' (*Letters* Tusitala Edition *31* p.88)

**Clarke, Rev. W.E.,** 'Robert Louis Stevenson in Samoa', *Yale Review*, January 1921

Clarke from the London Missionary Society was a close Vailima friend of the Stevensons and was with the unconscious Stevenson when he died. He describes their first meeting in Samoa in December 1889, walking along the shore at Apia, 'I met a little group of three European strangers – two men and a woman. The latter wore a print gown, large gold crescent earrings, a Gilbert-Island hat of plaited straw, encircled by a wreath of small shells, a scarlet silk scarf round her neck, and a brilliant plaid shawl across her shoulders; her bare feet were encased in white canvas shoes, and across her back was slung a guitar . . . The younger of her two companions [Lloyd] was dressed in a striped pyjama suit – the undress costume of most European traders in these seas – a slouch hat of native make, dark blue sun-spectacles, and over his shoulder a banjo. The other man was dressed in a shabby suit of white flannels that had seen many better days, a white drill yachting cap with a prominent peak, a cigarette in his mouth, a photographic camera in his hand. Both the men were bare-footed. They had, evidently, just landed from the little schooner now lying placidly at anchor, and my first thought was that, probably, they were wandering players en route to New Zealand, compelled by their poverty to take the cheap conveyance of a trading vessel.'

**'Classical Culture of Robert Louis Stevenson, The',** (*see* **Burris, Eli Edward**)

**Cleghorn, A.S.,** Scottish friend of the Stevensons married to a native princess and father of Princess Kaiulani, heiress-presumptive of Hawaii (*See also* **Kaiulani, Princess**)

**Clifford, Mrs W.K.**, 'The Sidney Colvins: Some Personal Recollections', *Bookman*, London, April 1928. Refers to their long friendship with Stevensons.

**Clouston, J. Storer**, 'About the Work of R.L.S.', in *A Cadger's Creel* (*see* **Douglas, Sir George**)

**Clunes, Andrew**, 'Could Unst have been Treasure Island?', *Scotsman*, 17 November 1962. Speculation upon Stevenson's inspiration for the island's location

**'Coast of Fife, The'**, an essay, first published in *Scribner's Magazine*, October 1888; in book form in *Across the Plains*, 1892; Tusitala Edition *30*.

**'Cockermouth and Keswick'**, an essay, first published in the Edinburgh Edition, 1896; Tusitala Edition *30*.

**Cockfield Rectory** (*see* **Babington, Rev. Churchill**)

**Colby, Frank Moore**, 'A Debated Charm', *Bookman*, New York, February 1902. Commenting on the Stevenson/Henley controversy, 'To have a friend like Henley must add greatly to the terrors of the grave.'

**Cole and Cox**, policemen who behaved with outstanding bravery during the Fenian bombing in London in the early 1880s, and to whom the Stevensons dedicated *The Dynamiter*, Tusitala Edition *3*

'To Messrs Cole and Cox, Police Officers. Gentlemen: In the volume now in your hands, the authors have touched upon the ugly devil of crime, with which it is your glory to have contended . . . Whoever be in the right in this great and confused war of politics; whatever elements of greed, whatever traits of the bully, dishonour both parties in this inhuman contest; – your side, your part, is at least pure of doubt. Yours is the side of the child, of the breeding woman, of individual pity and public trust. Courage and devotion, so common in the ranks of the police, so little recognised, so meagerly rewarded, have at length found their commemoration in an historical act. History, which will represent Mr. Parnell sitting silent under the appeal of Mr. Forster, and Gordon setting forth upon his tragic enterprise, will not forget Mr. Cole carrying the dynamite in his defenceless hands, nor Mr. Cox coming coolly to his aid.

Robert Louis Stevenson
Fanny Van de Grift Stevenson'

**Colgate, H.A.,** *Stevenson Library of H.A. Colgate, NY City*, sold by his order, New York 1928

**Colinton,** now a suburb of Edinburgh, in Stevenson's day it was a small outlying Edinburgh village on the picturesque Water of Leith

**Colinton Manse,** home of Stevenson's grandfather, Rev. Lewis Balfour. R.L.S. played in its gardens, an only child, supported by a regiment of young and boisterous cousins, exactly as had his mother in the previous generation. He wrote, 'It was a place like no other; the garden cut into provinces by a great hedge of beech, and overlooked by the church and the terrace of the churchyard, where the tombstones were thick and after nightfall "spunkies" might be seen to dance, at least by children; flower-pots lying warm in the sunshine; laurels and the great yew making elsewhere a pleasing horror of shade; the smell of water rising from all round, with an added tang of papermills; the sound of water everywhere, and the sound of mills, the wheel and the dam singing their alternate strain; the birds on every bush and from every corner of the overhanging woods pealing out their notes until the air throbbed with them; and in the midst of this, the manse.'

Inside there were many wonders for young 'Smout', as he was then called by the family. Several of the Balfour family had brought back from India exotic trophies, 'junks and bangles, beads and screens'.

(*See* **'Manse, The'**; **'Reminiscences of Colinton Manse'**; Plate 6)

**Collected Poems of R.L. Stevenson** (*see* **Smith, Janet Adam**)

*'Collecting of Stevensons,'* (*see* **Ellwanger, W.D.**)

**'College for Men and Women'**, an essay, first published in *The Academy*, 10 October 1874; Tusitala Edition *28*.

**'College Magazine, A'**, an essay first published in *Memories and Portraits*, 1887; Tusitala Edition *29*

**'College Papers'**, five essays, originally published individually in *Edinburgh University Magazine*, first published in book form in Edinburgh Edition, 1896; Tusitala Edition *25*

(*See* **'Debating Societies'**; **'Edinburgh Students in 1824'**; **'Modern Student Considered Generally, The'**; **'Philosophy of Nomenclature, The'**; **'Philosophy of Umbrellas, The'**)

**Colvin, Lady,** (*see* **Sitwell, Fanny**)

**Colvin, Sir Sidney,** (1845–1927), essayist and art critic. Slade Professor of Fine Art at Cambridge, later Curator of Prints at the British Museum. 'The Death of Mr. R.L. Stevenson', *Pall Mall Gazette*, 19 December 1894; *Memories and Notes of Persons and Places, 1852–1914,*

Edward Arnold, London, 1921; 'Robert Louis Stevenson at Hampstead', *Hampstead Annual*, 1902; *Robert Louis Stevenson, His Work and Personality*, by Sidney Colvin and others, Hodder & Stoughton, London, 1924; 'Some Letters of Mrs. R.L. Stevenson and One from Henry James', *Empire Review*, March-April 1924; 'More Letters of Mrs. R.L. Stevenson', *Scribner's Magazine*, April 1924.

A life-long friend of Stevenson, Colvin left the following vivid portrayal, (Introduction to *Letters*, Tusitala Edition *31*):
'There was yet another and very different side to Stevenson which struck others more than it struck myself, namely, that of the freakish or elvish, irresponsible madcap or jester which sometimes appeared in him. It is true that his demoniac quickness of wit and intelligence suggested occasionally a "spirit of air and fire" rather than one of earth; that he was abundantly given to all kinds of quirk and laughter; and that there was no jest (save the unkind) he would not make and relish . . . He would begin . . . perhaps with a jest at some absurd adventure of his own, perhaps with the recitation, in his vibrating voice and full Scotch accent, of some snatch of poetry that was haunting him, perhaps with a rhapsody of analytic delight over some minute accident of beauty or expressiveness that had struck him in some man, woman, child or external nature. And forthwith the floodgates would be opened, and the talk would stream on in endless, never importunate, flood and variety. A hundred fictitious characters would be invented and launched on their imaginary careers; a hundred ingenious problems of conduct and cases of honour would be set and solved; romantic voyages would be planned and followed out in vision, with a thousand incidents; . . . Imagine all this helped by the most speaking of presences: a steady, penetrating fire in the brown, wide-set eyes, a compelling power and richness in the smile; courteous, waving gestures of the arms and long, nervous hands, a lit cigarette generally held between the fingers; continual rapid shiftings and pacings to and fro as he conversed: rapid, but not flurried nor awkward, for there was a grace in his attenuated but well-carried figure, and his movements were light, deft, and full of spring. There was something for strangers, and even for friends, to get over in the queer garments which in youth it was his whim to wear – the badge, as they always seemed to me, partly of a genuine carelessness, certainly of a genuine lack of cash (the little he had was always absolutely at the disposal of his friends), partly of a deliberate detachment from any particular social class or caste, and partly of his love of pickles and adventures, which he thought befell a man thus attired more readily than another. But this slender, slovenly, nondescript apparition, long-visaged and long-haired, had only to speak in order to be recognised in the first minute for a witty and charming gentleman, and within the first five for a master spirit and man of genius. There were, indeed, certain

stolidly conventional and superciliously official kinds of persons, both at home and abroad, who were incapable of looking beyond the clothes, and eyed him always with frozen suspicion. This attitude used sometimes in youth to drive him into fits of flaming anger, which put him helplessly at a disadvantage unless, or until, he could call the sense of humour to his help. Apart from these his human charm was the same for all kinds of people, without distinction of class or caste; for worldly-wise old great ladies, whom he reminded of famous poets in their youth; for his brother artists and men of letters, perhaps, above all; for the ordinary clubman; for his physicians, who could never do enough for him; for domestic servants, who adored him; for the English policeman, even, on whom he often tried, quite in vain, to pass himself as one of the criminal classes; for the shepherd, the street arab, or the tramp, the common seaman, the beach- comber, or the Polynesian high-chief. Even in the imposed silence and restraint of extreme sickness the power and attraction of the man made themselves felt, and there seemed to be more vitality and fire of the spirit in him as he lay exhausted and speechless in bed than in an ordinary roomful of people in health.'

(*See also* **Clifford, Mrs. W.K.; Lucas, E.V.;** Part 4 (Letters))

*Colvins and their Friends, The* (*see* **Lucas, E.V.**)

**Committee for the Centenary Celebration of R.L. Stevenson's Travels in the Cévennes,** Alès, France, 1977-78; information leaflet ( *The Cévennes a hundred years later*) in Edinburgh Room, Edinburgh Central Library

*'Concerning the "Dead Man's Chest",'* (*see* **Kingsley, Martin**)

*Confessions of a Young Man,* (*see* **Moore, George**)

**Confessions of a Unionist, An Unpublished 'Talk on Things Current',** privately printed, Cambridge, Mass., 1921, outlining Stevenson's support of Lord Salisbury's line against Home Rule for Ireland. *See* **Curtin family**

**Connell, John,** (pseudonym J.H. Robertson), *W.E. Henley,* Constable, London, n.d. Refers to Henley's early friendship and long association with Stevenson. *The Return of Long John Silver, being a sequel to Treasure Island by Robert Louis Stevenson,* 1949

**Connelly, Willard,** 'Robert Louis Stevenson: A Reverie', from *Adventure in Biography,* 1956

**Cooper, Lettice,** *Robert Louis Stevenson,* 'The English Novelists Series', Home & Van Thal, London, 1947.

**Copeland, Charles Townsend,** 'Robert Louis Stevenson', *Atlantic Monthly*, April 1895. Valedictory article

**Cornford, L. Cope,** *Robert Louis Stevenson.* Wm. Blackwood, Edinburgh and London, 1899. A biography.

*Cornhill Magazine,* London, edited by Sir Leslie Stephen. Stevenson was a constant contributor between 1874 and 1882. The July 1894 issue carried an anonymous article entitled 'With Stevenson in Samoa'.

*'Cottage at Point Pleasant, The'* (*see* **Eaton, Charlotte**)

*'Could Unst have been Treasure Island?'* (*see* **Clunes, Andrew**)

*Country of Stevenson, The,* (*see* **Sharp, William**)

**Covenanters, The**
Childhood walks with Cummy in Greyfriars' Kirkyard, Edinburgh, were spiced with gory tales of the religious struggles of the seventeenth century and how on these very gravestones the National Covenant had been signed. (*See also* Part 2 ('Covenanting Profiles' and 'Covenanting Storybook'))

**Cowell, Henry J.,** *Robert Louis Stevenson: An Englishman's re-study after fifty years of R.L.S. the man,* Epworth Press, London, 1946

**Cowper, A.S.,** (*see* **Trinity Academy**)

**'Crabbed Age and Youth',** an essay, first published in *Cornhill Magazine*, March 1878; in book form in *Virginbus Puerisque*, 1881; Tusitala Edition *25.* Stevenson received £9 for this story.

**Crawshaw, E.A.H.,** 'R.L.S. and Music', *Musical Times*, 1932

*Critical Kit-Kats,* (*see* **Gosse, Sir Edmund William**)

*Critical Woodcuts,* (*see* **Sherman, Stuart**)

**Crockett, Samuel Rutherford,** (1860-1914), Scottish novelist.
'Apprenticeship of Robert Louis Stevenson', *Bookman*, London, March 1893; 'Stevenson's Letters', *Bookman*, London, December 1899; 'Stevenson's Books' (with earlier *Bookman* essays above), *Bookman* Extra Number, 1913
Greatly admired by Stevenson who in 1893, moved by a dedication to himself in one of Crockett's books, replied with the now famous 'Blows the wind to-day, and the sun and the wind are flying . . .' (Tusitala Edition *22,* p. 168) (*See also* (Part 4 (Letters))

*Cruise of the 'Janet Nichol', The, Among the South Sea Islands, A Diary,* (*see* **Stevenson, Fanny**)

**Cruse, Amy,** *Robert Louis Stevenson.* A biography. Harrap, London, 1915

**' "Cue" Stories of Stevenson',** (*see* **Hellman, George S.**)

**Cunningham, Alison, ('Cummy')** *Cummy's Diary: A Diary Kept by R.L. Stevenson's Nurse while travelling with him on the Continent during 1863.* With Preface and notes by Robert T. Skinner. Chatto & Windus, London, 1926

> Daughter of a Fife fisherman, she came to take care of the infant Stevenson when the family moved to Inverleith Terrace. Her love of him as a child was gratified in her old age when he dedicated to her *A Child's Garden of Verses.* By then she was ready to produce photographs for literary pilgrims and tell them that her 'laddie' was 'like other bairns, whiles very naughty'.
>
> Cummy's early influence on Stevenson doubtless sowed the seeds of the writer and he wrote of her lovingly caring for the sickly child, the wailing bundle of nerves and germs, 'troubled with a hacking exhausting cough and praying for sleep or morning from the bottom of my shaken little body'. And in 'Memoirs of Himself', from *Memories and Portraits,* 'She was more patient than I can suppose of an angel; hours together she would help console me in my paroxysms; and I remember with particular distinctness how she would lift me out of bed and take me, rolled in blankets, to the window, whence I might look forth into the blue night starred with street lamps and see where the gas still burned behind the windows of other sickrooms . . . where also, we told each other, there might be sick little boys and their nurses waiting, like us, for the morning'.
>
> After a fall in which she broke her hip, she died in Edinburgh in 1910, aged ninety-two.
>
> (*See* **Fowler, William; Guthrie, Lord James;** Part 4 (Letters); Plate 3)

*Current Opinion,* New York, contained anonymous articles entitled 'Stevenson Unwhitewashed' (review of Steuart's *Robert Louis Stevenson, Man and Writer*), December 1924; 'Stevenson from a New Point of View', December 1924

**Curry, George,** introduction and notes for a special film edition of *Catriona and Kidnapped* 1978. Omnibus film, 1972. (*See also* Part 6 (*Kidnapped*))

**Curtin family**

Farmer Curtin was killed by Fenians in Ireland, and his surviving family were 'boycotted'. Such injustice raised Stevenson's ire, he determined to fight for their cause and be martyred too if necessary. He wrote in April 1887 to Mrs. Anne Jenkin in Edinburgh, (Letters, Tusitala Edition *33* p.124), 'My work can be done anywhere; hence I can take up without loss a backgoing Irish farm . . . writers are so much in the public eye, that a writer being murdered would . . . throw a bull's eye light upon this cowardly business . . . I am not unknown in the States, from which the funds come that pay for these brutalities . . . Nobody else is taking up this obvious and crying duty. . . . Objection "You will not even be murdered, the climate will miserably kill you . . ." The purpose is to brave crime . . . My wife has had a mean life (1) loves me (2) could not bear to lose me . . . But what does she love me for? She must lose me soon or late . . . Am I not taken with the hope of excitement? I was at first. I am not much now. I see what a dreary, friendless, miserable, God-forgotten business it will be . . . Am I not taken with a notion of glory? I daresay I am . . . I see . . . a quite inglorious death by disease and from the lack of attendance; or even if I should be knocked on the head, as these poor Irish promise, how little anyone will care . . . I do not love this health-tending, housekeeping life of mine . . . The cause of England in Ireland is not worth supporting . . . Populations should not be taught to gain public end by private crime . . . for all men to bow before a threat of crime is to loosen and degrade beyond redemption the whole fabric of man's decency.'

Stevenson might well have set off for Ireland immediately except for a task of revision. And in May grave news from Edinburgh reached Bournemouth which had the Stevensons hastily packing. Thomas Stevenson, his 'dear, wild, noble father' was dying. With father dead and his own health intolerable, he listened to advice and, persuaded that another winter in Britain might be his last, he gathered up his household, including his widowed mother, and set forth on his second journey to America.

# D

**Daiches, David,** *Robert Louis Stevenson,* William MacLellan, Glasgow, 1947; *Robert Louis Stevenson and His World,* Thames & Hudson, London, 1973; *Stevenson and the Art of Fiction,* Folcroft, New York, 1951. Contributed an essay to *Stevenson and Victorian Scotland (ed.* Jenni Calder)

***Daily News,*** anonymous article entitled 'R.L. Stevenson's Love for Children', 22 December 1894

**Dalglish, Doris N.,** *Presbyterian Pirate: A Portrait of Stevenson,* Oxford University Press, 1937. A perceptive study of Stevenson's rebellion against Victorian society

**Damien, Father**

Belgian missionary priest who volunteered to spend his life in Hawaii's leper colony. In mid-nineteenth century leprosy was rife and once the lepers were isolated on to Molokai's Kalawao-Kalaupepa, they tended also to be banished from Hawaii's conscience. Father Damien tried to ease their lot and deal with the sin, squalor and violence which inevitably developed in the colony. For this he received no reward except becoming a leper himself. When he eventually died of the disease the proposal to erect a monument to his memory was ill-received by predominantly Protestant Hawaii. (Some years earlier Protestant missionaries had assisted with the forcible ejection of their Catholic colleagues.) Outraged by this injustice, Stevenson championed the old priest, 'Of old Damien, whose weaknesses and worse perhaps I heard fully, I think only the more. He was a European peasant, dirty, bigoted, untruthful, unwise, tricky, but superb with generosity, residual candour and fundamental good humour; convince him that he had done wrong (it might take hours of insult) and he would undo what he had done and like his corrector better. A man, with all the grime and paltriness of manhood, but a saint and hero all the more for that.'
(*See also* Part 4 (**Scots Observer**) for an open letter to the Rev. Dr. Hyde; **Kalawao-Kalaupepa** for full account of Stevenson's visit to the leper colony.)

**Damon, 'Father',** eminent Protestant missionary in Hawaii; became friend of the Stevensons

**Daplyn, A.J.,** 'Robert Louis Stevenson at Barbizon', *Chambers Journal,* 1917

**Dark, Sidney,** *Robert Louis Stevenson,* Hodder & Stoughton, London, 1932

**David Balfour: Memoirs of his Adventures at Home and Abroad,** original title of sequel to *Kidnapped.* (*See* **Catriona**)

*'David Balfour, Yr., of Shaws, Advocate',* (*see* **Anderson, Lord A.M.**)

**Davies, A.H.,** 'Poet's Tree at R.L. Stevenson's house in San Francisco', *Sunset Publications,* February 1928

**Davos,** This winter-sports village in north-east Switzerland was famous in the nineteenth century as a health resort for consumptives. In winter 1880 Stevenson took up residence, hoping for a 'cure' and encouraged by reports of Dr. Ruedi's clinic. Stevenson's health improved, although he suffered from mental inertia, but the climate made Fanny ill. In their second exile (winter 1881) he completed *Treasure Island,* begun that summer in Braemar, Scotland. He also developed a friendship with fellow-sufferer and writer J.A. Symonds.
He wrote, 'a world of black and white — black pine woods, and white snow . . . A few score invalids marching to and fro upon the snowy road, or skating on the ice rinks . . . The row of sunburned faces round the table would present the first surprise . . . In the rare air, clear cold and blinding light of Alpine winters . . . a man is stirringly alive.' Soon he hated the sterile wilderness 'where even the shopkeepers are consumptives'. For the professional writer, 'all his little fishes talk like whales'. Davos was '. . . a cage. The mountains are about you like a trap. You live in holes and corners and can only change one for the other.' (*See also* **Hotel Belvedere; Ruedi, Dr. Karl; Symonds, John Addington**)

**'Davos in Winter',** an essay, first published in *Pall Mall Gazette,* 21 February 1881; in book form in *Essays and Criticisms,* Herbert B. Turner, Edinburgh, 1903; 'Swiss Notes', *Further Memories,* Tusitala Edition *30*

**Davos Press**
While at school in California, Fanny's son Lloyd acquired a small printing press which accompanied him to Davos in 1881. He earned pocket-money printing menus for the hotel while Stevenson experimented with woodcuts and verses to match.
(*See also* **Stevenson Medley: Facsimiles of Davos Press**)

**'Davos Printing-Press, A',** (*see* **Stringer, Raymond**)

**Day, A. Grove,** (ed.) *Travels in Hawaii,* University Press of Hawaii, Honolulu, 1973. Collection of Stevenson's writings from and about Hawaii. His stay in Honolulu (1888/9) and friendship with the young Princess Kaiulani (daughter of A.S. Cleghorn)

'**Day After Tomorrow, The**', an essay, first published in *The Contemporary Review*, April 1887; Tusitala Edition 26

**Day with Robert Louis Stevenson, A,** (*see* **Claire, Maurice**)

**Deacon Brodie,** a play, written in collaboration with W.E. Henley, privately printed by T. and A. Constable, Edinburgh, 1880; first published in *Three Plays* by W.E. Henley and R.L. Stevenson, David Nutt, London, 1892; Tusitala Edition 24.

Deacon Brodie was a seventeenth-century Edinburgh cabinet-maker whose daytime respectability masked a nightlife of crime. Stevenson had been fascinated by Brodie since he learned as a child that the cabinet in his bedroom (now in Lady Stair's Museum, Edinburgh) had been made by those infamous hands. The play portrays the Deacon's last days. Retribution is at hand, played out by his sister Mary, ignorant of the Deacon's true nature, her lover Leslie, and the Deacon's faithful, ill-used mistress, Jean, supported by a cast of criminals, law officers, etc. It was first performed by the Haldane Crichton Company at Pullan's Theatre of Varieties, Bradford, 28 December 1882, in the following April at His Majesty's Theatre, Aberdeen, and at Princes Theatre, London, July 1884. Stevenson returned to Britain too late that month to see the performance but was sufficiently encouraged by its success to proceed with *Admiral Guinea* and *Beau Austin*.

**Deacon Brodie: Father to Jekyll & Hyde,** (*see* **Gibson, John S.**)

'**Dead Man's Chest, The: A Stevensonian Research**', (*see* **Starrett, David**)

'**Dear Andrew and Dear Louis**', (*see* **Green, Roger Lancelyn**)

**Death of Stevenson** (*see* **Obituaries** and **Stevenson, Robert Louis**)

'**Debated Charm, A**' (*see* **Colby, Frank Moore**)

'**Debating Societies**', an essay, first published in *Edinburgh University Magazine*, March 1871; in book form in Edinburgh Edition, 1896; Tusitala Edition 24.

**Deily, R.H.,** (*see* **Ehrsham, T.G.**)

**de Mattos, Katharine**
Sister of his cousin and great friend, Bob Mowbray Stevenson, both of whom possessed the family magnetic personality. Stevenson wrote two poems for her in 'Underwoods', entitled 'To K de M' and 'Katharine'. In the former he remembered their Scottish childhood together, 'A lover of the moorland bare, And honest country woods you are . . .' Katharine created a family scandal by marrying — and divorcing — Sydney de Mattos, a 'Cambridge atheist'. Without a husband and without money, she and her children were always made welcome at

Skerryvore. Like her brother — and her cousin — she had a vivid gift of expression and was encouraged to write pieces which Louis Stevenson was happy to criticise. One short story, 'The Nixie', was abandoned by her and taken up by Fanny who re-wrote and had it published under her own name. This 'plagiarism' became the subject of a bitter quarrel between Stevenson (who supported Fanny) and W.E. Henley. Their old relationship was never regained, especially as Fanny disliked Henley at the best of times and considered him a bad influence upon her husband. (*See* **Henley, William Ernest**)

Stevenson dedicated *Dr. Jekyll and Mr. Hyde* to Katharine,

It's ill to loose the bands that God decreed to bind;
Still will we be the children of the heather and the wind.
Far away from home, O it's still for you and me
That the broom is blowing bonnie in the north countrie.

He sent her a copy of the book with a letter written on New Year's Day 1886, 'Dearest Katharine, Here, on a very little book and accompanied with lame verses, I have put your name. Our kindness is now getting well on in years; it must be nearly of age, and it gets more valuable to me with every time I see you. It is not possible to express any sentiment, and it is not necessary to try, at least between us. You know very well that I love you dearly, and always will. I only wish the verses were better, but at least you like the story; and it is sent to you by the one that loves you — JEKYLL, AND NOT HYDE.' (*See Part 4* (Letters))

**'Devil and the Innkeeper, The'**, a fable, Tusitala Edition 5 (*see also* **Fables**)

***Devonia,*** ship of the Anchor line in which Stevenson set sail for America on his first visit, leaving Greenock on 7 August 1879

He went against the advice of his friends and in the face of hysterical denunciations from Heriot Row to persuade Fanny Osbourne to divorce her husband (with whom she was living meantime) and to marry him. He decided, poor as he was, to travel second-class rather than steerage as this would enable him to carry on writing. It was worth paying eight guineas for second class rather than six for steerage to gain little more than a table to write on. The food was inedible, tea 'with a flavour of boiling and dishcloths' and twice a week 'a saddlebag filled with currants under the name of plum-pudding'. Indifferent soup, porridge and bread kept him alive but he lost a stone in the course of the voyage and his health suffered lasting damage.
(*See also* **Amateur Emigrant, The**)

**Dhu Heartach (Isle of Earraid)**

Lighthouse constructed by brothers Thomas and David Stevenson and visited by Stevenson (with his father) in 1870 when they spent three weeks on the island. The impressions he gained were subsequently used

in *Kidnapped*, and their Bournemouth home was renamed after the lighthouse Skerryvore.
(*See* **Skerryvore; Buell, Llewellyn M.**)

*Diary*, (*see* **James, Alice**)

**Dickie, Francis,** 'The Tragic End of Stevenson's Yacht "Casco"', *World Magazine*, 4 January 1920

**Dickson, W.K.**, *The History of the Speculative Society*, privately printed for the Society, Edinburgh, 1905

**'Diogenes in London'**, an incomplete story, privately printed for John Howell, San Francisco, 1920; first published in Vailima Edition, 1923; Tusitala Edition 5

**'Diogenes at the Savile Club'**, a story, privately printed for David G. Joyce, Chicago, 1921; first published in Vailima Edition, 1923; Tusitala Edition 5

**Disraeli, Benjamin,** considered by Stevenson 'a nauseating opportunist, just a little better than Carlyle'. (*See also* **Carlyle, Thomas**)

**'Distinguished Stranger, The'**, a fable, Tusitala Edition 5 (*see also* **Fables**)

**Dobson, Austin,** 'R.L.S. in Memoriam', *Bookman* Extra Number, London, 1913

**Dr. Jekyll and Mr. Hyde, The Strange Case Of,** Longmans Green, London and Scribner's, New York, 1886; Tusitala Edition 5

Dr. Jekyll, fascinated by the warring elements of good and evil in man's personality, experiments with a drug which separates the two forces and thereby creates in him a monster, Mr. Hyde, who eventually gains ascendency over the doctor and murders Sir Danvers Carew. Jekyll loses control of the drug and Hyde takes over with tragic consequences. It had been intended to publish *The Strange Case of Dr. Jekyll and Mr. Hyde* in December 1885, but when the book was ready, the shops were full of the Christmas issue. Publication was therefore postponed until January 1886.

Fanny Stevenson's Prefatory Note contains an account of the book's origin, ' . . . Several . . . of my husband's friends fell into the habit of spending a couple of hours with us almost every evening [at Skerryvore] . . . These evenings of interesting, clever and brilliant talk were amongst the pleasantest experiences of my husband's life; but when they were prohibited by the doctor as being too exciting, he returned, with a pathetic acquiescence, to the "land of counterpane", where he played on his penny whistle; and when that, in turn, was forbidden, worked out problems in chess that we found in a newspaper. Chess problems hardly proved a panacea for brain and nerves exhausted by the day's work . . . My husband had always been able to sleep at will. He would say, "Call me in half an hour" and, laying his head on the pillow, would instantly drop into a refreshing slumber. For the first time in his life his sleep now became restless and broken. "The Brownies" busied themselves during all hours of the night, tormenting him with phantom problems on the chess-board, or more often reviving some almost forgotten train of thought. During an enforced cessation from dramatic collaboration [with W.E. Henley] *The Strange Case of Dr. Jekyll and Mr. Hyde* was thus inspired. My husband's cries of horror caused me to rouse him, much to his indignation. "I was dreaming a fine bogey tale," he said reproachfully, following with a rapid sketch of Jekyll and Hyde up to the transformation scene, where I had awakened him.

At daybreak he was working with feverish activity on the new book. In three days the first draft, containing thirty thousand words, was finished . . .'

This episode had its own drama glossed over by Fanny Stevenson but fully reported by Lloyd Osbourne, as Stevenson read aloud to him and his mother, 'I listened to it spellbound. Stevenson, who had a voice the greatest actor might have envied, read it with an intensity that made shivers run up and down my spine. When he came to the end, gazing at us in triumphant expectancy and keyed to a pitch of indescribable self-satisfaction — as he waited, and I waited for my mother's outburst of enthusiasm — I was thunderstruck at her backwardness. Her praise was constrained; the words seemed to come with difficulty; and then all at once she broke out with criticism. He had missed the point, she said; had missed the allegory; had made it merely a story — a magnificent bit of sensationalism — when it should have been a masterpiece.

Stevenson was beside himself with anger. He trembled; his hand shook on the manuscript; he was intolerably chagrined. His voice, bitter and challenging, overrode my mother's in a fury of resentment. Never had I seen him so impassioned, so outraged, and the scene became so painful that I went away, unable to bear it any longer. It was with a sense of tragedy that I listened to their voices from the adjoining room, the words lost but fraught with an emotion that struck at my heart.

When I came back my mother was alone. She was sitting, pale and desolate before the fire, and staring into it. Neither of us spoke. Had I done so it would have been to reproach her, for I thought she had been cruelly wrong. Then we heard Louis descending the stairs, and we both quailed as he burst in as though to continue the argument even more violently than before. But all he said was: "You are right! I have absolutely missed the allegory, which, after all, is the whole point of it — the very essence of it." And with that, as though enjoying my mother's discomfiture and her ineffectual start to prevent him, he threw

the manuscript into the fire. Imagine my feelings — my mother's
feelings — as we saw it blazing up; as we saw those precious pages
wrinkling and blackening and turning into flame!
'My first impression was that he had done it out of pique. But it was not.
He really had been convinced, and this was his dramatic amend. When
my mother and I both cried out at the folly of destroying the manuscript,
he justified himself vehemently. "It was all wrong," he said. "In trying
to save some of it I should have got hopelessly off the track. The only
way was to put temptation beyond my reach."
'Then ensued another three days of feverish industry on his part, and of a
hushed, anxious and tiptoeing anticipation on ours; of meals where he
scarcely spoke; of evenings unenlivened by his presence; of awed
glimpses of him, sitting up in bed, writing, writing, writing, with the
counterpane littered with his sheets. The culmination was the *Jekyll and
Hyde* that everyone knows; that, translated into every European tongue
and many Oriental, has given a new phrase to the world.
'The writing of it was an astounding feat, from whatever aspect it may
be regarded. Sixty-four thousand words in six days; more than ten
thousand words a day. To those who know little of such things I may
explain that a thousand words a day is a fair average for any writer of
fiction. Anthony Trollope set himself this quota; it was Jack London's; it
is — and has been — a sort of standard of daily literary accomplishment.
Stevenson multiplied it by ten; and on top of that copied out the whole in
another two days, and had it in the post on the third!
'It was a stupendous achievement; and the strange thing was that instead
of showing lassitude afterwards, he seemed positively refreshed and
revitalised; went about with a happy air; was as uplifted as though he
had come into a fortune; looked better than he had for months.'
Fanny Stevenson's account, 'That an invalid in my husband's condition
of health should have been able to perform the manual labour alone . . .
seems incredible. He was suffering from continual haemorrhages, and
was hardly allowed to speak, his conversation usually being carried on
by means of a slate and pencil. Two persons were not allowed in his
room at the same time, and when one was given that privilege by the
doctor, the interview was limited to fifteen minutes' duration. It was
my ungracious task to stand guard outside the door, watch in hand,
ready to warn the visitor.
'The success of *Jekyll and Hyde* was immediate and phenomenal, both in
England and in America, where it was pirated broadcast. The story was
used as a text by clergymen in churches [including St Paul's Cathedral]
and appeared on the stage as a play in at least three different versions . . .
It is strange how the public incline to identify an author with the
characters of his creation in one particular book. My husband's personal
appearance has been described as a sort of grotesque cross between Dr.
Jekyll and Mr. Hyde. One reviewer said: "He looks as if he had been

partially drowned and just dragged out of the water, his long hair still lank and clinging to his head". Even the artists who painted him tried, apparently, to force something spectral and strange into the portraits of the author of *Jekyll and Hyde* . . . Many peculiar letters were received by my husband, more particularly from spiritualists and theosophists, who fancied he must have had some supernatural guidance in his portrayal of the double life . . .'

Stevenson wrote of the monster he had created to Will Low, (*Letters*, Tusitala Edition *33*, p.67) 'I send you herewith a Gothic gnome . . . interesting, I think, and he came out of a deep mine, where he guards the fountain of tears. It is not always the time to rejoice.' And to J.A. Symonds (ibid., p.80), 'Jekyll is a dreadful thing, I own; but the only thing I feel dreadful about is that damned old business of the war in the members. This time it came out; I hope it will stay in, in future.' (*See also* Part 4 (Letters) and Part 6 (Media)

**Doughty, Leonard,** 'Answering R.L.S.', *Southwest Review*, Autumn 1928

**Douglas, Sir George** (ed.), *A Cadger's Creel. Book of the Robert Louis Stevenson Club Bazaar.* W. Brown, Edinburgh, 1925. Essays, etc. contributed to raise funds to purchase Stevenson's birthplace, 8 Howard Place and convert it into a museum.

(*See also* **Clouston, J. Storer; Drinkwater, John; McKenna, Stephen; Paul, Sir James Balfour; Roughead, William; Simpson, Rev. H.L.; Wakefield, Sir Charles; Walpole, Hugh; Watt, L.M.; Waugh, J.L.**)

**Doyle, Arthur Conan,** *Through the Magic Door.* Smith Elder & Co., London, 1907. Refers to admiration for Stevenson's *Pavilion on the Links* and its adaptation from serial to book form. 'Mr. Stevenson's methods in Fiction', *National Review*, 14 July 1889 (*see* Letters (Part 4))

**Drinkwater, John,** 'To R.L.S.', poem in *A Cadger's Creel* (*see* **Douglas, Sir George**)

**Droppers, Garrett,** 'Robert Louis Stevenson', *Harvard Monthly*, March 1887 (*see* Part 4 (Letters))

**Drummond, Dr.,** British doctor in Nice (1884)

Summoned by Fanny after her rescue of Stevenson from a carouse with convivial companions which ended in congestion of the lungs and kidneys. She wrote to his parents in Edinburgh, 'He says that Louis may well live to be seventy, only he must not travel about. He is steadily better and is reading a newspaper in bed at this moment. I, who have not slept a wink for two nights, am pretending to be the gayest of the gay, but in reality I am a total wreck, although almost off my head with relief and joy.'

Stevenson wrote to cousin Bob, 'I survived where a stronger man would not. Pain draws a lingering fiddle-bow. The doctor told me to leave off wine to regard myself as "an old man and sit by the fire". None of which I wish to do . . .'
(*See also* **Nice**)

**Drummond, Kate**

According to John A. Steuart's biography, *Robert Louis Stevenson: Man and Writer*, 1924, Kate Drummond was the first and greatest love of Stevenson's life, met while he was a student at Edinburgh University. She was 'a swooningly dark and lovely Highland girl whom he met in an Edinburgh brothel, whence he planned to rescue and marry her. His parents violently opposed the scheme'. Pressures were brought to bear upon him and he was persuaded to give her up. No valid evidence has ever been produced by biographers to substantiate the girl's identity — if she existed at all, outside the myth of bitter and lost first love.
(*See also* **'Claire'**)

**Drummond Street, Edinburgh,** Rutherford's howff (or inn) was a favourite haunt of Stevenson and his riotous student friends

Long afterwards from the *Casco*, voyaging in the South Seas en route for Samoa, he was to write to Baxter (*Letters*, Tusitala Edition *33*, p. 202) 'There was nothing visible but the southern stars, and the steersman there out by the binnacle lamp . . . the night was as warm as milk, and all of a sudden, I had a vision of — Drummond Street, It came to me like a flash of lightning: I simply returned thither, and into the past. And when I remembered all I hoped and feared as I pickled about Rutherford's in the rain and the east wind; how I feared I should make a mere shipwreck, and yet timidly hoped not; how I feared I should never have a friend, far less a wife, and yet passionately hoped I might; how I hoped (if I did not take to drink) I should possibly write one little book, etc., etc. And then now — what a change! I feel somehow as if I should like the incident set upon a brass plate at the corner of that dreary thoroughfare, for all students to read, poor devils, when their hearts are down.'
(*See also* **Barrie, Sir James Matthew**)

**Dunblane,** a town near Stirling, scene of Stevenson's early holidays with his parents (*See also* **Bridge of Allan**)

**Duncan, William Henry, Jr.,** 'Stevenson's Second Visit to America', *Bookman*, January 1900

**Dunn, James N.,** 'Robert Louis Stevenson', *Art and Literature*, June 1889

**Durham, Katharine,** (*see* **Osbourne, Katharine Durham**)

**Dynamiter, The,** a collection of stories, first published as *More New*

*Arabian Nights: The Dynamiter*, Longmans Green, London, 1885; Tusitala Edition *3*.

*The Dynamiter* was published in April 1885, and was reprinted in May and July of that year. Stevenson received £100 for this work. The stories, with a linking theme and characters, were begun in Hyères in 1884. Stevenson was seriously ill, confined to bed and Fanny wrote that these stories were devised as entertainment for him: 'I was to go out for an hour's walk every afternoon . . . and invent a story to repeat when I came in — a sort of Arabian Nights Entertainment where I was to take the part of Scheherazade and he the sultan. There had been several dynamite outrages in London' [Fenian in origin] 'the most of them had turned out fiascos. It occurred to me to take the impotent dynamite intrigue as the thread . . .' Stevenson's health improved but the stories were not written until they moved to Bournemouth later that year. 'Money was absolutely necessary, we cast about for something that could be done quickly and without too much strain; the Scheherazade stories came to mind and we both set to work to write what we could remember of them. We could recall only enough to write rather a thin book, so my husband added one more to the list, *The Explosive Bomb*.' Their economies stretched to using one of the central characters from *New Arabian Nights*, Prince Florizel of Bohemia.

**'Dynasty of the Shark, The,'** (*see* **Westminster Gazette**)

# E

*Early Home and Haunts of Robert Louis Stevenson, The,* (*see* **Patrick, John and Sons**)

*'Early Home of Robert Louis Stevenson, The',* (*see* **Ross, John A.**)

**Earraid, Isle of,** (*see* **Buell, Llewellyn M.; Dhu Heartach (Isle of Earraid)**)

**Eaton, Charlotte,** *A Last Memory of Robert Louis Stevenson,* Thomas Y. Crowell, New York, 1916; 'Stevenson at Manasquan', *Queen's Quarterly, 1931*; 'The Cottage at Point Pleasant', *Catholic World,* June 1926

**Ebb-Tide, The,** a Paramount production based on the story by R.L.S. and Lloyd Osbourne, appeared in *Screen Pictorial,* May 1938 (*see* below and Part 6)

**Ebb-Tide, The: A Trio and Quartette,** first published as a serial, with the title 'The Pearl Fisher' in *To-day,* 1893-4 and *McClure's Magazine,* 1894. (The title was later changed to 'The Schooner Farallone') in book form by Heinemann, London and Stone and Kimball, Chicago, 1894; Tusitala Edition *14.*

Richard Herrick, a penniless man of letters, teams up with Captain Davis and a villainous Cockney, Huish, in a desperate search for treasure. They meet more than their match in the religious fanatic, Attwater. The lonely Pacific island setting adds tension to a psychological drama.

Of their collaboration on this novel, Lloyd Osbourne wrote: 'try as I would I could not please R.L.S. I wrote and rewrote, and rewrote again, but always to have him shake his head. Finally, at his suggestion and in utter hopelessness, I laid the manuscript by, hoping to come back to it later with greater success. But I never did.'

So ended the first draft. Later Stevenson returned to it alone describing it as a 'brutal, brutal story about three first-class dead beats . . . a violent story, full of strange scenes and striking characters . . . a great and grisly tale.' Of the final draft: 'This forced, violent, alembicated style is most abhorrent to me; it can't be helped; the note was struck years ago on the *Janet Nicholl,* and has to be maintained somehow' (Letter to Colvin, Tusitala Edition *35,* p.27). In May 1893 he was 'grinding singly' and finished the manuscript in June ' . . . I have spent thirteen days about as nearly in Hell as a man could expect to live through'(p.35). Sidney Colvin did not share his enthusiasm for the sordid setting and did not feel that

Stevenson's readers would welcome stories about beachcombers and low-life in the Pacific Islands of the South Seas. Disappointed with the first chapters, he considered the last two had been 'done with astonishing genius'. Even Stevenson himself was mightily pleased with the result: 'I am afraid I think it excellent.'

*Echoes of Robert Louis Stevenson,* (*see* **Bay, J. Christian**)

**Edel, Leon,** *Henry James: The Middle Years*, London, 1963. Refers to his friendship and correspondence with Stevenson. (*See also* **James, Henry**)

**'Edifying Letters of the Rutherford Family'**, a previously unpublished short story by Stevenson, discovered in the Beinecke Collection, Yale University.
(*See also* **'Old Song, An'**)

**Edinburgh Academy,** Stevenson was entered at ten years old. The Academy was then a fairly new and fashionable school for the sons of gentlemen

While Stevenson was in good health he indulged in canoeing, riding, walking and swimming but had little inclination for competitive sports, or the rough-and-tumble of the Rugby field. His lack of enthusiasm to shine as a 'sportsman' also applied to Scotland's national game, golf, which was a raging fever in every town and hamlet north of the Tweed. He enjoyed the solitariness of fishing until having caught thirty trout in a day with his rod and line, he saw this not as a proud achievement but suffered for the misery of the dying fish on the bank beside him. He never fished again.

*Edinburgh and the Lothians* (*see* **Watt, Francis**)

**Edinburgh City Libraries,** the Edinburgh Room, Edinburgh Central Library, George IV Bridge, Edinburgh (Tel. 031-225 5584) contains a large collection of Stevenson material, including historical photographs, transparencies and translations.
*Robert Stevenson, 1722-1850: Notes on the Stevenson family*; privately printed, n.d.; *Robert Louis Stevenson Centenary, 1850-1894: Catalogue of the Stevenson Collection in the Edinburgh Room, Central Library*, illustrated, Edinburgh, 1950; Revised edition 1978; *R.L.S. Cévennes Centenary Tour (6-16 June, 1978)*, descriptive brochure, Edinburgh, 1978; *Stevenson Medley*, one of an edition of 300 copies — includes essays, facsimiles of the Davos Press cuts and verses, moral tales, etc., illustrated 1899

**Edinburgh Corporation, Education Department Museum Unit No. 2.**
Illustrated catalogue, Edinburgh, 1972. Contents: Part I, 'Robert Louis Stevenson and Lady Stair's House'; Part II, 'Life Among the Poor in

Edinburgh when Robert Louis Stevenson was Young'; Part III, 'Questionnaire on Robert Louis Stevenson (Lady Stair's House)'; Part IV, 'The Family Engineering Tradition'

**Edinburgh Edition,** *The Works of Robert Louis Stevenson* (ed.) S. Colvin 28 vols., Longmans Green, Cassell and Seeley, London and Scribner's New York, 1894–98

In 1893 Sidney Colvin and Charles Baxter had hoped to publish a complete and uniform edition of his works from which, as a popular author, he would also gain a steady income. Charles Baxter carried with him to Vailima the first volumes but Stevenson was already dead. He never had the thrill of pride in seeing the Edition which was to make him a famous and prestigious author.

*Edinburgh Eleven, An,* (*see* **Barrie, Sir James Matthew**)

**Edinburgh: Picturesque Notes,** first published in *The Portfolio*, an artistic periodical, June–December 1878; in book form by Seeley, Jackson & Halliday, London, 1879, with etchings by A. Brunet-Debaines from drawings by S. Bough, RSA, and W.E. Lockhart, RSA and vignettes by Hector Chalmers and R.K. Thomas; Tusitala Edition 26.

' . . . No situation could be more commanding for the head city of a kingdom; none better chosen for noble prospects. From her tall precipice and terraced gardens she looks far and wide on the sea and broad champaigns . . . But Edinburgh pays cruelly for her high seat in one of the vilest climates under heaven. She is liable to be beaten upon by all the winds that blow, to be drenched with rain, to be buried in cold sea fogs out of the east, and powdered with snow as it comes flying southward from the Highland hills. The weather is raw and boisterous in winter, shifty and ungenial in summer, and a downright meteorological purgatory in the spring. The delicate die early, and I, as a survivor, among bleak winds and plumping rain, have been sometimes tempted to envy them their fate . . . Happy the [train] passengers who shake off the dust of Edinburgh, and have heard for the last time the cry of the east wind among her chimney-tops! And yet the place establishes an interest in people's hearts; go where they will, they find no city of the same distinction; go where they will, they take a pride in their old home . . . Great people of yore, kings and queens, buffoons and grave ambassadors, played their stately farce for centuries in Holyrood. Wars have been plotted, dancing has lasted deep into the night, murder has been done in its chambers. There Prince Charlie held his phantom levées, and in a very gallant manner represented a fallen dynasty for some hours. Now, all these things of clay are mingled with the dust, the king's crown itself is shown for sixpence to the vulgar, but the stone palace has outlived these changes. . . . Few places, if any, offer a more barbaric display of contrasts to the eye. In the very midst

stands one of the most satisfactory crags in nature — a Bass Rock upon dry
land rooted in a garden, shaken by passing trains, carrying a crown of
battlements and turrets, and describing its warlike shadow over the
liveliest and brightest thoroughfare of the new town. From their smoky
beehives, ten stories high, the unwashed look down upon the open squares
and gardens of the wealthy; and gay people sunning themselves along
Princes Street, with its mile of commercial palaces all beflagged upon
some great occasion, see, across a gardened valley set with statues, where
the washings of the old town flutter in the breeze at its high windows. And
then, upon all sides, what a clashing of architecture! In this one valley,
where the life of the town goes most busily forward, there may be seen,
shown one above and behind another by the accidents of the ground,
buildings in almost every style upon the globe. Egyptian and Greek
temples, Venetian palaces and Gothic spires, are huddled one over
another in a most admired disorder; while, above all, the brute mass of the
Castle and the summit of Arthur's Seat look down upon these imitations
with a becoming dignity, as the works of Nature may look down upon the
monuments of Art . . . the lamps begin to glitter along the street, and faint
lights to burn in the high windows across the valley — the feeling grows
upon you that this also is a piece of nature in the most intimate sense; that
this profusion of eccentricities, this dream in masonry and living rock is
not a drop-scene in a theatre, but a city in the world of everyday reality,
connected by railway and telegraph wire with all the capitals of Europe,
and inhabited by citizens of the familiar type, who keep ledgers, and
attend church, and have sold their immortal portion to a daily paper. By
all the canons of romance, the place demands to be half-deserted and
leaning towards decay. . . . when the great exodus was made across the
valley, and the new town began to spread abroad its draughty
parallelograms and rear its long frontage on the opposing hill, there was
such a flitting, such a change of domicile and dweller, as was never
excelled in the history of cities; the cobbler succeeded the earl; the beggar
ensconced himself by the judge's chimney; what had been a palace was
used as a pauper refuge; and great mansions were so parcelled out among
the least and lowest in society, that the hearthstone of the old proprietor
was thought large enough to be partitioned off into a bedroom by the
new.'

**'Edinburgh Students in 1824'**    an essay, first published in *Edinburgh
University Magazine,* January 1871; in book form in Edinburgh Edition
1896; Tusitala Edition 25.

## Edinburgh University
It had long been the dream of Thomas and Margaret Stevenson that their
only son Louis would follow in the footsteps of the famous family of
engineers and lighthouse builders. Unprotesting, the young Stevenson

was enrolled and proceeded to enjoy the social life of a middle-class young Edinburgh gentleman, drinking in howffs, visiting dubious establishments in Leith Walk, and giving vent to general high spirits. On the more serious side he was active in the Speculative Society and the *Edinburgh University Magazine,* where the writings of this boy of twenty were outstanding in number as well as content and hinted at a great literary future. When his elder and adored cousin Bob, helped him shed the protective cocoon of Calvinism, horrifying whispers of atheism invaded the pious respectability of Heriot Row. The Stevenson parents were reassured when in 1870/1 Louis's academic efforts brought forth a paper 'On a new form of Intermittent Light for Lighthouses' (Tusitala Edition *28*). This was read before, and awarded a medal by, the Royal Scottish Society of Arts, but two weeks later on a walk to Cramond, Louis informed his father that he was finished with engineering. Stormy arguments followed and a compromise was reached: law, a respected vocation which also had a Scottish tradition of affinity with letters. And the elder Stevensons consoled themselves that it would be perfectly all right if their son, once his profession was firmly established, pursued his hobby of a little writing now and then. Thomas Stevenson further promised him one thousand pounds from his patrimony when he passed advocate, equivalent (at the Scottish bar) to an English barrister. In mid July 1875, wearing evening dress as custom required, and according to a fellow student looking 'like a drunken Irishman on the way to a funeral', Stevenson's competence was formally acknowledged. The ceremony over he drove back beside his proud parents in the open family carriage, sitting on the folded top shouting the news of his success to startled passersby. Thomas Stevenson had arranged for respectability to be further gratified by the dignified brass plate outside 17 Heriot Row which announced: 'R.L. Stevenson, Advocate'. (*See* Part 2 (Advocate's Thesis))

During his time with the Edinburgh firm of W.F. Skene and Peacock, where he was to learn conveyancing, he did not achieve spectacular success. In the one document which survives, five errors were found in its two pages. He clubbed together with several other new advocates to hire a clerk but apart from handling a complimentary brief from family friends took little interest in becoming actively professional. (For extracts from his journal as a law clerk, *see* **Arnold, William Harris; Balfour, Graham; Black, Margaret Moyes** )

(*See also* **'College Papers'; History, Chair of, Edinburgh University; Memories and Portraits; Skene, Edwards & Garson; Speculative Society**)

**Edinburgh University Magazine,** Numbers 1–4, 1871

The magazine was edited for the most part by Stevenson who also contributed several articles, his first in print (*see also* **'College**

**Magazine, A'; 'College Papers')**

**'Education of an Engineer, The'**, an essay, first published in *Scribner's Magazine*, November 1888; in book form in *Across the Plains*, 1892; Tusitala Edition *30*.

**Ehrsham, T.G. and Deily, R.H.**, *Bibliography of Twelve Victorian Authors*, Octagon Books, New York, 1968. Includes the works of R.L. Stevenson

**Eigner, Edwin M.**, *Robert Louis Stevenson and the Romantic Tradition.* Princeton University Press, New Jersey, 1966. His close relationship to the best of nineteenth century romantic prose with particular reference to the Gothic qualities of his short story 'Olalla'

**'Eilean Earraid: The Beloved Isle of Robert Louis Stevenson'.** (*see* **Buell, Llewellyn M.; Dhu Heartach (Isle of Earraid)**)

**'El Dorado'**, an essay first published in *London*, 11 May 1878; in book form in *Virginibus Puerisque*, 1881; Tusitala Edition *25*

**Eleven Thousand Virgins of Cologne,** barge bought and rechristened by Stevenson and friend Walter Simpson in 1875 to travel down the inland waterways of France

Her interior was to be decorated by Will Low, Stevenson's artist friend, with Watteau cherubs and pink clouds. Her cargo would be books, paints both for travelling artists and refurbishing, also wine, tobacco and friends in plenty who wished to enjoy peace and quiet. Stevenson mourned her passing in his dedication of *An Inland Voyage*, Tusitala Edition *17*

**Elina**

Vailima servant, who was ashamed of a wen on his neck. This disgraced his family, any deformity being shameful in Samoa. Persuaded that it was operable, Elina was terrified, refused to be moved by bribery or taunts of cowardice. Finally persuaded, Stevenson took him to Apia and personally administered the chloroform. As it took effect Elina repeated like a charm, 'I belong Tusitala, I belong Tusitala'. On Elinas's next visit to his clan village he returned with healed prestige and the glory of having been given a minor 'chief' name, well on the way to becoming a patriarch.

**Eliot, George,** (1819-80)

The English novelist was described by Stevenson as 'a high, but, may we not add? — a rather dry lady'. (*Letters*, Tusitala Edition *32*, p.36)

**Ellison, Joseph W.**, *Tusitala of the South Seas: The Story of Robert Louis Stevenson's Life on the South Pacific*, Hastings House, New York, 1953

**Ellwanger, W.D.**, 'Collecting of Stevensons'. *Bachelor of Arts*, July–August 1975. Together with a list of his contributions 1871-91 to English and American magazines; this is the first attempt at a bibliographical list of Stevenson's rarer writings

**Elwin, Malcolm,** *The Strange Case of Robert Louis Stevenson,* Macdonald, London, 1950. Explores the Stevenson legend — myth or reality, with particular reference to lay morals

*Emerson and Other Essays,* (*see* **Chapman, John Jay**)

*Emotional Discovery of America, The* (*see* **Sherman, Stuart**)

*Encyclopaedia Britannica,* After his commissioned article on Burns was rejected, Stevenson contributed 'Pierre Jean de Béranger' which appeared in 1875. (See Tusitala Edition *28*). Edmund Gosse was author of the entry on Stevenson. (*See also* **Burns, Robert**)

*Engineer's Outlook, An,* (*see* **Ewing, Sir Alfred**)

**England, G.A.**, 'The Real Treasure Island', *Travel,* January 1979. Claims that Stevenson's island is situated off the Cuban coast

**'English Admirals, The'**, an essay, first published in *Cornhill Magazine,* July 1878; in book form in *Virginibus Puerisque,* 1881; Tusitala Edition *25.*

*English Illustrated Magazine,* contained an anonymous article entitled 'Robert Louis Stevenson at Vailima, Samoa', May 1894

*Equator,* trading schooner of sixty-four tons whose San Francisco owners drew up a charter allowing the Stevensons to accompany them to Micronesia in 1889 and enjoy the scenery without hampering their trading business, as they picked up copra from the islands. (*See* **Tembinok, King;** South Seas map)

*Essays,* (*see* **Henley, William Ernest**)

*Essays in Little,* (*see* **Lang, Andrew**)

*Essays on Modern Novelists,* (*see* **Phelps, William Lyon**)

**'Ethics of Crime, The'**, an essay, first published in Vailima Edition 1923; Tusitala Edition *26.*

**Evans, Andrew J.**, *Across the Cévennes in the Footsteps of R.L. Stevenson and his Donkey,* Edinburgh Corporation Libraries and Museum Dept., 1965

**Ewing, Sir Alfred,** *An Engineer's Outlook,* Methuen, London, n.d.

A portrait of Stevenson drawn from life by V. Gribayédoff, October 1887. *Mansell Collection*

# F

'**Fables**' first published in *Longman's Magazine*, August, September 1895; in book form in *The Strange Case of Dr. Jekyll and Mr. Hyde With Other Fables, Longman's Green*, London, 1896 and in *Fables*, Scribner's, New York, 1896; Tusitala Edition 5 (except for 'The Persons of the Tale', which is in Tusitala Edition 2 because of its connections with *Treasure Island*)

In a Prefatory Note to the Tusitala Edition 5, Sidney Colvin states, 'The fable, as a form of literary art, had at all times a great attraction for Mr. Stevenson; and in an early review of Lord Lytton's *Fables in Song* he attempted to define some of its proper aims and methods. To this class of work, according to his conception of the matter, belonged essentially several of his own semi-supernatural stories, such as "Will of the Mill", "Markheim" and even "Jekyll and Hyde"; in the composition of which there was combined with the dream element, in at least an equal measure, the element of moral allegory or apologue. He was accustomed also to try his hand occasionally on the composition of fables more strictly so called, and cast in the conventional brief and familiar form. By the winter of 1887-88 he had enough of these by him, together with a few others running to greater length, and conceived in a more mystic and legendary vein, to enable him, as he thought, to see his way towards making a book of them . . . Then came his voyage in the Pacific and residence at Samoa. Among the multitude of new interests and images which filled his mind during the last six years of his life, he seems to have given little thought to the proposed book of fables. One or two, however, as will be seen, were added to the collection during this period. That collection, as it stood at the time of his death, was certainly not what its author had meant it to be. It may even be doubted whether it would have seen the light had he lived . . .'

(*See also* entries for individual fables)

**Fagan, J.B.,** 'Treasure Island' (play, 1936). A typescript in Edinburgh Room, Edinburgh Central Library

**Fairchild, Mr. and Mrs. Charles,** American 'patrons' of Stevenson who had John Singer Sargent paint his portrait
(*See also* **Newport; Sargent, John Singer;** Part 4 (Letters))

'**Faith, Half-Faith and no Faith at All**', a fable, Tusitala Edition 5 (*see also* '**Fables**')

**Faith of Robert Louis Stevenson, The,** (see **Kelman, John**)

**Fakarava,** picturesque Polynesian atoll visited by Stevenson on *Casco*
'A little eyot of dense, freshwater sand . . . delighting to hear the song of
the river on both sides and to tell myself that I was indeed and at last
upon an island'. Unfortunately their stay was cut short when Stevenson
took cold with complications and had to be hustled back on to the *Casco*
for Tahiti and the nearest doctor

**'Fall of Stevenson, The',** (see **Woolf, Leonard**)

**Familiar Studies of Men and Books,** nine essays, first published by
Chatto & Windus, London, 1882; Tusitala Edition 27.
*Dedication:* 'To Thomas Stevenson, Civil Engineer, by whose devices the
great sea lights in every quarter of the world now shine more brightly,
this volume is in love and gratitude dedicated by his son the author.'

**Family Tree of Robert Louis Stevenson of Edinburgh, The,** (see **Hill, Robin
Armstrong**)

**Fenian Violence,** (see **Curtin Family**)

**Ferguson, De Lancey, and Waingrow, Marshall,** *Robert Louis Stevenson's
Letters to Charles Baxter,* Yale University Press, New Haven, and
Oxford University Press, 1956 (*See* Part 4 (Letters))

**Fergusson, Robert,** (1750-74)
Scottish poet greatly admired and emulated by Stevenson in his student
days. He wrote that he identified with 'the poor, white-faced drunken,
vicious boy from St. Andrews'.

**Ferrier, 'Coggie',** sister of Walter, and friend of the Stevensons, who
visited them in France at Chalet La Solitude (*See also* Part 4
(Letters))

**Ferrier, James Walter,** boyhood friend and fellow student with
Stevenson
He lived in Dean Terrace, Edinburgh, and his dissolute drinking led to
his early death in 1883. His mother condemned Stevenson for the part he
played in the culmination of this tragedy and Stevenson wrote bitterly
to Henley, (*Letters*, Tusitala Edition 32, p.259) 'To think that he was
young with me, sharing the weather-beaten Fergussonian youth,
looking forward through the clouds to the sunburst; and now clean gone
from my path – silent, well, well . . . Last night, when I was alone in the
house, with the window open on the lovely still night, I could have
sworn he was in the room with me; I could show you the spot; and what
was curious, I heard his rich laughter; a thing I had not called to mind for
I know now how long.' (*See* Part 4 (Letters))

**Fetherstonhaugh, Frances Jane,** (*see* **Sitwell, Fanny**)

**Field, Edward,** second husband of Belle Strong, married in 1914

**Field, Isobel (Belle) Osbourne Strong,** *This Life I've Loved,* Michael Joseph, London, 1937; *Memories of Vailima* (as Isobel Strong with Lloyd Osbourne), Scribner's, New York, 1902; *Robert Louis Stevenson,* Stevenson Society of America, Saranac Lake, New York, 1920; 'Stevenson in Samoa', *Century Magazine,* 1899 (*See also* **Strong, Isobel (Belle);** *Catalogue* (**2**))

*Fifty-One Years of Victorian Life,* (*see* **Jersey, Countess of**)

**Findlay, J.P.,** *In the Footsteps of R.L.S.,* Nimmo, Hay and Mitchell, Edinburgh, 1911

**Finlay, Ian,** *The Young Robert Louis Stevenson,* Max Parrish, London, 1965

**'First Meeting between Meredith and Stevenson',** (*see* **Gordon, Alice**)

**Fisher, Annie,** *No More a Stranger.* Stanford University, California, 1946. Suggests evidence for Stevenson's alleged contribution of fifteen articles to weekly *Monterey Californian.*

**Fletcher, C. Brunsdon,** *Stevenson's Germany: the case against Germany in the Pacific,* Heinemann, London, 1920

**'Fontainebleau',** an essay, first published in *Magazine of Art,* May 1884; Tusitala Edition *30*

**'Footnote to History, A: Eight Years of Trouble in Samoa',** first published by Cassell, London and Scribner's, New York, 1892; Tusitala Edition *21* (*see also* **Tauchnitz**)

*Footnote to History of R.L. Stevenson and the German Dictatorship A',* (*see* **Thyne, C.A.M.**)

**Ford, R.C.,** 'Modestine's Shoes: A Bit of Stevensonia', *Atlantic Monthly,* April 1926

**'Foreigner at Home, The',** an essay, first published in *Cornhill Magazine,* May 1882; in book form in *Memories and Portraits,* 1887; Tusitala Edition *29*

**'Forest Notes',** an essay, first published in *Cornhill Magazine,* May 1876; Tusitala Edition *30*

**Fothergill, G.A.,** 'Relics of St. Giles and a Glimpse of R.L.S. at Swanston', in *Stones and Curiosities of Edinburgh,* 1912

**Foulis, T.N.,** *R.L. Stevenson Memories,* 1912

'**Four Reformers, The**', a fable, Tusitala Edition 5 (*see also* '**Fables**')

**Fowler, William,** 'Cummy', a paper read before a meeting of the R.L. Stevenson Club in Edinburgh, 14 February 1923, Selkirk, 1923

*Frail Warrior, The,* (*see* **Carré, Jean-Marie**)

**France,** Stevenson first visited France with his parents in 1863, the beginning of a love for that country which was never to end

Lloyd Osbourne wrote in *An Intimate Portrait,* 'France had a profound influence over Stevenson; mentally he was half a Frenchman; in taste, habits and prepossessions he was almost wholly French. Not only did he speak French admirably and read it like his mother-tongue, but he loved both country and people, and was more really at home in France than anywhere else. Of course, like all Scotsmen, he had an inordinate sentiment for his native land, but it was particularly a sentiment for the Scotland of the past — for the Scotland of history and romance, clanging with arms and resplendent in its heroic and affecting stories. Modern Scotland had less appeal, and though it held a very warm place in Stevenson's heart, he saw it always through that mist of bygone glory. What he praised most in the French as a national trait was their universal indulgence towards all sexual problems — their clear-sighted understanding and toleration of everything affecting the relations of men and women. He often said that in this the French were the most civilised people in Europe, and incomparably in advance of all others, ignoring as comparatively unimportant any criticisms of their irritating bureaucracy, their lottery bonds, their grinding *octrois*; their window-taxes, and so on. Britain to his mind was an infinitely better governed country, but with an intellectual outlook blinkered by caste, puritanism, and prejudice. He preferred France, with its mental and social freedom; its frankness; its lack of hypocrisy; its democratic and kindly acceptance of life as it is. He often pointed out that once French culture had taken root it could never be obliterated. "It has always conquered the conquerors," he said. "Get it started and it becomes ineradicable." '
(*See also* **Campagne Defli; La Solitude; Hotel Chevillon; Hyères**)

'**François Villon: Student, Poet and Housebreaker**', an essay, first published in *Cornhill Magazine,* August 1877; in book form in *Familiar Studies of Men and Books,* 1882; Tusitala Edition 27

**Fraser, Marie,** *In Stevenson's Samoa,* Smith Elder & Co., London, 1895
An actress, Marie Fraser, visited Vailima. 'Things are certainly allowed to occur here. Any attempt at order would be but coldly received', she wrote. Fanny heartily detested this glamorous but critical visitor.

**Freeman, John,** 'Robert Louis Stevenson' in *English Portraits and Essays,* Hodder & Stoughton, London, n.d.

'**French Legend, A**', an essay from *Hitherto Unpublished Prose Writings* first published by Boston Bibliophile Society, 1921; collected in Tusitala Edition *25*

*From a South Seas Diary*, (*see* **Luke, Sir Harrry**)

*From Saranac to the Marquesas and Beyond*, (*see* **Stevenson, Margaret**)

*From Scotland to Silverado, Robert Louis Stevenson*, (*see* **Hart, James D.**)

'**From the Clyde to Sandy Hook**', Part 1 of *The Amateur Emigrant*; written 1879, abridged 1894, first published in *Edinburgh Edition*, 1895; Tusitala Edition *18*.

On the 7th August 1879, Stevenson sailed from the Clyde on the *Devonia*, bound for New York. Immediately after his arrival he set out for the West, a journey that occupied the following week from Monday to Saturday. A year later, August 7, 1880, he sailed with his wife for Liverpool, having written down in the meantime his experiences as an emigrant. His father was insistent that the account should not be published, and, although it had been sold, the sum paid by the publishers was refunded by Stevenson and the book was withdrawn.

A prefatory note by Fanny Stevenson states, '*The Amateur Emigrant* was partly written in Monterey, and almost finished in San Francisco under the most depressing circumstances of ill health, poverty, and letters of adverse criticism from friends in England. In an unfinished letter dated Calistoga, June 4 1880, he writes: "Today at last I send the last of the Double Damned Emigrant. It was all written, after a fashion, months ago, before I caved in; yet I have not had the pluck and strength to finish copying these few sheets before today. The attempt has cost me many a heavy heart . . . I have sent three of my poems to *The Atlantic Monthly* and a fourth, heaven of heavens! to Stephen!" (editor of *Cornhill Magazine*) "I am not mad; only a poet."' The Dedication is to 'Robert Alan Mowbray Stevenson' (his cousin Bob), 'Our friendship was not only founded before we were born by a community of blood, but is in itself near as old as my life. It began with our early ages, and, like a history, has been continued to the present time. Although we may not be old in the world, we are old to each other, having so long been intimates. We are now widely separated, a great sea and continent intervening; but memory, like care, mounts into iron ships and rides post behind the horseman. Neither time nor space nor enmity can conquer old affection; and as I dedicate these sketches, it is not to you only, but to all in the old country, that I send the greeting of my heart.

R.L.S., 1879

**Funk, Doctor,** attended Fanny during her illness in Vailima

This mysterious affliction may well have been menopausal, as she was then in her early fifties and highly-strung, emotional at the best of times. Stevenson wrote to his mother, who had returned to Edinburgh, 'Fanny was devilish ill, no doubt she had an alarming illness. Old Funk did better than I could have hoped. The bother didn't exactly help my cold and for a long time I did a brisk business in spasmodic cough that's over now. In the midst of all this Belle' (Fanny's daughter was divorced and living with them meantime, acting as Stevenson's amanuensis) 'kind of bust up — I think it was only worry and overwork. I was mortal glad you weren't here.' ('Maggie' Stevenson was to return to Vailima later.) 'Now we are all recovered or recovering.' To this Belle added a note that her mother was *not* recovering, 'She lies in bed, does not smoke, doesn't want to eat, or speak; Louis does not want to alarm you but I think you should know what a really anxious time we are going through.'

**Furnas, J.C.**, *Anatomy of Paradise*, Gollancz, London, 1950. Contains reference to the author's stay in Vailima in 1946, with its close associations with Stevenson. *Voyage to Windward*, Faber & Faber, London, 1952, highly recommended as the definitive biography of Stevenson. Contributed an essay to *Stevenson and Victorian Scotland*, (ed.) Jenni Calder.

# G

**Garschine, Mme.**

With her sister Mme. Zassetsky fellow-boarder at the Hotel Mirabeau, Menton during Stevenson's stay there with Sidney Colvin in 1873. Stevenson was recovering from his 'heartbreak' over Fanny Sitwell (who was to remain a close friend). The two noble Russian ladies in their thirties captivated Stevenson. He indulged in a flirtation with the younger sister, Mme. Garschine. They entertained him to samovar-tea and caviar (which he found disappointing and dull) and Slav music (which he found stimulating and romantic). Both ladies were vivacious, temperamental (quite likely to erupt into shaming rows in public) and they told fortunes by palmistry. They also sang and danced in a wild and abandoned gipsy style.

**Gasson, R.,** *The Illustrated Robert Louis Stevenson*, Jupiter Books, London, 1977

**'Gathering of the Fragments, A: The Stevenson Family Revived'** (*see* **Roughead, William**)

**'Gavin Oglivy on Stevenson',** (*see* **Barrie, Sir James Matthew**)

**Geddie, John,** *The Home Country of R.L. Stevenson: The Water of Leith from Source to Sea*, Edinburgh, 1898

**'Genius of Robert Louis Stevenson',** (*see* **'Y.Y.'**)

**'Gentlemen',** an essay, first published in *Scribner's Magazine*, May 1888; Tusitala Edition 26

**Genung, John F.,** *Stevenson's Attitude to Life*, Thos. Y. Crowell, New York, 1901

**German 'Firm', The,** popular local name for Deutsche Handels-und Plantagengesellschaft für Südsee Inseln zu Hamburg, which played a considerable role in the affairs of the German 'territory' of Samoa and the South Pacific. (*See also* **German Interest in Samoa; Malietoa Laupepa, 'King'; Mataafa, 'King'; Samoa; Tamasese, 'King'**)

**German Interest in Samoa**

For twenty years before the Stevensons arrived, Samoa was the source of discord between Great Britain and the United States. Outbreaks of war

among native Samoan factions were brought about by foreign interventions and intrigues. The Tripartite Treaty of Berlin in 1889 added to discord and aggravated the situation by failing to recognise Germany's preponderance of interest and ambitions.
(*See also* **Thyne, C.A.M.**)

**Germany,** Stevenson visited Germany several times, in 1863 and 1875 with his parents, and he spent July/August 1872 in Frankfurt. Curiously for him, he left no written impression except for letters (1872) to his parents, (Letters, Tusitala Edition *31*, pp. 42-52).

**Gibson, John S.,** *Deacon Brodie; Father to Jekyll & Hyde.* Paul Harris, Edinburgh, 1977. Study of life, crimes and trial of Deacon Brodie upon whom Stevenson based his play.

**Gilbert Islands,** in Stevenson's time, noted for sharp-practice; a gathering place for riffraff of the Pacific. Used as setting for 'The Beach of Falesá' (*See* **'In the South Seas'; Apemama**)

**Gilder, Jeannette L.,** 'Stevenson — and After', *Review of Reviews*, February 1895

*Girlhood in the Pacific,* (*see* **Leslie, Mrs. Shane**)

**Gladstone, William Ewart,** (1809-98)

Britain's Prime Minister was detested by Stevenson, who described him as 'a man of fog, evasions and a general deliquescence of the spine'. He wrote to Colvin from Vailima (*Letters*, Tusitala Edition *34*, p.112), 'I wouldn't change my present installation for any post, dignity, honour or advantage conceivable to me . . . as for wars and rumours of wars . . . I like that also a thousand times better than decrepit peace in Middlesex. I do not quite like politics; I am too aristocratic, I fear, for that. God knows I don't care who I chum with; perhaps like sailors best; but to go round and sue and sneak to keep a crowd together — never. My imagination, which is not the least damped by the idea of having my head cut off in the bush, recoils aghast from the idea of a life like Gladstone's and the shadow of the newspaper chills me to the bone.'

**Glencorse,** Edinburgh 'hamlet' and favourite picnic-place in Stevenson's day
From Samoa eighteen months before his death (May 1893) he wrote to S.R. Crockett (Letters, Tusitala Edition *35*, p.28), 'Do you know where the road crosses the burn under Glencorse Church? Go there, and say a prayer for me . . . See that it's a sunny day; I would like it to be a Sunday . . . stand on the right-hand bank just where the road goes down into the water, and shut your eyes, and [see] if I don't appear to you!'

**Gordon, Alice,** 'First Meeting Between Meredith and Stevenson', *Bookman* Extra Number, London, 1913

**Gordon, General,** (1833-85)

Stevenson admired 'Chinese' Gordon and regarded his tragic end at Khartoum as a colossal political blunder. One of his treasures was Gordon's last message, written in Arabic on a cigarette paper, and proudly on display at Vailima.

**Gordon, T.C.,** *Robert Louis Stevenson in Atholl*, Kirkcaldy, 1936

**Gosse, Sir Edmund William,** (1845-1928). The English poet and critic was a lifelong friend of Stevenson. Fellow member of Savile Club, he described Stevenson 'of all men, the most clubbable'.
*Biographical Notes on the Writings of Robert Louis Stevenson*, Chiswick Press, London, 1908; Biographical Notes to the *Pentland Edition of the Works of Robert Louis Stevenson*, 1906-7; *Critical Kit-Kats*, Heinemann, London, 1913; 'Cummy' in *Leaves and Fruit*, Heinemann, London, 1927; 'Death of Mr. R.L. Stevenson', *St. James Gazette*, 17 December 1894; 'Mr. R.L. Stevenson as a Poet', *Longman's Magazine*, October 1887; *Questions at Issue*, Heinemann, London, 1893; 'Robert Louis Stevenson: An Early Portrait', *Bookman* Extra Number, Hodder & Stoughton, London, 1913; 'Robert Louis Balfour Stevenson, 1850-94', in *Encyclopaedia Britannica*, 10th edition; *Silhouettes*, Heinemann, London, 1925; *Some Diversions of a Man of Letters*, Heinemann, London, 1919; 'Stevenson's Relations with Children', *Chamber's Journal*, July 1899; 'To Tusitala in Vailima', *Bookman* Extra Number, London, 1913
(*See also* Part 4 (Letters))

**'Gossip about Robert Louis Stevenson, A',** (*see* **Ryan, J. Tighe**)

**'Gossip on a Novel of Dumas's, A',** an essay, first published in *Memories and Portraits*, 1887; Tusitala Edition *29*

**'Gossip on Romance, A',** an essay, first published in *Longmans Magazine*, November 1882; in book form in *Memories and Portraits*, 1887; Tusitala Edition *29*

**Grand Hotel Godam,** written in collaboration with Sidney Colvin, bilingual parody of French hotel advertising, 1873-74 (privately printed); published in E.V. Lucas *The Colvins and their Friends*, 1928

**'Great North Road, The',** a fragment of a proposed novel first published in *Illustrated London News*, December 1895 and in *The Cosmopolitan*, New York, December 1895, January 1896 with illustrations by R. Caton Woodville; Tusitala Edition *16*

**Green, Roger Lancelyn,** 'Dear Andrew and Dear Louis'. *Scots Magazine,* August 1945. Discusses collaboration of Lang and Stevenson on uncompleted project, 'Where is Rose?' *Stevenson in Search of a Madonna: Essays and Studies*, John Murray, London, 1950

**Greenaway, Kate,** (1846-1901) English illustrator of children's books

According to Stevenson's mother, 'I had Kate Greenaway's children's birthday book. Lou took it up one day and said, "These are rather nice rhymes, and I don't think they would be difficult to do." ' He proceeded to experiment and the result was *A Child's Garden of Verses*.

**Greenwood, Frederick,** 'An Impression of the Week', *Sphere*, 7 December 1901

Described Stevenson as having 'the most threateningly elfish face that I have ever seen in print or paint'.

**Gregg, Frederick James,** 'A Unique Collection of Stevenson', *Book Buyer*, April 1899

**Grez-Sur-Loing,** artists' colony near Paris which was the scene of Stevenson's first meeting with Fanny Osbourne in 1876

He allegedly declared his love in a boat floating below the bridge:
'. . . .On the stream
Deep, swift and clear, the lilies floated; fish
Through the shadows ran. There, thou and I
Read kindness in our eyes and closed the match.'
(*See also* **Hotel Chevillon**)

**Grolier Club,** (*see* **New York Grolier Club**)

**Gross, John,** *The Rise and Fall of the Man of Letters*, London, 1969

**Grundy J. Owen,** 'Robert Louis Stevenson in Greenwich Village', *New York Public Library Bulletin*, March 1963

***Guests and Memories: Annals of a Seaside Villa*** (*see* **Taylor, Una**)

**Guiney, L.I.,** (*see* **Brown, Alice**)

**Guthrie, Lord James,** lifelong friend of Stevenson's from student days and Speculative Society

'Alison Cunningham', *Scotia* 1909; *Cummy: The Nurse of R.L.S. - a Tribute to the Memory of Alison Cunningham*, Edinburgh, 1913; 'Robert Louis Stevenson, 13 November 1850 - 4 December 1894', *Juridical Review*, Vol. 31, 1919; *Robert Louis Stevenson: Some Personal Recollections by the late Lord Guthrie*, W. Green & Son Ltd., Edinburgh, 1920
(*See also* Part 4 (Letters))

**Gwynn, Stephen,** *Robert Louis Stevenson*, Macmillan & Co., London, 1939; 'The Posthumous Works of Robert Louis Stevenson', *Fortnightly Review*, April 1898

# H

**Haddon, Trevor,** 'Letters from R.L.S.' *Harper's Monthly*, 1901. Published in 1902 as *Some Letters*. (*See also* Part 4 (Letters))

**Haggard, Bazett M.**, British Land Commissioner in Samoa

Brother of Sir H. Rider Haggard, he was a friend of the Stevensons and a constant visitor to Vailima. (*See also* **Jersey, Countess of**)

*'Half-White, The'*, (*see* **Stevenson, Fanny**)

**Hamilton, Clayton,** *On the Trail of Stevenson*, Hodder & Stoughton, London, 1916. In search of Stevenson in Edinburgh, France and America.

**Hammerton, J.A.**, *In the Track of Stevenson and Elsewhere in Old France*, Arrowsmith, Bristol, 1907; (ed.) *Stevensoniana: An Anecdotal Life and Appreciation of Robert Louis Stevenson*, John Grant, Edinburgh, 1910

**Hampden, John,** (ed.) *Stevenson Companion*, Phoenix House, London, 1950

*'Handling the Words'* (*see* **Lee, Vernon**)

**Hanging Judge, The,** a play written in collaboration with Mrs. R.L. Stevenson; privately printed by R. and R. Clark, Edinburgh, 1887; first published in Vailima Edition 1922; Tusitala Edition *24*.

Justice Harlow discovers that he is bigamously wed as he passes the death sentence on Will Gillespie, his wife's real husband and the father of his beloved 'daughter', Eleanor.

Based on the career of 'Mr. Garrow, a counsel, whose subtle cross-examination of witnesses and masterly, if sometimes startling methods of arriving at the truth seemed to us more thrilling than any novel', wrote Fanny, claiming that she had suggested the idea to Louis and Henley and when it came to nothing, she had been 'emboldened by Louis's offer to give her any help needed'. Henley, on the other hand, claimed that the central character was suggested by a Sheridan Le Fanu short story. Whatever the origins of *The Hanging Judge*, Stevenson was to give him his ultimate portrayal in *Weir of Hermiston*, based on Lord Braxfield.

**Hanson, Rufe,** nearest neighbour of the Stevensons on honeymoon in Silverado

Hanson had a wife, children and an oafish brother-in-law, whom the

Stevensons nicknamed 'Caliban'. 'Beautiful as a statue' was Stevenson's opinion; 'Too lazy to spit', said the locals.
(*See also* **Silverado Squatters, The**)

**Happier for his Presence: San Francisco and Robert Louis Stevenson** (*see* **Issler, Anne Roller**)

**Hardy, H.F.,** 'Love Laughs at R.L.S.: Allan Breck as a Braw Wooer', *Scots Magazine*, 1938

**Hardy, Thomas,** (1840-1928)
During the Bournemouth period, Stevenson ventured to the West Country in August 1885 to meet the English novelist at Dorchester. Louis was anxious to dramatise *The Mayor of Casterbridge*, but found the author's reception rather diffident. Fanny considered Hardy 'modest, gentle and appealing' but said of Mrs. Hardy, 'What very strange marriages literary men seem to make . . . she is *very* plain, quite underbred, and most tedious' – three unforgivable sins in Fanny Stevenson's eyes. The visit ended with Louis taking ill in an Exeter hotel. Haemorrhages followed and there he had to remain in a hotel room, until he was fit to travel back to Bournemouth in September.

**Harrison, Birge,** 'With Stevenson at Grez', *Century Magazine*, December 1916
Harrison was an American artist who described Fanny Osbourne as 'a grave and remarkable type of womanhood, with eyes of a depth and somber beauty that I have never seen equalled – eyes, neverthless, that upon occasion could sparkle with humour and brim over with laughter . . . Had she been born a Medici, she would have held rank as one of the most remarkable women of all time . . .

**Hart, James D,** (ed.) *From Scotland to Silverado, Robert Louis Stevenson.* Harvard University Press, Cambridge, Mass., 1966. Contains excerpts from 'San Carlos Day' and 'Padre Dos Reales', written by Stevenson for *Monterey Californian. Private Press Ventures of Samuel Lloyd Osbourne and Robert Louis Stevenson*, Stanford University Press, 1966. Relates to the Davos Press operated by Stevenson and his stepson for their own amusement.

**Hawaii,** in 1889 still technically part of Polynesia but already heavily influenced by American missionary activities and large-scale agriculture dominated by American interests, where whites owned the best land, and cheap Chinese labour worked it in preference to the native Hawaiians.
Stevenson's first impressions at the end of a slow and tortuous voyage at the mercy of calms and headwinds,were expressed in a letter to Bob

Stevenson (Tusitala Edition *33*, p.233), 'It blew fair, but very strong . . .
The swell the heaviest I have ever been out in . . . came tearing after
us . . . We had the best hand – Old Louis – at the wheel . . . he did nobly,
and had noble luck, for it [the swell] never caught us once. At times it
seemed we must have it; Old Louis would look over his shoulder with
the queerest look and dive down his neck into his shoulders; and then it
missed us somehow, and only sprays came over our quarter . . . I never
remember anything more delightful and exciting. Pretty soon after we
were lying absolutely becalmed under the lee of Hawaii . . .' There they
were stranded for several days while rations ran perilously short. When
they eventually made port, Fanny's daughter Belle and her husband Joe
Strong came out to meet them in a shoreboat. A tearful reunion
followed, for the 'Casco' had been given up for lost.
(*See also* **Honolulu; Damien, Father; In the South Seas**)

**Hawaii, King of,** (*see* **Kalakaua, King**)

**Hayden, Mrs. Wm. B.,** (*see* *Catalogue* (**I**))

**Hayes, Michael,** (ed.) *The Supernatural Short Stories of Robert Louis
Stevenson,* 1976

**Hayes-McCoy, G.A.,** 'Centenary of Robert Louis Stevenson', *Studies*,
Dublin, December 1950; 'Robert Louis Stevenson and the Irish
Question', *Studies*, Dublin, June 1950

**Hazlitt, William,** (1778-1830)
The great essayist was a hero of Stevenson's boyhood, 'I was always
busy on my own private end, which was to learn to write . . . Whenever I read a book or a passage that particularly pleased me . . . I must sit
down and set myself to ape that quality. I was unsuccessful and I knew
it . . . but at least in these vain bouts, I got some practice in rhythm, in
harmony, in construction and the co-ordination of parts. I have thus
played the sedulous ape to Hazlitt, to Lamb, to Wordsworth, to Sir
Thomas Browne, to Defoe, to Hawthorne, to Montaigne, to Baudelaire
and to Obermann . . .' In Davos he had a biography of Hazlitt
tentatively commissioned. However the personality of his great hero
did not, in Stevenson's opinion, pay tribute to his literary abilities.
When he reached *Liber Amoris*, he gave up the idea entirely.
(*See also* Part 2 (William Hazlitt))

*He Wrote Treasure Island* (*see* **Stern, G.B.**)

**'Health and Mountains',** an essay, first published in *Pall Mall Gazette*,
17 February 1881; in book form in *Essays and Criticisms*, Herbert B.
Turner, Edinburgh, 1903; 'Swiss Notes', *Further Memories*, Tusitala
Edition *30*

**'Heathercat'**, an incomplete short story first published in *Edinburgh Edition* 1897; Tusitala Edition *16*

**Heine, Heinrich,** (1797-1856). The German poet and essayist was one of the young Stevenson's literary heroes
(*See also* **Jenkin, Henry Charles Fleeming**)

**Heintz, Dr. J.P.E.,** friend of Stevenson's Monterey days

**Hellman, George S.,** ' "Cue". Stories of Stevenson', *Bookman*, New York October 1925; *Lanes of Memory*, Alfred A. Knopf, New York, 1927; *The True Stevenson, A Study in Clarification*, Little, Brown & Co., Boston, 1925; 'R.L.S. and the Streetwalker', *American Mercury*, July 1936; 'Stevenson and Henry James', *Century Magazine*, January 1926; 'Stevenson Emerges and Stevenson Unwhitewashed' (review of Steuart's critical biography *Robert Louis Stevenson, Man and Writer*) *Bookman*, New York, January 1925; 'The Stevenson Myth', *Century*, December 1922; 'Stevenson's Annotated Set of Wordsworth', *Colophon*, 1931

**Henderson, James,** (ed.) *Poems of Robert Louis Stevenson*, Folcroft, New York, 1979 (*see* **Young Folks**)

**Henderson & MacFarlane, Sydney,** owners of the rigged steamer *Janet Nicholl* destined to carry the Stevensons from Australia to Vailima

Stevenson was ill and Fanny, encouraged by the Scots name of both steamer and owners, refused to take a negative answer. (The firm were reluctant to carry an apparently dying man and his eccentric determined wife.) Fanny's powers of persuasion once again prevailed.

**Henderson's School,** India Street, Edinburgh

Stevenson enrolled as a pupil at Mr. Henderson's School, which was just around the corner from Heriot Row. Five years old, he attended for two hours only each morning. His attendance until 1859 was very irregular due to frequent illness. A familiar sight was 'young Mrs. Stevenson [his mother] running the little fellow up and down sunny Heriot Row after breakfast to warm him before his school hours' (Rosaline Masson, *The Life of Robert Louis Stevenson*).

**Henley, Anthony,** artist brother of William Ernest with whom Stevenson became acquainted in France

**Henley, Edward ('Teddy'),** actor brother of William Ernest

Toured *Deacon Brodie* in the States with little success, suggested Stevenson guarantee the company's expenses for six weeks. For once Stevenson was firm and promised only to pay Mr. and Mrs. Henley's passage home.

With two fellow-actors Teddy was involved in a Philadelphia bar brawl, was arrested and fortunate to escape with only fines. The New York booking fell through also, which was a considerable blow to his brother, and to Stevenson, the play's authors, who had such high hopes of its success.

**Henley, William Ernest,** (1849-1903), *Essays,* Macmillan, London 1921; 'R.A.M.S.' (Obituary of Bob Stevenson), *Pall Mall Magazine,* July 1900; 'R.L.S.', *Pall Mall Magazine,* December 1901 (this article formed the literary sensation of the Christmas season of 1901 and was noticed by all the prestigious London and provincial newspapers).

Stevenson first met Henley in the Edinburgh Infirmary where Henley, having lost one foot through amputation for tuberculosis of the bone, had come as a last resort to consult the famous Dr. Joseph Lister, pioneer of antisepsis. Friendship was immediate and so there were constant visits to the infirmary by Stevenson who, as soon as Henley could sit up, brought him an armchair which he carried on his back all the way from Heriot Row, unable to afford the cab fare. He wrote an account of a carriage drive they had taken (Mrs. Sitwell, *Letters,* Tusitala Edition *31,* p.226). 'I had a business to carry him down the long stair, and more of a business to get him up again, but while he was in the carriage, it was splendid. It is now just the top of spring with us. The whole country is mad with green. To see the cherry-blossom bitten out upon the black firs, and the black firs bitten out of the blue sky, was a sight to set before a king. You can imagine what it was to a man who has been eighteen months in an hospital ward. The look on his face was wine to me.'

The huge, red-bearded, loud-talking, hard-drinking Henley was always regarded with suspicion by Fanny, who had great difficulty in concealing from Stevenson her cordial dislike of his favourite chum. She disliked him more than Stevenson's other early friends, who were prepared to accept her for her husband's sake, but Henley was different – a man unafraid to speak his mind. Whenever they met sparks flew. However, over the famous 'Nixie' short story (Saranac, March 1888) (*see* **de Mattos, Katharine**) Fanny got her chance and almost succeeded in removing Henley's bad influence entirely from her husband's life. And although the two men tried hard to regard it as a storm in a teacup, their relationship was irrevocably soured. In 1894 Henley's six-year-old daughter died; Margaret, an only child, golden-haired, her father's idol, was Barrie's model for Wendy in *Peter Pan.* Stevenson wrote immediately a loving letter saying that Margaret 'is the one thing I have always envied you, and envy you still.' Childless himself, he still knew the anguish (*see* **Children**). Henley was having a bad time financially and Stevenson authorised Charles Baxter to pay him a small allowance, adding 'if I gave him more, it would only lead to his starting a gig and a Pomeranian dog'.

In the Preface to *Plays* (Tusitala Edition 24), four of which were written by Stevenson in collaboration with Henley, Lloyd Osbourne writes, 'Never was there such another as William Ernest Henley; he had an unimaginable fire and vitality; he swept one off one's feet. There are no words that can describe the quality he had of exalting those about him, of communicating his own rousing self-confidence and belief in himself; in the presence of this demigod, who thrilled you by his appreciation, you became a demigod yourself, and felt the elation of an Olympian who never until then had known the tithe of what was in him. There is still a fellowship of those who proudly call themselves, "Henley's young men". I hope it will not sound presumptuous to say I was the first . . . Even after all these years there is a surge in my heart as I recollect Henley; he shines through the mist with an effulgence; that magic voice rises out of the grave with its unforgotten cadences. He was the first man I had ever called by his surname; the first friend I have ever sought and won; he said the most flattering things of me behind my back, and intoxicated me by his regard. How I idolised him! . . .' (*see* **Stevenson, Robert Louis**, 'Stevenson at Thirty-Five').

Stevenson dedicated *Virginibus Puerisque* to him, writing:
'My dear William Ernest Henley,

We are all busy in this world building Towers of Babel; and the child of our imaginations is always a changeling when it comes from nurse. This is not only true in the greatest, as of wars and folios, but in the least also, like the trifling volume in your hand. Thus I began to write these papers with a definite end: I was to be the *Advocatus*, not I hope *Diaboli*, but *Juventutis*; I was to state temperately the beliefs of youth as opposed to the contentions of age; to go over all the field where the two differ, and produce at last a little volume of special pleadings which I might call, without misnomer, *Life at Twenty-Five*. But times kept changing, and I shared in the change. I clung hard to that entrancing age; but, with the best will, no man can be twenty-five for ever. The old ruddy convictions deserted me, and, along with them, the style that fits their presentation and defence. I saw, and indeed my friends informed me, that the game was up. A good part of the volume would answer the long-projected title; but the shadows of the prison-house are on the rest.

It is good to have been young in youth and, as years go on, to grow older. Many are already old before they are through their teens; but to travel deliberately through one's ages is to get the heart out of a liberal education. Times change, opinions vary to their opposite, and still this world appears a brave gymnasium, full of sea-bathing, and horse-exercise, and bracing manly virtues; and what can be more encouraging than to find the friend who was welcome at one age, still welcome at another? Our affections and beliefs are wiser than we; the best that is in us is better than we can understand; for it is grounded beyond experience, and guides us, blindfold but safe, from one age onto another.

These papers are like milestones on the wayside of my life; and as I look back in memory, there is hardly a stage of that distance but I see you present with advice, reproof, or praise. Meanwhile, many things have changed, you and I among the rest; but I hope that our sympathy, founded on the love of our art, and nourished by mutual assistance, shall survive these little revolutions undiminished; and, with God's help unite us to the end.

R.L.S., Davos Platz, 1881.'

Stevenson was at that time completing _Treasure Island_, begun in Scotland. In a letter to Henley (National Library of Scotland) he reveals the origins of one famous character, '. . . John Silver is quite a kind of good third-rate part-creation. He has his moments, has Long John. Let the Heathen rage, Long John'll do.' And in a later letter from Hyères in May 1883 (Tusitala Edition _32_, p.242), 'I will now make a confession. It was the sight of your maimed strength and masterfulness that begot John Silver. Of course, he is not in any other quality or feature the least like you; but the idea of the maimed man, ruling and dreaded by the sound, was entirely taken from you.'

The famous 'Nixie' quarrel was still several years away but it has caused much speculation among biographers as to whether the grievance still rankled and influenced Henley's critique of Graham Balfour's authorised biography of _The Life of Robert Louis Stevenson_. His review in _Pall Mall Magazine_ (_see_ above) became notorious for its candour, 'I take a view of Stevenson which is my own, and which declines to be concerned with this Seraph in Chocolate, this barley-sugar effigy of a real man; that the best and most interesting part of Stevenson's life will never get written – even by me; and that the Shorter Catechist of Vailima, however authorised and acceptable as an artist in morals is not my old, riotous, intrepid, scornful Stevenson at all . . .'

That Balfour's _Life_ was restricted by the living, and very vigilant, Fanny Stevenson is sad but true. And Henley's own pen-portrait of 'R.L.S.', written in 1876 and published in his _Poems_, remains a marvellously evocative description of the young Stevenson,

'Thin-legged! thin-chested! slight unspeakably,
Neat-footed and weak-fingered; in his face –
Lean, large-boned, curved of beak, and touched with race,
Bold-lipped, rich-tinted, mutable as the sea,
The brown eyes radiant with vivacity –
There shines a brilliant and romantic grace,
A spirit intense and rare, with trace on trace
Of passion, impudence and energy,
Valiant in velvet, light in ragged luck
Most vain, most generous, sternly critical,

Buffoon and poet, lover and sensualist;
A deal of Ariel, just a streak of Puck,
Much Anthony, of Hamlet most of all,
And something of the Shorter Catechist.'

(*See* **Buckley, Jerome Hamilton; Connell, John;** Part 4 (Letters))

**Hennessy, James Pope,** *Robert Louis Stevenson,* Jonathan Cape, London, 1974. The posthumous publication of this biography carries an introduction by Nigel Nicholson

*Henry Adams and his Friends* (*see* **Adams, Henry**)

**Henry, Captain,** sailing master of the *Janet Nicholl*

**'Henry David Thoreau',** an essay, first published in *Cornhill Magazine,* June 1880; in book form in *Familiar Studies of Men and Books,* 1882; Tusitala Edition 27

*Henry James and Robert Louis Stevenson: A Record of Friendship and Criticism* (*see* **Smith, Janet Adam**)

*Henry James: The Middle Years* (*see* **Edel, Leon**)

**Heriot Row, No. 17,** Georgian terrace-house in Edinburgh's handsome New Town. Stevenson's home from age six. Last visited by him for his father's funeral in 1887. (*See also* **Edinburgh Public Library**; Plate 7)

**Herrick, Robert,** (1591-1674) English poet. Stevenson wrote to Henley from Hyères in 1883 (*Letters* Tusitala Edition *32,* p.246), 'You may be surprised to hear that I am now a great writer of verses . . . If I live till I am forty, I shall have a book of rhymes [*A Child's Garden of Verses* was published in 1885] . . . I have begun to learn some of the rudiments . . . and have written three or four pretty enough pieces of octosyllabic nonsense, semi-serious, semi-smiling. A kind of prose Herrick, divested of the gift of verse and you behold The Bard. But I like it.'

**Herries, J.W.,** 'R.L.S. as a Psychic Researcher: Spiritualism in Edinburgh in the Nineteenth Century', *Scots Magazine,* June 1938; 'R.L. Stevenson and Psychic Research' from *I Came, I Saw,* Edinburgh, 1937
The Psychical Society of Edinburgh had Stevenson briefly (1872) as Secretary and his cousin Bob as a Vice-President.

**Hesse, Hermann,** (1872-1962) German novelist and poet. 'A Journey with Stevenson', *Living Age,* November 1927

**Hewlett, Maurice,** (1861-1923), novelist, poet and essayist. 'The Renown of Stevenson', *The Times*, 13 April 1922

Hewlett always considered that Stevenson was overpraised and that such excess obscured his talents.

**Hill, Robin Armstrong,** *The Family Tree of Robert Louis Stevenson of Edinburgh, Novelist, 1850-94,* Chatto and Windus, London, 1934. 'Notes on the various members of the Stevenson family', 1950, unpublished; typescript in Edinburgh Room, Edinburgh Central Library

**Hillis, N.D.,** 'Stevenson's Pattern of the Ideal Life', *Young Man*, 1901. Suggested by quotations from his essays, etc.

**Hillman, Margaret,** 'In the Footsteps of "R.L.S."', A visit to the "Hills of Home".' *S.M.T. Magazine*, November 1928. A walk in the Pentland Hills with reminiscences of Stevenson's sojourn at Swanston Cottage.

**Hills, Gertrude,** 'Robert Louis Stevenson's Handwriting', Beinecke Collection, New York, privately printed, 1940

*Hills of Home,* (*see* **Watt, L.M.**)

**Hines, L.J. and King, Frank,** *Tusitala (Teller of Tales),* a play in four acts, 1934. Typescript in Edinburgh Room, Edinburgh Central Library

**Hinkley, Laura L.,** *The Stevensons: Louis and Fanny,* Hastings House, New York, 1950

**Hinsdale, Harriet,** *Robert Louis Stevenson,* a play, Caldwell, Idaho, 1947

*'His Oceanic Majesty's Goldfish'* (*see* **Strong, Austin**)

**History, Chair of, Edinburgh University**

While the Stevensons were on holiday *en famille* in Pitlochry in June 1881, Stevenson heard that Professor Aeneas Mackay was retiring from the Chair of History and Constitutional Law. Thomas Stevenson was very anxious that his son should apply, especially as there was a yearly salary of £250, for which the only obligation was a series of summer lectures. Thomas Stevenson argued that this would fill the bill health-wise, as his son could spend the killing Scottish winters abroad. In June Stevenson wrote to Sidney Colvin (*Letters*, Tusitala Edition *32*, p.153) 'Great and glorious news. Your friend, the bold unfearing chap,/Aims at a professorial cap,/And now besieges, do and dare,/The Edinburgh History chair./Three months in summer only it/Will bind him to that windy bit;/The other nine to range abroad,/Untrammel'd in the eye of

God./Mark in particular one thing:/He means to work that cursed thing,/And to the golden youth explain/Scotland and England, France and Spain./In short, sir, I mean to try for this chair. I do believe I can make something out of it. It will be a pulpit in a sense; for I am nothing if not moral, as you know. My works are unfortunately so light and trifling they may interfere. But if you think, as I think, I am fit to fight it, send me the best kind of testimonial stating all you can in favour of me and, with your best art, turning the difficulty of my never having done anything in history, strictly speaking . . . it would be a good thing for me, out and out good. Help me to live, help me to *work*, for I am the better of pressure, and help me to say what I want about God, man and life.

Heart-broken trying to write rightly to people.'                 R.L.S.

Despite his canvassing and receiving flattering testimonials from more eminent writer friends, he was not even called for interview.

**'History of Moses'**, privately printed for A.E. Newton, Daylesford, Pennsylvania, 1919; first published in Vailima Edition, 1923; Tusitala Edition *28*

Stevenson's earliest creative writing. When he was six a Balfour uncle offered a prize among the cousins for the best History of Moses. Stevenson dictated his entry to his mother, November–December 1856. He drew his own illustrations showing the Children of Israel wearing top hats and smoking pipes like his father. He won a special award, *The Happy Sunday School Book of Painted Pictures with Verses to each for Good Children*, Dean & Son, London, 1856

*History of Nineteenth Century Literature, A,* (*see* **Saintsbury, George**)

**Hitherto Unpublished Prose Writings** (ed.) H.H. Harper. Illustrated, Boston, 1921

450 copies were printed for members of the Boston Bibliophile Society, from material acquired when R.L.S.'s MSS, books, etc. were dispersed through a New York auction sale in November 1914 and January 1915

**Hogg W.D.**, 'Robert Louis Stevenson in Various Moods; Notes from Unpublished Letters', *Rymour Club Transactions*, Vol. 3, 1928

**Holland, Clive,** 'Robert Louis Stevenson at Bournemouth', *Chambers Journal*, December 1934

*Home and Early Haunts of Robert Louis Stevenson, The,* (*see* **Armour, Margaret**)

*Home Country of R.L. Stevenson, The,* (*see* **Geddie, John**)

*Home from the Sea: Stevenson in Samoa,* (*see* **Bermann, Richard A.**)

*'Homes of the Famous: Robert Louis Stevenson'*, (*see* **Mayne, L. Bruce**)

*'Honest John: The Shepherd Friend of R.L. Stevenson'*, (*see* **Waugh, J.L.**)

### Honolulu, Hawaii

Stevenson preferred to be at sea, no matter how stormy, to living on land, and wrote to Henry James (*Letters*, Tusitala Edition *33*, p.241), 'I have had more fun and pleasure of my life these past months than ever before and more health than at any time in ten long years. And even here in Honolulu I have withered in the cold; and this precious deep is filled with islands, which we may still visit, and though the sea is a deathful place, I like to be there, and like squalls (when they are over) and to draw near to a new island . . .'
He fared better than Fanny who was seasick all the time and wrote, 'To housekeep on a yacht is no easy thing'. Although Fanny was relieved to set foot on land, Stevenson did not care for Honolulu with its large houses and preference for white men, its degradation of the native and his sufferings. The treatment of lepers appalled him and his outspoken comments brought him enemies, especially in the press. (*See also* **Hawaii; In the South Seas; Damien, Father**)

*Honolulu Pacific Advertiser,* 24 June 1889, 'Robert Louis Stevenson and party leave today by the schooner Equator for the Gilbert Islands . . . It is to be hoped that Mr. Stevenson will not fall victim to native spears; but in his present state of bodily health, perhaps the temptation to kill him may not be very strong.'

*Honolulu Then and Now* (*see* **Baker, Ray Jerome**)

**Horne, John,** 'R.L. Stevenson in Wick.' Stevenson's early connections, his student days studying lighthouse building (1868). *Chambers Journal*, 1923. See *Letters* to his mother Tusitala Edition *31*, pp.18-26.

### Hotel Belvedere, Davos

The Stevensons arrived on 4 November 1880, after a tortuous train journey completed by diligence over frozen roads. While Fanny was inspecting the rooms, Louis waited downstairs and was informed by one of the friendly staff, 'Your mother will be down soon'. The difference in their years was beginning to show; Fanny was matronly, grey and stout, while Stevenson retained his look of 'blasted boy, blighted youth'. They had nothing in common with the other guests, who were mostly wealthy Britons, already biased against the Stevensons on account of Fanny's divorce, while Stevenson's long hair and 'un-British courtesy of manner' caused further comment. Despite the air of aggressive respectability, Stevenson reported that violent love affairs ensued, jealousies, cliques and intrigues among the mainly consumptive guests.

Many patients 'died discreetly' and were removed and buried at night. Fanny wrote to Mrs. Stevenson that 'it is depressing to live with dying and suffering people all about you'. Fellow-guests also thought it less than respectable that Lloyd Osbourne should call his stepfather 'Louis' and that he was bringing the boy up badly in his choice of reading-matter. 'Of course I let him read anything he wants, and if he hears things you say he shouldn't I am glad of it. A child should early gain some perception of what the world is really like.'

On the strict diet approved by Dr. Ruedi, with his smoking restricted, Stevenson worked on the essays which would be published as *Virginibus Puerisque*. The hotel offered evening entertainments of readings and concerts, and occasionally Stevenson would be lured to the billiard-room where 'he played with all the fire and dramatic intensity that he was apt to put into things. The balls flew wildly about, on or off the table as the case might be; but seldom indeed ever threatened a pocket or got within a hair's breadth of a cannon. "What a fine thing a game of billiards is," he remarked to the astonished onlookers, "– once a year or so."' (J. A. Hammerton (ed.) *Stevensoniana: An Anecdotal Life and Appreciation*).

(*See also* **Davos; 'Davos in Winter'**)

**Hotel Chevillon, Grez,** scene of Stevenson's first meeting with Fanny Osbourne, 1876

Alarmed by reports from Bob Stevenson that this summer sanctuary for male artists, their models and grisettes, had been invaded by a couple of American females, Stevenson arrived determined to help his cousin eject the intruders. Dinner was being served and he looked in at the half-door opening on the garden from the dining-room. The Americans were there, a married woman and her teenage daughter: Stevenson met the dark eyes 'full of sex and mystery' of Fanny Osbourne, and fell in love with her at first sight.

**Hotel Siron, Barbizon,** visited by Stevenson with his artist cousin Bob in the summer of 1875

Situated on the edge of the Forest of Fontainebleau, Siron's Hotel is described by Lloyd Osbourne in *An Intimate Portrait*: It was 'built around as court, a rambling structure giving evidence of gradual growth and added construction as necessity had arisen. The dining room looked on the village street and was panelled with wood,' on which the artist Will Low and a previous generation had painted rather indifferent sketches. There was a piano used to hard usage in one corner, a fireplace – and for five francs a day plus extras, the convivial easy-going clientele of artists could enjoy food and wine in abundance. Stevenson described Siron's as 'Theoretically . . . open to all comers; practically, it was a kind of club. The guests protected themselves, and, in doing so, they protected Siron.

Formal manners being laid aside, essential courtesy was the more rigidly exacted; the new arrival had to feel the pulse of the society; and a breach of its undefined observances was promptly punished. A man might be as plain, as dull, as slovenly, as free of speech as he desired; but to a touch of presumption or a word of hectoring these free Barbizonians were as sensitive as a tea-party of maiden ladies. I have seen people driven forth from Barbizon; it would be difficult to say in words what they had done, but they deserved their fate. They had shown themselves; they had "made their head", they wanted tact to appreciate the "fine shades" of Barbizon etiquette.'

(See also 'Fontainebleau'; Barbizon; Low, Will. H.)

'House of Eld, The', a fable, Tusitala Edition 5 (see also Fables)

Howard Place, No. 8, The Georgian terrace-house in the Canonmills district of Edinburgh where Robert Louis Stevenson was born on 13 November 1850 (See Plate 5)

'How Edith McGillicuddy met R.L.S.', (see Steinbeck, John)

Howells, W.D., (1837-1920), American novelist. Life in Letters of William Dean Howells, ed. Mildred Howells, Heinemann, London, 1928

Editor-in-Chief of Atlantic Monthly from 1872-81, Howells had corresponded with Stevenson about contributions to the magazine and had received an invitation to visit them in St. Marcel. However, when Howells expressed his strict notions about marriage in A Modern Instance Stevenson addressed him sternly, 'Dear Sir, I have just finishd' reading your last book; it has enlightened (or darkened?) me as to your opinions . . . I find myself under the unpleasant necessity of intruding on your knowledge a piece of my private life. My wife did me the honour to divorce her husband in order to marry me. This, neither more nor less, is at once my duty and my pleasure to communicate . . . after the kindness you showed me in your own country and the sympathy with which many of your books have inspired me, it will be a sincere disappointment to find that you cannot be my guest. I shall bear up, however; for I assure you I desire to know no one who considers himself holier than my wife. With best wishes, however it goes, believe me Yours truly, Robert Louis Stevenson.'
The visit never took place.

'How the Biography of Robert Louis Stevenson Came To Be Written', (see Balfour, Michael)

Hubbard, Elbert, Little Journeys to the Homes of English Authors, Putnam, London, 1903. Includes a Stevenson pilgrimage. Robert Louis Stevenson and Fanny Osbourne, Hartford Lunch Co., New York, n.d.

*Human Personality and its Survival of Bodily Death,* (*see* **Myers, Frederick W.H.**)

**'Humble Remonstrance, A'**, an essay, first published in *Longmans Magazine*, December 1884; in book form in *Memories and Portraits*, 1887; Tusitala Edition 29

**Hume, David,** (1711-1776), Scottish philosopher, historian and political economist

One of the 'Four Great Scotsmen' in the work projected by Stevenson which materialised only in fragments over the ten years from 1873. (The other three were Burns, Knox and Scott)

**Hutchinson, Allen,** 'Stevenson's only Bust from Life', *Scribner's Magazine*, August 1926. The sculptor's reminiscences of Stevenson sitting for him in Honolulu

**Hyde, Rev. Dr.**

Father Damien had devoted his life to the lepers of Molokai. At the suggestion of a memorial to him, a Protestant missionary, Rev. Dr. Hyde, publicly accused the priest of being 'a coarse, dirty man, headstrong and bigoted'. He further hinted that as the priest was 'not a pure man in his relations with women, the leprosy of which he died should be attributed to his vices and carelessness.' Outraged by this injustice, Stevenson replied in 'An Open Letter to the Rev. Dr. Hyde of Honolulu'. For the gist of his defence (*see* **Damien, Father**; Part 4 (Letters))

**Hyères,** (*see* **La Solitude,**)

In 1883 Hyères was a renowned resort for consumptives. The old town, however, was very dirty and Stevenson wrote to the mayor complaining about the state of the streets. The rubbish was cleared and dumped in front of the cottage of an absent Englishman. The Stevensons had to negotiate this unsightly heap going up and down the hill to the town. In another protest Stevenson mentioned that the road outside La Solitude needed repair, and the pile of refuse was moved from outside the Englishman's cottage to his own. From the filthy dust blowing off the street, Stevenson contracted ophthalmia. This further setback was more than Fanny could bear; she wrote to his mother, 'I am not very good at letter writing since I have been doing blind man's eyes, but here is a note to say that the blind man is doing very well, and I consider the blindness a real providence. Since he has been unable to read or do anything at all a wonderful change has come over his health, spirits, and temper, all for the better . . . I wish you could see him with his eyes tied up and singing away like mad; truly like mad, as there is neither time nor method in it, only a large voice . . . Our Wogg' [another name for the Skye terrier

Bogue] 'is an invalid, having got himself badly mangled in several fights, the maid is ill with symptoms of pleurisy and altogether we are a forlorn household, but with all this Louis and I are in high spirits. [Stevenson continued to write, even silent, lying down in a darkened room with his right arm bound to his side to prevent haemorrhage.] 'Across his bed, a board was laid on which large sheets of paper were pinned,' wrote Fanny, 'on these, or on a slate fastened to the board, he laboriously wrote out in the darkness, with his left hand, many more of the songs of his childhood.' [for *A Child's Garden of Verses*.] To encourage Fanny to leave the sickroom he insisted she take an hour's walk each day and make up a tale to tell him on her return. And so *The Dynamiter* came into being based on the Irish bomb outrages in London.

One day they observed a mysterious cloud gathering over the horizon above nearby Toulon. Ominous and depressing, it hung heavy and lowering for several days. They learned that great fires were burning in the streets and that it was soon cholera not 'angels' which 'frequented the magic garden'. In the frightful death toll, Fanny decided that Hyères must be abandoned as too dangerous a place for them to live. Stevenson wrote to Colvin. (*Letters* Tusitala Edition *32*, p.315) 'My life dwindles into a kind of valley of the shadow picnic'. And heart-broken by the quarrel over 'The Nixie' with Henley he wrote to Baxter from Saranac Lake, 12 April 1888, 'The bottom wish of my heart is that I had died at Hyères; the happy part of my life ended there . . .' (See Plate 16)

# I

*I Can Remember Robert Louis Stevenson,* (*see* **Masson, Rosaline**)

**Ide, Annie,** elder daughter of Henry C. Ide, U.S. Land Commissioner and later Chief Justice of Samoa

Annie was born on Christmas Day and regarded herself as defrauded of her natural right to a private anniversary. On 19 June, 1891 Stevenson drew up a Deed which gave her his own birthday (*Letters*, Tusitala Edition *34*, p.86),

'Dear Mr. Ide: Herewith please find the Document which I trust will prove sufficient in law. It seems to me very attractive in its eclecticism: Scots, English and Roman law phrases are all indifferently introduced, and a quotation from the works of Haynes Bayly can hardly fail to attract the indulgence of the bench:

I, Robert Louis Stevenson, Advocate of the Scots Bar, author of *The Master of Ballantrae* and *Moral Emblems*, stuck civil enginer, sole owner and patentee of the Palace and Plantation known as Vailima, in the island of Upolu, Samoa, a British subject, being in sound mind, and pretty well, I thank you, in body:

In consideration that Miss Annie H. Ide, daughter of H.C. Ide, in the town of Saint Johnsbury, in the county of Caledonia, in the State of Vermont, United States of America, was born, out of all reason, upon Christmas Day, and is therefore out of all justice denied the consolation and profit of a proper birthday;

And considering that I, the said Robert Louis Stevenson, have attained an age when O, we never mention it, and that I have now no further use for a birthday of any description;

And in consideration that I have met H.C. Ide, the father of the said Annie H. Ide, and found him as about as white a land commissioner as I require:

*Have transferred* and *do hereby transfer,* to the said Annie H. Ide, *all and whole* my rights and privileges in the thirteenth day of November, formerly my birthday, now, hereby and henceforth, the birthday of the said Annie H. Ide, to have, hold, exercise, and enjoy the same in the customary manner, by the sporting of fine raiment, eating of rich meats, and receipts of gifts, compliments, and copies of verse, according to the manner of our ancestors;

*And I direct* Annie H. Ide to add to the said name of Annie H. Ide the name Louisa – at least in private; and I charge her to use my said birthday with

moderation and humanity, *et tamquam bona filia familiae*, the said birthday
not being so young as it once was, and having carried me in a very
satisfactory manner since I can remember;
And in case the said Annie H. Ide shall neglect or contravene either of
the above conditions, I hereby revoke the donation and transfer my
rights in the said birthday to the President of the United States of
America for the time being: In witness whereof I have hereto set my
hand and seal . . .' He wrote to her in November 1891 (*Letters*, Tusitala
Edition *34*, p.115), 'My dear Louisa: Your picture of . . . your very witty
and pleasing letter . . made me feel I had my money's worth for that
birthday. I am now, I must be, one of your nearest relatives; exactly
what we are to each other, I do not know, I doubt if the case has ever
happened before – your papa ought to know and I don't believe he does;
but I think I ought to call you . . . my name-daughter . . You are thus
become a month and twelve days younger than you were, but will go on
growing older for the future in the regular and human manner from one
13th November to the next. The effect on me is more doubtful; I may, as
you suggest, live for ever; I might, on the other hand, come to pieces like
the one-horse shay at a moment's notice; doubtless the step was risky,
but I do not the least regret that which enables me to sign myself your
revered and delighted name-father,

Robert Louis Stevenson.'

(*see* Part 4 (Letters))

'**Ideal House, The**', an unfinished essay, first published in the Edinburgh
Edition, 1898; Tusitala Edition *25*

**Iles, George,** 'A Note upon Stevenson'. Valedictory article, stressing
Stevenson's value as a modern writer. *Book Buyer*, February 1895

***Illustrated London News,*** serialised *The Beach of Falesá* in six weekly
instalments, 1883. Apart from one essay 'A Winter's Walk in Carrick
and Galloway', Stevenson's 'projects' for them, mentioned in letters,
did not materialise. Their issue of 22 December 1894 contained an
anonymous article entitled 'R.L.S.: with Sketches of Mr. Stevenson's
Home in Vailima'

***Illustrated Robert Louis Stevenson, The*** (*see* **Gasson, R.**)

'***Impression of the Week, An***', (*see* **Greenwood, Frederick**)

**Indianapolis, Indiana,** birthplace of Fanny Osbourne, 10 March 1840

**Inland Voyage, An,** C. Kegan Paul, London, 1878; Tusitala Edition *17*.
Stevenson's first published book.
The First Edition contains one of Stevenson's rare prefaces, 'To equip so
small a book with a preface is, I am half afraid, to sin against proportion.
But a preface is more than an author can resist, for it is the reward of his

labours. When the foundation stone is laid, the architect appears with his plans, and struts for an hour before the public eye. So with the writer in his preface: he may have never a word to say, but he must show himself for a moment in the portico, hat in hand, and with an urbane demeanour. It is best, in such circumstances, to represent a delicate shade of manner between humility and superiority: as if the book had been written by some one else, and you had merely run over it and inserted what was good. But for my part I have not yet learned the trick to that perfection; I am not yet able to dissemble the warmth of my sentiments towards a reader; and if I meet him on the threshold, it is to invite him in with country cordiality.

To say truth, I had no sooner finished reading this little book in proof than I was seized upon by a distressing apprehension. It occurred to me that I might not only be the first to read these pages, but the last as well; that I might have pioneered this very smiling tract of country all in vain, and find not a soul to follow in my steps. The more I thought, the more I disliked the notion; until the distaste grew into a sort of panic terror, and I rushed into this Preface, which is no more than an advertisement for readers. What am I to say for my book? Caleb and Joshua brought back from Palestine a formidable bunch of grapes; alas! my book produces naught so nourishing; and for the matter of that, we live in an age when people prefer a definition to any quantity of fruit.

I wonder, would a negative be found enticing? for, from the negative point of view, I flatter myself this volume has a certain stamp. Although it runs to considerably upwards of two hundred pages, it contains not a single reference to the imbecility of God's universe, nor so much as a single hint that I could have made a better one myself – I really do not know where my head can have been. I seemed to have forgotten all that makes it glorious to be man. 'Tis an omission that renders the book philosophically unimportant; but I am in hopes the eccentricity may please in frivolous circles.

To the friend who accompanied me I owe many thanks already, indeed I wish I owed him nothing else; but at this moment I feel towards him an almost exaggerated tenderness. He, at least will become my reader – if it were only to follow his own travels alongside of mine.

R.L.S.'

*Dedication* To Sir Walter Grindlay Simpson, Bart.: 'My dear "Cigarette", It was enough that you should have shared so liberally in the rains and portages of our voyage; that you should have had so hard a paddle to recover the derelict "Arethusa" on the flooded Oise; and that you should thenceforth have piloted a mere wreck of mankind to Origny Sainte-Benôite and a supper so eagerly desired. It was perhaps more than enough, as you once somewhat piteously complained, that I should have set down all the strong language to you, and kept the appropriate reflections for myself. I could not in decency expose you to share the disgrace of another and more public shipwreck. But now that this voyage of ours is going into a cheap edition, that peril, we shall hope, is at an end, and I may put your name on the burgee.

But I cannot pause till I have lamented the fate of our two ships . . . For a while . . . the world looked smilingly. The barge was procured and christened, and, as the "Eleven Thousand Virgins of Cologne", lay for some months, the admired of all admirers, in a pleasant river and under the walls of an ancient town . . . you will not have forgotten the amount of sweet champagne consumed at the inn at the bridge end, to give zeal to the workmen and speed to the work [of re-decoration]. On the financial aspect, I would not willingly dwell. The "Eleven Thousand Virgins of Cologne" rotted in the stream where she was beautiful. She felt not the impulse of the breeze, she was never harnessed to the patient track-horse . . . at length she was sold . . . along with her the "Arethusa" and the "Cigarette" . . . Now these historic vessels fly the tricolour and are known by new and alien names.

R.L.S.'

The last words of this account of his canoeing trip down the inland waterways of France are prophetic, 'Now we were to return, like the voyager in the play, and see what rearrangements fortune had perfected the while in our surroundings; what surprises stood ready made for us at home; and whither and how far the world had voyaged in our absence. You may paddle all day long; but it is when you come back at nightfall, and look in at the familiar room, that you find Love or Death awaiting you beside the stove; and the most beautiful adventures are not those we go to seek.'

It was love Stevenson found awaiting him in the shape of Fanny Osbourne at the Hotel Chevillon in Grez.

(*See also* Part 6 (Radio))

'*In Memoriam R.L.S.*', (*see* **Archer, William; MacLaren, Ian**)

*In Stevenson's Samoa*, (*see* **Fraser, Marie**)

'*Interview with Mrs. Robert Louis Stevenson, An*', (*see* **Burgess, Gelett**)

'*In the Cévennes without a Donkey*', (*see* **Skinner, R.T.**)

*In the Footsteps of R.L.S.* (*see* **Findlay, J.P.**)

'*In the Footsteps of "R.L.S.": A visit to the Hills of Home*' (*see* **Hillman, Margaret**)

'**In the Latin Quarter. No. I — A Ball at Mr. Elsinare's**', an essay, first published in *London*, 10 February 1877; reprinted in *The Stevensonian*, London, 1965

'**In the Latin Quarter. No. II. — A Studio of Ladies**', an essay, first published in *London*, 17 February, 1877

**In the South Seas: A Record of Three Cruises,** first published by
Cassell, London, 1890. Tusitala Edition *20*. 'Being an account of
Experiences and Observations in the Marquesas, Paumotos, and
Gilbert Islands in the Course of two Cruises, on the yacht CASCO
(1888) and the schooner EQUATOR (1889) by Robert Louis
Stevenson.'

During the writing of this book, Stevenson informed Colvin (*Letters,*
Tusitala Edition *33*, p.259) that he had 'material for a very singular book
of travels: names of strange stories and characters, cannibals, pirates,
ancient legends, old Polynesian poetry, – never was so generous a
farrago . . . The Pacific is a strange place; the nineteenth century only
exists there in spots; all round, it is a no man's land of the ages, a stir-
about of epochs and races, barbarisms and civilisations, virtues and
crimes.'
Fanny too was anxious regarding the outcome of this book and wrote
privately to Colvin, 'Louis has the most enchanting material that any
one ever had in the whole world for this book, and I am afraid that he is
going to spoil it all. He has taken it into his Scotch Stevenson head that
his book must be a sort of scientific and historical impersonal thing
comparing the different languages (of which he knows nothing, really)
and the different peoples . . and the whole thing to be impersonal,
leaving out all he knows of the people themselves. And I believe there is
no one living who has got so near or who understands them as he does . .
I am going to ask you to throw the weight of your influence as heavily as
possible in the scales with me, otherwise Louis will spend a good deal of
time in Sydney actually reading other people's books on the Islands.
What a thing it is to have a "man of genius" to deal with. It is like
managing an overbred horse. Why with my own feeble hand I could
write a book that the whole world would jump at . . Even if I thought it
a desirable thing to write what he proposes, I should still think it
impossible unless after we had lived and studied here for some twenty
years or more.' Colvin agreed with her; the result is the published
volume.(*See* Part 6 (Radio))

*In the Track of Stevenson and Elsewhere in Old France,* (*see* **Hammerton,
J.A.**)

*Intimate Portrait of Robert Louis Stevenson, An,* (*see* **Osbourne, Lloyd**)

**Inverleith Terrace, No. 1,** now No. 9; Stevenson's infant home in
Edinburgh; the property was renumbered in the 1880s when
additional houses were built

His parents moved there when he was three, considering the site would
be healthier for both child and mother, who suffered from chest

troubles. The house looked across the circles and squares of Edinburgh's New Town to the Castle and Arthur's Seat from its back windows and faced onto the Botanic Gardens. It did not fulfil its early promise of better health; it was so damp that clothes mildewed in the closets.

*Island Boy, Robert Louis Stevenson and his Step-grandson in Samoa,* (*see* **Mackay, Margaret**)

**Island Nights' Entertainments,** Cassell, London and Scribner's, New York, 1893. Tusitala Edition *13*.Dedicated to 'Three old Shipmates among the Islands: Harry Henderson, Ben Hird, Jack Buckland – Their Friend, R.L.S.' Contains three stories, 'The Beach of Falesá', 'The Bottle Imp' and 'The Isle of Voices'; all published separately. (*See* Part 6 (Radio))

*Island Treasure: A Visit to Samoa,* (*see* **Simpson, Rev. H.L.**)

**'Isle of Voices, The',** a short story, an atmospheric folk-tale of the South Seas, first published in *National Observer*, 4-25 February 1893, illustrated by W. Hatherell; in book form in *Island Nights' Entertainments*, 1893; Tusitala Edition *13*. (*See* Part 6 (Radio))

**Issler, Anne Roller,** the one-time Curator of the Stevenson Museum at Monterey, and an acknowledged authority on Stevenson in California. *Happier for His Presence: San Francisco and Robert Louis Stevenson*, Stanford University Press, n.d.; *Our Mountain Heritage*, Stanford University Press, n.d.; 'Robert Louis Stevenson in Monterey'. *Pacific Historical Review*, August 1965. Reference to Stevenson contributions to *Monterey Californian; Stevenson in Silverado*, Caxton Printers, Caldwell, Idaho, 1939

# J

**James, Alice,** Unmarried sister of Henry James (*see below*). *Diary* (ed. Leon Edel), Hart-Davies, London, 1965. Her diary indicates that she was shocked by the forthright, unconventional Fanny Stevenson

**James, Henry,** (1843-1916) 'Robert Louis Stevenson' from *Partial Portraits*, Macmillan, London, 1888; *Letters* (ed. Percy Lubbock), 2 vols., Macmillan, London, 1920; 'Robert Louis Stevenson', *Century Magazine*, April 1888

When the American novelist first visited the Stevensons in Bournemouth in 1885 he was mistaken for an expected tradesman and kept waiting at the door. Fanny wrote (Mackay, *The Violent Friend*), 'We have had a very pleasant visitor. One evening a card was handed in with "Henry James" upon it. He spent that evening, asked to come again the next night, arriving almost before we had got done with dinner, and staying as late as he thought he might, and asking to come the next evening, which is tonight. I call that very flattering. I had always been told that he was the type of an Englishman, but, except that he looks like the Prince of Wales, I call him the type of an American . . I think there is no question but that he likes Louis; naturally, I have hardly been allowed to speak to him, though I fain would. He seems very gentle and comfortable and I worship in silence.' James was in Bournemouth visiting his invalid sister Alice (*see above*); soon he was an almost daily visitor, with his own chair, a favourite big blue armchair which had come to Skerryvore with furnishings from Heriot Row in Edinburgh; it became 'Henry James's Chair'. Soon Fanny was writing, 'We are devoted to him'. He shared their taste for the macabre and declared 'Thrawn Janet' a masterpiece. Of Stevenson himself, 'Character, character is what he has! His feelings are always his reasons.' He praised Fanny's 'elegant letters' and in a note of introduction to accompany Owen Wister, the American author of *The Virginian* on a visit to the Stevensons in Saranac, said, ' . . You will find him a young, unique, dishevelled, undressed, lovable fellow. There is a fresh, youthful, complacent Scotch mother, a poor sightless (or almost so) American stepson and a strange Californian wife, 15 years older than Louis himself, but almost as interesting. If you like the gulch and the canyon you will like *her* . . .'

(*See* **Edel, Leon; Hellman, George S.; Smith, Janet Adam;** Part 4 (Letters))

**Janet Nicholl,** mis-spelt by Fanny Stevenson as *Nichol*

Trading steamer which she negotiated to take the 'dying Stevenson' from Sydney back to the South Seas. 'Louis was laid out on a board, rolled like a mummy in a blanket; [Fanny] sat beside him, silent and watchful of his comfort.' The iron-screw steamer of about 600 tons was long, low and rakish, blackened by coal-dust and even at anchor she rolled – Fanny later learned that the vessel was known throughout the islands as 'Jumping Jenny'. It was not easy to get Stevenson over the high bulwarks, 'some half-naked blackmen carried him up the narrow gangway . . a red-faced, red-bearded man, somewhat the worse for drink, lurched about the slippery deck, making a nuisance of himself in his efforts to help'. Belle Strong added, 'We were heavy-hearted . . Louis looked so ill we thought we might never see him again. It seemed terrible for him to be going away in that sloppy ship with drunken men and inky-black savages, and I didn't like the thought of my mother being the only woman on board with not even Ah Fu to look after her.' Unfortunately the steamer also picked up a cargo of fireworks and soon after they left the first port of call, Auckland, Fanny heard 'a spitting puff, followed by gorgeous flames and the most horrible chemical stench'. Blue, green and red rockets burst into the saloon and high over the deck. The captain and crew were taken by surprise and only Fanny seemed capable of seizing a blanket to deal with the emergency. At last with blanket, rug and hose the captain succeeded in smothering the flames, but had the wind been in a different quarter, or the cartridges exploded, the ship would have been a total loss.

During these operations Fanny saw a couple of black boys about to throw a blazing trunk overboard and ran forward just in time to stop them depositing the contents, four large boxes full of her husband's manuscripts, into the ocean. Personally they lost everything, even toothbrushes, retaining only the clothes they were wearing, and sadly most of their precious photographs were destroyed.

(*See also* **Henderson & MacFarlane, Sydney; In the South Seas;** *Cruise of the 'Janet Nichol', The*)

**Japp, Alexander H.,** 'A Master of Romance, R.L. Stevenson', *Atalanta*, 1892/3; 'A Memorial of R.L.S.', *Old and Young*, February 1923; 'Mr. R.L. Stevenson and the "Cornhill"' *Daily Chronicle*, 19 December 1894; 'Robert Louis Stevenson', *Argosy*, February 1895; 'Robert Louis Stevenson's Death', *Daily Graphic*, 18 December 1894; *Robert Louis Stevenson, a record, an estimate and a memorial*, T. Werner Laurie, London 1905
(*See also* (Part 4 (Letters)))

**'J.E.B.B.',** *Recollections of a Visit to Samoa and the Home of Mr. R.L. Stevenson*, n.d.

**Jekyll and Hyde,** (*see* **Dr. Jekyll and Mr. Hyde, The Strange Case of**)

**Jenkin, Henry Charles Fleeming** (1833-1885) and **Anne**

Fleeming Jenkin was Professor of Engineering at Edinburgh University from 1868 to 1885. That he befriended Stevenson was the result of a chance meeting with Anne Jenkin while she was having tea with Mrs. Thomas Stevenson in Heriot Row. She was greatly impressed by the 'student's brilliant conversation'. Returning home she described him to her husband as 'a young Heine with a Scottish accent'. Mrs. Jenkin was an amateur actress of some standing and ran a salon carefully selected from Edinburgh's professional class who shared her own and Fleeming's pleasure in the arts, widely interpreted as theatre, music, philosophy and literature. To this purpose their house was equipped for ready conversion into a theatre and they produced an annual play for which Jenkin designed the Greek costumes. For young Stevenson the Jenkin household offered 'an oasis in a desert of convention'. Stevenson's acting ability in no way lived up to his growing brilliance as a talker; a poor actor, he was allowed only minor roles, but the rich costumes and the champagne-supper afterwards were adequate compensation. Fleeming Jenkin was a man of remarkable talents. Before his professorship he had laid submarine cables and pioneered electricity applied to transportation. He was also enough of a biologist to have corrected Charles Darwin on a minor point and to have written a significant work on fecundity and in the more social scene he was a splendid ice-skater, dancer and actor. He constructed a phonograph into which Stevenson talked 'broad Scots' and wished to 'teach it how to swear'.

Edmund Gosse wrote, 'In Jenkin's presence, Stevenson seemed to be resisting an instinctive tendency towards veneration, which Jenkin, to do him justice, was on his part always anxious to break down.'

The young Stevenson, now atheistic, mocking at the establishment, could be neatly curbed by Jenkin. To retain his place in the University Stevenson had to produce certificates of class attendance from several professors, 'It is quite useless for you to come to me, Mr. Stevenson', said Professor Jenkin when he was approached, 'There may be doubtful cases, there is no doubt about yours. You have simply not attended my class.' On the grounds of Thomas Stevenson's despair and disappointment, Professor Jenkin brought forth the certificate with the stern injunction that Stevenson was never to use it to qualify for a degree. 'That was the bitter beginning of my love for Fleeming,' wrote Stevenson, 'I never thought lightly of him afterwards'. Another passage in the *Memoir of Fleeming Jenkin* is illuminating, Stevenson put to the professor a problem of conduct, to which he received the evasive reply, 'What would Christ have advised?' 'Nothing unkind or cowardly', said Stevenson carefully. 'True, Mr. Stevenson, nor anything amusing'. Years later, Stevenson was to write (*Letters* Tusitala Edition *33*, p.237),

'My dear Colvin, I owe you and Fleeming Jenkin, the two older men who took the trouble, and knew how to make a friend of me, everything that I have or am.'
It was indeed fortunate that Anne Jenkin had been impressed by the student Stevenson and that her husband saw some merit and likeable quality in the young rebel. As for Anne herself, in her mid-thirties, she was very attractive and cultured. The possessor of an expressive though not conventionally beautiful face, her grand manner earned her the family nickname of 'Madam'. Her encouragement and kindliness, her patient ear, soothed the frustrations of Heriot Row and a tortured home life. She became the first of the older women whom Stevenson found far more interesting and agreeable than 'some dull, good girl' from middle-class Edinburgh whom his parents hoped earnestly would some day curb his rebellion in marriage.

In 1878 Jenkin was a juror at the International Exhibition in Paris and engaged Stevenson as his private secretary, which greatly helped further his romance with Fanny Osbourne.

When Fleeming died in 1885 Stevenson wrote his obituary in *The Academy* (20 June). Anne Jenkin came down to Skerryvore to help him to write the *Memoir*. 'She is not generally liked, but I like her', wrote Fanny, who was apt to be acid about her husband's former loves.
(*See* **Memoir of Fleeming Jenkin**; Part 4 (Letters))

**Jersey, Margaret Elizabeth (Leigh) Child-Villiers, Countess of,** wife of the Governor of New South Wales. *Fifty-One Years of Victorian Life,* John Murray, London, 1922. With special reference to Stevenson's work on *Object of Pity or, the Man Haggard* (the latter being Bazett Haggard, British Land Commissioner at Samoa (brother of the author H. Rider Haggard)

'I shall never forget the moment when I first saw him [Stevenson] and his wife standing at the door of the long, wood-panelled room in Ruge's Building. A slim, dark-haired, bright-eyed figure in a loose black velvet jacket over his white vest and trousers, and a scarlet silk sash. By his side the short, dark woman with cropped curly hair and the strange piercing glance which had won for her the name in native tongue, "The Witch Woman of the Mountain".'
In order that his aristocratic visitor might discreetly visit the rebel 'king' Mataafa, Stevenson invented for Lady Jersey the incognito of 'his cousin, Amelia Balfour'. He wrote to Colvin, (*Letters*, Tusitala Edition *34*, p.224). 'It is all nonsense that it can be concealed; Miss Amelia Balfour will be at once identified with the Queen of Sydney, as they call her; I would not in the least wonder if the visit proved the signal of war . . . the thing wholly suits my book and fits my predilections for Samoa.'

Later Lady Jersey wrote, 'Stevenson was not only a writer of romance, but a hero of romance'.
(*See also* Part 4 (Letters))

**'John Knox and his Relations to Women'**, an essay, first published in *Macmillan's Magazine*, September and October 1875; in book form in *Familiar Studies of Men and Books*, 1882; Tusitala Edition 27

*John o'London's Weekly,* contained an anonymous article entitled 'Robert Louis Stevenson' (Centenary Number) 24 November 1950

*John Sargent,* (*see* **Charteris, Evan**)

**Johnstone, Arthur,** *Recollections of Robert Louis Stevenson in the Pacific,* Chatto & Windus, London, 1905. Includes comments on Stevenson's desire to write stories in French

**'Journal Written Aboard the "Pharos" '**, first published in *Scribner's Magazine*, January 1889. Account of voyage with his father and Commissioners of the Northern Lights through the Orkney and Shetland Isles.

*Journals of Arnold Bennett,* (*see* **Bennett, Arnold**)

*'Journey with Stevenson, A',* (*see* **Hesse, Hermann**)

**'Jules Verne's Stories'**, an essay, first published in *The Academy,* 3 June 1876; collected in Tusitala Edition 28

**Julian, Atelier,** Paris art school attended by Fanny Osbourne and her daughter Belle, the former chaperoning the latter in the life class with its nude models. Fanny's drawing received praise for its charm and simplicity

# K

**Kahn, Edgar M.**, *R.L.S.: a Warm-hearted Friend of Humanity*, privately printed, San Francisco, 1964. Stevenson's affection for Hawaii

*Kaimiloa*, **H.H.M.S.**, Kalakaua, King of Hawaii, deciding that his country would acquire esteem by the possession of a Navy, equipped this rather ancient steamer with a few small guns and manned her with young delinquents from the royal reform school. Joe Strong (Belle's husband) accompanied the 'delegation' sent to confer with the three powers, Germany, Britain and the United States in Samoa, but the *Kaimiloa* made a poor show among the antique but imposing men-of-war that the powers kept in the Pacific. All that was achieved was an abnormal consumption of alcohol by the crew, with the result that a local ship master had to be hired to see that she found her way safely back to Honolulu

**Kaiulani, Princess,** daughter of A.S. Cleghorn, Stevenson's Scottish friend, and the heiress-presumptive of Hawaii

Her mother, King Kalakaua's sister, had died when Kaiulani was twelve. A year later she was sent to England by her father to a boarding-school for education befitting her royal station. Stevenson wrote in her album:

> When she comes to my land and her father's, and the rain beats upon the window (as I fear it will), let her look at this page; it will be like a weed gathered and pressed at home; and she will remember her own islands, and the shadow of the mighty tree; and she will hear the peacocks screaming in the dusk and the wind blowing in the palms; and she will think of her father sitting here alone.

They never met again. When she returned in 1898 Stevenson had been dead for four years and her own health had been ruined by the cold climate with its cruel winters. She died a year later, aged twenty-two. (*See also* **Cleghorn, A.S.**)

**Kalakaua, King,** Belle and Joe Strong, with their son Austin, had established themselves at his court in Honolulu, and Belle had designed the Royal Order of the Star of Oceania while Joe was 'official' artist. They became closely identified with the 'royal crowd' before the Stevensons arrived. Stevenson took a liking to the King and soon *Casco* was entertaining royalty, at which Stevenson read poetry and Belle danced. Stevenson at their next meeting presented His Hawaiian Majesty with a set of verses and a large yellow pearl from Taumotu. From then on the royal carriage was frequently to be seen outside the Stevensons' house denoting that the King was a visitor. ' . . . What a crop for the drink', wrote Stevenson to Baxter (*Letters* Tusitala Edition *33*, p.229) 'He carries it, too, like a mountain with a sparrow on its shoulders. We calculated five bottles of champagne in three hours and a half (afternoon), and the sovereign quite presentable, although perceptibly more dignified at the end . . . ' In a further letter (Tusitala Edition *33*, p.235) Stevenson continued admiringly, 'A bottle of fizz is like a glass of sherry to him; he thinks nothing of five or six in an afternoon as a whet for dinner. You should see a photograph of our party after an afternoon with H.H.M.: my! what a crew!' Kalakaua aped Western royalty with his stone palace which resembled a mid-Western courthouse complete with verandas, a miniature opera house with electric lighting and a royal box. His 'national anthem' was played by a German bandmaster and he had a complete wardrobe of frock coats and musical comedy style uniforms. He also possessed, as well as a 'Navy', characterised by the H.H.M.S. *Kaimiloa* (*above*), an army consisting of a few score soldiers and a battery of out-of-date field guns, and his ambition for a miniature imperialism contributed heavily towards the ruinous national debt.

## Kalawao-Kalaupepa

Stevenson visited the leper colony of Molokai in 1889. The inter-island steamer reached the colony at sunrise, as he wrote to Fanny (*Letters* Tusitala Edition *33*, p.256) 'Bleak and harsh, a little town of wooden houses, two churches . . . lying athwart the sunrise, with the great wall of the pali cutting the world out on the south . . . I do not know how it would have been with me if the sisters had not been there. My horror of the horrible is about my weakest point; but the moral loveliness at my elbow blotted all else out; and when I found that one of them was crying, poor soul, quietly under her veil, I cried a little myself; then I felt as right as a trivet, only a little crushed to be there so uselessly. I thought it was a sin and a shame she should feel unhappy; I turned round to her and said something like this: "Ladies, God Himself is here to give you welcome. I'm sure it is good for me to be beside you; I hope it will be blessed to me; I thank you for myself and for the good you do me" . . . a great crowd, hundreds of (God save us) pantomime masks in poor human flesh, waiting to receive the sisters and the new patients. Every hand was offered: I had gloves, but I had made up my mind on the boat's voyage *not* to give my hand; that seemed less offensive . . . '
For eight days he lived in a passion of pity among faces melting into bestiality. Daily he played croquet, without gloves, with leper-children

and yarned with 'old, blind, leper beachcombers in the hospital, sickened with the spectacle of abhorrent suffering, touched to the heart by the sight of lovely and effective virtues in their helpers; no stranger time have I ever had, nor any so moving'.
(*See also* **Damien, Father; Hyde, Rev. Dr.; Vailima Papers.**)

**Kegan Paul, C.:** (*see* **Paul, C. Kegan**)

**Kelman, John,** *The Faith of Robert Louis Stevenson,* Oliphant & Co., London and Edinburgh, 1903. Stevenson as a Christian, his beliefs and morals; *Robert Louis Stevenson,* Famous Edinburgh Students Series, 1914

**Kennedy, Maud,** 'A Passing Glimpse of Robert Louis Stevenson', *St. Paul's,* 26 January 1895

**Kidnapped,** first published as a serial in *Young Folks,* 1 May to 31 July 1886; in book form Cassell, London and Scribner's, New York 1886; Tusitala Edition 6. 'Being Memoirs of the adventures of David Balfour in the Year MDCCLI. How he was kidnapped and cast away; his sufferings in a desert isle; his journey in the wild Highlands: his acquaintance with Alan Breck Stewart and other notorious Highland Jacobites; with all that he suffered at the hands of his Uncle, Ebenezer

A woodcut from *The Bookman. Mansell Collection*

Balfour of Shaws, falsely so-called; written by himself, and now set forth by Robert Louis Stevenson.'

The story is based on an historical incident just after the Jacobite Rebellion of 1745, the murder of Colin Campbell of Glenure, 'the Red Fox'. When Alan Breck is accused of the murder, he and David Balfour flee to safety through the West Highlands whose scenery, political and social conditions are described with understanding and compassion. Begun early in 1885 at Bournemouth 'partly as a lark, partly as a pot-boiler' for *Young Folks*. Editor Henderson had specified an avoidance of 'much broad Scotch in it, as a little of that goes a long way with our readers'. Stevenson wrote that the work took probably five months actual writing, and one of these months entirely over the last chapters, which had to be put together without interest or inspiration, 'almost word by word, for I was entirely worked out'. He was worried about 'the Highland part. I don't think it will be so interesting to read, but it is curious and picturesque'. The idea had taken root long ago, from his childhood fascination with Scottish history, particularly the Jacobite cause and the Appin Murder. (*See also* **Baxter, Charles; Cameron, D.L.; Cameron, John; MacKay, D.N.;** (Part 6 (Media))

**'Kidnapped Walk, The'**, (*see* **Nimmo Ian, and Seaton, Jim**)

**Kiely, Robert,** *Robert Louis Stevenson and the Fiction of Adventure,* Harvard University Press, Cambridge, Mass., 1965. Discusses similarity to Conrad's *Aesthetics of Adventure* (boy's daydream; modern epic; comic satire and fable of faraway places)

**King, F.,** (*see* **Hines, L.J. and King, Frank**)

**Kingsley, Martin,** 'Concerning the "Dead Man's Chest", *Book Buyer,* 12 March 1895. Claims that this piece of *Treasure Island* came from his father Charles Kingsley's *At last: A Christmas in the West Indies,* 1871

**Kingussie,** the Stevensons spent part of the summer of 1882 in this Inverness-shire village

**Kinnaird Cottage** (*see* **Pitlochry**)

**Knight, Alanna,** *The Passionate Kindness: the Love Story of Robert Louis Stevenson and Fanny Osbourne,* Milton House Books, Aylesbury, 1974; 'The Private Life of R.L.S.' (play), Wilfion Books, Paisley, 1984

**Knox, John,** (c.1505-72), Scottish reformer and historian, whom Stevenson intended to include in a projected work 'Four Great Scotsmen', the other three were Burns, Hume and Scott. His researches materialised in **'John Knox and his Relations to Women'** (*Familiar Studies of Men and Books*) and **'John Knox and the**

**Almoner of the Galley'** ('Stevenson's Companion to the Cook Book')

**Ko-o-amua, Chief**

Of their visit to the Marquesas, Stevenson wrote to Colvin (*Letters, Tusitala Edition 33*, p.202), 'It is all a swindle: I chose these isles as having the most beastly population, and they are far better, and far more civilised than we. I know one old chief Ko-o-amua, a great cannibal in his day, who ate his enemies even as he walked home from killing 'em, and he is a perfect gentleman and exceedingly amiable and simple-minded . . . '

'He looked such a mild and benevolent old gentleman,' wrote Stevenson's mother to relatives in prim and seemly Edinburgh, 'It is difficult to believe he was till recently a cannibal. Now he has a large European house.'

(*See* **Moanatini; Vaekehu, 'Queen'**)

# L

**Lady Stair's House Museum,** Lawnmarket, Edinburgh (Tel. 031-225-1131), contains many original Stevenson manuscripts of letters, poems, printed works, etc.

**Lafaele (Raphael),** native Samoan servant at Vailima

There was a saying ' on the beach' that the only place where anyone saw a Samoan run was in Vailima. Lafaele proved his devotion in practical manner when hostilities broke out. He had been lured to a neighbour for a larger wage, 16s. a week, but anxious for the welfare of the Vailima womenfolk of his former employer (as both sides took heads from captives, whether male or female) Lafaele begged to return for his old wage of 13s. 'Never mind money. I no care for that. I like come back because I love Madam (Tamatai) too much'

**La Farge, John,** (1835-1910), American artist, born New York of French parentage, friend of Henry Adams and Will Low, visitor to Vailima in early stages of building. (*See also* **Adams, Henry**)

**Laird, George,** 'R.L.S. and the Law', *Journal of the Law Society of Scotland,* Edinburgh, July 1974

*Lancet, The*

In Hyères, the home physician Fanny Stevenson subscribed to *The Lancet* and assiduously applied herself to every health fad. She decided, long before medical science proved the point, that colds were infectious. Since colds were always associated with Stevenson's illness, a person with a cold was humorously declared 'a pizon sarpint' and Fanny went to great lengths to isolate them from her invalid. In 1880 this infuriated visitors who had no reason to believe Fanny's theory. Eyed suspiciously, pronounced 'sniffly', they were firmly ejected from the house.

*Lanes of Memory,* (*see* **Hellman, George S.**)

**Lang, Andrew,** (1844-1912), *Adventures Among Books,* Longmans Green, London, 1905. Discusses proposed collaboration on 'Where is Rose?', a work which never materialised; *Essays in Little,* Henry & Co. (Whitefriars Library), London, 1891; 'The Late Mr. R.L. Stevenson', *Illustrated London News,* 5 January 1895; 'Modern Men: Mr. R.L. Stevenson', *Scots Observer,* 26 January 1889; Review of Graham Balfour's 'Life of Robert Louis Stevenson', *Morning Post,* 18 October 1901; 'Robert Louis Stevenson', *Longman's Magazine,* February 1895

The Scottish scholar was introduced to Stevenson by Sidney Colvin at Menton in 1873. The 'man of letters' was not greatly impressed at first sight by his fellow-countryman. ' More like a lass than a lad, with a rather long, smooth, oval face, brown hair worn at greater length than is common, large lucid eyes, slender agile frame . . . clad in a wide blue cloak, he looked nothing less than English, except Scotch . . . Here, I thought, is one of your aesthetic young men, though a very clever one . . .' Stevenson's odd costume may have been responsible, since he scorned the conventional and was wearing a new hat, 'a brigand sort of arrangement' and a Parisian cloak, specially sent at his request by Colvin, ' . . . a sort of pensive Roman stateliness, sometimes warming into Romantic guitarism . . .' Although a deep friendship was destined for himself and Lang, Stevenson was similarly unimpressed, dismissing Lang as 'too good-looking, delicate, Oxfordish . . . a la-de-dady Oxford kind of Scot.' Later when Lang became an 'addict' of Stevenson's novels and short stories he was to declare the author 'the most ingenious and refined writer of his generation'.

(*See also* **Green, Roger Lancelyn;** Part 4 (Letters))

**Lanier, Charles D.,** 'Robert Louis Stevenson'. Valedictory article. *Review of Reviews,* New York, February 1895

**'Lantern Bearers, The',** an essay, first published in *Scribner's Magazine,* February 1888; collected in Tusitala Edition *30*

**La Solitude, Hyères**

From Campagne Defli's fevers the Stevensons fled to Hyères in 1883, and took up residence in Chalet La Solitude romantically situated in the Rue de la Pierre Glissante, the Street of the Sliding Stone. In a Prefatory Note to *The Dynamiter* Fanny described the chalet as 'an incongruous object in Hyères, and it was made more conspicuous by its position, clinging to a low cliff almost at the entrance of the old town. From this cliff the ground rose with a gentle gradient and just outside our garden gate, where it became more rugged and steep, breaking out near the summit into rocky crags that were crowned with the ruins of an ancient Saracen Castle. Our tiny châlet was the result of a visit of the owner to the Paris Exposition of 1878. There, amidst Chinese pagodas, Turkish mosques, and the like in miniature, stood a model Swiss châlet that so fascinated [him] that he bought it outright and had it removed to be again erected on his property in Hyères. It was like a doll's house, with rooms so small that we could hardly turn round in them, but the view from the verandas was extensive, the garden was large and wild, with winding paths and old grey olive trees where nightingales nested and sang. Looking in one direction we could see the Iles d'Or, and in another, the hills beyond Toulon. So quiet and secluded was our life here that we heard almost nothing of the outside world except through an occasional English correspondent . . . We made almost no new acquaintances . . . with the exception of Dr. Vidal, our physician, and a local English chemist, Mr. Powell . . . Near the foot of one of these stairways was [his] pharmacy, very conveniently placed for us, as was afterwards proved . . . Our life in the châlet was of the utmost simplicity. With the help of one untrained maid I did the cooking myself. The kitchen was so narrow that I was in continual danger of being scorched by the range on one side, and at the same time impaled by the saucepan hooks on the other, and when we had a guest at dinner our maid had to pass on the dishes over our heads, as our chairs touched the walls of the dining-room . . . The markets of Hyères were well supplied, and the wine both good and cheap. so we were able, for the first time, to live comfortably within out limited income. My husband usually wrote from very early morning until noon, while my household duties occupied the same time. In the afternoon the work of the morning was read aloud, and we talked it over, criticising and suggesting improvements. That finished, we walked in our garden, listened to the birds, and looked at our trees and flowers; or, accompanied by our Scotch terrier,' (Wogg) 'wandered up the hill to the ruins of the castle . . . the châlet was well named, as far as we were concerned, for it was almost a solitude à deux, but the days slipped by with amazing celerity . . .' With three tiny rooms above and four rooms downstairs, it had everything in miniature to make it comfortable.

Stevenson called it, 'the loveliest house you ever saw, with a garden like a fairy story and a view like a classical landscape . . . Eden and Beulah and the Delectable Mountains and Eldorado and the Hesperidean Isles and Bimini'. He wrote to Will Low, (Letters, Tusitala Edition 32, p.268) '. . . a most sweet corner of the universe, sea and fine hills before me, and a rich variegated plain; and at my back a craggy hill, loaded with' vast feudal ruins. I am very quiet; a person passing by my door half startles me; but I enjoy the most aromatic airs, and at night the most wonderful view into a moonlit garden. By day this garden fades into nothing, overpowered by its surroundings and the luminous distance; but at night and when the moon is out, that garden, the arbour, the flight of stairs that mount the artificial hillock, the plumed blue-gum trees, that hang trembling, become the very skirts of paradise. Angels I know frequent it; and it thrills all night with the flutes of silence. Damn that garden – and by day it is gone.'

The threat of typhus and cholera from Toulon, three miles away, destroyed their 'Paradise'. But despite the ending and ophthalmia and another haemorrhage, a plaque on the wall reminds present-day visitors that Stevenson also wrote, '. . . I was only happy once; that was at Hyères'. (Letters (to Colvin) Tusitala Edition 34, p.59)
(See also **Hyères;** Plate 16)

*Last Memory of Robert Louis Stevenson, A,* (*see* **Eaton, Charlotte**)

*Last Witness for Robert Louis Stevenson,* (*see* **Caldwell, Elsie Noble**)

*'Late Mr. R.L. Stevenson, The',* (*see* **obituaries**)

*'Late Mr. R.L. Stevenson, The: A Schoolfellow Remembers',* (*see* **Baildon, H. Bellyse**)

**'Late Sam Bough, R.S.A., The'**, an obituary, first published in *The Academy*, 30 November 1878; collected in Tusitala Edition *28* (*See* **Bough, Samuel**)

*'Late Sir W. Simpson, Bart., The, and Robert Louis Stevenson',* (*see* **Bookman**)

**Lavenue's,** restaurant (long-departed) in Montparnasse patronised by Stevenson; for him it symbolised the best in French cuisine, expensive and elegant

**Lawrence, R.M.,** *A Stevenson Scrapbook,* Aberdeen, 1926

**Lawson, McEwan,** *On the Bat's Back: The Story of Robert Louis Stevenson,* Lutterworth Press, London, 1950

**'Lay Morals',** an essay, first published in Edinburgh Edition 1896; Tusitala Edition *26*

**Leatham, James,** *The Style of Robert Louis Stevenson,* Deveron Press, Aberdeen, n.d.

**Lee, Albert,** 'An Unique Bit of Stevensonia', *Book Buyer,* February 1897
An account of the Samoan version of 'The Bottle Imp', with a facsimile page from the Samoan newspaper *O le Sulu Samoa* (printed in monthly instalments, May to December 1891)

**Lee, Vernon** (pen name of **Violet Paget**), (1856–1935), novelist and critic. 'Handling the Words', *Contemporary Review,* September 1895. *Catriona* considered as a masterpiece of constructive craft

**Le Gallienne, Richard,** (1866–1947), English poet and critic. *The Romantic Nineties,* Putnam's Sons, London, 1925; *Robert Louis Stevenson: An Elegy,* 1895
Le Gallienne hailed Stevenson as the 'Virgil of prose'. (*See* Part 4 (Letters))

**Leigh, Captain Rupert,** brother of Lady Jersey (*see* **Jersey, Countess of**)

*Leisure Hour,* included an anonymous article entitled 'Robert Louis Stevenson in his Letters', 1899

## Leith Walk, Edinburgh

From infant walks with nurse Cummy, through boyhood's ploys to the more sophisticated student carousings in its howffs, Stevenson was always nostalgic about this area, and wrote to Baxter from exile in Davos (*Letters,* Tusitala Edition *32,* p. 180), '. . . what would I not give to steal this evening with you through the big, echoing, college archway and away south under the street lamps, and away to dear Brash's, now defunct! But the old time is dead, also never, never to revive. It was a sad time too, but so gay and hopeful, and we had such sport with all our low spirits and all our distresses, that it looks like a kind of lamp-lit fairyland behind me. O for ten Edinburgh minutes – sixpence between us, and the ever-glorious Lothian Road, or dear mysterious Leith Walk!'

**Le Monastier,** village visited by Stevenson en route for the Cévennes and where he bought the donkey, Modestine

**Leslie, Mrs. Shane,** (née **Marjorie Ide**), *Girlhood in the Pacific,* Macdonald, London, n.d.

**'Leslie Takes Tea with a Friend of Long John Silver',** (*see* **Longstreth, T.M.**)

**'Letter to a Young Gentleman who Proposes To embrace the Career of Art'**, an essay, first published in *Scribner's Magazine,* September 1888; Tusitala Edition *28*

**'Letter to Mr. Stevenson's Friends, A: in Memory of R.L.S.',** (*see* **Osbourne, Lloyd**)

**'Letter to R.L.S., A',** (*see* **Walpole, Hugh**)

**'Letter to The Times Literary Supplement',** (*see* **Osbourne, Alan**)

**'Letter to the Same Young Gentleman, A',** (*see* **Low, Will H.**)

**Letters,** (ed.) Sidney Colvin, 1863–1894, Tusitala Edition *31*–35 (*See* Part 4)

**Letters,** (*see* **Adams, Henry; James, Henry; Meredith, George**)

**Letters and Papers,** (*see* **Symonds, John Addington**)

**Letters from Samoa: 1891–95,** (*see* **Stevenson, Margaret Isabella Balfour**)

**Letters of James Barrie** (*see* **Barrie, Sir James Matthew**)

**Letters of Mrs. R.L. Stevenson, Some** (*see* **Colvin, Sidney**)

## 'Libbelism'

'John Libbel' was a character invented by Stevenson and his cousin Bob and in student days they also invented a cult of 'Libbelism' to fit the image, with shabbily printed calling-cards inscribed with strange messages from John Libbel. They left messages for him at shady lodging-houses and harrassed eminent Edinburgh folk with communications purporting to be from him. They also circulated a rumour that he was being sought as an heir to 'the great Libbel fortune'.

*Life and Letters of Edmund Gosse,* (*see* **Charteris, Evan**)

*Life and Letters of Leslie Stephen, The,* (*see* **Maitland, Frederick William**)

*'Life and Limitations of Stevenson, The'* (*see* **Wallace, William**)

*Life in Letters of William Dean Howells,* (*see* **Howells, W.D.**)

*Life of Mrs. Robert Louis Stevenson, The* (*see* **Sanchez, Nellie Vandegrift**)

*Life of Robert Louis Stevenson, The,* (*see* **Balfour, Graham**)

*Life of Robert Louis Stevenson, The* (*see* **Masson, Rosaline**)

*Life through Tusitala's Glasses,* (*see* **Mackerchar, E.M.**)

**Liliuokalani, Queen of Hawaii,** sister of king Kalakaua
She succeeded at his death and Stevenson supported her when she was deposed by 'missionaries' in 1893, calling on her frequently. The Kingdom of Hawaii was no more but the romance of dethroned royalty appealed to Stevenson, who disapproved of the mean way the royal family had been deposed.
(*See also* **Johnstone, Arthur; Kalakaua, King**)

**Literary Digest,** contained an anonymous article entitled 'Stevenson in Extremis' (a review of Steuart's *Robert Louis Stevenson, Man and Writer*), 6 December 1924

*'Literary Leprosy',* (*see* **Saturday Review**)

**Literary Opinion,** contained an anonymous article entitled 'Robert Louis Stevenson', September 1891

*Little Journeys to the Homes of English Authors,* (*see* **Hubbard, Elbert**)

**L.J.R. Club**
Organised by R.A.M. (Bob) Stevenson in September 1872, the founding principles of this miniature club, were Liberty, Justice, Reverence, and one object was the abolition of the House of Lords. Another item on the Constitution was 'Disregard everything our parents have taught us'. The few meetings were begun with great earnestness by the Stevenson cousins, Charles Baxter and Walter Ferrier, in a pub in Advocate's

Close, Edinburgh, which had connections with another rebel, Robert
Burns.
(*See also* **Christianity of Stevenson; Stevenson, Bob**)

'**Local Conditions Influencing Climate**', a paper delivered by
Stevenson on 2 July 1873. Notice of this paper appears in *Journal of the
Scottish Meteorological Society,* 4 July 1873

**Lockett, W.G.**, *Robert Louis Stevenson at Davos,* Hurst & Blackett,
London, 1934

**Lockhart, W.E.**, (*see* **Edinburgh: Picturesque Notes**)

'**Lodging for the Night, A: A Story of Francis Villon**', first short
story, first published in *Temple Bar,* October, 1877; in book form in
*New Arabian Nights,* 1882; Tusitala Edition *1*

A dissolute evening's drinking ends with a murder and the 16th-century
French poet, François Villon, escapes from the scene to seek shelter from
the Lord of Brisetout, who has much to impart on moral issues.

*London: The Conservative Weekly Journal,* founded in 1877 by Robert
Glasgow Brown, who was a student friend of Stevenson
Brown was *London's* first editor and proprietor until he died of
tuberculosis in 1879. Fanny wrote, 'It was foredoomed to failure, as Mr.
Brown was not possessed of suffcient means to carry the venture far, and
about a year after his death it ceased to exist. Meanwhile Mr. Henley
was performing prodigies to keep it afloat. His own salary (as editor)
was small and the limited funds at his disposal allowed him to pay next to
nothing to contributors. Both his and my husband's friends helped so far
as they could, but a weekly publication made too heavy a drain on their
good-nature. It often happened that an entire number of *London* was
written by Mr. Henley and my husband alone . . . circulation was
extremely small, and . . . there were occasions when the journal
presented the odd appearance of being almost wholly composed of
verses. This occurred when the too sanguine editor found himself disappointed in hoped-for contributions and had to make up his pages at the
very moment of going to press. Verses filled space more readily than
prose, and were easier to do; in such emergencies poem after poem
would be dashed off by Mr. Henley and my husband until the blanks
were filled. "Hurry, my lad," Mr. Henley would shout; "only six more
lines now!" My husband would scratch off the six lines, hand them to the
printer's devil, who stood waiting with outstretched hand, and the
situation was saved for another week.'
*London* achieved immortality in its brief life by serialising *Latter-Day
Arabian Nights* (1878) and some of Stevenson's earliest essays. His other
contributions were a sketch of Belle Osbourne, Fanny's daughter, and a

description of the Paris Bourse and other anonymous pieces. Professor
Fleeming Jenkin strongly disapproved of Stevenson's participation in
this kind of journalism. Stevenson wrote at *London*'s demise, '. . . deeply
regretted by none who knew it, except myself, its author, founder and
slave'. And to Charles Baxter '*London* is rapidly hustling me into the
abhorred tomb, I do write such damn rubbish in it, that's a fact, and I
hate doing it so inconceivably. I declare I would ten times rather break
stones or – in short do anything that didn't involve an office'. However,
he did try to fit the 'image' by wearing a respectably conventional blue
suit, travelling in cabs which he could not afford, and carrying a loaded
walking-stick to add a touch of melodrama.
(*See also* **Henley, William Ernest; 'Old Song, An'**)

*London Quarterly Review, The,* contained an anonymous article entitled
    Robert Louis Stevenson', October 1895

**Long John Silver,** reference to character's conception, (*see Letters* (to
    Henley) Tusitala Edition *32*, p.242)

*Longman's Magazine,* London. First publisher of many of Stevenson's
    works, including 'The Treasure of Franchard' (April-May 1883),
    'Across the Plains' (July-August 1883), *Prince Otto* (April-October
    1885)

**Longstreth, T.M.,** 'Leslie Takes Tea with a Friend of Long John Silver',
    *St. Nicholas Magazine,* November 1925

**Lothian Road, Edinburgh**
    To Charles Baxter, from 'exile' in Saranac, New York, November
    1887, Stevenson wrote, (*Letters* Tusitala Edition *33*, p.157), 'Times are
    changed since the Lothian Road. Well, the Lothian Road was grand fun
    too; I could take an afternoon of it with great delight. But I'm awfu'
    grand noo, and long may it last.'
    (*See also* **Leith Walk**)

**Lovat-Fraser, J.A.,** 'Stevenson and the Jacobite Tradition', paper read to
    the Robert Louis Stevenson Club of London. Privately printed,
    Inverness, n.d.

*'Love Laughs at R.L.S.: Allan Breck as a Braw Wooer',* (*see* **Hardy,
    H.F.**)

**Lovett, Rev. R.,** 'R.L. Stevenson in relation to the Christian Life and
    Christian Missions', *Sunday at Home,* 1901–02

**Low, Will H.,** American artist friend of Stevenson. 'A Letter to the Same
    Young Gentleman', *Scribner's Magazine,* September 1888; 'Robert
    Louis Stevenson's Letters', *Book Buyer,* December 1899; *A Chronicle of*

*Friendships, 1873*–1900, Hodder & Stoughton, London, 1908; *Stevenson and Margarita,* Mayflower Press, New York, 1922.

He described Barbizon days, 'Louis, quite unconsciously, exercised a species of fascination whenever we were together. Fascination and charm are not qualities which Anglo-Saxon youths are prone to acknowledge, in manly avoidance of their supposedly feminizing effect, but it was undoubtedly this attractive power which R.L.S. held so strongly through life; and which, gentle though it may have been, held no trace of dependence or weakness . . .' (from *A Chronicle of Friendships,* in which Low makes particular reference to the friendship of Stevenson and Rodin.). Lloyd Osbourne described this book as one in which '. . . Stevenson is more illuminatingly revealed than in anything ever written of him. Here is the true Stevenson – the Stevenson I would fain have the reader know and take to his heart – boyish, gay, and of all things approachable to the poorest and shabbiest; a man bubbling over with talk and no less eager to listen; a man radiating human kindness and good will, in whom the gift of genius had not displaced the most winning, the most lovable of personal qualities'
Stevenson dedicated the Epilogue of *The Wrecker* to Will Low.
(*See* Part 4 (Letters))

**Lowe, Charles,** 'Robert Louis Stevenson: A Reminiscence', *Bookman,* New York, November 1891; also *Bookman* Extra Number, London, 1913

**Lübeck,**

In February 1890, while the site for Vailima was being cleared of jungle and a temporary dwelling erected, the Stevensons sailed in this German ship for Sydney, Australia, where they were to be reunited with Belle Strong, Fanny's daughter

**Lucas, E .V.,** *The Colvins and their Friends,* Methuen & Co., London, 1928. Contains many references to their long friendship with Stevenson.
(*See also* **Grand Hotel Godam**)

**Ludgate Hill,**

On 22 August 1887 Stevenson left Britain for the last time in this ship. This was his second voyage to America and he was accompanied by Fanny, Lloyd, the maid Valentine Roch, and his fifty-eight-year-old mother, Margaret Stevenson. Gallant in starched widow's cap, she had shed the comfort and security of an Edinburgh middle-class lifetime to go into voluntary exile with her only son. Before she saw Edinburgh again, she would entertain cannibals and face shipwreck in the South Seas. Edmund Gosse was among the friends who suspected that this was a final parting with Stevenson, '. . . looking rather white, and a little dazzled in the eyes, but otherwise much better and less emaciated than I feared . . . he is in mourning for his father and was quite stylishly dressed in a black velvet coat and waistcoat and black silk neck-tie and dark trousers, so that instead of looking like a Lascar out of employment, as he generally does, he looked extremely elegant and refined, his hair over his shoulders, but very tidy, and burnished like brass with brushing. He prowled about the room, in his usual noiseless panther fashion, talking all the time, full of wit and feeling and sweetness, as charming as ever he was, but with a little more sadness and sense of crisis than usual.' To Henry James, Stevenson wrote (Tusitala Edition *33*, p.143), '. . . enjoyed myself more than I could have hoped on board our strange floating menagerie: stallions and monkeys and matches made our cargo; and the vast continent of these incongruities rolled the while like a haystack; and the stallions stood hypnotised by the motion, looking through the ports at our dinner-table, and winked when the crockery was broken; and the little monkeys stared at each other in their cages, and were thrown overboard like little bluish babies; and the big monkey, Jacko, scoured about the ship and rested willingly in my arms, to the ruin of my clothing.'

His arrival in New York coincided with publicity for a stage version of *Jekyll and Hyde.* Journalists besieged him, for the book was a best-seller in the United States, and he was famous. A contrast indeed to his first arrival eight years earlier, dripping-wet in a rain storm, with six volumes of Bancroft's *History of the United States* and his bedroll. (*See also* **New York**)

**Luke, Sir Harry,** *From a South Seas Diary,* Nicolson & Watson, London, 1943. Includes reminiscences of Stevenson

**Lysaght, Sidney,** poet, friend of Meredith, visitor to Vailima

# M

**Macaire,** a play, written in collaboration with W.E. Henley, privately printed 1885; first published in *The Chap Book*, 1 and 15 June 1895; in book form, Stone and Kimball, Chicago, 1895; Tusitala Edition *24*

An escaped prisoner, Robert Macaire, finds the prospect of gain in claiming the false identity of Charles Dumont's father on the eve of the young man's marriage to Ernestine Goriot. His plans are foiled by the appearance of Charles's true father, the Marquis de la Cherté de Médoc.

**MacCallum, Thomas Murray,** *Adrift in the South Seas: Including Adventures with Robert Louis Stevenson,* Wetzel Publishing Co., Los Angeles, n.d.

**McCleary, G.F.,** 'Stevenson's Early Writings', *Fortnightly Review,* November 1950. With particular reference to *The Pavilion on the Links*

**McClure, S. S.,** ex-patriate Scots editor of *McClure's Magazine*

His offer of $10,000 a year for a weekly contribution to his magazine was met with caution by Stevenson who had just arrived off the *Ludgate Hill* in New York. Although bemused by a celebrity's welcome, he considered Scribner's offer of $3,500 (with a choice of his own subject material) more realistic.

'Stevenson received me in bed', from *My Autobiography* by S.S. McClure. Mansell Collection

*My Autobiography,* John Murray, London, 1914. How McClure offered to publish *Black Arrow* (as *Outlaws of Tunstall Forest*), illustrated by W.H. Low, 'It brought in more than any other serial we ever syndicated.' (*See also* **Scribner, Charles**)

**McClure's Magazine,** New York. Serialised novels, *St. Ives* (1897) and *The Ebb-Tide* (1894), as well as publishing occasional essays, etc.

**MacCulloch, J.A.,** *Stevenson and the Bridge of Allan: With Other Stevenson Essays,* John Smith & Son, Glasgow, 1927. Comments on Stevenson's *Appeal to the Clergy of the Church of Scotland* with a Note for the Laity

**McGaw, Sister Martha Mary,** *Stevenson in Hawaii.* With particular reference to his visit to the lepers of Molokai and his defence of Father Damien. University of Hawaii Press, Honolulu, 1950

**MacGregor, A.A.,** 'Who Shot the Red Fox?', *Cornhill Magazine,* December 1939. Relates to the controversy raised by this historic incident (known as 'The Appin Murder') which Stevenson incorporated into *Kidnapped*

**McIntosh, R.J.,** 'Random Memories of Robert Louis Stevenson', *Scots Magazine,* June 1945

**Mackaness, George,** *Robert Louis Stevenson: His Association with Australia,* privately printed, 1935. Describes Stevenson's visits to Sydney in 1890, 1891 and 1893

**MacKay, D.N.,** *The Appin Murder: The Historical Basis of 'Kidnapped' and Catriona',* Edinburgh, 1911

**McKay, George L.,** *The Stevenson Library of the Edwin J. Beinecke Collection* (6 volumes), Yale University Press, New Haven, CT, 1964. Catalogue of immense collection of Stevenson material, especially useful for listing of unpublished letters by Stevenson and others in which opinions of his work are expressed. *Some Notes on Robert Louis Stevenson, His Finances, His Agents and Publishers,* Yale University Press, New Haven, 1958. A pamphlet of tremendous interest and value to Stevensonians (*See* Part 8)

**Mackay, Margaret,** *Island Boy, Robert Louis Stevenson and his Step-grandson in Samoa,* 1969; *The Violent Friend: The Story of Mrs. Robert Louis Stevenson,* Doubleday, New York, 1968; Dent, London, 1969

**McKenna, Stephen,** 'Stevenson', an essay in *A Cadger's Creel* (*See* **Douglas, Sir George**)

**Mackenzie, Compton,** 'Robert Louis Stevenson', *International Profiles,*

1968; 'Robert Louis Stevenson: Heir of the Romantics', *Picture Post*, 11 November 1950

**Mackerchar, E.M.**, *Life through Tusitala's Glasses.* Privately printed, n.d. 366 quotations

**MacLaren, Ian,** 'In Memoriam', *Bookman* Extra Number, London, 1913

**McLaren, Moray,** *Stevenson and Edinburgh: A Centenary Study,* Chapman & Hall, London and Folcroft, New York, 1950; 'Stevenson's Scottish Characters', *Scotland's Magazine,* November 1950; *The Unpossessed,* Chapman & Hall, London, 1949

**Macmillan's Magazine,** London. Published Stevenson's first essay, 'Ordered South', May 1874.

**MacPherson, Harriet D.**, *Robert Louis Stevenson: A Study in the French Influence,* Institution of French Studies, New York, 1930

**Magazine of Art,** London, published several of Stevenson's essays between 1881-1883

**magazines and newspapers,** Stevenson contributed serials, essays and reviews to more than sixty magazines and newspapers from 1863-94. Those marked ** indicate sufficient importance to merit individual entries.
(*See also* Part 4 (Letters))

** Academy, The
** Atalanta
** Athenaeum, The
** Black and White
Blackwood's Magazine
** Bookman
British Weekly
Cassell's Christmas Annual
** Century Magazine
Chap Book, The
Chicago Tribune
Church of Scotland
    Home and Foreign
    Missionary Record
Contemporary Review
** Cornhill Magazine
Cosmopolis
Cosmopolitan, The

Court and Society Review
Current Opinion
Daily Chronicle
** Daily News
** Edinburgh University
    Magazine
** Encyclopaedia Britannica
** English Illustrated Magazine
Fortnightly Review
Fraser's Magazine
Herald, The (London)
Idler, The
** John o'London's Weekly
** London
** London Quarterly Review
** Longman's Magazine
** McClure's Magazine
** Macmillan's Magazine

**Magazine of Art
**Monterey Californian
National Observer
Nature
New Quarterly
New Review
New York Herald
New York Sun
New York Tribune
Outlook, The
Pacific Commercial Advertiser
**Pall Mall Gazette
Portfolio, The
Presbyterian, The (Sydney)
Royal Scottish Society of
Arts, Transactions of the
Royal Society of Edinburgh,
Proceedings of the

Samoa Times and South
Seas Advertiser
**Saturday Review
School Boys Magazine
Scots Observer
Scottish Church, The
Scottish Meteorological Society,
Journal of the
**Scribner's Magazine
Stirling Observer
Studio, The
Sunbeam, The
Temple Bar
Times, The
**Today
Vanity Fair
**Young Folks

**Mahaffy, A.W.,** 'A Visit to the Library of R.L. Stevenson at Vailima, Samoa', *Spectator,* 30 November 1895

**Mair, Craig,** *A Star for Seamen: The Stevenson Family of Engineers,* John Murray, London, 1978. Biographical material on Stevenson family.

**Maitland, Frederick William,** *The Life and Letters of Leslie Stephen,* Duckworth & Co., London, 1906 (*see also* **Stephen, Sir Leslie**)

**Maixner, Paul,** (ed.) *Robert Louis Stevenson: The Critical Heritage,* Routledge and Kegan Paul, London, 1981. Collection of reviews of many well-known Stevenson novels and short stories

**Makin Island**

In July 1890 the Stevensons on *Equator* put in for supplies in this tiny island in the Gilberts. Unfortunately their arrival coincided with recent Fourth of July celebrations when the native 'king' had been persuaded to relax the taboo on selling spirits to his subjects. The Stevensons came ashore to find the 'king', his wives, his council and naked bodyguard armed with repeating rifles which they were firing indiscriminately with the cheerful disregard of the very inebriated. The Stevensons were committed to going steadily forward portraying a courage they did not feel and, armed with presents, as well as revolvers, they considered it judicious to show off their own markmanship. Fanny, who had learned all about guns in her early days in the 'Wild West', was an excellent shot and made short work of a row of target bottles. This earned them attention from the storekeeper and respect from the 'king'. They were regally entertained before they took ship again.

**Malietoa Laupepa, 'King'**, puppet 'king' of Samoa, installed by Germans and brought back from exile to which they had sentenced him some years earlier, for being a tool of Britain and the United States (*See also* **Mataafa, 'King'; Tamasese 'King'**)

**'Man and his Friend, The'**, a fable, Tusitala Edition 5 (*see also* **'Fables'**)

**Manasquan, New Jersey**, visited by Stevenson in the spring of 1887

It was popular with his artist friend Will Low, and Stevenson enjoyed the sea and sailing with Lloyd Osbourne. The sculptor Augustus St. Gaudens also visited him there.

**'Man in Portsmouth Square, The'**, (*see* **Chalmers, Stephen**)

**'Manse, The'**, an essay, first published in *Scribner's Magazine*, May 1887; in book form in *Memories and Portraits*, 1887; Tusitala Edition 29 (*See also* **Reminiscences of Colinton Manse**)

**'Manuscripts of Records of a Family of Engineers: The Unfinished Chapters'**, introduction by J. Christian Bay, Walter H. Hill, Chicago, 1929

**'Markheim'**, a short story, first published in *Unwin's Annual*, December 1886; in book form in *The Merry Men and Other Tales*, 1887; Tusitala Edition 8 (*See* Part 6 (Radio))

Markham murders an antique dealer who is avenged by a ghostly visitor who makes him see the error of his ways.

**Marquesas**, (*see* **Kooamua, Chief; Paaaeua, Chief**)

**Marriage**, views expressed by Stevenson in *Virginibus Puerisque.*

'Marriage is terrifying, but so is a cold and forlorn old age. The friendships of men are vastly agreeable, but they are insecure. You know all the time that one friend will marry and put you to the door; a second accept a situation in China, and become no more to you than a name, a reminiscence, and an occasional crossed letter, very laborious to read; a third will take up with some religious crochet and treat you to sour looks thenceforward . . . Marriage is certainly a perilous remedy. Instead of on two or three, you stake your happiness on one life only . . . you have not to fear so many contingencies; it is not every wind that can blow you from your anchorage; and so long as Death withholds his sickle, you will always have a friend at home. People who share a cell in the Bastille, or are thrown together on an uninhabited isle, if they do not immediately fall to fisticuffs, will find some possible ground of compromise . . . The discretion of the first years becomes the settled habit of the last; and so, with wisdom and patience, two lives may grow indissolubly into one. But marriage, if comfortable, is not at all heroic. It certainly narrows and damps the spirits of generous men. In marriage, a man becomes slack and selfish, and undergoes a fatty degeneration of his moral being . . . Marriage is of so much use to a woman, opens out to her so much more of life, and puts her in the way of so much more freedom and usefulness, that, whether she marry ill or well, she can hardly miss some benefit . . . the rule is none the less certain: if you wish the pick of men and women, take a good bachelor and a good wife . . . To deal plainly, if they only married when they fell in love, most people would die unwed; and among the others, there would be not a few tumultuous households. The Lion is the King of Beasts, but he is scarcely suitable for a domestic pet. In the same way, I suspect love is rather too violent a passion to make, in all cases, a good domestic sentiment. Like other violent excitements, it throws up not only what is best, but what is worst and smallest, in men's characters . . . One is almost tempted to hint that it does not much matter whom you marry; that, in fact, marriage is a subjective affection, and if you have made up your mind to it, and once talked yourself fairly over, you could 'pull it through' with anybody . . . matrimony at its lowest . . . is no more than a sort of friendship recognised by the police . . .

Certainly, if I could help it, I would never marry a wife who wrote. The practice of letters is miserably harassing to the mind; and after an hour or two's work, all the more human portion of the author is extinct; he will bully, backbite, and speak daggers. Music, I hear, is not much better. But painting, on the contrary, is often highly sedative . . . A ship captain is a good man to marry if it is a marriage of love, for absences are a good influence in love and keep it bright and delicate; but he is just the worst man if the feeling is more pedestrian, as habit is too frequently torn open and the solder has never time to set. Men who fish, botanise, work with the turning-lathe, or gather sea-weeds, will make admirable husbands; and a little amateur painting in water-colour shows the innocent and quiet mind.

It is to be noticed that those who have loved once or twice already are so much the better educated to a woman's hand; the bright boy of fiction is an odd and most uncomfortable mixture of shyness and coarseness, and needs a deal of civilising.

Marriage is a step so grave and decisive that it attracts light-headed, variable men by its very awfulness . . . It seems as if marriage were the royal road through life, and realised, on the instant, what we have all dreamed on summer Sundays when the bells ring, or at night when we cannot sleep for the desire of living . . . but this is a wile of the devil's. To the end, spring winds will sow disquietude, passing faces leave a regret behind them, and the whole world keep calling and calling in their ears. For marriage is like life in this – that it is a field of battle and not a bed of roses. Times are changed with him who marries; there are no more by-path meadows, where you may innocently linger, but the road lies long and straight and dusty to the grave . . . To marry is to domesticate the Recording Angel. Once you are married, there is nothing left to you, not even suicide, but to be good . . . ere you marry, you should have learned the mingled lesson of the world: that dolls are stuffed with sawdust, and yet are excellent playthings; that hope and love address themselves to a perfection never realised, and yet, firmly held, become the salt and staff of life . . .'

Of his own impending marriage in May 1880, he wrote that he was 'a very withered bridegroom . . . my doctor took a desponding fit about me, and scared Fanny into blue fits; but I have talked her over again'. And afterwards, 'It was not my bliss that I was interested in when I was married; it was a sort of marriage *in extremis*; and if I am where I am, it is thanks to care of that lady, who married me when I was a mere complication of cough and bones, much fitter for an emblem of mortality than a bridegroom'. (*See* **Oakland**)

'Marriage is one long conversation, chequered by disputes', Stevenson wrote in 'Talk and Talkers'. 'The disputes are valueless; they but ingrain the difference; the heroic heart of woman prompting her at once to nail her colours to the mast. But in the intervals, almost unconsciously and with no desire to shine, the whole material of life is turned over and over, ideas are struck out and shared, the two persons more and more adapt their notions one to suit the other, and in process of time, without sound of trumpet, they conduct each other into new worlds of thought.' Their marriage lasted fourteen years, until Stevenson's death in Samoa, and their friend Henry James described their relationship as 'a fable, strange and romantic as one of Louis's own'.

**Martin, A. Patchett,** Stevenson's first 'fan' – an Australian who had read his contributions to *Cornhill Magazine* and in 1877 sent Stevenson a volume of his own verses, entitled *A Sweet Girl Graduate and Other Poems*. Stevenson was delighted and replied enthusiastically. (*See* Part 4 (Letters))

**Masson, Flora,** *Victorians All,* Chambers, London and Edinburgh, 1931. Flora and her sister Rosaline (*see below*) were daughters of David Masson, Professor of Rhetoric and English Literature at Edinburgh University

She left a description of the student Stevenson in his home at Heriot Row, 'Our end of the table was, to me, almost uncomfortably brilliant. Mr. Stevenson [Thomas] had taken me in and Louis Stevenson was on my other side. Father and son both talked, taking diametrically opposite points of view on all things under the sun. Mr. Stevenson seemed to me, on that evening, to be the type of kindly, orthodox Edinburgh father. We chatted of nice, concrete comfortable things, such as the Scottish highlands in autumn; and in a moment of Scottish fervour he quoted – I believe sotto voce – a bit of versified psalm. But Louis Stevenson, on my other side, was on that evening in one of his most recklessly brilliant moods. His talk was almost incessant. I remember feeling quite dazed at the amount of intellection he expended on each subject, however trivial in itself, that we touched upon. He worried it as a dog might worry a rat, and then threw it off lightly, as some chance word of allusion set him thinking, and talking, of something else. The father's face at certain moments was a study – an indescribable mixture of vexation, fatherly pride and admiration, and sheer bewilderment at the boy's brilliant flippancies, and the quick young thrusts of his wit and criticism.'

Many years later, Flora Masson was also to record the sight of Stevenson leaving Edinburgh in 1887. His father dead, he was never to return: 'An open cab, with a man and a woman in it, seated side by side, and leaning back – the rest of the cab piled high with rather untidy luggage – came slowly towards us . . . As it passed us . . . a slender, loose-garbed figure stood up . . . and waved a wide-brimmed hat. "Goodbye!" he called to us, "Goodbye!" '

**Masson, Rosaline,** sister of Flora Masson (*see above*), (ed.) *I Can Remember Robert Louis Stevenson,* Chambers, London and Edinburgh, 1922; *The Life of Robert Louis Stevenson,* Chambers, London and Edinburgh, 1923; 'The Religion of R.L. Stevenson' in *Poets, Patriots and Lovers,* Clarke, London, 1933; *Robert Louis Stevenson,* T.E. & E.C. Jack, London, n.d.; 'Robert Louis Stevenson', *S.M.T. Magazine,* April 1929; 'Robert Louis Stevenson and the Home of his Heart', *S.M.T. Magazine,* May 1938

**Master of Ballantrae, The: A Winter's Tale,** first published in *Young Folks,* 12 monthly instalments, November 1888 to October 1889; in book form, Cassell, London and Scribner's, New York 1889; Tusitala Edition *10*

The tragic story of the family's downfall is narrated by their steward, Mackellar. The Master, James Durie, is handsome but unscrupulous, his younger brother Henry plain but honest. Both are in love with the same girl, Alison Graeme. James joins Prince Charles Edward and is believed killed at Culloden. Some time later he returns a hunted man, to find that brother Henry has succeeded to the title and has also married Alison. Revenge leads him on a trail of destruction from Scotland to America which succeeds in destroying both brothers.

*Dedication:* To Sir Percy Florence [son of the poet Percy Bysshe Shelley] and Lady Shelley

'Here is a tale which extends over many years and travels into many

countries. By a peculiar fitness of circumstance the writer began, continued it, and concluded it among distant and diverse scenes. Above all, he was much upon the sea. The character and fortune of the fraternal enemies, the hall and shrubbery of Durrisdeer, the problem of Mackellar's homespun and how to shape it for superior flights; these were his company on deck in many star-reflecting harbours, ran often in his mind at sea to the tune of slatting canvas, and were dismissed (something of the suddenest) on the approach of squalls. It is my hope that these surroundings of its manufacture may to some degree find favour for my story with seafarers and sealovers like yourselves. And at least here is a dedication from a great way off; written by the loud shores of a subtropical island near upon ten thousand miles from Boscombe Chine and Manor: scenes which rise up before me as I write, along with the faces and voices of my friends. Well, I am for the sea once more; no doubt Sir Percy also. Let us make the signal B.R.D.!'
Inspired by Robert Marryat's 'The Phantom Ship' which Stevenson read at Saranac Lake, '. . . this was to be a story on a great canvas; it was to cover many years, so that I might draw my characters in the growth and decay of life; and many lands so that I might display them in changing and incongruous surroundings.' Begun in December 1887, interrupted by the *Casco* cruise it was completed in May 1889, but not without problems. As with all Stevenson's work, once the initial enthusiasm ended he found the writing troublesome: 'The first half was already in type when I made up my mind to have it thrown down, and recommence the tale in the third person; friends advised, one this way, one that; my publishers were afraid of the delay; indolence has doubtless a voice; I had besides a natural love for the documentary method in narration and I ended by committing myself to the impersonation of Mackellar, and suffering the publication to proceed . . . Months passed before I saw how to tackle the problem, how the pen of Mackellar was to relate a series of incidents so highly coloured, so excessive, and so tragic; the magazine was already on my heels, when desperation helped me; and in a few days of furious industry the novel was, for good or evil, rushed to its last word.

Waikiki, May 17, 1889 R.L.S.'

(*See also* Part 6 (Media))

*'Master of Romance, R.L. Stevenson, A.'* (*see* **Japp, Alexander H.**)

**Mataafa, 'King'**, one of the three Samoan chiefs used as political pawns in the German fight for ascendency in the South Seas
Mataafa was a kinsman of the exiled Malietoa, ablest and most personable of the three contenders, and described by Stevenson as a 'beautiful, sweet old fellow' when he defied social comment among the whites by taking sides and visiting Mataafa. Stevenson regarded himself

as one chief advising another, searching for a way to end the rebellion and seeking Mataafa's backing for a coconut-fibre mill which would provide Samoa with a desperately needed cash crop. Samoa was soon afire with rumour that Stevenson's visits were concerned with arrangements to buy arms for the rebels, especially as Mataafa gave Stevenson the 'royal' *kava*, highest honour in Samoan etiquette and of considerable political import. It brought forth comments from the Foreign Office that 'Mr. Stevenson would do better if he stuck to novel-writing and left politics alone'. When Mataafa's rebellion broke out in July 1893, Stevenson arranged for Apia's public hall to be used as a hospital and personally assisted at operations on wounded partisans of Mataafa. Stevenson wrote to Mark Twain, 'I wish you could see my "simple and sunny heaven" now; war has broken out, "they" have long been making it, "they" have worked hard, and here it is – with its concomitants of blackened faces, severed heads and men dying in hospital . . . the government troops have started a horrid novelty; taking women's heads. If this leads to reprisals, we shall be a fine part of the world. Perhaps the best that could happen would be a complete and immediate suppression of the rebels; but alas! all my friends (bar but a few) are in the rebellion'.

Defeated, Mataafa and his higher chiefs were exiled to the German-controlled Marshall Islands, where Stevenson tried to ease their imprisonment by supplies of gifts via Graham Balfour, his cousin, who was visiting in the area.

In November Stevenson's birthday coincided with a Samoan festival and with Fanny, Belle Strong and Lloyd, Stevenson defied comments and drove openly to the gaol where Mataafa's minor chiefs had been imprisoned in Apia. He took them gifts of tobacco and *kava* and in the following month the chiefs showed their appreciation by giving a return feast for Stevenson and family – in gaol where the courtyard was heaped with gifts brought by the prisoners' families, and presented to Stevenson item by item, as their 'only' friend. Their gratitude stretched wider, for when in 1894 they were released they decided personally to make him a new road from the cross-island track to the main Vailima stream; no food was to be provided for them by Stevenson, and no presents, only the necessary tools. They kept their promise and in early October 1894 the road was completed. Less than two months later the same natives would help carry Stevenson, their beloved Tusitala, up Mt. Vaea for burial on its summit.

(*See* **'Footnote to History, A'; Malietoa Laupepa, 'King'; Road of the Loving Heart; Tamasese, 'King'**)

**Matthews, H.,** (*see* **Skelt's Juvenile Drama**)

**Mattos, Katharine de,** (*see* **de Mattos, Katharine**)

**Mayne, L. Bruce,** 'Homes of the Famous: Robert Louis Stevenson', *Britannia,* 5 October 1958

**'Measure of a Marquis, The',** a review, published in *Vanity Fair,* 25 November 1875, of the Marquess of Lorne's 'Guido and Lita: A Tale of the Riviera'

**Mehew, Ernest J.,** (*see* **Stevensonian, The** )

**Memoir of Fleeming Jenkin,** Scribner's, New York, 1887; Tusitala Edition *19*

'On the death of Fleeming Jenkin, his family and friends determined to publish a section of his various papers; by way of introduction, the following pages were drawn up; and the whole, forming two considerable volumes, has been issued in England. In the States, it has not been thought advisable to reproduce the whole; and the memoir appearing alone, shorn of that other matter which was at once its occasion and justification, so large an account of a man so little known may seem to a stranger out of all proportion. But Jenkin was a man much more remarkable than the mere bulk or merit of his work approves him. It was in the world, in the commerce of friendship by his brave attitude towards life, by his high moral value and unwearied intellectual effort, that he struck the minds of his contemporaries. His was an individual figure, such as authors delight to draw, and all men to read of, in the pages of a novel. His was a face worth painting for its own sake. If the sitter shall not seem to have justified the portrait, if Jenkin, after his death, shall not continue to make new friends, the fault will be altogether mine.

R.L.S.

Saranac,
Oct., 1887.'

(*See* **Jenkin, Henry Charles Fleeming and Anne**)

**'Memoirs of an Islet',** an essay, first published in *Memories and Portraits,* 1887; Tusitala Edition *29*

**'Memoirs of Himself',** an autobiographical fragment, first published in *The Cornhill Booklet,* 1914; Tusitala Edition *29*
(*See also* **Childhood Notes**)

**'Memorial of R.L.S., A',** (*see* **Japp, Alexander H.**)

**Memories,** (*see* **Paul, C. Kegan**)

**Memories and Notes of Persons and Places, 1852–1914** (*see* **Colvin, Sir Sidney**)

**Memories and Portraits,** a collection of essays, Chatto & Windus, London and Scribner's, New York, 1887; Tusitala Edition *29*

*Dedication:* 'To my Mother in the name of past joy and present sorrow, I dedicate these memories and portraits. S.S. "Ludgate Hill" within sight of Cape Race.
NOTE. This volume of papers, unconnected as they are, it will be better to read through from the beginning, rather than dip into at random. A certain thread of meaning binds them. Memories of childhood and youth, portraits of those who have gone before us in the battle – taken together, they build up a face that "I have loved long since and lost awhile", the face of what was once myself. This has come by accident; I had no design at first to be autobiographical; I was but led away by the charm of beloved memories and by regret for the irrevocable dead; and when my own young face (which is a face of the dead also) began to appear in the well as by a kind of magic, I was the first to be surprised at the occurrence. My grandfather the pious child, my father the idle eager sentimental youth, I have thus unconsciously exposed. Of their descendant, the person of today, I wish to keep the secret; not because I love him better, but because, with him, I am still in a business partnership, and cannot divide interests . . .                    R.L.S.'

*Memories of George Meredith,* (*see* **Butcher, Lady Alice Mary**)

*Memories of Vailima,* (*see* **Field, Isobel Osbourne Strong; Osbourne, Lloyd**)

**Menton**

In the 1870s this French coastal town to the east of Nice acquired fame as a health resort for consumptives. Since the enclosures of the ancient château perched high above the town had been converted into a cemetery, the centre for Catholics, the lower ramps for heretics, invalids could not escape melancholy associations of recorded deaths, many tragically young. Stevenson, climbing by carriage or carried on a donkey to rest in the open air, had no alternative but to view this 'Château des Morts'. Despite the perfume of lemon blossom drifting down upon him, he was depressed and wrote to Mrs. Sitwell, 'I have been tired all day; lying outside my bed and crying in a feeble way that you recollect . . . I walked about the streets in such a rage with every person who came near me, that I felt inclined to break out upon them with all sorts of injurious language . . . If you knew how old I felt! I am sure that this is what age brings with it – this carelessess, this disenchantment, this continual bodily weariness. I am a man of seventy: O Medea, kill me, or make me young again!'
(*See also* **Garschine, Mme.**)

**Meredith, George,** (1828—1909). *Letters of George Meredith,* collected and edited by his son, Constable, London, 1912
The English novelist held Stevenson in high regard and made him the

basis of the unorthodox character Gower Woodseer, hero of *The Amazing Marriage.* Their friendship lasted all Stevenson's life and Meredith was the recipient of many of his most moving letters, such as the one written from exile in Vailima, in 1893 (*Letters,* Tusitala Edition 35, p.74). 'For fourteen years I have not had a day's real health; I have wakened sick and gone to bed weary, and I have done my work unflinchingly. I have written in bed, and written out of it, written in hemorrhages, written in sickness, written torn by coughing, written when my head swam for weakness . . . I am better now, have been rightly speaking since first I came to the Pacific; and still, few are the days when I am not in some physical distress. And the battle goes on – ill or well, is a trifle; so as it goes. I was made for a contest, and the Powers have willed that my battlefield should be this dingy, inglorious one of the bed and the physic bottle . . . I would have preferred a place of trumpetings and the open air over my head.'
(*See also* **Butcher, Lady Alice Mary; Part 4** (Letters))

**'Merry Men, The'**, a story, first published in *Cornhill Magazine,* June and July 1882; in book form in *The Merry Men and Other Tales,* 1887; Tusitala Edition *8*

The story recaptures the magic and legend of the Western Isles, with treasure from the Spanish Armada, a shipwreck and the guilt-stricken conscience of Gordon Darnaway, which drives him to his death.

**Merry Men, The, and Other Tales,** a collection of stories first published by Chatto & Windus, London and Scribner's, New York, 1887; Tusitala Edition *8*

*Dedication:* 'My dear Lady Taylor: To your name, if I wrote on brass, I could add nothing; it has been already written higher than I could dream to reach, by a strong and a dear hand; and if I now dedicate to you these tales, it is not as the writer who brings you his work, but as the friend who would remind you of his affection.

Skerryvore,                                                    Robert Louis Stevenson.
           Bournemouth.'
(*See* **Taylor, Sir Henry and Lady**)

In a prefatory Note, Stevenson writes, 'I am given to understand that days of prefaces are now quite over, and those who still care to read such things – or even write them – a despised minority. A preface then is like the top of a high mountain, seemingly a spot of much publicity, truly as private as a chamber; where a person of defective ear may stand up in the view of several counties and sing without reproof. Or we may say again that what a man writes there is singly for himself, like those loving legends and beloved names that we engrave on the sea-sand before the return of the flood.

Nothing is more agreeable to the writer than to let his pen move *ad libitum* and without destination; careless where he shall pass by or whither, if anywhere, he shall arrive. I question if it be equally pleasing to a reader; but in a preface I am safe from their intrusion and may run on, and gratify myself – and to some extent gratify my publisher, who is bewailing the thinness of the volume – like the singer on the mountain top, without offence.

The stories here got together are somewhat of a scratch lot. Three of them seem to me very good and in the absence of the public, I may even go to the length of saying that I very much admire them; these three are *Will o' the Mill, Thrawn Janet* and *Markheim. Thrawn Janet* has two defects; it is true only historically, true for a hill parish in Scotland in old days, not true for mankind and the world. Poor Mr. Soulis's faults we may equally recognise as virtues; and feel that by his conversion he was merely coarsened; and this, although the story carries me away every time I read it, leaves a painful feeling on the mind. I hope I should admire *Will o' the Mill* and *Markheim* as much if they had been written by someone else; but I am glad no one else wrote them.

One is in a middle state; some persons of good taste finding it pizzicato and affected to the last degree; others finding in it much geniality and good nature.

Thus *Eilean Aros,* first under that name, and more recently under its true name *Eilean Earraid,* has done me yeoman's service. First it was the backbone of *The Merry Men,* then it made a tolerable figure in *Kidnapped*: and now (its last appearance) it is to supply the present volume with a preface.

The author sees in his work something very different from the reader; the two parts are incompatible; that unhappy man who has written and re-written every word with inky fingers, and then passed through the prolonged disgust of proof sheets, has lost all touch with his own literature. They are presumably the books he would like to read, since they are those he has been pleased to write; yet he can never read them. To him they speak only of disappointment and defeat, and are the monuments of failure. I have long had a desire to read *Treasure Island,* which cannot be gratified; I might read the *Rig Veda* in the original – never *Treasure Island*: and think of the sad case of Mr. Meredith who can never read *Rhoda Fleming,* Mr. Anstey who can never read *A Fallen Idol,* or Mr. Lang who is debarred from the *Letters to Dead Authors!*

Yet there is an intimate pleasure, hard to describe, and quite peculiar to the writer of imaginative work. It is in some sense the fulfilment of his life; old childish daydreams here have taken shape – poignant and vague aspirations.'

**Mew, Egan,** 'Robert Louis Balfour Stevenson', *Literature,* 27 July 1901

**Mind of Robert Louis Stevenson, The,** (*see* **Ricklefs, Roger**)

**Minto, Charles Sinclair,** Robert Louis Stevenson Club Collection of Stevensonia, 1964. Typescript in Edinburgh Room, Edinburgh Central Library

**'Misadventures of John Nicholson, The',** 'The Misadventures of John Nicholson; A Christmas Story', originally published in *Yule-Tide*, Cassell's Christmas Annual, 1887 in book form in Edinburgh Edition, 1897; Tusitala Edition *13*
Young Nicholson robs his father of four hundred pounds, is disinherited and sails to San Francisco. He returns to Scotland and, after considerable misunderstanding, is reinstated with his father and his lost love.

**'Misgivings of Convalescence',** an essay, no. 5 in the series 'Swiss Notes', published *Pall Mall Gazette*, 17 March 1881. Not collected with other four

*'Miss Pringle's Neighbours',* (*see* **Stevenson, Fanny**)

**'Missions in the South Seas',** an address, read by his mother to the Women's Missionary Society and members of the General Assembly of the Presbyterian Church of New South Wales, Sydney, March 1893. Stevenson was unable to be present, due to illness; published in *The Presbyterian*, Sydney, March 1893; in book form in Balfour's *Life*, 1901

**'Mr. Baskerville and his Ward',** an unfinished short story, first published in Tusitala Edition *16*, 1924

**'Mr. Browning Again!',** a review in *Vanity Fair*, 11 December 1875 of 'The Inn Album' in which Stevenson slates Browning 'pretty handsomely'.

**'Mr. Tennyson's "Harold": Book of the Week',** a review in *London*, 3 February 1877.

**Moanatini, 'Prince' Stanislas,** cultured, European-educated high chief of Hiva-Oa, in the Marquesas Islands
He learned that beneath the gilded surface of hospitality, of feasts, dances, good manners and a cultured chief, the natives, who until recently had been the 'most inveterate cannibals of Polynesia', still hankered for the return of their ritual life and the eating of the 'long pig', as the cannibal feast was termed.
(*See* **Vaekehu, 'Queen'**)

**'Mock Trial, A',** an essay, written 1881, first published in *Columbia Library Columns*, 17 February 1968. It is in the form of a literary joke, Stevenson giving 'evidence' at the trial of a Mr. Cornish, a Davos acquaintance.

**'Model of R.L.S.?: Adam Blackadder's Flight from Sweden, A', (see Ramsay, M.P.)**

**'Modern Men: Mr. R.L. Stevenson',** (see **Lang, Andrew**)

**Modern Scottish Writers,** (see **Parker, M.W.**)

**'Modern Student Considered Generally, The',** an essay, first published in *Edinburgh University Magazine,* February 1871; in book form in Edinburgh Edition 1896; Tusitala Edition 25

**'Modestine's Shoes: A Bit of Stevensonia',** (see **Ford, R.C.**)

**Moë, 'Princess'**

During the voyage of the *Casco,* Stevenson took ill in Papeete, Tahiti and was finally transported, thanks to Fanny's determination and insistence, to the island of Tautira, where they were welcomed by the local aristocracy. Princess Moë insisted on caring for Stevenson personally, tempting his appetite with a South Seas speciality, raw fish marinated in lime juice and coconut milk. Stevenson miraculously began to mend; he swam in the lagoon, put on weight, demanded second helpings at the innumerable feasts. He was known as 'Ona' – the Rich One.
(*See* **Ori à Ori; Papeete,**)

**Moffat, John,** ten photographs of R.L.S. and his parents (1852–70) in the Edinburgh Room, Edinburgh Central Library, taken by J. Moffat

**Molokai,** leper colony (see **Kalawao-Kalaupepa**)

**'Monmouth: A Tragedy',** a play, first published by William Edwin Rudge, New York, 1928. A student attempt at collaboration by Stevenson and his cousin Bob
(*See also* **Catalogue (3)**)

**'Monterey',** an essay, first published in *Fraser's Magazine,* November 1880; appeared with 'San Francisco' under the joint title of 'The Old and New Pacific Capitals', Edinburgh Edition, 1895; Tusitala Edition 18

After his journey half-way across the world to persuade Fanny to divorce her husband Sam Osbourne and marry him, the tides of misfortune finally washed up Stevenson at Fanny's lodgings in Monterey. The 'pre-Gringo' capital of California was an unprepossessing place in 1879, composed of missions, soldiers and cattle and a few down-at-heel Mexican families trying desperately to cling to the *hacienda* tradition which demanded lace mantillas and serenades by guitar. To Stevenson's jaundiced eyes, the town unfolded as a Mexican fishing village whose life centred around the main street, a shabby thoroughfare deep in sand which made walking for even a fit strong man difficult and his own progress was as unsteady as that of the drunks who staggered out of the saloon. Apart from these lively gentlemen the entire male population appeared to be composed of a few sad-looking Indians leaning against the walls of the adobe houses, with the sole purpose of preventing them from falling down. Other recreations consisted of indifferent guitars practising raucous serenades and several alarming scuffles where knives as well as fists were clearly in evidence. (*See also* **Amateur Emigrant, The** (Fanny Stevenson's Prefatory Note); plate 15)

## Monterey Californian

A conspiracy among Stevenson's fellow-boarders at Simoneau's raised two dollars a week to enable the *Californian* editor Bronson to hire the impoverished Stevenson as a part-time reporter. He had fallen among friends, although the idea of a 'reporter' in a place where "the population is about that of a dissenting chapel on a wet Sunday . . . mostly Mexican and Indian", was of considerable amusement to him.

**Moore, George,** (1852—1933), the Anglo-Irish novelist's *Confessions of a Young Man* contains an assessment of Stevenson as an author of fiction

**Moorman, Lewis J.,** *Tuberculosis and Genius,* University of Chicago Press, n.d. Describes how this condition affected the famous, and how they dealt with it

**Moors, H.J.,** *With Stevenson in Samoa,* Fisher Unwin, London, 1910. Personal recollections of his friendship with Stevenson, the building of Vailima and daily life there; also the writing of 'The Bottle Imp'

**'Moral Emblems',** a selection of poems, illustrated by R.L. Stevenson, published by S.L. Osbourne & Co., Davos Press, 1882 (private printing venture of Stevenson and Lloyd Osbourne); first published in *Edinburgh Edition,* 1898; Tusitala Edition *22*

**'Morality of the Profession of Letters, The',** an essay, first published in *Fortnightly Review,* April 1881; Tusitala Edition *28*
(*See also* Part 4 (Letters: Academy, The))

## Morals

'It is probable that nearly all who think of conduct at all, think of it too much; it is certain that we all think too much of sin . . . To make our ideal of morality centre on forbidden acts is to defile the imagination and to introduce into our judgements of our fellow-men a secret element of gusto. If a thing is wrong for us, we should not dwell upon the thought of it; or we shall soon dwell upon it with inverted pleasure. If we cannot drive it from our minds – one thing of two: either our creed is in the wrong and we must more indulgently remodel it; else, if our morality be in the right, we are criminal lunatics and should place our persons in restraint . . . Gentleness and cheerfulness . . . are the perfect duties. And it is the trouble with moral men that they have neither one nor other . . . If your morals make you dreary, depend upon it they are wrong. I do not say "give them up", for they may be all you have; but conceal them like a vice, lest they should spoil the lives of better and simpler people.' ('A Christmas Sermon'. *Ethical Studies,* Tusitala Edition *26*)

And to cousin Bob, he wrote in September 1894, three months before his death (*Letters*, Tusitala Edition *35* p. 168): 'If I had to begin again – I know not – *si jeunesse savait, si vieillesse pouvait* ... I know not at all – I believe I should try to honour Sex more religiously. The worst of our education is that Christianity does not recognise and hallow Sex. It looks askance at it, over its shoulder, oppressed as it is by reminiscences of hermits and Asiatic self-tortures. It is a terrible hiatus in our modern religions that they cannot see and make venerable that which they ought to see first and hallow most. Well, it is so; I cannot be wiser than my generation'.

**More New Arabian Nights,** (*see* **Dynamiter, The**)

**Morris, David B.,** *Robert Louis Stevenson and the Scottish Highlander,* Aeneas Mackay, Stirling, 1929. Stevenson's sympathy with the Jacobite cause from his early absorption of Highland history

**Morrison, Alexander,** *Robert Louis Stevenson's Ancestral, Personal and Literary Associations with Bridge of Allan,* n.d.; 'The Three David Balfours of Powis and their Friends', Aeneas Mackay, Stirling, 1929. A paper read to the Robert Louis Stevenson Club, Edinburgh, 17 January 1929

**Morse, Hiram G.,** 'Robert Louis Stevenson as I Found him in his Island Home'. Privately printed, 1902. Stevenson's living habits, his daily routine at Vailima. 20pp

**'*Most Unforgettable Character I've Met, The*'**, (*see* **Strong, Austin**)

**'Mountain Town in France, A'**, an essay, first published in *Studio*, Winter 1896–97; in book form, as opening chapter of *Travels with a Donkey in the Cévennes*, Tusitala Edition *17*

**Mrantz, Maxine,** *R.L. Stevenson: Poet of Paradise,* Aloha Graphics, Honolulu, Hawaii, 1977. Stevenson in Honolulu 1889. His friendship with King Kalakaua and Princess Kaiulani; his visit to the leper colony at Molokai

**Muir, Edwin,** 'Robert Louis Stevenson', *Modern Scot*, Autumn 1931;

critical assessment of Stevenson's value to modern literature. *Scott and Scotland: The Predicament of the Scottish Writer*, Routledge & Sons, London, 1936

**Muirhead, J.H.**, *Robert Louis Stevenson's Philosophy of Life*, 1902

**Munro, D.G. Macleod**, *The Psychopathology of Tuberculosis*, Oxford Unviversity Press, n.d. Contains interesting theories relating to this medical condition in writers, artists, etc.

**Munro, Neil**, 'Stevenson: The Man and his Work', essay from *Bookman* Extra Number, Hodder & Stoughton, London, 1913

*My Autobiography*, (*see* **McClure, S.S.**)

**'My First Book'**, Stevenson's Preface to *Treasure Island*, Tusitala Edition 2
Stevenson writes: 'Sooner or later, somehow, anyhow, I was bound to write a novel. It seems vain to ask why. Men are born with various manias: from my earliest childhood it was mine to make a plaything of imaginary series of events; and as soon as I was able to write, I became a good friend to the paper-makers . . . and it is consolatory to remember that these reams are now all ashes, and have been received again into the soil . . . the succession of defeats lasted unbroken till I was thirty-one. By that time I had written little books and little essays and short stories, and had got patted on the back and paid for them – though not enough to live upon. . . . I was the successful man. I passed my days in toil, the futility of which would sometimes make my cheek to burn, . . . and yet could not earn a livelihood; and still there shone ahead of me an unattained ideal . . . I had not yet written a novel. . . . Anybody can write a short story – a bad one, I mean – who has industry and paper and time enough; but not everyone may hope to write even a bad novel. It is the length that kills . . . There must be something for hope to feed upon. The beginner must have a slant of wind, a lucky vein must be running. . . . For so long a time the slant is to continue unchanged . . . for so long a time you must hold at command the same quality of style; for so long a time your puppets are to be always vital, always consistent, always vigorous . . . a feat – not possibly of literature – but at least of physical and moral endurance and the courage of Ajax.'

*'My Meeting with Stevenson'*, (*see* **Wakefield, Sir Charles**)

*'My Stevenson Find'*, (*see* **Waugh, J.L.**)

*'My Stevensons'*, (*see* **Arnold, William Harris**)

**Myers, Frederick W.H.**, *Human Personality and its Survival of Bodily Death*, Longmans Green, London, 1903
Myers, an eminent psychical researcher, was introduced by Sir Henry and

Lady Taylor. He was intrigued by the supernatural aspects suggested by the nightmare which produced *Jekyll and Hyde*.

**'Myth of Robert Louis Stevenson, The'**, (*see* **Benson, E.F.**)

# N

**National Library of Scotland,** George IV Bridge, Edinburgh (Tel. 031-226 4531), contains a large amount of Stevenson material, including a considerable number of unpublished manuscripts

*'Native of Torryburn, A: More Leaves from the Diary "of the beloved nurse Cummy"'*, (*see* **Skinner, R.T.**)

**Neider, Charles,** (ed.) *Our Samoan Adventure* by Fanny and Louis Stevenson, Weidenfeld & Nicolson, London, 1956. Compiled from Journals kept at Vailima

**Nerli, Count,** visitor to Vailima who painted several controversial portraits of Stevenson

**New Arabian Nights,** first published as *Latter-Day Arabian Nights* in *London*, June-October 1878; in book form by Chatto & Windus, London, 1882; Tusitala Edition *1*

Comprises 'The Suicide Club' and 'The Rajah's Diamond', as well as four short stories, 'The Pavilion on the Links', 'A Lodging for the Night', 'The Sire de Malétroit's Door', 'Providence and the Guitar'. *Dedication:* 'To Robert Alan Mowbray Stevenson, in grateful remembrance of their youth and their already old affection'

**newspapers, contributions to** (*see* **magazines and newspapers**)

**'New View of R.L.S., A',**(*see* **Safroni-Middleton, A.**)

**New York**

Stevenson's first impressions of the city were contained in Part I of *The Amateur Emigrant*, 'From the Clyde to Sandy Hook', (Tusitala Edition *18*). 'As we drew near to New York I was at first amused, and then somewhat staggered by the cautious and the grisly tales that went the round. You would have thought we were to land upon a cannibal island. You must speak to no one in the streets as they would not leave you till you were rooked and beaten. You must enter a hotel with military precautions; for the least you had to apprehend was to awake next morning without money or baggage, or necessary raiment, a lone forked radish in a bed; and if the worst befell, you would instantly and mysteriously disappear from the ranks of mankind . . . Jones and I issued into West Street, sitting on some straw in the bottom of an open

baggage-wagon. It rained miraculously; and from that moment till on the following night I left New York, there was scarce a lull, and no cessation of the downpour. The roadways were flooded; a loud strident noise of falling water filled the air; the restaurants smelt heavily of wet people and wet clothing . . . Jones was well known [at Reunion House]; we were received warmly and two minutes afterwards I had refused a drink from the proprietor and was going on, in my plain European fashion, to refuse a cigar when Mr. Mitchell sternly interposed, and explained the situation. He was offering to treat me, it appeared; whenever an American bar-keeper proposes anything, it must be borne in mind that he is offering to treat; and if I did not want a drink, I must at least take the cigar. I took it bashfully, feeling I had begun my American career on the wrong foot. I did not enjoy that cigar; but this may have been from a variety of reasons, even the best cigar often failing to please if you smoke three-quarters of it in a drenching rain...
I suppose we had one of the "private rooms for families" . . . It was very small, furnished with a bed, a chair, and some clothes-pegs; and it derived all that was necessary for the life of the human animal through two borrowed lights; one for looking into the passage, and the second opening, without sash, into another apartment, where three men fitfully snored, or in intervals of wakefulness, drearily mumbled to each other all night long . . . I pitched my camp upon the floor . . . and never closed an eye. At sunrise I heard a cannon fired . . . the men in the next room gave over snoring for good, and began to rustle over their toilettes. The sound of their voices as they talked was low and moaning, like that of people watching by the sick . . . I found myself growing eerier and eerier, for I daresay I was a little fevered by my restless night, and hurried to dress and get downstairs. You had to pass through the rain, which still fell thick and resonant, to reach a lavatory on the other side of the court. There were three basin-stands, and a few crumpled towels and pieces of wet soap, white and slippery like fish; nor should I forget a looking-glass and a pair of questionable combs. Another Scots lad was here, scrubbing his face with a good will. He had been three months in New York and had not yet found a single job nor earned a single halfpenny . . . I began to grow sick at heart for my fellow-emigrants. Of my nightmare wanderings in New York I spare to tell. I had a thousand and one things to do; only the day to do them in, and a journey across the continent before me in the evening. It rained with patient fury; every now and then I had to get under cover for a while in order, so to speak, to give my mackintosh a rest; for under this continued drenching it began to grow damp on the inside. I went to banks, post-offices, railway offices, restaurants, publishers, booksellers, money-changers, and wherever I went a pool would gather about my feet, and those who were careful of their floors would look on with an unfriendly eye. Wherever I went, too, the same traits struck me; the people were all surprisingly rude and

surprisingly kind. The money-changer cross-questioned me like a French commissary, asking my age, my business, my average income and my destination, beating down my attempts at evasion and receiving my answers in silence; and yet when all was over, he shook hands with me up to the elbows, and sent his lad nearly a quarter of a mile in the rain to get me books at a reduction. Again, in a very large publishing and bookselling establishment, a man, who seemed to be the manager, received me as I had certainly never before been received in any human shop, indicated squarely that he put no faith in my honesty, and refused to look up the names of books or give me the slightest help or information, on the ground, like the steward, that it was none of his business. I lost my temper at last, said I was a stranger in America and not learned in their etiquette; but I would assure him, if he went to any bookseller in England, of more handsome usage . . . like many a long shot, it struck the gold. The manager passed at once from one extreme to the other . . . from that moment he loaded me with kindness . . . I was so wet when I got back to Mitchell's towards the evening, that I had simply to divest myself of my shoes, socks and trousers, and leave them behind for the benefit of New York City. No fire could have dried them ere I had to start; and to pack them in their present condition was to spread ruin among my other possessions. With a heavy heart I said farewell to them as they lay in the middle of a pool upon the floor of Mitchell's kitchen. I wonder if they are dry by now.' (Plate 14).

Eight years later in 1887, New York had a very different reception in store for Mr. Robert Louis Stevenson, the celebrated and famous author of *Dr. Jekyll and Mr. Hyde*. Eulogistic accounts of interviews were published in the newspapers, 'A Writer about whom Critics agree. If there is any writer of the time about whom critics of England and America substantially agree, it is Mr. Robert Louis Stevenson. There is something in his work, precisely what, it is not easy to say, which engages and fixes the attention from the first page to the last, which shapes itself before the mind's eye while reading, and which refuses to be forgotten long after the book which revealed it has been closed and put away . . . The quality by which Mr. Stevenson is chiefly distinguished, and which differentiates his writing from the story-writing of the period, is imagination – the power of creating characters which are as real as creatures of flesh and blood, and of devising and shaping events which are as inevitable as fate. Beyond all the writers of his time, he is remarkable for clearness and accuracy of vision, he seems to see, and we believe he *does* see, all that he describes and he makes all his readers see likewise. How he accomplishes this last feat, which is a very uncommon one, we have never been able to discover, for on returning to a scene or a chapter which has impressed us deeply, which has sent the blood tingling through our veins, or has darkened our souls with foreboding, we have always failed to detect the secret of his power. It can hardly be in his language, which is always of the simplest, nor in the feeling that he depicts, which is always natural, and often common, but it is there all the same.'

Stevenson wrote to Colvin (*Letters,* Tusitala Edition *33,* p.142), 'My reception here was idiotic to the last degree . . . it is very silly, and not pleasant, except where humour enters; and I confess the poor interview lads pleased me. They are too good for their trade; avoided anything I asked them to avoid, and were no more vulgar in their reports than they could help. I liked the lads . . .' The 'lads' obviously liked Stevenson. 'There were a great many things on Stevenson's bed – things to eat and to smoke, things to write with and to read. I have seen tidier sickbeds, and also invalids more modishly attired . . . I call him an invalid chiefly because, as I remember him, the term has such a picturesque unfitness. His body was in evil case, but his spirit was more bright, more eager, more ardently and healthily alive than that of any other mortal,' wrote one reporter.

Another wrote, 'His dress suited his face, which was not that of an ordinary man. I have seldom seen eyes further apart or more striking, as they were coal-black, or at least, had that appearance in contrast with his pale complexion. He was as lively and full of spirits as though he had never known what it was to have an ill day. His conversation – which was entirely unbookish, as befitted the occasion – bubbled over with fun, and altogether he suggested anything rather than an invalid in the vain search for health.'

To another who asked, 'What is your object in now visiting America?' Stevenson said, 'Simply on account of my health, which is wretched. I am suffering from catarrhal consumption, but am sanguine that my sojourn here will do much to restore me to my former self . . . I certainly did not expect to make the voyage with one hundred horses . . . The company's agent was most impertinent to us, but the horses behaved themselves exceedingly well. And I feel pleased to add that the ship's officers were particularly nice, and everything was most pleasant after we got used to the stables.'

'Where do you propose to go?'

'Well, the Lord only knows; I don't. I intend to get out of New York just as fast as I can. I like New York exceedingly. It is to me a mixture of Chelsea, Liverpool and Paris, but I want to get into the country –' (*See* **Ludgate Hill**)

**New York Grolier Club,** an exhibition of first editions of Robert Louis Stevenson with other Stevensoniana, was held at the New York Grolier Club, 5—28 November 1914

**New York State University,** *Robert Louis Stevenson, a Catalogue of his Works and Books Relating to him in the Rare Book Collection,* State University of New York at Buffalo, Amherst, NY, 1972

**Newell, Rev. J.E. and Mrs.**, respected and well-liked missionary couple who were visitors to Vailima

**Newport, Rhode Island**

When the Stevensons arrived in New York off the *Ludgate Hill* in September 1887, they were met by the Fairchilds, wealthy friends of the artist John Sargent (whom they had commissioned to paint Stevenson). Undismayed by the party having appeared from the gangway of a cattle boat, they offered the hospitality of their summer home in Newport. Louis had taken another cold and was glad of the chance to be cosseted. A firm friendship ensued.

(*See also* **Fairchild, Mr. and Mrs. Charles; Sargent, John Singer**)

**Nice**

This French resort was almost the scene of Stevenson's death in 1884. His friends Baxter and Henley came to Hyères and Fanny, trying to keep a strict eye on her invalid, was not at all pleased by the amount of carousing in her 'doll's house'. Her dislike of Henley increased, especially as Stevenson wished to pay him for services as unofficial literary agent. Finally Stevenson decided to accompany his chums on a jaunt to Nice, some distance along the coast, to escape the tense atmosphere and Fanny's nagging once the bedroom door was closed. In Nice Stevenson caught cold, and although he made light of it to his friends departing for Britain, acute congestion of the lungs and kidneys swiftly followed. Fanny, two doctors and a nurse fought to save his life; he was delirious and out of his mind with pain. Fanny managed to write to his parents through it all, '. . . when the doctor came he beckoned me to follow him, and told me Louis was dying and could not be kept alive until you could get here. That was yesterday. I watched every breath he drew all night in what sickening apprenhension you may guess . . .' She did not add that the doctor advised her to send for some male friend or relative to stand by and help with the funeral arrangements. She wired for Stevenson's cousin Bob, and sought the advice of yet another doctor, who was more hopeful.

(*See also* **Drummond, Dr.**)

**Nicoll, W. Robertson**, 'Robert Louis Stevenson', *Bookman*, London, October 1901 (The Stevenson Number); 'Robert Louis Stevenson: Home from the Hill', *Bookman* Extra Number, London, 1913

**Nicolson, Nigel,** (*see* **Hennessy, James Pope**)

**'Night in France, A'**, an essay from 'Hitherto Unpublished Prose Works', first published by Boston Bibliophile Society, 1921; collected in Tusitala Edition *30*

**Nimmo, Ian and Seaton, Jim,** 'The Kidnapped Walk', *Weekly Scotsman,* 5 January–2 February 1961. Follows the route taken by David Balfour and Alan Breck in *Kidnapped*

*'The Nixie',* (*see* **de Mattos, Katharine; Henley, William Ernest; Stevenson, Fanny**)

**Noble, James Ashcroft,** 'Robert Louis Stevenson: In Memoriam', *Westminster Gazette,* 18 December 1894

**'Noctes Ambrosianae',** a review, first published in *The Academy,* 22 July 1876; Tusitala Edition *28*

**Nolan, J.B.,** 'The Stevenson Museum, Edinburgh', *Mentor,* May 1928

*No More a Stranger,* (*see* **Fisher, Annie**)

**Norman, Henry,** 'Robert Louis Stevenson, Man and Artist', *Daily Chronicle,* 18 December 1894. Valedictory article

**North Berwick**

By 1860 this East Lothian seaside town had already expanded into a fashionable resort, made accessible to Edinburgh by the railway. When Stevenson's grandfather Rev. Lewis Balfour died, the days at Colinton Manse were also at an end and the Stevensons rented a 'summer' house in North Berwick.. Young Stevenson made many friends among other children on holiday and indulged in 'Crusoe-ing . . . a word that covers all extempore eating in the open air: digging perhaps a house under the margin of the links, kindling a fire of the seaware [sic], and cooking apples there'. By night he met his new friends after dark with bull's eye lanterns. There was scope for imagination, the Bass Rock on which David Balfour was to be imprisoned and the sinister domain of Tod Lapraik; there were hints of Treasure Island-to-come as the companions became smugglers, pirates and hunted buried treasure. He was remembered by his companions as the one who 'always led the band, was always the master-spirit and inspiring force. A kind of magnetism seemed to emanate from him, some great, though then undeveloped personality . . . a strange boy, a thin elfin lad with brilliant eyes.'

**North Bridge,** in *Edinburgh: Picturesque Notes,* Stevenson wrote, 'They lean over the great bridge which joins the New Town with the Old – that windiest spot, or high altar, in this northern temple of the winds – and watch the trains smoking out from under them and vanishing into the tunnel on a voyage to brighter skies. Happy the passengers who shake off the dust of Edinburgh, and have heard for the last time the cry of the east wind among her chimney-tops!'

**'North, Captain George',** pseudonym of Stevenson (*see* **Young Folks**)

**Northern Light,** Stevenson and Lloyd Osbourne planned to go into business when they first reached Samoa, to buy or build a schooner to be called *Northern Light*. However, Stevenson decided to buy and plant land as a more profitable venture, and so the Vailima estate came into being

**No Son of Mine,** (*see* **Stern, G.B.**)

'**Note at Sea, A**', an essay from 'Hitherto Unpublished Prose Works', first published by Boston Bibliophile Society, 1921; collected in Tusitala Edition *30*

'**Note on Realism, A**', an essay, first published in *Magazine of Art,* November 1883; Tusitala Edition *28*

'**Note on Robert Louis Stevenson, A – 1850–1894**' (*see* **Bailey, Mrs. H.S.**)

'**Note upon Stevenson, A**', (*See* **Iles, George**)

'**Notes on the Movements of Young Children**', an essay, first published in *The Portfolio,* August 1874; Tusitala Edition *25*

'**Notes on the various members of the Stevenson family**', (*see* **Hill, Robin Armstrong**)

'**Nuits Blanches**', an essay, first published in *Edinburgh Edition* 1896; Tusitala Edition *30*

'**Nurses**', an essay, first published in *Edinburgh Edition* 1896; Tusitala Edition *30*

# O

### Oakland, California

Fanny's marital home with Sam Osbourne was described by Stevenson as a 'flimsy wooden cottage, which seemed indissoluble from the green garden in which it stood'. Its sides blew in and out like a balloon on windy nights, as no solid stone house he had ever encountered in Scotland. It was in the cottage at East Oakland that Stevenson sought refuge when he took seriously ill in San Francisco in 1879. For the sake of the proprieties and since Californian law required that a husband support his wife and family during divorce proceedings, Stevenson was moved into an Oakland hotel. Fanny was in no hurry and in the following May, Stevenson made the journey across the Bay back to San Francisco by horse-car and ferry. He found a clergyman, a fellow Scot, to perform the ceremony and armed with a marriage licence, bought two plain silver wedding rings, the kind worn by French peasants, which seemed appropriate to himself and Fanny especially as he could not afford gold. On 19 May the still sick man crossed the Bay again, accompanied by Fanny and unable to afford the cab fare, took the cable car uphill to the house of their friends, the Williams. As they had not been warned of the impending event, Virgil was away from home but his wife Dora accompanied them to the Post Street home of Rev. Dr. William Scott, the minister of St John's Presbyterian Church. Dora is described as 'guardian angel, and our Best Man and Bridesmaid rolled into one'. She was also witness with the minister's wife. The marriage register read:

'Married by me at my residence 19th May 1880, Robert Louis Stevenson, born Edinboro', Scotland, white, single, 30 years old, resides in Oakland, Calif.

Fannie Osbourne, born Indianapolis, Indiana, 40 years, widowed, white, resides in Oakland.

Certificate to be sent to Mrs. Virgil Williams, 719 Geary Street, City.'

It is interesting to note that although Fanny gave her true age, she shied away from 'divorced' and became 'widowed'.

(*See also* **Osbourne, Samuel; Silverado Squatters, The**)

**Obituaries.** Many of the notable magazines and newspapers to which Stevenson had contributed during his lifetime, printed anonymous obituaries in December 1894, including *The Academy, The Athenaeum, Edinburgh Evening News, The Scotsman, The Times, Westminster Gazette.*

There were many more, in many places throughout the world where Stevenson was known and loved.
(*See also* **Colvin, Sir Sidney; Gosse, Sir Edmund William; Japp, Alexander H.; Lang, Andrew**)

*Object of Pity, or, The Man Haggard, A Romance,* 'by Many Competent Hands'. Privately printed in Edinburgh, November 1898; 25 copies uniform with the Edinburgh Edition; first published in an edition of 110 copies by Dodd, Mead & Co., New York, 1900.

A humorous piece in which Stevenson, Fanny, Belle Strong, Graham Balfour, Lady Jersey and her brother Rupert Leigh, each had to draw a portrait of himself or herself in the style of 'Ouida' (to whom the booklet was dedicated by Stevenson), while Bazett Haggard was to be the hero of a romance running through the whole.
(*See* **Jersey, Countess of**)

*Of Making Many Books,* (*see* **Burlingame, Roger**)

*Ogilvy, Gavin* [**J.M. Barrie**] *on Stevenson,* (*see* **Barrie, Sir James Matthew**)

'**Olalla**', a short story, first published in *Court and Society Review*, December 1885; in book form in *The Merry Men and Other Tales*, 1887; Tusitala Edition *8*
A Gothic horror story, set in Spain with overtones of Edgar Allan Poe, of beautiful but doomed Olalla, her brother Felipe and the narrator who falls in love with her.

'**Old and New Pacific Capitals, The**', (*see* '**Monterey**'; '**San Francisco**')

'**Old Mortality**', an essay, first published in *Longman's Magazine*, May 1884; in book form in *Memories and Portraits*, 1887; Tusitala Edition *29*

'**Old Scots Gardener, An**', an essay, first published in *Edinburgh University Magazine*, March 1871; in book form in *Memories and Portraits*, 1887; Tusitala Edition *29*

**Old Song, An**, a story, first published in *London*, 24 February–17 March 1877; in book form with *Edifying Letters of the Rutherford Family*, Wilfion Books, Paisley, 1982. A remarkable piece of literary detection on the part of Roger G. Swearingen (who edits and introduces the book), led to the recent discovery of this early Stevenson story

**O'Meara, Frank**
Irish artist who became enamoured of Belle, Fanny's daughter, while they were in Grez. With Bob Stevenson, he was a constant visitor to the

Paris apartment, at 5 Rue Douay, which Fanny and Stevenson shared in the autumn of 1876

**'Ona'**,   name given to Stevenson by Polynesian natives, indicating 'owner' of the *Casco*, which signified power and wealth. It could also be translated as 'The Rich Man'

**'On a Hill in Samoa'**, (*see* **Brown, Hilton**)

**'On a New Form of Intermittent Light for Lighthouses'**, first published in Transactions of the Royal Scottish Society of Arts, Vol. 8, Edinburgh, 1871; collected in Tusitala Edition *28*. Paper read before the R.S.S.A. on 27 March 1871, for which Stevenson was awarded the Society's Silver Medal.

**'On Falling in Love'**,   an essay,   first   published   in   *Cornhill Magazine,* February 1877; in book form in *Virginibus Puerisque,* 1881; Tusitala Edition *25*.

'Falling in love is the one illogical adventure, the one thing of which we are tempted to think as supernatural, in our trite and reasonable world. The effect is out of all proportion with the cause. Two persons, neither of them, it may be, very amiable or very beautiful, meet, speak a little, and look a little into each other's eyes. That has been done a dozen or so of times in the experience of either with no great result. But on this occasion all is different. They fall at once into that state in which another person becomes to us the very gist and centre-point of God's creation, and demolishes our laborious theories with a smile; in which our ideas are so bound up with the one master-thought that even the trivial cares of our own person become so many acts of devotion, and the love of life itself is translated into a wish to remain in the same world with so precious and desirable a fellow-creature. And all the while their acquaintances look on in stupor, and ask each other, with almost passionate emphasis, what so-and-so can see in that woman, or such-an-one in that man? I am sure, gentlemen, I cannot tell you . . . Of the misbegotten changelings who call themselves men, and prate intolerably over dinner-tables, I never saw one who seemed worthy to inspire love — no, nor read of any, except Leonardo da Vinci, and perhaps Goethe in his youth . . .
Love should run out to meet love with open arms. Indeed, the ideal story is that of two people who go into love step for step, with a fluttered consciousness, like a pair of children venturing together into a dark room. From the first moment when they see each other, with a pang of curiosity, through stage after stage of growing pleasure and embarrassment, they can read the expression of their own trouble in each other's eyes. There is here no declaration properly so called; the feeling is so plainly shared, that as soon as the man knows what is in his own heart, he

is sure of what is in the woman's. This simple accident of falling in love is as beneficial as it is astonishing. It arrests the petrifying influence of years, disproves cold-blooded and cynical conclusions, and awakens dormant sensibilities . . . the essence of love is kindness; and indeed it may be best defined as passionate kindness; kindness, so to speak, run mad and become importunate and violent . . . [the] pre-existence of both occurs to the mind as something indelicate. To be altogether right, they should have had twin birth together, at the same moment with the feeling that unites them . . . Then they would understand each other with a fulness impossible otherwise. There would be no barrier between them of associations that cannot be imparted. They would be led into none of those comparisons that send the blood back to the heart . . . Some one has written that love makes people believe in immortality, because there seems not to be room enough in life for so great a tenderness, and it is inconceivable that the most masterful of our emotions should have no more than the few spare moments of a few years . . .

"The blind bowboy", who smiles upon us from the end of terraces in old Dutch gardens, laughingly hails his birdbolts among a fleeting generation. But for as fast as ever he shoots, the game dissolves and disappears into eternity from under his falling arrows; this one is gone ere he is struck; the other has but time to make one gesture and give one passionate cry; and they are all the things of a moment. When the generation is gone, when the play is over, when the thirty years' panorama has been withdrawn in tatters from the stage of the world, we may ask what has become of these great, weighty, and undying loves, and the sweethearts who despised mortal conditions in a fine credulity; and they can only show us a few songs in a bygone taste, a few actions worth remembering, and a few children who had retained some happy stamp from the disposition of their parents'

'On Lord Lytton's *Fables in Song*,' an essay, first published in *Fortnightly Review*, June 1874; Tusitala Edition 28

'On Morality', an essay, first published in Vailima Edition 1923; Tusitala Edition 26

'On Some Technical Elements of Style in Literature', an essay, first published in *Contemporary Review*, April 1885; Tusitala Edition 28

*On the Bat's Back,* (*see* **Lawson, McEwan**)

'On the Choice of a Profession', an essay, written 1887–88 and rejected by *Scribner's Magazine* as too cynical and sombre in tone; eventually published by them, 1915; Tusitala Edition 28

'On the Enjoyment of Unpleasant Places', an essay, first published in *The Portfolio*, November 1874; Tusitala Edition 25

**'On the Thermal Influence of Forests'**, a paper, read before the Royal Society of Edinburgh, 19 May 1873; reprinted from the *Proceedings of the R.S.E.*; Tusitala Edition 28

*On the Trail of Stevenson*, (*see* **Hamilton, Clayton**)

**'Ordered South'**, his first published essay, appeared in *Macmillan's Magazine*, May 1874; in book form in *Virginibus Puerisque*, 1881; Tusitala Edition 25

**'O'Rell, Max'**, nom-de-plume of Paul Blouet, (1848–1903), French author, journalist and traveller, who visited Vailima

**Ori à Ori**, (also known as **Teriitera**), member of the Tautira aristocracy who lent the Stevensons one of his 'dwellings' and became a staunch friend during their stay

At an emotional parting when the *Casco* sailed, the Stevensons' 'exchanged' names with Ori and Princess Moë, a gesture which initiated them as tribal members and symbolised mutual regard and goodwill. (*See also* **Moë, 'Princess'; Papeete**)

**Orr, Christine**, *Witness in Danger* (play) from *Catriona*, 1955. Information in Edinburgh Room, Edinburgh Central Library ·

**Osbourne, Alan**, son of Lloyd, born 1897. Letter to *The Times Literary Supplement*, 25 March 1960, about the writing of the official biography of R.L. Stevenson

**Osbourne, Fanny Vandegrift**, (*see* **Stevenson, Fanny**)

**Osbourne, Hervey**, Fanny's third child, born in 1871

He was described as a beautiful, ethereal sweet-natured child with large dark eyes and golden hair, which his mother patiently trained into curls. When Hervey was four, Fanny found her husband Sam's continuing unfaithfulness intolerable and decided to go to Europe to study art, taking the children with her. In Antwerp, Hervey took a fever and Fanny was advised to see a children's specialist in Paris. For a little while he improved, then early in 1876 he died a slow and terrible death from 'scrofulous tuberculosis'. Heart-broken, Fanny, his sister Belle and brother Lloyd followed his coffin to the burial ground of Père Lachaise, where they could afford only one of the temporary French graves, 'surely the cruellest in the world', wrote Lloyd later, 'from which the bones are flung into the catacombs at the expiration of five years.'

**Osbourne, Isobel (Belle)**, (*see* **Strong, Isobel (Belle)**))

**Osbourne, Katharine Durham**, *Robert Louis Stevenson in California*, A. C. McClurg, Chicago, 1911; 'The Best Thing in Edinburgh', privately printed for John Howells, San Francisco, 1923. Contains an inaccurate version of Stevenson's valedictory address to the Speculative Society, March 1873

Katharine Durham married Lloyd Osbourne in Honolulu in 1896, when he was twenty-eight years old. The Durhams, from Springfield, Missouri, were Quakers, and Katharine's mother was a descendant of Puritan Vermonters, many of them Congregational missionaries. Katharine had been teaching in a New Mexico mission school. 'Her life,' said her future mother-in-law, Fanny Stevenson, (Mackay, *The Violent Friend*) 'has been very grey and filled with self-sacrifice of which she was not conscious. Samoa will not, therefore, be a dull place for her as it would be for so many girls, and I believe she will be quite happy there . . . I have still to see whether my new daughter-in-law is able to take my place and leave me free to go when I like. She is a very good, sensible, capable girl, and not too young, so I am hoping more, perhaps, than I should from her. She will arrive here on the ninth of April and they will be married at once.' One of the guests at that wedding wrote ' . . . it seemed to me that the grey mare was decidedly the better in that team'. Later stripped of first illusion, Katharine was to describe Fanny as 'colourful . . . fascinating, if one didn't have to live with her'.

**Osbourne, Lloyd, (Samuel Lloyd Osbourne),** (1868–1947). Born in San Francisco. Son of Sam and Fanny Osbourne, stepson of and collaborator with Stevenson. Married (1) Katharine Durham (two sons, Alan Herbert and Louis Wolfert) and (2) Ethel Head (no children). *A Letter to Mr. Stevenson's Friends: In Memory of R.L.S.*, privately printed, 1894; *An Intimate Portrait of Robert Louis Stevenson*, Scribner's, New York, 1924; (with R.L. Stevenson) *The Ebb-Tide; The Wrecker; The Wrong Box*; (with Isobel Strong) *Memories of Vailima*, Scribner's, New York, 1902; *Stevenson Reader: Selected Passages from the Works of R.L.S.* (ed.), Chatto & Windus, London, 1898

Some of his descriptions of his stepfather (*see* **Stevenson, Robert Louis**) from *An Intimate Portrait of Robert Louis Stevenson* are reproduced as prefatory notes in the Tusitala Edition.

**Osbourne, Samuel,** Fanny's first husband

She was seventeen and Sam not quite twenty when they were married in Indianapolis on 5 December 1857. They made a handsome pair and 'looked like two children'; Fanny with her 'tiger-lily' beauty and the young Lieutenant (as he then was), six feet tall, with yellow curls and a Vandyke beard. To extreme good looks were added charms in abundance and, what Fanny was yet to discover, an eager eye for the ladies. He fought in the Civil War and was made Captain; a true adventurer, he was the prototype of the 'movie Westerner', oblivious to danger, a pioneer who was game for any wanderlust. He frequently went prospecting for gold and silver and Fanny spent a considerable part of those early years making homes for herself and Belle, who had been born nine months after the wedding. Fanny quickly learned to set up house in improbable places such as mining camps, where she mastered the masculine arts of rolling and smoking cigarettes and became a crack shot with a heavy revolver; such was a necessity of a wild life where Indians were by no means confined to reservations and frequently roving bands stared in at her through the cabin windows. Afraid that pulling the shutters would offend them, she placated their curiosity with cups of coffee. Her early training in survival was invaluable when as Mrs. Fanny Stevenson she accompanied her husband and family on jaunts to South Sea islands where the genteel 'royalty' who greeted them were just one step removed from a generation who had killed and eaten their enemies at 'the feast of the long pig'.

Although it was his constant infidelities which originally led to their separation, Sam behaved in a remarkably gallant and gentlemanly fashion over the divorce and appears to have tolerated – and even liked – Stevenson. He bore no ill-feelings and his generosity extended to helping the impoverished pair out with a little cash, which was sorely needed in San Francisco and Silverado. Soon after the divorce he remarried and Belle, who was always devoted to her father, liked her stepmother 'Paulie' – Miss Rebecca Paul, 'a slim, black-eyed, curly-haired woman who adored him' (and who sounded not unlike Fanny in appearance). Twice Sam came to Europe to see his son and take him on holiday. He acquired a vineyard near Silverado in the Napa Valley and was keen that Lloyd should return to California with him and work 'on the ranch'. This turn of events did not please Fanny. However, Fate intervened with an ending as dramatic and colourful as the other strange circumstances of his life. Paulie had his supper awaiting his return from the San Francisco office. He never arrived home that night. In the days and weeks that followed all her exhaustive enquiries brought no clue to his disappearance. Although much later there came a hardly credible rumour that he had been seen in South Africa, as far as Paulie and his family were concerned he had simply vanished off the face of the earth. A more likely theory is that he had been a 'victim' of the 'mafia' who ruled San Francisco, and had ended his life in the murky waters of the Bay. Stevenson and Fanny too were deeply concerned for Paulie's welfare, to the extent of financial help which they could ill afford. (*See* **Stevenson, Fanny**)

**Otis, A.H. Captain,** master of the *Casco*

He showed understandable reluctance to take on his cruise of the Polynesian islands three women, one young (the maid Valentine Roch), one middle-aged and one an old lady. All were wearing native dress, the voluminous *holoku* or 'Mother Hubbard' which missionaries had imposed upon the islanders' handsome nudity. To the conventionally minded Captain Otis, this uncorseted gown verged on indecency for European women. The middle-aged Fanny Stevenson further shocked his sensibilities by smoking incessantly and wearing her greying hair in a short crop of boyish curls, while her mother-in-law (known as Aunt Maggie) topped her weird apparel with the 'widow's cap' beloved of Queen Victoria, complete with starched white streamers. As for 'the frail stick of a man, the author R.L. Stevenson', Captain Otis, who was a practical man, checked carefully before sailing that the ship was also equipped with everything proper for burial at sea. The Captain was a devoted and ruthless seaman, his heart was in his ship and admiration of the *Casco*'s beauty and performance was the only common ground he found with his strange passengers. Secretly he regarded them as Jonahs and sea-lawyers, for they knew nothing of sea discipline. Fanny Stevenson would involve the helmsman in long conversations oblivious of the Captain's sarcastic 'Please don't talk to him today, Mrs. Stevenson. Today I want him to steer'. Neither of the women, nor their maid, took seriously his orders to keep deadlights firmly fastened, until the *Casco* heeled over in a sudden squall and deposited hundreds of gallons of the Pacific Ocean into their cabin. 'Aunt Maggie' infuriated Otis by her attempts to convert him, her constant quoting from the Bible and insistence on grace at meals. She also tried to discuss her son's writing with him until Otis told her sharply that he had read only *Treasure Island*; hinting that as its seamanship was 'not all square,' he saw no reason to read another book by the same author. When Fanny Stevenson asked him teasingly what he would do if Aunt Maggie fell overboard, he snapped, 'Put it in the log'.

As the voyage progressed there were many storms and squalls, many emergencies, and the women gained his grudging admiration for not once did any of them take the vapours or show the slightest fear. He was further and unexpectedly delighted to discover that Aunt Maggie was a splendid and ruthless whist-player. And although the author's wife was constantly seasick – twenty thousand miles of the Pacific never cured her – she gamely helped the cook and attended to cuts and bruises and minor ailments among the crew. As for the frail stick of a man, he blossomed, gaining weight, a fine tan, and a splendid appetite. 'I was never well but at sea,' was his proud boast. When Stevenson was taken ill with an unexpected haemorrhage on Fakarava and had to be rushed to Tahiti where there was a doctor, the Captain was summoned to his cabin, where he was given precise orders about ship and charter by Stevenson and what to do if he died. All the while, the sick man was smoking a cigarette with such an air of nonchalance and lack of drama that Otis felt he regarded the whole grim business of dying with no more concern than deciding on the next port. Stevenson had

some experience in facing imminent death but even tough Captain
Otis marvelled at his courage.

When they were leaving Tautira, with Stevenson well again thanks to
Princess Moë's nursing, Aunt Maggie gave a farewell thanksgiving
party on board the *Casco*, at which the visitors were earnestly sought not
only to give thanks but to sing hymns of praise as they sat in neat rows,
the service and prayers conducted by Aunt Maggie. One woman rose
and prayed for the safety of the ship, especially that if anything were to
go wrong, 'it might be discovered in time'. Captain Otis stamped off in
disgust; it was really the last straw suggesting that his beloved ship
might have some failing, however small. He disliked pious folk and was
eager to get under way. To his horror, as he made the final inspection, he
discovered that the main topmast was sprung – the spars were hollow
with dry rot. That the *Casco* had survived storms and squalls they had
encountered without the topmast falling, with loss of all hands, was a
miracle – and a fine moral tale for Aunt Maggie's dinner parties when
they trooped back on shore for another two weeks while the repair was
made

**'Our City Men. No. 1. A Salt-Water Financier',** an essay, published in
*London*, 3 February 1877

*Our Life in the Swiss Highlands,* (*see* **Symonds, John Addington**)

*Our Mountain Heritage,* (*see* **Issler, Anne Roller**)

*Our Samoan Adventure,* (*see* **Stevenson, Fanny**)

**'Owl, The',** an unfinished short story, first published in Vailima
Edition, 1923; Tusitala Edition *16*

# P

### Paaaeua, Chief

His family at Atuona in the Marquesas Islands exchanged names with the Stevensons. In Polynesia this was a great honour and formally recognised a stranger's standing in the community. Louis Stevenson's name would be 'Paaaeua' and the Chief's new name as close a version of 'Louis' as was pronounceable.

**'Padre Dos Reales'**, 200 copies of this broadsheet were printed by Creole M. Bronson (*Monterey Californian*). 3 copies survive (in Margaret Stevenson's scrapbook, Monterey Museum; Widener Collection; and Huntington Library)

During Stevenson's short stay in Monterey in 1879, he became champion of the underdog. In typical fashion he befriended a half-mad alcoholic old Indian who was tormented by local thugs. Then delightedly he helped plaster the town with placards to denounce the penurious parish priest as 'Padre Dos Reales' (Father Two-Bits). Such behaviour guaranteed him a warm place in the hearts of Simoneau's lodgers and fellow-drinkers, and earned him the extreme disapproval of Monterey's staid and respectable citizens.

**Pagan, G.H.**, 'Some Memories of "Cummie": a Link with R.L.S.', *Chambers Journal*, September 1939

***Pall Mall Gazette***, contained an anonymous article entitled 'Mr. R.L. Stevenson on Literature', 14 June 1893
(*See also* Part 4 (Letters))

**'Pan's Pipes'**, an essay, first published in *London*, 4 May 1878; in book form in *Virginibus Puerisque*, 1881; Tusitala Edition *25*

### Papeete, Tahiti

Voyaging on the *Casco* (1888), Stevenson took a haemorrhage and Captain Otis made haste for the nearest 'civilisation'. What passed for a hotel was considerably less salubrious than the *Casco* and Fanny, suspecting that their stay might be long, moved into 'a little bare one-twentieth furnished house'. With grated verandahs it stood near the calaboose. Papeete was the capital of France's eastern Pacific possessions, slack and corrupt, a woeful place in which to live – or to die. They considered leaving at the risk of being doctorless, especially as drunkenness and sickness were spreading among the *Casco*'s crew. They

crawled back aboard and sailed on to the other end of Tahiti – Tautira, and Princess Möe's skilful nursing.
(*See also* **Möe, Princess**)

*'Paradox and Antithesis in Stevenson's Essays'*, (*see* **Snyder, Alice D.**)

**Paris,** in January 1877 Stevenson was giving his address as No. 5 rue Douay, the lodging of Fanny Osbourne. In September they stayed together at No. 5 rue Ravignan
(*See also* **St. Germain**)

**'Paris Bourse, The'**, an essay, first published in *London*, 24 February 1877; reprinted in *The Stevensonian*, 1965

**Parker, M.W.,** *Modern Scottish Writers*, Wm. Hoyt & Co., Edinburgh, 1917

*Passages from the Journal of T.R. Sullivan,* (*see* **Sullivan, Thomas Russell**)

*'Passing Glimpse of Robert Louis Stevenson, A'*, (*see* **Kennedy, Maud**)

*Passionate Kindness, The,* (*see* **Knight, Alanna**)

**'Pastoral'**, an essay, first published in *Longman's Magazine*, April 1887; in book form in *Memories and Portraits*, 1887; Tusitala Edition *29*

**Patrick, John & Sons,** *The Early Home and Haunts of Robert Louis Stevenson*, a set of 12 platino-types, Edinburgh, n.d.

**Paul, C. Kegan,** *Memories*, Kegan Paul, Trench, Trubner & Co., London, 1899

He paid Stevenson twenty pounds each for *An Inland Voyage* and *Travels with a Donkey in the Cévennes*. He followed this with an invitation to dinner where, Fanny writes, 'the shy young man [Stevenson] suffered agonies of embarrassment over the claret that was served to the guests alone, Mr. Paul being an abstainer from principle. Would the acceptance, at his invitation, of the wine Mr. Paul thought it wrong to take, put Mr. Paul in a false position? And yet, on what grounds to refuse? This delicate question became so harassing to the Scotch conscience that, as my husband has told me, he would have infinitely preferred to dine not at all'.

**Paul, Sir James Balfour,** 'A Boy's Adventure with RLS', an essay in *A Cadger's Creel* (*see* **Douglas, Sir George**)

**'Pavilion on the Links, The'**, a short story, first published in *Cornhill Magazine*, September/October 1880; in book form in *New Arabian Nights*, 1882; Tusitala Edition *1*

Frank Cassilis returns to North Berwick, scene of a student summer spent with the enigmatic Northmour. He finds himself involved in mysterious and sinister activities in a deserted pavilion with a damsel in distress, Clara Huddlestone, and her villainous father.

**Pears, Sir Edmund Radcliffe,** 'Some Recollections of Robert Louis Stevenson', *Scribner's Magazine*, January 1923

**Peattie, Donald and Louise,** 'The Treasure of Robert Louis Stevenson', *Reader's Digest*, November 1952

**Peebles,** Stevenson spent several summer holidays in this small country town to the south of Edinburgh. He and Fanny spent part of the summer of 1882 with his parents at Stobo Manse. During boyhood holidays there, fond of 'real' games, he fought another boy, challenged him to a duel with real pistols, powder, but luckily without bullets, although redcurrant jelly was used to add a splendidly gory effect

**'Penitent, The',** a fable, Tusitala Edition *5* (*see also* **Fables**)

**Pennell, Joseph,** 'Comment on R.L.S. as illustrator of "A Mountain Town in France" ', *The Studio*, Winter 1896-7. (*See also* Part 4 (Letters))

***Penny Piper of Saranac, The, An Episode in Stevenson's Life*** (*see* **Chalmers, Stephen**)

**'Penny Plain and Twopence Coloured, A',** an essay, first published in *Magazine of Art*, April 1884; in book form in *Memories and Portraits*, 1887; Tusitala Edition *29*

**'Penny Whistles',** projected title for *A Child's Garden of Verses*

**Pentland Edition,** *The Works of Robert Louis Stevenson,* With Biographical Notes by Edmund Gosse, 20 vols., Cassell, London, 1906-7

**Pentland Hills,** (*see* **Swanston Cottage**)

**'Pentland Rising, The',** 100 copies of a 16-page pamphlet printed at Thomas Stevenson's expense by Andrew Elliott, Edinburgh, 1866; collected in Tusitala Edition *28*

**'Persons of the Tale, The',** a fable connected with *Treasure Island*, Tusitala Edition *2* (*see also* **Fables**)

**Phelps, William Lyon,** *Essays on Modern Novelists*, Macmillan, New York, 1910. Includes Stevenson

**Philip, Sir James Randall,** 'R.L.S.: a character study from his writings', *University of Edinburgh Journal*, Vol. 15, No. 4, 1951

**'Philosophy of Nomenclature, The',** an essay, first published in *Edinburgh University Magazine*, April 1871; in book form in Edinburgh

Edition, 1896; Tusitala Edition 25

**'Philosophy of Umbrellas, The'**, an essay, first published in *Edinburgh University Magazine*, February 1871; in book form in Edinburgh Edition, 1896; Tusitala Edition 25

**Pinero, Sir Arthur Wing,** (1855-1934), 'Robert Louis Stevenson as a Dramatist'. Privately printed for the Dramatic Museum of Columbia University, 1914

*Pioneer Missionary and Explorer, (see* **Brown, George**)

**Pitlochry** In the early summer of 1881, the Stevensons spent some time in this small town in the Perthshire hills, before moving on to Braemar in search of kindlier weather

In a Prefatory Note to *The Merry Men and Other Tales*, Fanny Stevenson writes, 'In a vague quest for "a house . . . a burn within reach; heather and a fir or two," we came upon "Kinnaird Cottage", near Pitlochry, where Professor Blackie, a picturesque and well-known figure in Scotland, had been in the habit of spending his vacations. For some reason the cottage was vacant during the summer of 1881; we were very glad indeed to engage it, though our landlady and her daughter, who were to attend to our domestic affairs, made it plain to us that we were not to be considered in the same breath with the eccentric professor. Kinnaird Cottage possessed more advantages than my husband had demanded when he agreed to go to the Highlands with his people, for the house stood a few yards from "a little green glen with a burn, – a wonderful burn, gold and green and snow white, singing loud and low in different steps of its career, now pouring over miniature crags, now fretting itself to death in a maze of rocky stairs and pots; never was so sweet a little river. Behind, great purple moorlands reaching to Ben Vrackie".

Although it was the seventh of June when we moved into the cottage, as yet we had had nothing but cold rains and penetrating winds; and in all innocence (this being my first season in this beautiful and inclement region) I asked when the spring would begin. "The spring!" said my mother-in-law; "why, *this* is the spring." "And the summer," I enquired anxiously, – "when will the summer be here?" "Well," returned my mother-in-law doubtfully, "we must wait for St. Swithin's day, it all depends on what kind of weather we have then." St. Swithin's day came and went in a storm of wind and rain. "I am afraid," confessed my mother-in-law, "that the summer is past, and we shall have no more good weather." And so it turned out. Between showers she and I wandered over the moor and along the banks of the burn, but always with umbrellas in our hands, and generally returning drenched. My husband, who had come to the Highlands solely for the sunshine and bracing air, was condemned to spend most of his time in our small, stuffy sitting-room, with no amusement or occupation other than that afforded by his writing materials. The only books we had with us were two large volumes of the life of Voltaire, which did not tend to raise our already depressed spirits. Even these, removed from us by my husband's parents one dreary Sunday as not being proper "Sabba'-day reading", were annexed by the elder couple, each taking a volume. Thrown entirely on our own resources for amusement we decided to write stories and read them to each other; naturally these tales, coloured by our surroundings, were of a sombre cast.

As my husband was then writing only for our mutual entertainment, without thought of publication, he put his first tale, *Thrawn Janet*, in the vernacular of the country. "I doubt if this is good enough for my father to hear," he said, as he began reading it to me . . . That evening is as clear in my memory as though it were yesterday – the dim light of our one candle, with the acrid smell of the wick we forgot to snuff, the shadows in the corners of the "lang, laigh, mirk chalmer, perishing cauld," the driving rain on the roof close above our heads, and the gusts of wind that shook our windows . . . sent a "cauld grue" along my bones. By the time the tale was finished my husband had fairly frightened himself, and we crept down the stairs clinging hand-in-hand like two scared children. My father-in-law's unexpected praise . . . caused my husband to regard it with more favour; and after a few corrections he began to feel that he had "pulled it off" . . . *The Merry Men* was soon under way . . . The continual cold rains having seriously affected my husband's health, we finally left Kinnaird Cottage, and by the doctor's orders settled for a time in Braemar . . . '
(*See also* **Braemar**)

**'Playful Stevenson, The'**, (*see* **Bok, Edward W.**)

**Plays,** first collected together in *The Edinburgh Edition* 1894–98; Tusitala Edition *24*
Written in collaboration with W.E. Henley: *Deacon Brodie, or the Double Life; Beau Austin; Admiral Guinea; Macaire* (*see also* **Three Plays**)
Written in collaboration with Mrs. R.L. Stevenson: *The Hanging Judge*. (*See also* individual entries for these)
Projected plays with W.E. Henley (1884) never written: 'The Admirable Crichton: Romantic comedy in Five Acts'. 'Ajax: Drama in Four Acts'. According to Henley (*Pall Mall Magazine*, 25 December 1901) 'our hero Sir Robert Trelawney, an elderly Anglo-Indian engineer who – brave, honest, magnificent – plays the unconscious criminal as one of several directors in a fraudulent bank.' 'The Atheists: Comedy'. 'Farmer George: Historical Play [on reign of Mad George III] in Five Acts'. 'Honour and Arms: Drama in Three Acts and Five Tableaux', described

by Henley as 'English, Jacobitish romance'. 'King of Clubs: Drama in Four Acts'. Henley took the idea from Dickens' *Old Curiosity Shop*. 'Madame Fate: Drama in a Prologue and Four Acts'. 'Marcus Aurelius: Historical play'. 'The Mother-in-Law: Drama' (which was, according to Henley, to have been a tragedy). 'Pepys Diary: Comedy'. 'The Passing of Vanderdecken: Legend (!) in Four Acts'. 'The Gunpowder Plot: Historical Play'.

**'Plea for Gas Lamps, A'**, an essay, first published in *London*, 27 April 1878; in book form in *Virginibus Puerisque*, 1881; Tusitala Edition *25*

**'Plot in Stevenson, The'**, (*see* **Brown, Hilton**)

**Plotz, Helen** (ed.), *Poems of Robert Louis Stevenson,* Crowell, New York, 1973

**'Poe, Edgar Allan'**, (*see* **'Works of Edgar Allan Poe, The'**)

**Poems,** first collected together in *Edinburgh Edition* 1894–98; with additional material in Tusitala Edition *22,23* (*See also* Part 5 (Poems))

**'Poems Hitherto Unpublished'**, (with an introduction by George S. Hellman and William P. Trent) first published by Boston Bibliophile Society, 1916

**Poems of Robert Louis Stevenson** (*see* **Plotz, Helen**)

**'Poets and Poetry of Scotland, The'** an essay, first published in *The Academy*, 12 February 1876; collected in Tusitala Edition *28*

**Poet's Tree at R.L. Stevenson's House in San Francisco,** (*see* **Davies, A.H.**)

**Polynesian Dress**

On the advice of Belle, Fanny's daughter, who had been living with her artist husband Joe Strong in Honolulu, Fanny, 'Aunt Maggie' Stevenson and the maid Valentine invested in a wardrobe of garments of cool lawn or muslin which the missionaries had thrust upon the male and female nudity of the natives. These garments consisted of a *holoku*, a long loose gown flowing waistless from a yoke and underneath a *muumuu*, a straight chemise flounced around the hem which also did service as a nightgown. Fanny found this fashion extremely comfortable as it made corsets unnecessary and she wore it in one style or another for the rest of her life. It was the perfect cruising costume; the men wore singlets and trousers, and all went barefoot. Even the conventional Edinburgh-bred Maggie Stevenson succumbed to the fashion and is described by Will Low as, '...the demure Scots lady, seated erect in a chair, wherever procurable, spick and span, as though newly issued from her Heriot Row home for an afternoon visit to a friend of her own social rank, [the

*holoku*] coiffed by the widow's cap which became her so well. This cap
she carried...even on journeys in an open boat around the islands, in a
box, ready to don on the first occasion of ceremony...' A large box
accompanied her travels and there was always a fresh cap ready, with
organdie streamers starched and immaculately ironed. She found the
natives as intriguing as they did her and wrote: 'They were in every state
of undress. The display of legs was something we were not accustomed
to; but as they were all tattooed in the most wonderful patterns, it really
looked quite as if they were wearing open work silk tights.'

The natives were further intrigued by the sights of the *Casco*'s
interior. Fourteen of them swarmed over the deck while the Captain
and the menfolk had gone ashore. According to Mrs. Stevenson: 'We
women were a little frightened.' However, they were interested only in
the luxuries, posturing before mirrors, fingering velvets and shining
brass. One lady was so overwhelmed, she lifted her *holoku* and 'bare-
breeched' rubbed her tattooed posterior against the crimson velvet
cushions.

The King of Hawaii imitated European royalty in his splendid garden
parties, the ladies arriving in smart carriages with liveried servants, and
dressed in the latest Paris fashions; wasp-waisted gowns of satin and
lace, complete with parasols and 'wheel' hats. One day, however, when
an unexpected rain-storm had everyone rushing for shelter, the ladies
calmly removed their elegant clothes, bundled them into calabashes for
protection, and sprinted across the lawns to the Palace *au naturel*. In
Samoa, the Vailima servants on special occasions wore striped blazers
and *lavalavas* (loin-cloths) of Royal Stewart tartan, which Stevenson
chose specially to blend with their skin hues. Thus they served dinner
and greeted the Vailima guests. On such occasions Fanny would
abandon the *holoku* for grey silk, or black velvet (purchased in Sydney).
At her side, Stevenson was gravely elegant in starched white mess
jacket, pleated Sydney-made silk shirt, black trousers and wearing
pumps on his slender feet. He wrote, 'Slovenly youth, all right – not
slovenly age. So really now I am pretty spruce...fresh shave, silk socks,
O, a great sight.' He presented a less elegant sight on his trips to Apia, in
a battered white yachting cap, survivor of the Pacific cruises, white
shirt, white trousers tucked into lace-up high boots. And his 'at home'
dress was as little as possible and always barefoot.

**Poor, Henry,** Stevenson's nearest neighbour at Waikiki. Half-native, a
   local politician, he interested Stevenson in Hawaiian, and thence in
   Samoan, affairs

*Poor Stevenson, This',* (*see* **Ridge, Antonia**)

**'Poor Thing, The',** a fable, Tusitala Edition 5 (*see also* **Fables**)

**'Popular Authors'**, an essay, first published in *Scribner's Magazine*, July 1888; collected in Tusitala Edition *28*

*'Popularity of Robert Louis Stevenson, The'*, (*see* **Chambers Journal**)

*'Porto Bello Gold'*, (*see* **Smith, Arthur D. Howden**)

*Portrait of a Rebel, Robert Louis Stevenson*, (*see* **Aldington, Richard**)

*'Posthumous Works of Robert Louis Stevenson'*, (*see* **Gwynn Stephen**)

**Powell, Mr.**, English chemist with a desire to write, and a pharmacy conveniently situated close to La Solitude, at Hyères

**Pratt, Tinsley,** *Alan Breac Stewart and his Associates*. With Some Account of Scottish Soldiers under French Kings; 1916. Interesting for Stevenson's interpretation of this character in *Kidnapped*

**'Prayers Written for Family Use at Vailima'**, first published in *Edinburgh Edition* 1896; Tusitala Edition *21*
(*See* Part 6 (Radio))

**'Preface, By Way of Criticism'**, an essay, first published in *Familiar Studies of Men and Books*, 1882; Tusitala Edition *27*

*Presbyterian Pirate: A Portrait of Stevenson*, (*see* **Dalglish, Doris N.**)

**Prideaux, Col. W.F.**, *A Bibliography of the Works of Robert Louis Stevenson*, The first comprehensive account of the collected works. Hollings, London, and Scribner's, New York, 1917; *Stevenson at Hyères*, privately printed, 1912

**Prince Otto,** a novel, first published in *Longman's Magazine*, 7 instalments April-October 1885; in book form, Chatto & Windus, London, 1885; Tusitala Edition *4*

> The story is set in an imaginary German principality. Prince Otto and his estranged wife, Princess Seraphina, sort out their domestic and national differences against a background of intrigue and unscrupulous courtiers.
> Dedicated to Nellie Vandegrift (*see* **Sanchez, Nellie Vandegrift**). Stevenson received £100 for this story from Chatto & Windus, although he had asked for £250.
> The first chapter was written at Kingussie, Scotland in August 1882, the bulk at Hyères and in all the writing took 'about five months' . . .
> 'OTTO was my hardest effort for I wished to do something swell, which did not quite come off. Whole chapters were written as often as five or six times, and one chapter, that of the Countess and the Princess, eight times by me and once by my wife — my wife's version was second last'.
> (*See also* **Stevenson, Bob**)

*'Private Life of R.L.S., The'*, (*see* **Knight, Alanna**)

*Private Press Ventures of Samuel Lloyd Osbourne and Robert Louis Stevenson*, (*see* **Hart, James D.**)

*Prose Writings of Robert Louis Stevenson, The, A Guide.* (*see* **Swearingen, Roger C.**)

**'Protest on Behalf of Boer Independence'** an essay, first published in *Hitherto Unpublished Prose Writings*, Boston Bibliophile Society, 1921; Tusitala Edition 28

Stevenson wrote to W.E. Henley, (National Library of Scotland, Edinburgh), 'This is a damned, dirty, foul job of ours in the Transvaal . . .', and he began an indignant letter to a newspaper (which was not sent), 'I am literally grilling in my own blood about this wicked business . . . It is no affair of ours if the Boers are capable of self-government or not . . . that we have been fairly beaten is occasion for honourable submission'. This was a characteristic attitude of Stevenson, who considered all politics a dirty business, whether men fought for power in South Africa, Ireland, or the South Seas.
(*See also* **Curtin Family; Gladstone, William Ewart; Mataafa, 'King'**)

**Proudfit, Isabel,** *The Treasure Hunter: The Story of Robert Louis Stevenson*, Julian Messner, New York, n.d.

**'Providence and the Guitar'**, a short story, first published in *London*, 2–23 November, 1878; in book form in *New Arabian Nights*, 1882; Tusitala Edition 1

*Psychopathology of Tuberculosis The,* (*see* **Munro, D.G. Macleod**)

**'Pulvis et Umbra'**, an essay, first published in *Scribner's Magazine*, April 1888; Tusitala Edition 26

# Q

*Quarterly Review,* contained an anonymous article entitled 'Robert Louis Stevenson', April 1895

*Questions at Issue, (see* **Gosse, Sir Edmund William**)

'**Quiet Corner of England, A**', a review, first published in *The Academy,* 5 December 1874; Tusitala Edition *28*

**Quiller-Couch, Sir Arthur Thomas,** (1863-1944), *Adventures in Criticism,* Cassell, London, 1896

He completed the unfinished *St. Ives,* and wrote of Stevenson, 'Put away books and paper and pen . . . Stevenson is dead, and now there is nobody left to write for'.
(*See* **St. Ives**)

# R

**Rackin, Martin,** (*see* **Tennant, Kylie**)

**Raeburn,** (*see* **'Some Portraits by Raeburn'**)

**'Rajah's Diamond, The',** four stories, first published (with 'The Suicide Club') as 'Latter-Day Arabian Nights', 17 weekly instalments, *London*, 8 June–26 October 1878, for which Stevenson received forty-two guineas; in book form in *New Arabian Nights*, 1882; Tusitala Edition *1*

Further adventures of Prince Florizel (from 'The Suicide Club') and others, with the theft and recovery of the Rajah's Diamond which contaminates the lives of all those into whose hands it falls. (See also Part 6 (TV))

**Raleigh, Sir Walter,** *Robert Louis Stevenson*, lecture to the Royal Institution of Great Britain, 17 May 1895. Edward Arnold, London, 1895

**'R.A.M.S.'** *(Obituary of Bob Stevenson)*, (*See* **Henley, William Ernest**)

**Ramsay, M.P.,** 'A Model of R.L.S.? Adam Blackadder's Flight from Sweden', *Scots Magazine*, 1939

**'Random Memories of Robert Louis Stevenson',** (*see* **McIntosh, R.J.**)

**'Reader, The',** a fable, Tusitala Edition *5* (*see also* **Fables**)

**Real Robert Louis Stevenson, The,** (*see* **Thompson, Francis**)

**'Real Treasure Island, The',** (*see* **England, G.A.; Stewart, George R.**)

**Recollections of a Happy Life,** (*see* **Symonds, John Addington**)

**Recollections of a Visit to Samoa and the Home of Mr. R.L. Stevenson** (*see* **'J.E.B.B.'**)

**Recollections of Robert Louis Stevenson in the Pacific,** (*see* **Johnstone, Arthur**)

**Records of a Family of Engineers,** first published in *Edinburgh Edition* 1896; Tusitala Edition *19*

In Vailima, Stevenson regarded himself as 'chieftain' and became particularly anxious to unearth a 'Clan Stevenson'. To this end he carried on various research correspondence.
(*See also* **Bay, J. Christian; Hill, Robin Armstrong; Roughead, William**); Part 4 (Letter to R.A.M. Stevenson))

'**Reflections and Remarks on Human Life**', an essay, first published in *Edinburgh Edition* 1898; Tusitala Edition *26*

**Reid, Alex**, 'R.L.S.: A Psychological Novelist?', *Scotland's Magazine*, January 1960

**Reid, Denis Captain,** Master of the trading schooner *Equator* in which the Stevensons voyaged from Honolulu to the Gilbert Islands in June 1889 and had their first sight of Samoa on 7 December 1889

Captain Reid was young, and described by Fanny as 'a small fiery Scotch-Irishman, full of amusing eccentricities, and always a most gay and charming companion'. He combined skill of seamanship with skill at draughts, which delighted the Stevensons, and he wore his national bonnet even in the tropics, where he was also addicted to spirited but tuneless renderings of 'Annie Laurie' and 'In the Gloaming'.

'*Relics of St. Giles and a Glimpse of R.L.S. at Swanston*', (*see* **Fothergill, G.A.**)

*Religion of R.L.Stevenson, The*, (*see* **Masson, Rosaline**)

'**Reminiscences of Colinton Manse**', an essay, first published in Balfour's *Life*, 1901; probably contributed to 'The Manse' (*See also* '**Manse, The**')

'*Reminiscence by One who Knew R.L.S., A*', (*see* **Westminster Gazette**)

'*Renown of Stevenson, The*' (*see* **Hewlett, Maurice**)

**Requiem,** on Stevenson's grave in Samoa (*see* Plate 24):
        1850 ROBERT LOUIS STEVENSON 1894
            Under the wide and starry sky,
            Dig the grave and let me lie.
            Glad did I live and gladly die,
            And I laid me down with a will.

            This be the verse you grave for me:
            Here he lies where he longed to be,
            Home is the sailor, home from sea,
            And the hunter home from the hill.

The original version of this Requiem appears in a letter to Sidney Colvin from San Francisco, dated February 1880 (*Letters*, Tusitala Edition *32*, p.108), when Stevenson had few expectations of survival. He ends the letter declaring his fascination with the seamy side of the city, ' . . . were I stronger, I should try to sugar in with some of the leaders: a chield amang 'em takin' notes; one, who kept a brothel, I reckon, before she started socialist, particularly interests me. If I am right as to her early industry, you know she would be sure to adore me. I have been all my days a dead hand at a harridan, I never saw the one yet that could resist me. When I die of consumption, you can put that on my tomb.

> Sketch of my tomb follows:—
> ROBERT LOUIS STEVENSON
> BORN 1850, OF A FAMILY OF ENGINEERS,
> DIED....
> "NITOR AQUIS."
> HOME IS THE SAILOR, HOME FROM SEA,
> AND THE HUNTER HOME FROM THE HILL.
> You, who pass this grave, put aside hatred; love kindness; be all services remembered in your heart and all offences pardoned; and as you go down again among the living, let this be your question: can I make some one happier this day before I lie down to sleep? Thus the dead man speaks to you from the dust: you will hear no more from him.

Who knows, Colvin, but I may thus be more use when I am buried than ever when I was alive? The more I think of it, the more earnestly do I desire this. I may perhaps try to write it better some day; but that is what I want in sense. The verses are from a beayootiful poem by me.

R.L.S.

**'Retrospect, A'**, an essay, first published in Edinburgh Edition, 1896; Tusitala Edition *30*

**'Return of Long John Silver, The, being a Sequel to Treasure Island'**, (*see* **Connell, John**)

**Review of Reviews,** contained a review of Graham Balfour's 'Life of Robert Louis Stevenson', 1901

**Reviews by Stevenson of 'Shamrock and Rose'**, **'Kilcorran'**, **'Mottiscliffe'**, **'Against Her Will'**, first published in *The Academy*, 2 August 1877; Tusitala Edition *28*

**Rice, Richard Ashley,** *Robert Louis Stevenson: How to Know Him*, Bobbs-Merrill, Indianapolis, n.d.

**Ricklefs, Roger,** *The Mind of Robert Louis Stevenson*, Arno Press, New York, 1962

**Ridge, Antonia,** 'This Poor Stevenson', *Good Housekeeping*, 1946

**Ridley, Maurice Roy,** *R.L. Stevenson: a selection and commentary*, Sheldonian English Series, 1953.

**Ringaroona, H.M.S.**

When the ship came into Apia in October 1892, to pick up sealed orders, this gave rise to speculation that they contained instructions for the deportation of Stevenson for his support of the 'rebels'. Stevenson took the initiative and called on the *Ringaroona*'s commander and made friends with the ship's company so that he would have a comfortable voyage if the worst came to the worst – which it did not, fortunately.

**Rise and Fall of the Man of Letters, The,** (*see* **Gross, John**)

**Rivenburgh, Eleanor,** 'Stevenson in Hawaii', *Bookman*, New York, October-December 1917. Deals with writing of 'The Bottle Imp' in particular

**R.L.S./Teuila,** a collection of poems by Stevenson, privately printed for Isobel Strong by the Gillis Press, 1899

**'Road of Loving Hearts to Stevenson's Tomb, The',** (*see* **Carothers, Alva**)

**Road of the Loving Heart**

J.C. Furnas in *Voyage to Windward* states, 'This has often been stickily misinterpreted as a matter of all Samoa thanking nice, kind Tusitala for his help . . . it was nothing of the sort. Louis's championing of the Mataafas was not likely to rouse gratitude among Malietoas or Tamaseses, so the Road of the Loving Heart was the work of a single faction in temporary eclipse. But – neither must this be lost sight of – the extraordinary nature of the gesture points to extraordinary emotions affecting the chiefs concerned. Faction they might be . . . but this was a thing that they would not have done spontaneously, or even voluntarily, for any other white man . . .'

The signboard at the highway entrance of the road states, 'We bear in mind the surpassing kindness of Mr. R.L. Stevenson and his loving care during our tribulations while in prison. We have therefore prepared a type of gift that will endure without decay for ever – the road we have constructed'. The names of 22 Samoans follow. Six weeks later some of these men helped carry their beloved Tusitala up Mt. Vaea for burial. (*See* **Carothers, Alva; Thyne, C.A.M.; Mataafa, 'King'**)

**'Roads',** an essay, first published in *The Portfolio*, December 1873; Tusitala Edition 25

**Robert, Louis,** (*sic*) Lloyd Osbourne's tutor during the Stevensons' stay at Hyères

**'Robert Louis Stevenson: A Reminiscence',** (*see* **Lowe, Charles**)

**Robert Louis Stevenson Club, The,** Honorary Secretary: A.J.R.

Ferguson, W.S., 5 Albyn Place, Edinburgh EH2 4NJ; no regular meetings apart from an annual luncheon on or about Stevenson's birthdate, 15 November
(*See also* **Stevensonian, The**)

**Robert Louis Stevenson Companion,** (*see* **Calder, Jenni**)

**Robert Louis Stevenson in California,** (*see* **Osbourne, Katharine Durham**)

**Roberts, M.,** 'With Stevenson last May', *Saturday Review*, 12 January 1895

**Robertson, J.H.,** (*see* **Connell, John**)

**Robertson, Margaret H.,** 'Robert Louis Stevenson in Wick', *Wick Literary Society Magazine*, Christmas 1903

**Roch, Valentine,** maid who joined Stevenson household in Hyères
Born in Switzerland into a large French family, her father was a local railway employee. Untrained, she learned quickly and was, according to Lloyd, 'a charming girl, far above her class, with a sparkling sense of humour, who reviewed the whole neighbourhood and nightly brought its annals up to date'. Strong and blonde, Stevenson called her 'Joe' when she was good and 'Thomasina' when she was in a bad mood. She soon learned English and in her six years with them at home and abroad, she joined the circle of family literary criticism. However, she occasionally shocked British visitors by exclaiming 'My God', a literal translation of 'Mon Dieu' and delivered in an equally casual manner. Although sparks flew from the kitchen in lively encounters with her sharp-tongued mistress, when Valentine became ill Fanny nursed her devotedly. At Bournemouth, when Fanny was absent, Valentine defied the local gossips by sleeping in Stevenson's bedroom by the fire, to be instantly on hand should he have a haemorrhage during the night. Accepted as one of the family, she endured all the hardships of seasickness during their South Seas voyages. When at last they reached Honolulu, she helped them settle into a temporary home and then abruptly took a steamer back to California. Stevenson hinted to Colvin that it was 'the usual tale of the maid on board the yacht'. Valentine took a housekeeper's job in a San Francisco hotel, married and called her only son Louis.

**Rodin, Auguste,** (1840-1917). The sculptor was a close friend of Stevenson and they corresponded in French. Stevenson was given a plaster cast of the famous 'Le Printemps' by him as a gift for the house at Vailima. (See Part 4 (Letters))

**Romantic Nineties, The,** (*see* **Le Gallienne, Richard**)

**'Romantic Stories of Books, The: Treasure Island',** (*see* **Winterich, J.T.**)

'**Rosa Quo Locorum**', an essay, first published in *Edinburgh Edition* 1896;
Tusitala Edition *30*

**Rosebery, A.P. Primrose, Lord,** (1847-1929), 'Robert Louis Stevenson' in *Miscellanies, Literary and Historical,* Vol. 2 Aeneas Mackay,
Stirling, 1921

**Rosenblatt, L.M.,** 'The Writer's Dilemma: A Case History and
Critique of R.L.S.', *International Journal of Ethics,* Vol. 46, 1936

**Ross, Dr. Fairfax,** friend of Belle Strong who attended Stevenson in
Sydney
Visiting London later, he confided in Sidney Colvin that Stevenson's
'weak lung is doing its best to recover, and would almost certainly do so,
if he gave it any chance; by freedom, that is, from exposure, malaria,
worry and overwork; all of which things, he says, are doing him harm,
so as to make the issue doubtful; but under good conditions, he might yet
get quite well and live as long as any of us.' Referring to Fanny
Stevenson's mysterious breakdown at this time (1893), Dr. Ross
considered her, 'ill . . . both as to body and mind'

**Ross, John A.,** 'The Early Home of Robert Louis Stevenson', *Good
Words,* March 1895

**Roughead, William,** 'A Gathering of the "Fragments"', an essay in *A
Cadger's Creel (see* **Douglas, Sir George**)

**Royal Scottish Society of Arts** (*see* '**On a New Form of Intermittent
Light for Lighthouses**')

**Royat, France** In the Prefatory Note to *Black Arrow* Fanny Stevenson
describes this spa near Clermont-Ferrand as 'an enchanting little
watering-place . . . Caesar himself had bathed in the healing water of
the Royat springs . . . The baths were more or less arsenical; some so
strongly impregnated that they were dangerous, and only given out to
drink, in limited quantities, by virtue of the doctor's prescription. One
*source* had a flavour that reminded you of weak chicken broth, and
another effervesced, when you plunged into it, like champagne. There
were two ways to reach the baths from our hotel; we might choose an
exceedingly steep street, or go more directly down an immense flight of
precipitous stairs. As it was our stately, though uncomfortable, custom
to be carried in sedan chairs, we generally went by way of the street.
There had already been accidents on the stairs; should a bearer slip or
lose his hold the consequences would be disastrous. It was against the
law for chairs to be taken down the stairs; but if the bearers had several
fares in view they were apt to ignore the regulation. When you ordered

a chair . . . it was brought into your bedroom. You stepped inside, usually in your dressing-gown; the door was closed and the curtains drawn until you arrived at your destination, where you alighted in front of your bath-tub. The privacy was absolute and the discomfort extreme. As you could not see out, you were always nervously uncertain what route your bearer had taken, and you might unexpectedly find yourself in the middle of the forbidden stairs. The air space was limited, and in warm weather the interior of the chair became very stuffy. There were two bearers to each chair, who went at a jog-trot, purposely refraining from keeping step, which would swing their burden from side to side. The uneven movement gave a jolting effect that was the most tiring thing imaginable.

Here amid these romantic, almost theatrical surroundings, *The Black Arrow* was continued . . .'

(*See also* **Black Arrow, The**)

## Ruedi, Dr. Karl

In the autumn of 1880, the Stevensons left Scotland for Davos, where the already famous Dr. Ruedi had established a clinic for consumptives. Stevenson was put on a diet stressing milk and red meat, plus the wine of the country, which was considered particularly beneficial. Stevenson found this part of the diet gratifying and developed a taste for good red wine which he was never to lose. He was less delighted at being forbidden cigarettes entirely and allowed to smoke only three pipes per day and indulge in only three hours' writing. Dr. Ruedi assured Fanny that the cure would take eighteen months but when it became obvious that a second winter in Davos would put a considerable strain on both the Stevensons' health, the doctor recommended as an alternative the South of France, 'fifteen miles as the crow flies from the sea, and if possible near a fir-wood'. Eventually he approved the move to the United States on the grounds that he had seen lung-rotten farmers completely restored to vigorous life by the mountain air of Colorado.

(*See also* **Davos**)

**Ryan, J. Tighe,** 'A Gossip about Robert Louis Stevenson', *The Antipodean*, Sydney 1894. Stevenson's visits to Sydney, 1890–93

# S

**Safford, Mrs. W.E.,** (*see Catalogue (5)*)

**Safroni-Middleton, A,** 'A New View of R.L.S.', *John o'London's Weekly*, 20 January 1950; 'With Stevenson in Old Samoa', *Journal of the Robert Louis Stevenson Club*, London, May, 1950

**St. Gaudens, Augustus,** (1848-1907)

Born in Dublin, a French shoemaker's son, he was taken to America as a baby. He trained as a cameo-cutter and later studied sculpture in Paris and Rome, being greatly influenced by the Italian renaissance. Returning to America, he was acclaimed as the foremost sculptor of his time. Will H. Low introduced him to Stevenson and they became firm friends. In Manasquan, St. Gaudens began a medallion of Stevenson, in his favourite old red poncho, cigarette in hand. This original pose was later changed to 'pen in hand' for the reproduction in St. Giles' Cathedral, Edinburgh.
(*See* Part 4 (Letters); Plates 26 and 27)

**St. Germain, France**

In the spring of 1881, Stevenson, worn-out by the sterility of Davos, decided to risk another summer in Scotland with his parents. En route, in a wave of nostalgia Fanny and he visited the forest of Fontainebleau, but faulty drains and an epidemic scare sent them scurrying onward to Paris. There, in traditional manner, Stevenson spent their last sou on an antique watch Fanny had admired – and then, with Fanny at her wits' end, he came upon an uncashed cheque in the pocket of an old coat. They were captivated by St. Germain, where for the first time, they heard a nightingale sing. Their buoyancy did not last long; Stevenson caught a chill, which was followed by another haemorrhage. He was penniless and unable to meet the hotel bill, and the landlord became threatening, suspicious of Stevenson's eccentric wardrobe, and his coloured flannel shirt. The situation was saved by a donation from the elder Stevensons in Edinburgh and their dignified exit from the hotel, 'left the landlord in the belief that he had turned from his doors the eccentric son of a wealthy English nobleman'.

**St. Ives,** a novel first published in *Pall Mall Magazine*, London,

November 1896 to November 1897; *McClure's Magazine*, March–
November 1897; and in book form by Scribner's, New York, 1897,
Chatto & Windus, London, 1898; Tusitala Edition *15*

The adventures of the Vicomte Anne de Kéroual de Saint-Yves (alias
Champdivers and Edward Ducie), an aristocratic French prisoner in the
Napoleonic Wars held captive in Edinburgh Castle. He escapes and
after sundry adventures, including a romantic encounter with Miss
Flora Gilchrist, he succeeds in regaining his inheritance.

'The following tale was taken down from Mr. Stevenson's dictation by
his step-daughter and amanuensis, Mrs. Strong, at intervals between
January 1893 and October 1894. About six weeks before his death he laid
the story aside to take up *Weir of Hermiston*. The thirty chapters of *St. Ives*
which he had written (the last few of them apparently unrevised)
brought the tale within sight of its conclusion, and the intended course
of the remainder was known in outline to Mrs. Strong. For the benefit of
those readers who do not like a story to be left unfinished, the delicate
task of supplying the missing chapters has been entrusted to Mr. Quiller-
Couch, whose work begins at Chapter XXXI.' (From Tusitala Edition,
*15*.)

St. Ives was written against a background of Stevenson's ill-health and
the Samoan war. January 1893 began in Samoa with an epidemic of
influenza brought by a passing ship; Stevenson caught a severe cold and
although forbidden to talk or make the least physical effort, he had two
slight haemorrhages. His mother and Lloyd Osbourne took turns
entertaining their most impatient patient in the mornings. In the
afternoons, he played draughts and halma with Belle Strong, who knew
how he longed to continue *St. Ives*. During her schooldays, Belle had
learned the deaf-and-dumb alphabet. Stevenson mastered this new
technique quickly and with its assistance triumphantly dictated fifteen
pages of the manuscript.

There were other dramas beyond Vailima's threshold. At family
prayers, a passing band of hostile warriors, with blackened faces stared
in at them through the open windows, drowning their prayers with the
strange, savage beat of native war drums. One morning during the
dictating of *St. Ives*, Belle Strong paused anxiously at some interruption
outside and asked, 'Louis, have we a pistol or a gun in the house that will
shoot?' 'No,' he replied calmly, 'but we have friends on both sides', and
he returned to the story.

(*See also* Part 6 (Media))

**St. John's Presbyterian Church, San Francisco,** Stevenson and Fanny
Osbourne were married by the church's minister, Rev. Dr. W. Scott,
on 19 May 1880

(*See also* **Oakland**)

**St. Marcel,** the suburb of Marseilles which was the Stevensons' first home in France.
(*See also* **Campagne Defli**)

**Saintsbury, George,** *A History of Nineteenth-Century Literature (1780-1895),* Macmillan, London, 1896. Includes assessment of Stevenson as a writer
(*See* Part 4 (Letters))

**'Salvini's *Macbeth*',** an essay, first published in *The Academy,* 15 April 1876; Tusitala Edition *28*

**Samoa**

The Stevensons' introduction to Samoa was brought about by Belle Osbourne's husband, Joe Strong, who had been sent there by King Kalakaua as official artist with a Hawaiian delegation. The mission was a farce but the parts played by Joe and the King aroused the Stevensons' interest, especially as there was a good mail steamer service which would make serialisation of *The Wrecker* feasible.

On the morning of 7 December 1889 they had their first sight of the long narrow island of Upolu, mountainous amid thick jungle. The land breeze brought the smell of copra, wood smoke, tropical flowers and fruits, plus the wholesome smell of baking breadfruit on the hot stones. The masts and low rooftops of Apia became visible at the foot of Mt. Vaea and as they entered the bottle-necked coral harbour, the island's only port, they observed the wrecks of foreign warships destroyed in a hurricane earlier that year. Then came the canoes to greet the *Equator,* crewed by brown men and pretty girls garlanded in wreaths and flowers. There was no wharf; they disembarked by clambering over the side and down a steep rope ladder into the whale-boat belonging to Harry J. Moors, an American trader. The islanders who assisted them sang as they pulled for the jetty, behind which the shabby town wandered along the beach, half-concealed by coconut palms. Facing the sea were squat white wooden houses with verandahs, the local 'shops' where the traders lived and sold their wares. There were also several large churches of coral blocks, white-plastered, squatting imposingly among the thatched roofs of the basket-shaped native Samoan houses. Another touch of the white man's civilisation lay in the scattered bars and the long pier and warehouse of the German 'Firm', with its monopoly in trading and planting.

The Stevensons' arrival was greeted with some curiosity. Fanny, in her *holoku,* wore a wide-brimmed native straw hat and carried a guitar, Lloyd Osbourne in addition to his dark glasses now wore big round earrings and carried a fiddle, while Stevenson was carelessly dressed as usual, in calico shirt, cotton trousers and a shabby yachting cap, barefoot. Small wonder that Rev. W.E. Clarke of the London

1. Mrs M. I. Stevenson.
*Mansell Collection*

2. Stevenson as a boy of
seven with his father,
Thomas Stevenson.
*Edinburgh Library photograph*

*Above:*
**3. Alison Cunningham, Stevenson's nurse 'Cummy'.**
*Edinburgh Library photograph*

*Right:*
**4. Stevenson at 26, after a drawing by his wife.**
*Mansell Collection*

5. 8, Howard Place,
Edinburgh, birthplace
of Stevenson,
13 November 1850.
*Mansell Collection*

*Below:*
6. Colinton Manse,
home of Stevenson's
grandfather, Rev. Dr.
Lewis Balfour.
*Mansell Collection*

COLINTON MANSE—AN EARLY HOME OF R.L.S.

**7. 17 Heriot Row, Edinburgh, the Stevenson home from 1857 to 1887.**
*Mansell Collection*

*Below:*
**8. Shop at corner of Antigua Street, Edinburgh, mentioned by Stevenson in 'A Penny Plain and Twopence Coloured'.**
*Mansell Collection*

*Above:*
9. Swanston Cottage, a country retreat for the Stevenson family in the Pentland Hills.
*Mansell Collection*

*Left:*
10. Skerryvore, Bournemouth. '... ivy-covered yellow brick and blue slates and a garden growing towards the brink of steep Alum Chine.'
*Edinburgh Library photograph*

11. Stevenson in 1879, taken after he followed Fanny Osbourne to California.

12. Fanny Osbourne, before
her marriage in 1880.
*Edinburgh Library photograph*

*Right:*
13. The Knox portrait, 1887.
*Mansell Collection*

14. 10 West Street, New York, where Stevenson briefly stayed in
August 1879 *en route* for California.

15. Stevenson House Museum, Monterey, California. Stevenson
lived here from September to December 1879.

**16. Chalet La Solitude,
Hyères, France, 1883-84.**
*Edinburgh Library photograph*

*Below:*
**17. The Stevensons,
Belle Strong and Margaret
Stevenson in Sydney, 1893.**
*Edinburgh Library photograph*

**18. A road near Apia, Samoa.**
*Mansell Collection*

*Below:*
**19. Vailima, Stevenson's house on Samoa.**
*Mansell Collection*

20. Stevenson with (left to right) Lloyd Osbourne,
a Vailima visitor (name unknown), and Samoan
chief Tuimalealiifono.

**21. The Vailima household, 31 July 1892.**
*Left to right:* Joe Strong, Margaret Stevenson, Lloyd Osbourne,
Stevenson and Fanny. Seated in front of Fanny are Belle Strong
and Austin, her son.

*Below:* **22. Another group of family and servants on the Vailima
verandah.**

**23.** The last photograph taken of Stevenson, Vailima, **1894.**

24. One of the panels on Stevenson's tomb, Mount Vaea, Samoa.
'Under the wide and starry sky...'

25. The tomb was constructed, Samoan fashion, from slabs of
cement. The panel bears the words 'The Tomb of Tusitala'
followed by Ruth's words to Naomi, in Samoan, 'Whither thou
goest I will go...'.

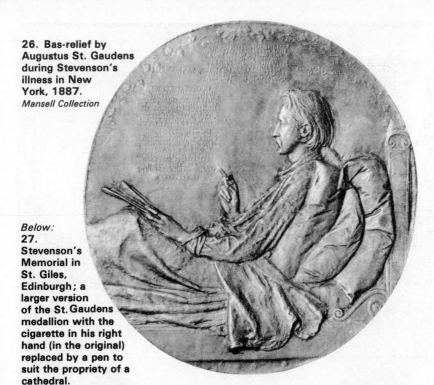

**26. Bas-relief by Augustus St. Gaudens during Stevenson's illness in New York, 1887.**
*Mansell Collection*

*Below:*
**27. Stevenson's Memorial in St. Giles, Edinburgh; a larger version of the St. Gaudens medallion with the cigarette in his right hand (in the original) replaced by a pen to suit the propriety of a cathedral.**
*Edinburgh Library photograph*

·TO REMEMBER
ROBERT·LOVIS
·STEVENSON·
TO BE HONEST·TO BE
KIND·TO EARN A LIT-
TLE·TO SPEND A LIT-
TLE LESS·TO MAKE
VPON THE WHOLE A
FAMILY HAPPIER FOR
HIS PRESENCE·TO RE
NOVNCE WHEN THAT
SHALL BE NECESSARY
AND NOT BE EMBIT
TERED TO KEEP A FEW
FRIENDS BVT THESE
WITHOVT CAPITVLAT
ION·ABOVE ALL ON
THE SAME GRIM CON
DITION TO KEEP FRIE
NDS WITH HIMSELF
HERE IS A TASK FOR
ALL THAT A MAN HAS
OF FORTITVDE AND
DELICACY

28. Stevenson's Memorial in Portsmouth Square, San Francisco.

Missionary Society assumed he was witnessing the arrival of a troupe of
poor out-of-work entertainers hoping to pick up a few dollars
performance money.

Stevenson was intrigued and impressed by the smiling Samoans, the tall
handsome men dressed in what he called 'the kilt', the *lavalava* which the
men wore fastened at the waist. Brown skins were polished with
perfumed coconut oil and the men were tattooed from waist to knee, 'as
if they wore lacy drawers'. The population of white and half-castes was
about three hundred, and two-thirds of these were British, most of the
remainder German. Stevenson bubbled over with delight and enthusiasm. 'It's grand! It's grand!'

After they had settled in Vailima, 'Aunt Maggie' Stevenson, assisted by
Fanny and Belle, founded the Vine-ula Club of Apia, a social organisation for the half-castes, and the Samoan wives of white men. Once a
week they met in Vailima where Fanny was president and the aims were
instruction in the social graces of European society and how to ballroom
dance sedately in Vailima's 'hall'. Criticism and advice were given on
progress and on deportment. Sometimes activities were extended
beyond Vailima and the three ladies would go to 'the village' and give
instructions in various useful or decorative arts and sciences. Alas, the
snobbery of half-castes who objected to the Stevensons' cook being
allowed membership, brought a rapid decline in activities. During 1893-
94 *The Samoa Times* frequently reported social functions at Vailima, 'The
private ball given by Mr. and Mrs. Stevenson at their residence,
Vailima, on Wednesday evening, was a most successful one. The
weather being fine, the guests derived great pleasure from their journey
to and fro, independent of their entertainment. About forty couples
engaged in dancing, which was kept up with great spirit until three
o'clock in the morning. The music was exceptionally good, which
partly accounts for the late hour mentioned. We have not heard of a
single guest who did not enjoy himself or herself, and it therefore must
be said that the hospitable entertainers cannot be otherwise than
gratified at the result of their ball.'

(*See also* **Clarke, Rev. W.E.; German 'Firm', The; Moors, H.J.;
Vailima**; Plate 18)

## Samoa and Scotland

In the Prefatory Note to *Catriona* Fanny Stevenson wrote, 'It might seem
a far cry from Samoa to Scotland, and yet in many ways one recalled the
other. There were days when the clouds driving about the summit of
Mount Vaea dropped in soft grey mist that almost obliterated the
intervening trees; the tinkling of a little rushing stream, and its
accompanying waterfall a few yards from our door, made the illusion so
nearly complete that for a moment my husband would feel himself
transported to his own beloved Scotland. Nor was it the scenery alone

that reminded the exile of his home. The fatherly rule of the Samoan chief, and the loyalty of the clan to a name more than to an individual, were extraordinarily in the Scottish spirit, and the simple dignity of the high chief was the same in both countries. The ramifications of a Scotch family are bewildering to a stranger, who would hardly go beyond a second cousin twice removed in his search for kindred; in Samoa even the most distant relations of an adopted child must not marry within the family of its adoption.

When the war drums sound and the native warriors of the different factions "go to the bush" (which is preliminary to fighting in the islands) the easy discipline of peace is at once discarded; the chief now becomes a real leader of men, his "sons" rendering him an absolute obedience in all things. In times not so remote affairs were so ordered in the Highlands of Scotland. I remember the astonished pride of the native men of our household when they discovered that the crest on our silver was not a meaningless ornament, but a symbol of the family. The large dish covers were thereafter always produced when we had Samoan visitors, and the crest pointed out and explained. Even the fact that my husband's ancestors built lighthouses redounded to the glory of our family; for house-building of any description is one of the fine arts in Samoa, and a most suitable occupation for a chief.'

**Samoa Times, The** (*see* **Samoa**)

**Samoan War**

The Stevensons discovered that Vailima was situated on a historic battlefield at the border between the opposing forces and at any moment they might expect a confrontation upon their very doorstep. They had no reason to fear from either side but were made rather nervous in the knowledge that Samoans took no prisoners. Even a wounded prisoner was instantly decapitated and no exception was made for women. One suspects that Stevenson found exhilaration in such dangerous living, as he wrote to Sidney Colvin on 1 May, 1892 (*Letters*, Tusitala Edition *34*, p.187), 'I have endured some two and forty years without public shame, and had a good time as I did it. If only I could secure a violent death, what a fine success! I wish to die in my boots; no more Land of Counterpane for me. To be drowned, to be shot, to be thrown from a horse, – ay, to be hanged, rather than pass again through that slow dissolution.'

One part of his wish did come true. He did die in his boots – of a cerebral haemorrhage brought about by overwork.

(*See also* **'Footnote to History, A'**; **Mataafa, 'King'**; **Vailima Papers**)

**'Samuel Pepys'**, an essay, first published in *Cornhill Magazine*, July 1881; in book form in *Familiar Studies of Men and Books*, 1882; Tusitala Edition *27*

'**San Carlos Day**', an essay, first published (anonymously) in the *Monterey Californian*, 11 November 1879; reprinted in *Scribner's Magazine*, August 1920 (*See also* **Hart, James D.**)

**Sanchez, Adolfo,** married Fanny's sister, Nellie Vandegrift

Adolfo was a matrimonial prize – the most popular man in Monterey, son of one of the old aristocratic Spanish-Mexican families, who had lost their wealth with the advent of the 'gringos'. Adolfo made his living as the local saloon-keeper, and the marriage was short-lived, for he died of galloping consumption. Nellie was left with a son 'Louie', the same age as her niece Belle's son, Austin Strong.

**Sanchez, Nellie Vandegrift,** Fanny's sister. *The Life of Mrs. Robert Louis Stevenson*, Chatto & Windus, London, 1920; 'Some Stevenson Legends', *Overland Monthly*, January 1930

Stevenson dedicated *Prince Otto*: 'To NELLY VAN DE GRIFT (MRS. ADULFO SANCHEZ, OF MONTEREY): 'At last, after so many years, I have the pleasure of reintroducing you to *Prince Otto*, whom you will remember a very little fellow, no bigger in fact than a few sheets of memoranda written for me by your kind hand. The sight of his name will carry you back to an old wooden house embowered in creepers; [Fanny's house in East Oakland, San Francisco] a house that was far gone in the respectable stages of antiquity and seemed indissoluble from the green garden in which it stood, and that yet was a sea-traveller in its younger days, and had come round the Horn piecemeal in the belly of a ship, and might have heard the seamen stamping and shouting and the note of the boatswain's whistle. It will recall to you the nondescript inhabitants now so widely scattered:– the two horses, the dog and the four cats, some of them still looking in your face as you read these lines; – the poor lady, so unfortunately married to an author; – the China boy, by this time, perhaps, baiting his line by the banks of a river in the Flowery Land; – and in particular the Scot who was then sick apparently unto death, and whom you did so much to cheer and keep in good behaviour. You may remember that he was full of ambitions and designs: so soon as he had his health again completely, you may remember the fortune he was to earn, the journeys he was to go upon, the delights he was to enjoy and confer, and (among other matters) the masterpiece he was to make of *Prince Otto*!
Well, we will not give in that we are finally beaten. We read together in those days the story of Braddock, and how, as he was carried dying from the scene of his defeat, he promised himself to do better another time: a story that will always touch a brave heart, and a dying speech worthy of a more fortunate commander. I try to be of Braddock's mind. I still mean to get my health again; I still purpose, by hook or crook, this book or the next, to launch a masterpiece; and I still intend – somehow, some

time or other – to see your face and to hold your hand. Meanwhile, this little paper traveller goes forth instead, crosses the great seas and the long plains and the dark mountains, and comes at last to your door in Monterey, charged with tender greetings. Pray you, take him in. He comes from a house where (even as in your own) there are gathered together some of the waifs of our company at Oakland; a house – for all its outlandish Gaelic name and distant station – where you are well-beloved.

Skerryvore,                                                                 R.L.S.
Bournemouth
(*See also* **Vandegrift family**)

'**San Francisco**', an essay, first published as 'A Modern Cosmopolis' in *Magazine of Art*, 1883; appeared with 'Monterey' under the joint title of 'The Old and New Pacific Capitals', Edinburgh Edition, 1895; Tusitala Edition *18*

**San Francisco,** Stevenson lodged with Mrs. Carson at 608 Bush Street late 1879 to May 1880 and, while he waited for Fanny's divorce to come through, he earned a few dollars with occasional contributions to the local newspapers. There is a monument to him in Portsmouth Square (*see* Plate 28) and he left these impressions of the city, 'The streets lie straight up and down the hills, and straight across at right angles, these in sun, those in shadow, a trenchant pattern of gloom and glare; and what with the crisp illumination, the sea-air singing in your ears, the chill and glitter, the changing aspects both of things and people, the fresh sights at every corner of your walk – sights of the bay, of Tamalpais, of steep descending streets, of the outspread city – whiffs of alien speech, sailors singing on shipboard, Chinese coolies toiling on the shore, crowds brawling all day in the street before the Stock Exchange – one brief impression follows and obliterates another, and the city leaves upon the mind no general and stable picture, but a profusion of airy and incongruous images, of the sea and shore, the east and west, the summer and the winter'
(*See also* **Carson, Mrs; Oakland; St. John's Presbyterian Church; Plate 28**)

**Saposnik, Irving S.,** *Robert Louis Stevenson.* Twayne's English Authors Series, New York, 1974. Short biography which assesses man and writer

**Saranac (Lake).** In 1887 the Stevensons stayed in this isolated logging and trapping village in the Adirondack Mountains in New York State where Dr. E.L. Trudeau had founded a sanatorium for consumptives. They rented half of a guide-trapper's white wooden cottage, with green shutters and a verandah. Set high on a forested ridge it looked down on the backwoods village of frame houses and log cabins, 'a hatbox on a hill'. One room was converted into a study for Louis, with a garret for visitors. They christened their new abode 'Hunter's Home', and Fanny described the housekeeping as 'very like camp life'. When she learned that cold in Saranac meant '40 below', she went to Montreal and returned with a supply of strange garments made by the Canadian Indians. Their sole purpose was not to pander to vanity but to keep out the cold; shaggy, bulky buffalo coats, huge sealskin boots and monumental fur caps. Stevenson was daunted by the scenery, or lack of it. He found writing difficult when, in order to pace the narrow verandah in search of inspiration, it was necessary to don his entire fur wardrobe, and he was rationed to 'a dash of sleighing' and forbidden to skate.

(*See also* **Bakers (of Saranac); Trudeau, Dr. E.L.**)

**Sargent, John Singer,** (1856-1925) Born in Florence of American parents, he studied painting in Italy and in France, where he first gained recognition. In England, he became the most fashionable portrait painter of his age and was elected an R.A. in 1897. He was introduced to Stevenson by Mr. and Mrs. Charles Fairchild, wealthy Bostonians who commissioned him to paint the 'famous author'. Stevenson described him as 'a charming, simple, clever, honest young man . . . he delighted us'. They were not quite so enthusiastic about Stevenson's likeness, 'a poetical but very chicken-boned figurehead'. The artist shared their feelings but the portrait remains of the tall thin man with the stringy moustache, pacing the dark room, with his wife in the background in Indian dress 'for a touch of colour'.

(*See also* **Charteris, Evan; Fairchild, Mr. and Mrs. Charles**)

**Sarolea, Charles,** *Robert Louis Stevenson and France*, R.L.S. Fellowship, Edinburgh, 1922

**'Satirist, The',** an essay, first published in *Edinburgh Edition* 1896; Tusitala Edition *30*

**Saturday Review,** contained an anonymous article entitled 'Literary Leprosy', 30 November 1901. Refutes W.E. Henley's savage attack on Graham Balfour's official biography of Stevenson

**Savile Club, London,** Stevenson was elected to membership in July 1874, through Sir Sidney Colvin's recommendation rather than his services to literature

This literary club had been founded in 1868 with an informality surprising for the times. One of the rules was that members were obliged to chat with one another without benefit of introduction. Conversation, wit and argument were encouraged and such agreeable necessities of life led Stevenson to make it his 'headquarters' while in London

*School Boys Magazine, The* (*see* **Burlington Lodge Academy**)

**Schultz, Myron G.**, *The Strange Case of Robert Louis Stevenson, Journal of American Medical Association*, 5 April 1971. Suggests that *Jekyll and Hyde* was the result of Stevenson taking cocaine for his respiratory condition

**Schuyler, Montgomery**, 'The Canonisation of Stevenson', *Century Magazine*, 1899

**Schwob, Marcel**, (1867–1905), French writer and scholar; he did research on François Villon and translated *Hamlet* and *Moll Flanders*. 'R.L.S.', *New Review*, February 1895. He corresponded with Stevenson and translated some of his works into French
(*See also* Part 4 (Letters))

*'Scotland, Stevenson and Mr. Henley'*, (*see* **Wallace, William**)

*'Scotland's Lament (for R.L.S.)'*, (*See* **Barrie, Sir James Matthew**)

*Scotland's S.M.T. Magazine*, Stevenson Centenary Number, November 1950

**Scott, Dr. Thomas Bodley,** receives particular mention for his services to Stevenson in Skerryvore, among the many doctors to whom 'Underwoods' is dedicated
(*See* Part 4 (Letters))

**Scott, Rev. Dr. W.**, (*see* **St. John's Presbyterian Church**)

**Scott, Sir Walter,** (1771-1832)
His novels coloured Stevenson's boyhood and the discovery, during his membership of the Speculative Society of Edinburgh University, that Sir Walter, his favourite novelist, had his own ill-spelled minutes of a 'Spec. Soc.' meeting framed on the walls of the 'snug room' added to his delight. He planned to include Scott in the projected 'Four Great Scotsmen' in the company of Burns, Hume and Knox. Conscious that the financial burden of Vailima was to him what Abbotsford had been to Scott, he wrote to Colvin (Letters, Tusitala Edition *34*, p.166), 'Is not this Babylon the Great which I have builded? Call it *Subpriorsford*'

*Scott and Scotland* (*see* **Muir, Edwin**)

**'Scott's Voyage on the Lighthouse Yacht'**, an essay, first published in *Scribner's Magazine*, October 1893. Contains reminiscences of Sir Walter Scott's tour of northern lighthouses as Sheriff of Selkirk

*Scottish Hogmanay Annual 1950-51,* R.L. Stevenson Centenary Number

**'Scottish Rivers',** an essay, first published in *The Academy,* 15 August 1874; Tusitala Edition *28*

**Scottish Thistle Club of Honolulu,** made Stevenson an honorary chieftain and he proudly wore the tiny thistle in his lapel. A speech delivered in October 1893, published in the *Pacific Commercial Advertiser,* refers to 'the long brawl which is Scottish history'.

**Scott-Moncrieff, George,** *Robert Louis Stevenson,* Gateway Editions, Chicago, 1959

**Scribner, Charles,** head of New York publishing firm, Charles Scribner's Sons. When Stevenson arrived in New York in 1887. Charles Scribner offered him $3,500 for twelve monthly contributions to their *Scribner's Magazine* and offered to buy *The Black Arrow,* voluntarily paying royalties for the earlier books published, although no international copyright was involved. Stevenson was delighted and jubilantly signed a contract giving Scribner's rights in all his work in the United States. Other publishers were interested. McClure brought an offer from Joseph Pulitzer of $10,000 for a year's weekly essays for New York *World.* Later, visiting Stevenson at Saranac, he made an offer on behalf of his own newspaper syndicate *McClure's Magazine* of $8,000 for a projected sequel to *Kidnapped.* The agreement signed, Stevenson remembered too late that he had already signed a contract with Scribner's. Promptly he wrote an apology to McClure, confessing that his absent-mindedness regarding business matters extended to forgetting to sell American rights in *Jekyll and Hyde,* so that this story was constantly pirated. Scribner was very displeased. Tough, hard-headed editors like himself and Sam McClure (who reported Stevenson's reaction to his offer was "he didn't feel he ought to take so much money, and was he worth it? . . . He was unlike any other author I ever met . . .") could hardly be expected to realise they were dealing with a writer who thrust cheques into coat pockets and repeatedly forgot to cash those on his desk, scratching through piles of paper in a frantic search when Fanny declared that they were unable to meet current bills. (*See* **Bok, Edward W.; Burlingame, Roger; McClure, S.;** Part 4 (Letters))

*Scribner's Magazine* published many of Stevenson's essays, etc., between 1879 and 1882; also serialised *The Wrecker* and *The Master of Ballantrae* (1891–92)

**Sea Cook, The,** (*see* **Treasure Island**)

**Seaton, Jim,** (*see* **Nimmo, Ian and Seaton, Jim**)

**Seed, J.**

In 1875, during difficult days with his parents, there came a visitor to 17 Heriot Row, Mr. Seed, a New Zealand governor, who kept young Stevenson up until dawn with wondrous tales of the South Seas, especially Samoa, known to be ideal for sufferers from respiratory diseases. Stevenson wrote to Mrs. Sitwell from Edinburgh in 1875 (*Letters*, Tusitala Edition *31*, p.235) 'beautiful places, green forever; perfect climate; perfect shapes of men and women, with red flowers in their hair; and nothing to do but to study oratory and etiquette, sit in the sun, and pick up the fruits as they fall. Navigator's Island is the place; absolute balm for the weary . . .' Again fifteen years later in 1890 he refers to the prophetic visit of Mr. Seed in a letter to Mrs. Fairchild from Sydney (*Letters*, Tusitala Edition *33*, p.315)' . . . he told me that I had no business to stay in Europe; that I should find all I cared for and all that was good for me, in the Navigator Islands . . . I go there only to grow old and die; but when you come, you will see it as a fair place for the purpose'

**'Selections from his Notebook'**, first published in Vailima Edition, 1923; Tusitala Edition *29*

**Sewall, Harold Marsh,** U.S. consul in Samoa and friend of Stevensons during Vailima days

**Sharp, William,** (1855–1905). Scottish writer. 'The Country of Stevenson', *Literary Geography*, Pall Mall Press, 1907. Sharp left this interesting account of his first meeting with Stevenson

'The first time I saw Robert Louis Stevenson was at Waterloo Station . . . when my attention was attracted by a passenger, of a strangeness of appearance almost grotesque, emerging from a compartment in the Bournemouth train which had just arrived . . . He was tall, thin, spare – indeed, he struck me as almost fantastically spare; I remember thinking that the station draught caught him like a torn leaf flowing at the end of a branch. His clothes hung about him, as the clothes of a convalescent who has lost bulk and weight after long fever. He had on a jacket of black velveteen . . . a flannel shirt with a loose necktie negligently bundled into a sailor's knot, somewhat fantastical trousers, though no doubt this effect was due in part to their limp amplitude about what seemed rather the thin green poles familiar in dahlia-pots than the legs of a human creature. He wore a straw hat, that in its rear rim suggested forgetfulness on the part of its wearer, who had apparently in sleep or heedlessness, treated it as a cloth cap . . . The long, narrow face, then almost sallow with somewhat long, loose, dark hair, that draggled from beneath the yellow straw hat well over the ears, along the dusky hollows of temple and cheek, was what immediately attracted

attention . . . the impression was of a man who had just been rescued
from the sea or a river . . . Except that his clothes did not drip, this
impression . . . was overwhelming . . . proved by the exclamation of a
cabman, who was standing beside me expectant of a "fare" . . . "Looks
like a sooercide, don't he, sir? One o' them chaps as takes their down-on-
their-luck 'eaders inter the Thames!" And truth to tell, my fancy was
somewhat to the same measure . . . Our eyes met, I was struck by their
dark luminousness below the peculiar eyebrows. [I] was impressed by
their sombre melancholy. Some poor fellow, I thought, on the last coasts
of consumption, with Shadow-Ferry within hail.
. . . Suddenly the friend whom he was expecting came forward. The
whole man seemed to change. The impression of emaciation faded; the
'drowned' look passed; even the damaged straw hat and the short
velveteen jacket and the shank-inhabited wilderness trousers shared in
this unique 'literary renascence'. But the supreme change was in the
face. The dark locks apparently receded, like the weedy tangle in the
ebb; the long sallow oval grew rounder and less wan; the sombre
melancholy vanished like cloud-scud on a day of wind and sun, and the
dark eyes lightened to a violet-blue and were filled with sunshine and
laughter. An extraordinary winsome smile invaded the face . . .
pervaded the whole . . .
Who was this puzzling and interesting personality . . . this stranger, like
a consumptive organ-grinder, with such charm of manner? . . . This
problem was solved for me by the sudden appearance on the scene of my
French friend . . . "I thought you should have known . . . why, it is your
*homme-de-lettres vraiment charmant*, Robert Louis Stevenson! . . .

### Shaw, George Bernard, (1856–1950)

In Saranac (1887) Stevenson received from William Archer *Cashel
Byron's Profession*, the Irish dramatist's first novel, published when he was
21. Stevenson wrote Archer (*Letters*, Tusitala Edition *33*, p.175), ' . . .
have read your friend's book with singular relish . . . full of promise; but
I should like to know his age . . . It is *horrid fun*. All I ask is more of it . . .
(I say, Archer, my God, what women!) . . .'

### Shelley, Sir Percy and Lady, formed part of the Bournemouth élite
society while the Stevensons occupied Skerryvore

Sir Percy, elderly son of the poet, was an addict of amateur photography
and theatricals, while his wife became obsessed with the idea that
Stevenson was her father-in-law's reincarnation. She found
considerable likenesses in both men which Stevenson utterly failed to
understand or appreciate.
(*See* Dedication of **The Master of Ballantrae**)

### Sherman, Stuart, *Critical Woodcuts*, Scribner's, New York, 1926.
Discusses Stevenson's 'modern attitudes. *The Emotional Discovery of*

*America*, Farrer & Rinehart, 1932. The controversy over W.E. Henley and Balfour's official biography

**Shipman, Louis Evan,** 'Stevenson's First Landing in New York'. Description of Stevenson's brief and disastrous visit in August 1879. *Book Buyer*, February 1896

**'Sick Man and the Fireman, The',** a fable, Tusitala Edition 5 (*see also* **Fables**)

*'Sidney Colvins, The',* (*see* **Clifford, Mrs. W.K.**)

*Silhouettes,* (*see* **Gosse, Sir Edmund William**)

**Silverado Squatters, The,** first published in *Century Magazine*, 7 November, 27 December 1883; in book form by Chatto & Windus, London, 1884; Tusitala Edition *18* (with 'The Silverado Diary', first published in Vailima Edition, 1923)

Journal of the Stevensons' honeymoon and their stay in the Napa Valley, May-July 1880.

'Immediately after his marriage, Stevenson and his wife and stepson went to the country fifty miles north of San Francisco, there to seek health in the mountains. How they took possession of a deserted mining-camp and lived in isolation and independence among the ruins, is told once for all in *The Silverado Squatters*. The book was finished, however, in Switzerland (Davos), whence he wrote to his mother, "I work, work away, and get nothing or but little done: it is slow, slow, slow: but I sit from four to five hours at it, and read all the rest of the time from Hazlitt." ' (From Introduction to Tusitala Edition, *18*).

Dedication: 'To Virgil Williams and Dora Norton Williams these sketches are affectionately dedicated by their friend THE AUTHOR.'

The honeymoon-house 'consisted of three rooms, and was so plastered against the hill, that one room was right atop of another, that the upper floor was more than twice as large as the lower, and that all three apartments must be entered from a different level. Not a window-sash remained. The door of the lower room was smashed, and one panel hung in splinters . . . sand and gravel had been sifted in there by the mountain-winds; straw, sticks and stones; a table, a barrel, a plate-rack on the wall; two home made bootjacks, signs of miners and their boots . . . The window was choked with sweet smelling foliage of a bay and through a chink in the floor, a spray of poison-oak had shot up and was handsomely prospering in the interior.'

Fanny Stevenson was undaunted; she had not pioneered with her first husband Sam and learned nothing. Soon she was writing to her mother-in-law in Edinburgh, '. . . I was told nothing else would save his life, and I believe it was true. We could not afford to go to a 'mountain resort'

place and there was no other chance . . . I put in doors and windows of
light frames covered with white cotton, with bits of leather from the old
(miners) boots for hinges, made seats and beds and got things to look
quite homelike. We got white and red wine, dried peaches and fruits
which we kept cool in the tunnel and which we enjoyed extremely.'
Fanny omitted to mention that a load of hay which had to be carted up
the mountain side had formed their nuptial couch and that their wedding
breakfast which she had cooked for her new husband and her son was
porridge, bacon and coffee. Fanny had a survivor's instinct and had used
the materials available, scattered outside, old wood, nails, rails and the
like to make their shack habitable. Stevenson's letter to Mrs. Sitwell,
however, was in a more subdued mood (National Library of Scotland,
Edinburgh), 'My dear, we have had a miserable time. The first night I
had a cramp and was quite worn out after it, the second day Fanny
mashed her thumb while carpentering and had a nervous chill; the third
day she had another form of sleeplessness; the sixth day she and Lloyd
began to have diphtheria. I got them down in an open cart; the cases
were slight; Lloyd's especially but F has been pretty sick and a little
light-headed for forty-eight hours. You may fancy I am tired. I am
homesick for Europe . . .'
(*See also* **Carrington, James B.; Issler, Anne Roller**)

**Simele, Henry,** Samoan servant at Vailima
A young chief from Savaii, he was anxious to learn English, which he
called 'long explessions'. Like all the other servants, he was devoted to
the Stevensons

**Simoneau, Jules,** big-hearted Frenchman who ran a restaurant in
    Monterey and befriended the poor and sick Stevenson
'A dear and kind old man', he also nursed Stevenson on occasion, played
chess with him and became a symbol of comradely benevolence.
Knowing that the Scotsman would never accept charity, Simoneau
became part of a conspiracy among the fellow-boarders who, not much
better off, clubbed together to make up a salary of two dollars a week
which Bronson, editor of the town's newspaper then paid him to write
articles.
(*See* **Monterey; Blanch, Josephine Mildred;** Part 4 (Letters))

**Simpson, Eve Blantyre,** sister of Walter (*see below*); friend of
    Stevenson's Edinburgh days
*Robert Louis Stevenson*, 'Spirit of the Age' Series, Luce, London, 1906;
*Robert Louis Stevenson Originals*, Foulis, Edinburgh, 1912; *Robert Louis
Stevenson's Edinburgh Days*, Hodder & Stoughton, London, 1914; 'R.L.
Stevenson's Two Mothers', *Bookman*, September 1897 and *Bookman*

Extra Number, London, 1913; 'Some Notes on Stevenson's Childhood', *Book Buyer*, May 1899

**Simpson, Rev. H.L.**, 'Island Treasure: A Visit to Samoa', an essay in *A Cadger's Creel* (*see* **Douglas, Sir George**)

**Simpson, Sir Walter Grindlay,** friend of Stevenson's from student days; fellow voyager in France

Affectionately known as 'The Bart'; He came into the baronetcy in 1870 on the death of his father. Sir James Young Simpson was obstetrician/physician to the Queen in Scotland, the pioneer of chloroform as an anaesthetic (used by Queen Victoria at the birth of Prince Leopold in 1853).

(*See also* **Inland Voyage, An**; Part 4 (Letters))

**Simpson, 'Willie',** eccentric brother of Walter, artist in the Barbizon colony

**'Sinking Ship, The',** a fable, Tusitala Edition 5 (*see also* **Fables**)

**'Sire de Malétroit's Door, The',** a short story, first published in *Temple Bar*, January 1878; in book form in *New Arabian Nights*, 1882; Tusitala Edition 1

Originally called 'The Sire de Malétroit's Mousetrap'

**Siron's,** (*see* **Hotel Siron**)

**Sitwell, Rev. Albert,** Church of England minister and estranged husband of Fanny Sitwell (*see below*)

Distantly related to the literary Sitwell family, he was referred to as 'a man of unfortunate temperament and uncongenial habits'. There are hints of the alcoholic who physically abused his wife

**Sitwell, Bertie,** elder son of Fanny and Albert Sitwell

In common with all children, he became great friends with Stevenson when they met at Cockfield Rectory in 1873. Seven years later, when he was eighteen, he accompanied his mother to join the Stevensons in Davos. Dr. Ruedi's cure for him was too late; he was in the last throes of galloping consumption and died in his mother's arms on 3 April 1881. She remained a little while with the Stevensons, who shared her personal agony of loss, and Stevenson wrote his touching 'In Memoriam: F.A.S.' (*Poems*, Tusitala Edition 22, p.89):

> 'Yet, O stricken heart, remember, O remember
> How of human days he lived the better part.
> April came to bloom and never dim December
> Breathed its killing chills upon the head or heart . . .'

I think now, this 5th an 6th of April 1873, that I can see my future life. I think it will run stiller and stiller year by year; a very quiet, desultarilly studious existence If god only gives me tolerable health, I think now I shall be very happy; work and science calm the mind and stop gnawing in the brain; and as I am glad to say that I do now recognise that I shall never be a great man, I may set myself peacefully on a smaller journey; not without hope of coming to the inn before nightfull

Oclass auein lehen nach diesem ziel ein ewig wandeln seg!

Desiderata.

I  good - Health
II  2 to 3 hundred a year.
III  « O du lieber gott, freunds!

A M E N

Robert Louis Stevenson

Extract from letter to Mrs Fanny Sitwell, written from Edinburgh 'Late Autumn 1874' and containing copy of Desiderata 'in which I sketched out my life before I knew you . . .' *Mansell Collection*

**Sitwell, Fanny** (Frances Jane Fetherstonhaugh). Born in Ireland. Wife
of the Rev. Albert Sitwell (*see above*), she was a friend of another
minister's wife, Stevenson's cousin Maud Babington (née Balfour) with
whom she took refuge from her 'uncongenial husband'. An unhappy
Stevenson also sought refuge at Cockfield Rectory in Suffolk in the
summer of 1873, from the miseries of illness and the oppressive
intolerance of Heriot Row. Men of all ages fell wildly in love with
Fanny Sitwell, who aroused them to statements such as 'Beauty like hers
was genius . . . Divining intuition like hers was genius. Vitality like hers
was genius.' (Lucas, *The Colvins and their Friends*).

Sidney Colvin, whom she was eventually to marry, wrote of her, 'In the
fearlessness of her purity, she can afford the frankness of her affections,
and shows how every fascination of her sex may in the most open
freedom be the most honourably secure. Yet in a world of men and
women, such an one cannot walk without kindling once and again a
dangerous flame before she is aware . . . she never foresees these
masculine combustions, but has a wonderful tact and gentleness in
allaying them, and is accustomed to convert the claims and cravings of
passion into a lifelong loyalty of grateful and contented friendship.'

Colvin's statement shows remarkable insight into Fanny's relationship
with Stevenson, in whom she certainly kindled both a 'dangerous flame'
and 'masculine combustion' and diverted them into calmer waters of a
lifelong friendship and correspondence. Stevenson also captivated
Colvin and he did not object when she became Louis's cherished 'older
woman', his Madonna, his Consuelo. In 1875 from Edinburgh he
confided in Mrs. Sitwell (*Letters*, Tusitala Edition *31*, p.218) that he had
been glad to take Madame Garschine 'by the hand as a mother and make
a mother of her at the time, so far as it would go. You do not know
perhaps – I do not think I knew myself, perhaps, until I thought it out
today – how dear a hope, how sorry a want this has been for me. For my
mother is my father's wife; to have a French mother, there must be a
French marriage; the children of lovers are orphans. I am very young at
heart – or (God knows) very old – and what I want is a mother, and I
have one now, have I not?' He began this letter and the next 'Dearest
Mother'. 'I am to be a son, you must be a mother; and surely I am a son in
more than ordinary sense, begotten of the sweet soul and beautiful body
of you, and taught all that I know fine or holy or of good report, by the
contact of your sweet soul and lovely body – transmuted and
transfigured and made a new creature, even though at times I may still
stumble, by the knowledge of your goodness and beauty; if this is so, and
it is so, my mother, in a real mild way, that is more real than
commonplace realities, you have your duties to me as certainly as ever a
fleshly mother had, and for these duties you must be true to me, and
happy for me, and the brave, good, beautiful, happy mother I want.'
When he met Fanny Osbourne he must have been conscious of the hand

of coincidence. They not only shared the same first name, they were of an age. Both were dark and had striking features, beautiful eyes, small hands and feet. Both had married at seventeen and had suffered at the hands of those first husbands. Both were mothers of two small sons and both had been bereaved of the second-born and thereby shocked into illness (Fanny Sitwell suffered from a respiratory weakness).

Since divorce was an unthinkable social disaster for a minister's wife, Fanny Sitwell, although acknowledged as Sidney Colvin's hostess at literary evenings – he was then Slade Professor of Fine Art at Cambridge – had to wait patiently to become his wife after a courtship of three decades. Even when her husband died at last, Colvin by then had an old and dependent mother. When at last death removed the final barrier and they married in 1903, Fanny was sixty-two and Sidney fifty-six. The devotion and constancy of these elderly lovers which had lasted half a lifetime were rewarded by a cultivated, harmonious and happy marriage which lasted for more than twenty years.

(*See* **Colvin, Sir Sidney; Babington, Rev. Churchill;** Part 4 (Letters))


**Skae, Hilda,** 'Atween the Pentland's Muckle Knees: With R.L.S. at Swanston', *S.M.T. Magazine*, September 1934; 'The Auld Kirk in the Glen: Memories of Glencorse', *S.M.T. Magazine*, August 1933


**Skelt's Juvenile Drama,** a collection of characters, scenery and mostly anonymous texts is retained in the Edinburgh Room, Edinburgh Central Library, n.d., comprising:

*The Battle of Waterloo: A Drama in Three Acts*, 18 pp. Illus. n.d.

*Cock-a-doodle-doo; or The Lady bird's Bower*, 12 pp, n.d.

*The Falls of Clyde: A Drama in Two Acts*, 20 pp. Illus. n.d.

*Jacob Faithful: A Drama in Three Acts*, 20 pp. Illus. n.d.

*Pizarro: A Drama in Five Acts*, 18 pp. Illus. n.d.

*My Poll and My Partner Joe: A Drama in Three Acts*, Illus. n.d.

*The Miller's Maid: A Drama in Two Acts*, 12 pp. Illus. n.d.

*Robinson Crusoe; or The Bold Buccaneers* by H. Matthews, 1886

Skelt entered Stevenson's life when he received a model theatre as a sixth birthday present. 'In the Leith Walk window, all the year round there stood displayed a theatre in working order, with a "forest set", a "combat", and a few "robbers carousing" in the slides; and below and about, dearer tenfold to me! the plays themselves, those budgets of romance, lay tumbled one upon another. Long and often have I lingered there with empty pockets. One figure, we shall say, was visible in the first plate of characters, bearded, pistol in hand, or drawing to his ear the clothyard arrow . . . Oh, how I would long to see the rest! how – if the name by chance were hidden – I would wonder in what play he figured, and what immortal legend justified his attitude and strange

apparel! And then to go within, to announce yourself as an intending
purchaser, and, closely watched, be suffered to undo those bundles and
breathlessly devour those pages of gesticulating villains, epileptic
combats, bosky forests, palaces and war-ships, frowning fortresses and
prison vaults – it was a giddy joy. That shop, which was dark and smelt
of Bibles, was a loadstone rock for all that bore the name of boy . . . they
kept us at the stick's end, frowned us down, snatched each play out of
our hand ere we were trusted with another . . . these were the dragons
of the garden; but for such joys of paradise we could have faced the
Terror of Jamaica himself. Every sheet we fingered was another
lightning glance into obscure, delicious story; it was like wallowing in
the raw stuff of story-books. I know nothing to compare with it save
now and then in dreams, when I am privileged to read in certain unwrit
stories of adventure, from which I awake to find the world all
vanity . . . What am I? What are life, art, letters, the world, but what
my Skelt has made them? He stamped himself upon my immaturity. The
world was plain before I knew him, a poor penny world; but soon it was
all coloured with romance.' (From 'A Penny Plain and Twopence
Coloured', *Memories and Portraits*, Tusitala Edition *29*).
(*See* Plate 8)

**Skene, Edwards & Garson;** present name of the Edinburgh firm of
solicitors where Stevenson received legal training from autumn 1871
until mid-1873. It was at that time W.F. Skene & Peacock, having
been founded by W.F. Skene, well-known for his writing on
Highland history.
(*See also* **Black, Margaret Moyes; Edinburgh University**)

**Skerryvore, Bournemouth**

Fanny's son Lloyd was studying science at Edinburgh University, living
in Heriot Row with his step-grandparents. She and Stevenson had
'wintered' in Bournemouth and found the climate mild. From
Edinburgh came alarms that clearly indicated Thomas Stevenson was
failing. In a desperate bid to keep his only son in Britain, he offered to
buy them a house, and in 1885 they took possession of a handsome villa
on the cliffs at Bournemouth called 'Sea View'. They renamed it
'Skerryvore' in honour of the famous lighthouse in the Inner Hebrides,
built by Stevenson's uncle. An unpretentious two-storey house with
ivy-covered yellow brick and blue slates and a garden growing towards
the brink of steep Alum Chine . . . According to Lloyd: 'It was typical of
an old sailor [its previous owner]; it was so trim, so well-arranged, so
much thought had been given to its many conveniences. One felt it was a
dream-come-true of long years passed at sea – even to the natty little
stable, the miniature coach-house, and the faultlessly bricked court,
faultlessly slanted to the central drain. Of course, it had a pigeon-cote;

what old seaman would be happy ashore without one? And through all my memories of "Skerryvore" runs that melodious cooing and the flutter of wings on the lawn. The house and five hundred pounds towards furnishing it were a wedding present to my mother from R.L.S.'s parents. The wanderers were now anchored; over their heads was their own roof-tree; they paid rates and taxes, and were called on by the vicar . . . Respectability, dullness, and similar villas encompassed him for miles in every direction . . . '

Fanny was a gifted home-maker; in Skerryvore she could now indulge the talent Stevenson was to describe later to Barrie as 'can make anything from a home to a row, all fine and large of their kind'. The drawing-room blossomed with yellow silk cushions on the window-seat. The dining-room became 'The Blue Room', with Turner's painting of 'The Bell Rock Lighthouse' above the fireplace and a collection of 'buccaneering weapons' on the wall. Stevenson had a partiality for the popular blue and white china mass-produced in imitation of Chinese Ming. There were also a Rodin sculpture, photographs of Colvin, Henley and Fleeming Jenkin; later Sargent's 'peripatetic painting' of Stevenson in mid-stride, quizzical, moustache-tugging. A model lighthouse was installed at the entrance which was lit every evening as darkness fell. Fanny's inexhaustible energy extended beyond the interior to 'a seductive little labyrinth' of paths, stairs and arbours with seats where Stevenson could pause and write his notes. She planted fruit trees, roses and hydrangeas and introduced Indian corn and tomatoes, then rare in England. 'It is very comfortable to know that we have a home really and truly, and will no more be like Noah's dove, flying about with an olive branch . . .' Stevenson was readily converted to being a householder. He described the drawing-room as '. . . so beautiful that it's like eating to sit in it . . . there I sit like an old Irish beggarman's cast-off bauchle in a palace throne-room . . . I blush for the figure I cut in such a bower..,'

Skerryvore was their last home in Britain; they left when Thomas Stevenson died in 1887 to return no more. It was the birthplace of *Dr. Jekyll and Mr. Hyde*, of *Kidnapped*, and many of his best short stories, as well as *Memoir of Fleeming Jenkin*. It also saw his poorest health and lowest spirits. Fanny was heartbroken to leave her 'little nest . . . Life had been too happy at Skerryvore – the envying gods had struck it down'. Lloyd's opinion differed, 'In his heart I doubt if (Stevenson) ever really liked Skerryvore; he never spoke of it with regret; left it with no apparent pang. The Victorianism it exemplified was jarring to every feeling he possessed, though with his habitual philosophy he not only endured it, but even persuaded himself that he liked it . . .'

The sale of Skerryvore brought £1,500 towards the purchase of Vailima. During World War II, in 1943, a German land-mine exploded nearby and rendered Skerryvore so unsafe that it was demolished. Stevenson's

Bournemouth sojourn is marked by the Avenue named after him. (*See also* **Boodle, Adelaide; Holland, Clive; Stevenson, Alan;** Plate 10)

**Skerryvore Edition,** *The Works of Robert Louis Stevenson,* 30 vols. Illustrated, maps, Heinemann, London, 1924-26

**Skinner, R.T.,** 'Alison Cunningham: R.L.S. Reminiscences, an Unwritten Chapter', *The Scotsman,* 29–31 December 1935; 'A Cévennes Link with R.L.S.', Edinburgh, privately printed, 1924; 'In the Cévennes without a Donkey', *Scots Magazine,* 1924; 'A Native of Torryburn: More Leaves from the Diary of "the beloved nurse Cummy" ', *Yesterday and Today,* Edinburgh, 1931; 'Stevenson and the Cévennes', *Scots Magazine,* 1924, *Graphic* 1924, *Sphere,* 1926 (extracts); 'Treasure Island: Stevenson at Braemar', *Figures and Figureheads,* Edinburgh, 1931

**Slate, The,** play projected, but never finished, during his San Francisco stay in 1880. 'Both Fanny and I have condemned it utterly; it is too morbid, ugly and unkind; better starvation'

**Slater, J.H.,** *Robert Louis Stevenson: a bibliography of his complete works,* 1914 (*See also* **Bibliographies of Stevenson's writings**)

**Smith, Arthur D. Howden,** *Alan Breck Again,* Coward-McCann, New York, 1934; 'Porto Bello Gold', *Brentano's,* New York, n.d.

**Smith, A.W.,** 'Stevenson's Haunts in their Winter Garb.' A description of the Pentland Hills, Swanston. *S.M.T. Magazine,* January 1932

**Smith, Janet Adam,** *R.L. Stevenson,* 'Great Lives' Series, Duckworth, London, 1937; (ed.) *Henry James and Robert Louis Stevenson: A Record of Friendship and Criticism,* Rupert Hart-Davies, London, 1948; (ed.) *Collected Poems of R.L. Stevenson,* Rupert Hart-Davis, London, 1971

**Smith, Thomas and Jean,** Stevenson's paternal great-grandparents. (*See* **Stevenson, Robert**)

**Snyder, Alice D.,** 'Paradox and Antithesis in Stevenson's Essays', *Journal of English and German Philology,* Vol. XIX

**Social conscience of Stevenson**
According to Fanny Stevenson's Preface to *The Amateur Emigrant* Stevenson was sensitive upon this score, '[He] sympathised with the socialists. He could not think of the innocent victims of civilisation – the men who only asked for work and could get none, while their children were starving . . . while his own comfortable circumstances filled him with shame when he contemplated the hardships of those less fortunate than himself. But . . . he could suggest no remedy; the assassination of

individuals and bomb-throwing seeming to him not only barbaric, but silly and futile.

While he could see no royal road for others, the path for himself showed plainly enough before him, and it was his duty to swerve neither to the right nor the left. He believed he had no rights, only undeserved indulgences. He must not eat unearned bread; but must pay the world, in some fashion, for what it gave him – first, materially, then in kindness, sympathy and love. Class distinctions, so strictly observed in England, he could not tolerate and never gave the slightest heed to their limitations. "Ladies?" he said in reply to an observation by a visitor, "one of the truest ladies in Bournemouth, Mrs. Watts, is at this moment washing my study windows". Once, coming upon a crowd of young roughs who were tormenting a wretched drunken creature of the streets, he pushed his way through them, and amid their jeers offered his arm to the woman and escorted her to the place she called home . . . Too much ease frightened him; he would occasionally insist on some sharp discomfort, such as sleeping on a mat on the floor, or dining on a ship's biscuit, to awaken him, as he said, to realities; and nothing pleased him more than to risk his life or health to serve another. Yet he never succeeded in wholly subduing the "old Adam" within him. Meanness or falsity or cruelty set his eyes blazing, and his language on such occasions became far from parliamentary.

Naturally his first visit to America, a land without class distinctions, was to him an event of extraordinary interest. The privations he endured as an amateur emigrant caused him much less suffering than his friends, who could not imagine themselves in a similar position, supposed. It was not the first time he had associated with the working-man on terms of equality; nor did it occur to him that it was a condescension on his part to join with his fellow-passengers in their attempts to make the time pass pleasantly, or to do for them what little kindly offices came in his way. One thing he did resent with bitterness – the visits of the first-class passengers, who came out of curiosity into the steerage, looking about as though they were passing through a menagerie . . . For street musicians and wandering performers – acrobats, jugglers, etc. – my husband showed an understanding and sympathy that always won their confidence. "We're in the same boat," he would say, "earning our bread by amusing the public. I always divide with a brother artist," he would remark as he emptied his pockets into their hands. His acquaintance with such people and his knowledge of the lives they led, gave him an almost morbid sense of the pitiless cruelty of modern civilisation. It was only his strong intelligence and common-sense that kept him from the ranks of the anarchists. He came to America . . . believing that there he would find the ideal social as well as political life. In the beginning he encountered many rude shocks, but he soon readjusted his point of view, though he never ceased regretting that this

great country should have been lost to England. The name of George the Third was hardly to be spoken in his presence. "Had it not been for that idiot," he would cry, "we should now be one nation" . . .'
(*See* **Curtin family; 'Amateur Emigrant, The'; Mataafa, 'King'; 'Footnote to History, A'**)

**'Some Aspects of Robert Burns'**, an essay, first published in *Cornhill Magazine*, October 1879; in book form in *Familiar Studies of Men and Books*, 1882; Tusitala Edition 27

**'Some College Memories'**, an essay, first published in *Memories and Portraits*, 1887; Tusitala Edition 29

Appeared for the first time in *The New Amphion*, the book of the Edinburgh University Union fancy fair (*sic*), by David Douglas, Edinburgh, 1886. Illustrated. *The New Amphion* contained original contributions from many eminent writers, and was produced as part of an enterprise organised by the Students' Representative Council to defray the cost of the University Union.

***Some Diversions of a Man of Letters,*** (*see* **Gosse, Sir Edmund William**)

***Some Further Recollections of a Happy Life,*** (*see* **Symonds, John Addington**)

**'Some Gentlemen in Fiction'**, an essay, first published in *Scribner's Magazine*, June 1888; Tusitala Edition 26

***Some Letters,*** (*see* **Haddon, Trevor**)

**'*Some Memories of "Cummie": a Link with R.L.S.'*,** (*see* **Pagan, G.H.**)

***Some Notes on Robert Louis Stevenson, his Finances, his Agents and Publishers*** (*see* **McKay, George L.**)

**'*Some Notes on Stevenson's Childhood'*,** (*see* **Simpson, Eve Blantyre**)

**'*Some of the Rarer Stevensons'*,** (see **Ellwanger, W.D.**)

**'Some Portraits by Raeburn'**, an essay, first published in *Virginibus Puerisque* 1881; Tusitala Edition 25

***Some Recollections of Robert Louis Stevenson,*** (*see* **Baildon, H. Bellyse; Pears, Sir Edmund Radcliffe**)

**'*Some Stevenson Gleanings'*,** (*see* **Westminster Gazette**)

**'*Some Stevenson Legends'*,** (*see* **Sanchez, Nellie Vandegrift**)

**'*Some Stevenson Pictures'*,** (*see* **Book Buyer**)

**'Something In It'**, a fable, Tusitala Edition 5 (*see also* **Fables**)

'**Song of the Morrow, The**', a fable, Tusitala Edition 5 (*see also* **Fables**)

'**Songs of Travel**', a collection of poems, first published by Chatto & Windus, London, 1896; Tusitala Edition 22

**Sophia Scarlett,** projected novel by Stevenson (1892). It was to involve three heroines and to be written after *Weir of Hermiston* was completed

**Sosimo,** Samoan servant, Stevenson's devoted right-hand man at Vailima. Sosimo was with him at the end and held vigil beside his master, reciting the Catholic prayers for the dead, in mingled Latin and Samoan, all through the night prior to his burial on 4 December 1894

*'So This is Ballantrae',* (*see* **Williams, Alan**)

*'South Sea Memories of R.L.S.',* (*see* **Allen, Maryland**)

**South Seas Edition,** The *Works of Robert Louis Stevenson*, 32 vols., Scribner's, New York, 1925

*South Seas Trader, A,* (*see* **Balfour, Graham**)

**Speculative Society, The,** Edinburgh University's literary and debating society. *Address to the Speculative Society, Edinburgh, March 1873*; first published in *The Outlook*, 19 February 1898

Election was – and is still – on intellectual merit. In Stevenson's days meetings were held weekly, by candlelight, evening dress compulsory. Strictly for the sons of gentlemen, the eccentric student from Heriot Row gained admittance on the strength of his minister grandfather, Rev. Lewis Balfour of Colinton, and his lighthouse-builder grandfather, Robert Stevenson. Elected 16 February 1869, enrolled as a member on 2 March. His first meeting was a dismal failure; his maiden speech ignored, he was further snubbed when members adjourned in the interval to 'The Pump'. However, he proved himself a worthy member on his literary merit and was elected one of five rotating presidents; in his days of fame the 'Spec. Soc.' was pleased to honour him as one of its famous sons. He contributed eight papers, unpublished except for No. 6: *Address to Spec. Soc.*, (as above)
1. The Influence of the Covenanting Persecution on the Scottish Mind; 8 March 1870
2. Notes on *Paradise Lost*; 14 March 1871
3. Notes on the Nineteenth Century; 9 January 1872
4. Two Questions on the Relation between Christ's Teaching and Modern Christianity; 12 November 1872
5. Law and Free Will: Notes on the Duke of Argyll; 11 February 1873 (Mentioned by Lord Dunedin in Masson's *I Can*

*Remember . . .'* and in *Letters,* Tusitala Edition *31,* p. 78, to
Mrs. Sitwell)
7. John Knox; 3 November 1874
8. John Knox and Women; 19 January 1875
(*See* **Edinburgh University; Dickson, W.K.; Osbourne, Katharine Durham**)

*Speculative Society 1764-1904, The History of the,* (*see* **Dickson, W.K.**)

**Star for Seamen, A: The Stevenson Family of Engineers,** (*see* **Mair, Craig**)

**Starrett, David,** 'The Dead Man's Chest: A Stevensonian Research' Claims for the real location of Treasure Island. *Colophon,* No. 17, 1934

**Steinbeck, John,** 'How Edith McGillicuddy met R.L.S.', *Harper's,* August 1941

**Stephen, Sir Leslie,** (1832-1904), English man of letters, 'Robert Louis Stevenson', *National Review, Studies of a Biographer,* Duckworth, London 1902. As editor of the *Cornhill Magazine,* he published Stevenson's early work, including his first essay on 'Victor Hugo's Romances'

**Stern, G.B.,** *No Son of Mine,* Cassell, London, 1948. Novel based on fiction of an illegitimate son of Stevenson. *He Wrote Treasure Island,* Heinemann, London 1954; *Robert Louis Stevenson,* Supplement to *British Book News,* No. 27, 1952; *Robert Louis Stevenson: An Omnibus,* Cassell, London, 1950; *Robert Louis Stevenson: Writers and their Work,* Longmans, London, n.d.

**Steuart, John A,** *The Cap of Youth: The Love Romance of Robert Louis Stevenson,* Low, London, 1927; *Robert Louis Stevenson: Man and Writer,* 2 vols, Low, London, 1924

**Stevenson, Alan,** Bob Stevenson's father
After showing early brilliance with the family firm of engineers (he was the designer of the Skerryvore Lighthouse), he was struck down at forty-five by 'a sudden shattering of the nervous system'. He lived a half-mad recluse for his remaining thirteen years

**'Stevenson at Play: War Correspondence from Stevenson's Notebook',** first published in *Scribner's Magazine,* December 1898; Tusitala Edition *30*

**Stevenson, Bob,** (Robert Alan Mowbray)
Bob and his sister Katharine (*see* **de Mattos, Katharine**) were Stevenson's favourite cousins, children of Alan Stevenson (*see above*). They

stayed one winter at Heriot Row when Stevenson was seven and Bob
ten years old. As the attractive pair also combined considerable charm
and magnetism in their make-up, Stevenson fell a little in love with
Katharine and hero-worshipped Bob for the rest of his life. He wrote of
those childhood days, 'We lived together in a purely visionary state. We
had countries where we ruled and made wars and inventions, and
maps . . . We were never weary of dressing up . . .'
Soon they were to be taken by their still healthy father to a life in
France. Educated abroad, Bob returned to Scotland and passed on to his
young cousin the continental fashion of a 'wide-awake' hat and velvet
jacket which not even the derision of Edinburgh gangs of children could
make him discard. Bob went to Cambridge and returned in 1870 with a
degree, to enter the Edinburgh College of Art. 'The mere return of Bob
changed at once and for ever the course of my life . . . I was at last able
to breathe . . . [He was] the man likest and most unlike to me that I have
ever met. Our likeness was one of tastes and passions . . . Laughter was
at that time our principal affair, and I doubt if we could have had a
better.' The cousins proceeded to get into many wild scrapes together in
Leith Walk howffs and other insalubrious Edinburgh institutions. A
young cousin lay dying and felt obliged to summon Stevenson's father to
his bedside to impart the grave news that Bob was wantonly corrupting
his trusting cousin (this was the period of the L.J.R. Club; p. 114). He
wrote to Charles Baxter, 'The war began with my father accusing Bob
of having ruined his house and his son. Bob answered that he didn't
know where I had found out that the Christian religion was not true but
that he hadn't told me. And I think from that point the conversation
went off into emotion and never touched shore again . . . My views
according to my father are a childish imitation of Bob, to cease the
moment the mildew is removed, all that was said was that I had ceased to
care for my father and that my father confessed he was ceasing, or had
greatly ceased, to care for me'. Later, he confided to Mrs. Sitwell
(*Letters*, Tusitala Edition *31*, p.70). 'They shook hands; my father . . .
wished him (Bob) all happiness, but prayed him . . . that he should never
see him between the eyes again . . . no practical issue except the
ludicrous one that Bob promised never to talk Religion to me any
more . . . he had no idea that there was that sort of thing in the world,
although I had told him often enough – my father on his knees and that
kind of thing.'
It was directly through Bob Stevenson and their holidays together in
France that Stevenson met Fanny Osbourne in Grez; Lloyd Osbourne
describes how the two Scottish cousins 'were the ringleaders in
everything. Nobody who failed to please the "two Stevensons" could
possibly stay in Grez. That was the risk we had to face . . . that the two
Stevensons might force us to leave . . . Some of the artists had already
arrived, amiable young fellows who painted in the fields under

prodigious white umbrellas and who seemed to find nothing especially
affronting in the presence of my very pretty mother and very pretty
sister. At last . . . I can recall my mother and myself gazing down from
our bedroom window at Isobel (Belle) who was speaking in the court
below to the first of the arriving Stevensons – "Bob" as he was always
called – a dark, roughly dressed man as lithe and graceful as a Mexican
vaquero and evoking something of the same misgiving. He smiled
pleasantly, hat in hand, with a mocking expression that I learned
afterwards was habitual with him, and which reminded me of the wolf
in Little Red Riding Hood. I suffocated, with terror and suspense. In my
innocence I thought he might suddenly strike Isobel . . . Then she ran up
to our room, laughing with excitement, to tell us that "Bob" was a most
agreeable and entertaining man, who was much amused at the way he
had been misrepresented to us. In fact, he had been most deferential to
her, and my sister's eyes were shining at the most obvious impression she
had made. With "Bob" on our side – and he soon became very much a
friend – all our trepidations subsided, and a curious reversal took place
in our attitude towards that other Stevenson, that unknown "Louis" as
everyone called him.' (From *An Intimate Portrait*). Fanny Osbourne wrote
to her sister Nellie Sanchez of Bob rather than Louis, 'He is exactly like
one of Ouida's heroes, with the hand of steel in the glove of velvet . . .
He is the best painter here, a charming musician, speaks all languages,
does all sorts of feats of strength and has no ambition . . . Bob Stevenson
is the most beautiful creature I ever saw in my life . . . He spent a large
fortune at the rate of eight thousand pounds a year, and now he has only
a hundred pounds a year left; he graduated from Cambridge with high
honours and won all the boat races and everything of that sort, studied
music and did wonderful things as a musician, took holy orders to please
his mother, quit in disgust, studied painting and did some fine work, and
is now dying from the effects of dissipation and is considered a little
mad.' When the two cousins returned to Scotland, Fanny received a
letter from Bob, 'I implore you to write a little letter to my poor cousin
in that prison house of his in Edinburgh. I am only a poor cad but Louis is
a true and good man and your letters may cheer him for he is said to be
dying, God help me.' She received a similar epistle from Louis Stevenson
that 'dear Bob is not long for this world . . . and you need not fear to
write to him. Pray do, to please me as well as for his sake.'
In the Prefatory Note to *New Arabian Nights*, which is dedicated to him,
Fanny wrote, 'It seems incredible that a genius so unusual as that of
Robert Alan Stevenson should pass out of existence, [he died in 1900]
leaving nothing more for posterity than a single brilliant volume,
[*Velasquez*] and a few desultory papers on music and painting; but he was
a dreamer of dreams, without ambitions, who dwelt alone in a world of
fantasy, from which he would sometimes emerge to dazzle his friends
with wild theories, sound philosophy, unexpected learning, and

whimsical absurdities, all jumbled together and presented with such pertinent reasoning and certainty of the truth of his premises that his hearers would be swept off their feet. Running through the contradictory tangle of his mind was a consistent thread of religion . . . Expiating on the glories of the future world, he once led his listeners to the very gates of heaven. If they knew, he continued, that this enchanting region lay in the next country, free to all who chose to expend a few shillings, who would refuse to accompany him? Why shrink from using the equivalent of a railway ticket – just a few pennies' worth of prussic acid. How exhilarating for several friends . . . – to make the journey in company . . . and embark on a voyage that would end in paradise . . . He went on to describe the advantages of a suicide train where persons weary of life might engage compartments. There would be no depressing preparations necessary; only the choice of a route either quick or slow, and the companions, if one cared for companions, suited to such an enterprise. The subject, thus begun, was taken up again . . . resulting in the invention of *The Suicide Club*, Robert Alan figuring in the beginning as the young man with the cream tarts, while the Prince of Wales was taken as the model for Prince Florizel . . .'

And in the Prefatory Note to *Prince Otto*, '*Prince Otto* was originally modelled on the character of his cousin . . . but fell insensibly into what my husband conceived himself. In some respects his friends could detect a superficial resemblance, but the fundamental character of the man was not there . . . It never seemed to me that either my husband or Robert Alan Stevenson quite belonged to their century. In some indefinable way they differed in appearance from the majority of mankind as much as they differed in character . . . [later] . . . we had several visitors in the little châlet [La Solitude] . . . Robert Alan Stevenson, whose remarkable personal attraction alone would have made him every moment of his stay a delight to us both; his talk, of a rare intelligence, witty, wise, gay, full of surprises and extravagances, did my husband more good than all the drugs in the chemist's shop.'

In 1881, Bob Stevenson married Louisa Purland, an emancipated lady who shared his artistic interests.

(*See also* Dedications to **New Arabian Nights** and **Prince Otto; Barbizon; Christianity of Stevenson; Henley, William Ernest;** Part 4 (Letters))

**Stevenson Club,** (*see* **Robert Louis Stevenson Club**)

**Stevenson, Fanny,** (Frances Matilda Vandegrift Osbourne) (1840–1914), Mrs. Robert Louis Stevenson, born 10 March 1840 in Indianapolis,

Indiana. In 1857 she married Samuel Osbourne; they had three children, Isobel (Belle), (Samuel) Lloyd and Hervey (who died in Paris in 1876). In 1880 she divorced Osbourne and married Robert Louis Stevenson on 18 May. They had no children. Fanny's ancestors on both sides – Swedish Kyns (Keens) and Dutch Van de Grifts – had settled near Philadelphia in the 17th century; she also claimed descent from Captain Cook. 'Some Letters of Mrs. R.L. Stevenson and one from Henry James', (ed.) Sidney Colvin, *Empire Review*, March–April, 1924; 'More Letters of Mrs. R.L. Stevenson', (ed.) Sidney Colvin, *Scribner's Magazine*, April 1924; *The Cruise of the 'Janet Nichol' among the South Sea Islands, A Diary*, Chatto and Windus, London, 1915; 'The Half-White', *Scribner's Magazine*, March 1891; 'Miss Pringle's Neighbours', *Scribner's Magazine*, June 1887; 'The Nixie', *Scribner's Magazine*, March 1888 (see **de Mattos, Katharine**); 'Too Many Birthdays', *St. Nicholas Magazine*, July 1878 (first published story); 'Under Sentence of the Law', *McClure's Magazine*, June 1893; With R.L. Stevenson: *Our Samoan Adventure* (ed.) Charles Neider, Weidenfeld & Nicholson, London, 1956

Fanny began life at a disadvantage, black-haired and swarthy-complexioned at a time when golden-haired, blue-eyed beauties were the fashion. She was the despair of her grandmother who tried washing the child's face with scouring soap only to give up at last with the words, 'She is that colour by nature – God made her ugly.' Her dark looks were no disadvantage as she grew up with compensating vitality and vivacity. When her daughter Belle was a teenager she noticed the attention her mother attracted in Oakland, or on the San Francisco ferry, 'I realised how very pretty she was with her pale face, her regular features cut like a delicate cameo, and her lovely eyes "of gold and bramble dew" ' (as Stevenson was to describe their glittering depths) 'Her figure was slender, with the hourglass effect slightly accented; and with her nicely shod little feet and dainty gloves she well repaid the many glances cast her way!'

A compatriot at Grez (see **Harrison, Birge**) described her as 'a woman of profound character and serious judgment, who could, if occasion called, have been the leader in some great movement. But she belonged to the quattrocento rather than to the nineteenth century . . . Mrs. Osbourne was in no sense ordinary. Indeed she was gifted with a mysterious sort of over-intelligence, which is almost impossible to describe, but which impressed itself upon everyone who came within the radius of her influence . . . She was therefore both physically and mentally the very antithesis of the gay, hilarious, open-hearted Stevenson, and for that reason perhaps the woman in all the world best fitted to be his life comrade and helpmate.'

Stevenson mentions her in a letter to his parents at this time, 'One of the matrons was a very beautiful woman indeed; I played old fogy and had a great deal of talk with her which pleased me.'

Her first mention of Louis Stevenson at Grez (Mackay, *The Violent Friend*), ' . . . the hysterical fellow, who wrote the article about Belle, is a tall, gaunt Scotsman with a face like Raphael, and between over-education and dissipation has ruined his health, and is dying of consumption. Louis reformed his habits a couple of years ago, and Bob [Stevenson] this winter. Louis is the heir to an immense fortune which he will never live to inherit. His father and mother, cousins, are both threatened with insanity, and I am quite sure the son is. His article about Belle was written as she says, for the five pounds which he wanted to give a pensioner of his in the hospital and was done when he had a headache, and badly enough we knew as well as he . . .'

At her first meeting with Sidney Colvin and Fanny Sitwell in London, pre-marriage, she demonstrated a spectacular ability to roll her own cigarettes which she then offered to teach her host and hostess. Colvin remembered, 'Her personality was almost as vivid as Stevenson's. She was small, dark-complexioned, eager, devoted; of squarish build – supple and elastic; her hands and feet were small and beautifully modelled, though busy; her head had a crop of close-waving thick black hair. She had a build and character that somehow suggested Napoleon, with a firm setting of jaw and beautifully precise and delicate modelling of the nose and lips; her eyes were full of sex and mystery as they changed from fire or fun to gloom or tenderness . . . a fine pearly set of small teeth, and the clear metallic accents of her intensely human and often quaintly individual speech.' This was the voice Nellie Sanchez, her sister referred to in her biography, 'Her speaking voice was low, modulated, and sweet, but with few inflections, and her husband once compared it to the pleasantly monotonous flow of a running brook under ice'. Colvin was among the majority of Stevenson's friends who opposed the marriage; however, he was waiting, loyally supporting the elder Stevensons, when the newly-wed pair arrived in Liverpool, on 17 August 1880. He wrote to W.E. Henley, '. . . Louis's mother looked the fresher of the two women . . . whether you or I will ever get reconciled to the little determined brown face and white teeth and grizzling (for that's what it's up to) hair, which we are to see beside him in future – that is another matter.' In due course Fanny won him over and later he was to write, 'She had deep and rich capacities alike for tragedy and humour. All her moods, thoughts, and instincts were vividly genuine and her own, and in her daily talk, like her letters, there was a play of character and feeling and choice and colour of words.'

'Please remember that my photograph is flattering,' (Plate 12) wrote Fanny to her future mother-in-law in Edinburgh, 'unfortunately all photographs of me are; I can get no other. At the same time Louis thinks me, and to him I believe I am, the most "beautiful creature in the world." It is because he loves me that he thinks that, so I am very glad. I do so earnestly hope that you will like me, but that can only be for what I am to you after you know me, and I do not want you to be disappointed in the beginning in anything about me, even in so small a thing as my looks.' Stevenson's mother confided in a woman-cousin, '...doubtless she is not the daughter-in-law that I have always pictured to myself', while Stevenson implored his parents from California, 'If you can love my wife, it will, I believe, make me love both her and you the better'. At that first momentous meeting in Liverpool, Margaret Stevenson wrote, 'Fanny is very entertaining...' and later 'Fanny fitted into our household from the first . . . it was quite amusing how entirely she agreed with my husband on all subjects, even to looking on the dark side of most things, while Louis and I were more inclined to take the cheery view'. The Stevenson family approved of Fanny; Louis's uncle, Dr. George Balfour, remarked 'I married a besom [Scottish term of contempt for a woman] myself and have never regretted it', while her stern father-in-law, Thomas Stevenson, teased her, 'I doot ye're a besom' and allotted her a series of pet names including 'Cassandra' for her gloomy prophecies, and 'The Vandegrifter'. She teased him in return, calling him Uncle Tom, or Mr. Tommy.

In pre-marriage days, Stevenson had written, ' . . . the woman I love is somewhat of my handiwork; and the great lover, like the great painter, is he who can so embellish his subject as to make her more than human . . . the woman can go on being a true woman, and give her character free play, and show littleness or cherish spite, or be greedy of common pleasures, and he continue to worship without a thought of incongruity.' ('The Story of a Lie', Tusitala Edition *14*, p. 143).

His attitude was less cynical in *Songs of Travel*, when he wrote:


TO MY WIFE


Trusty, dusky, vivid, true,
With eyes of gold and bramble-dew,
Steel-true and blade straight
The great artificer
Made my mate.

Honour, anger, valour, fire;
A love that life could never tire,
Death quench or evil stir,
The mighty master
Gave to her.

> Teacher, tender, comrade, wife.
> A fellow-farer true through life,
> Heart-whole and soul-free
> The august Father
> Gave to me.

Newly-wed in Heriot Row, her black silk stockings, short boyish hair and tendency to chain-smoking caused a sensation among servants used to conventional Victorian middle-class behaviour from their 'betters'. 'Mrs. Louis speaks English well for a foreigner, ye ken,' was overheard by Fanny, and from two servants gossiping in the kitchen about a Scot newly returned from foreign parts, 'He's merrit on til a black woman, ye ken'. Embarrassment was complete as they stared open-mouthed at Mrs. Louis's dark complexion. Too late one maid shook her head in warning, raised a finger to her lips. When Fanny was introduced to Stevenson's London literary circle, Edmund Gosse described her as '. . . one of the strangest people who have lived in our time, a sort of savage nature in some ways, but very lovable – extraordinarily passionate and unlike everyone else in her violent feelings and unrestrained way of expressing them – full of gaiety, and with a genius for expressing things picturesquely, but not literary. I think R.L.S. must have caught some of his ways of feeling from her . . . ' When Fanny returned to her husband in California from France in 1878 with the future between herself and Stevenson still uncertain, he wrote to Colvin (Beinecke Collection) ' . . . to F I never write letters . . . All that people want by letters has been done between us. We are acquainted; why go on with more introductions; I cannot change so much, but she would still have the clue and recognise every thought . . . ' Seldom parted once married, their letters were short and Stevenson's often began, 'My dear fellow,' 'My dear Dutchman,' 'My dearest little man', rather than the more conventional, 'My dearest girlie'. Most ended with conventional enough sentiments, 'I shall be damn glad to get you back and meanwhile send you a kiss', or 'as for yourself, I adore you – on the whole and I am Ever your Louis'.

That the marriage was stormy was witnessed in Bournemouth days by their neighbour and constant visitor, Adelaide Boodle (*R.L.S. and his Sine Qua Non*), 'Of course, there were fleeting tragedies at Skerryvore. There were moments when the casual looker-on might have felt it his duty to shout for the police – hastening their steps perhaps with cries of "murder!" But seasoned playgoers knew that neither the daggers nor the arrows were poisoned, and we soon became cheerfully confident that our hero and heroine would live happily ever afterward.'

Henry James was another constant visitor to Skerryvore and Stevenson wrote him, (*Letters*, Tusitala Edition 33, p.115), 'My wife is peepy and dowie . . . She is a woman (as you know) not without art; the art of

extracting the gloom of the eclipse from the sunshine; and she has
recently laboured in this field not without success or (as we used to say)
not without a blessing. It is strange: "we fell out my wife and I" the
other night; she tackled me savagely for being a canary-bird; I replied
(bleatingly) protesting that there was no use in turning life into *King
Lear*; presently it was discovered that there were two dead combatants
upon the field, each slain by the arrow of truth, and we tenderly carried
off each other's corpses. Here is a little comedy for Henry James to
write! The beauty was that each thought the other quite unscathed at
first. But we had dealt shrewd stabs . . . here are the kindest
recollections from the canary-bird and from King Lear; from the Tragic
Woman and the Flimsy Man.'
Henry James, who had first-hand knowledge, described Fanny as 'a
poor, barbarous and merely *instinctive* lady'.
To Henley, Stevenson was a little less loyal, 'I got my little finger into a
steam press called the Vandegrifter (patent) and my whole body and
soul had to go through after it. I came out as limp as a lady's novel, but
the Vandegrifter suffered in the process, and is fairly knocked about . . .
I am what *she has made me*, the embers of the once gay R.L.S.' That her
physical attractions aroused his sensual nature is stated in the poem
'Dark Women', by R.L.S., privately printed in 1899 by Belle Strong
under her Samoan name Teuila:

> I must not cease from singing
> And leave their praise unsung,
> The praise of the swarthy women
> I have loved since I was young.
> The hue of heather honey,
> The hue of honey bees,
> Shall tinge her golden shoulder,
> Shall tinge her tawny knees.
>
> Dark as a wayside gipsy,
> Lithe as a hedgewood hare,
> She moves a glowing shadow
> Through the sunshine of the fair;
> And golden hue and orange,
> Bosom and hand and head
> She blooms, a tiger lily,
> In the snowdrift of the bed.
>
> Tiger and tiger lily,
> She plays a double part,
> All woman in the body,
> And all the man at heart.

She shall be brave and tender,
She shall be soft and high,
*She* to lie in my bosom
And *he* to fight and die.

Take, O tiger lily,
O beautiful one – my soul.
Love lies in your body
As fire slumbers in coal.
I have been young and am old,
I have shared in love and strife
And the touch of a dusky woman
Is the dear reward of life.

In Vailima she was 'Tamatai' (Madame), also 'The Witch Woman of the Mountain'. Loved and feared by the Samoan servants, she wrote, 'I am glad to say that the gossip among the natives is that I have eyes all around my head and am in fifty places at once, and that I am a person to be feared and obeyed.'

Rev. W.E. Clarke, who came to Vailima when Stevenson was dying, remembered Fanny's small figure standing by the foot of the great redwood staircase. 'Without Louis, I am nothing,' she said. Stevenson left her his greatest tribute in the Dedication to *Weir of Hermiston*:

'TO MY WIFE:
I saw rain falling and the rainbow drawn
On Lammermuir. Hearkening I heard again
In my precipitous city beaten bells
Winnow the keen sea wind. And here afar,
Intent on my own race and place, I wrote.

Take thou the writing: thine it is. For who
Burnished the sword, blew on the drowsy coal,
Held still the target higher, chary of praise
And prodigal of counsel – who but thou?
So now, in the end, if this the least be good,
If any deed be done, if any fire
Burn in the imperfect page, the praise be thine.

                                                              R.L.S.'

She devoted the rest of her life to 'the Stevenson legend' and died in Santa Barbara, California, in February 1914 shortly before her seventy-fourth birthday, like Stevenson, of a cerebral haemorrhage. Her sister Nellie Sanchez wrote, (*Life of Mrs. Robert Louis Stevenson*) '..., even in her last days, a picture . . . of dainty, lacy, silken prettiness in which she sat enshrined. She was pretty as a young woman, but as she grew older she was beautiful . . . She kept her spirit young to the last, so that no one

could ever think of her as an old woman, and young people always enjoyed her company. Her ashes were interred beside Stevenson in the tomb on Mt. Vaea and an old Samoan chief told Belle, 'Tusitala is happy now. His true love has come back to him'.
(*See* Part 4 (Letters))

**Stevenson, Katharine,** daughter of Alan, sister of R.A.M. (Bob). (*See also* **de Mattos, Katharine; Henley, William Ernest**)

**Stevenson, Margaret,** Aberdeen-born girl, allegedly mistress of young Stevenson during Swanston Cottage days. There were rumours that she bore him a son, which biographers have been unable to substantiate. (*See* **Steuart, John A.**)

**Stevenson, Margaret Isabella Balfour,** (Mrs. Thomas Stevenson) Stevenson's mother. *From Saranac to the Marquesas and Beyond*, being letters written to her sister, Jane Whyte Balfour, 1887-88, (ed.) Marie Clothilde Balfour, Methuen, London, 1903; *Letters from Samoa: 1891-95*, ed. as above, Methuen, London, 1906

A minister's daughter, she was a frail young woman with a weak chest which required her to visit spas in Germany, the South of France and English resorts, when her son was small (Plate 1). Despite this early weakness at fifty-eight, newly widowed, she left respectable middle-class Edinburgh in 1887 to throw in her lot with her son, on his travels, first to the United States where she found herself in Saranac. A year later, she was voyaging on a yacht to the 'cannibal islands'. An excellent sailor, she drank champagne and wore the *holoku*, abandoning the corseted Victorian shape of 'proper womanhood'. She was only a decade older than Fanny Stevenson and when she was in her sixties she rode a horse for the first time and mastered the bicycle. Her back ramrod straight, her widow's caps crisply starched, she never forgot the pious upbringing of her early days and earnestly pressed conversion upon tough sea-captains and Polynesian 'savages' with equal zeal. The 'Popeys', i.e. Catholic converts, were a deadly challenge to her Presbyterianism and she constantly wrestled with their beliefs, urging their feet on to the reformed path. Before reaching Vailima, she again crossed half the world to nurse a sick sister in Edinburgh and returned to Samoa via Sydney. Discovering that Vailima was not yet ready for habitation, she prudently decided on a visit to relatives in New Zealand. As 'Aunt Maggie' she was a solid, reliable character in the Vailima regime. Utterly devoted to 'her boy', when he died she returned again to Scotland and lived with her sister until her death of pneumonia, in 1897 at the age of sixty-eight. 'Thinking she saw her son at the foot of the bed, she exclaimed, "There is Louis! I must go," and fell back, unconscious, though she did not actually breathe her last until the next day.'

(*See also* **Balfour, Dr. Lewis; Stevenson, Thomas;** Part 4 (Letters))

*Stevenson Medley: Facsimiles of Davos Press*, Chatto & Windus, London, 1899

*'Stevenson Museum, Edinburgh, The'* (*see* **Nolan, J.B.**)

*Stevenson Reader: Selected Passages from the Works of R.L.S.*, (*see* **Osbourne, Lloyd**)

**Stevenson, Robert,** (1772–1850), Stevenson's grandfather, son of a Glasgow merchant, lost his father in infancy. At 19 he was apprenticed to Thomas Smith, first engineer of the Lighthouse Board, a widower, who married Robert's mother Jean in 1792. Robert succeeded his stepfather in 1796. During 47 years as consultant engineer, he was responsible for 23 lighthouses, and invented the system of 'intermittent' and 'flashing' lights. He received a coat-of-arms with a lighthouse and the motto *Coelum non solem*

**Stevenson, Robert Louis,** for details of Stevenson's life, see Chronology pp. xix-xxii. He was described at various ages by his stepson, Lloyd Osbourne in *An Intimate Portrait of Robert Louis Stevenson* and some of these descriptions were included in the Tusitala Edition as prefaces:

*'Stevenson at Twenty-Six* (Plate 4): It was at the old inn at Grez-sur-Loing that I first saw Robert Louis Stevenson. I was eight years old, a tousled-haired, barefoot child who was known to that company of artists as "Pettifish" . . . At Hotel Chevillon, Louis [Stevenson], . . . was everybody's hero; Louis was the most wonderful and inspiring of men; his wit, his sayings, his whole piquant attitude towards life were unending subjects of conversation. Everybody said: "Wait till Louis gets here," with an eager and expectant air . . . Then in the dusk of a summer's day as we all sat at dinner about the long table d'hôte, some sixteen or eighteen people, of whom my mother and sister were the only women and I the only child, there was a startling sound at one of the open windows giving on to the street, and in vaulted a young man with a dusty knapsack on his back. The whole company rose in an uproar of delight, mobbing the newcomer with outstretched hands and cries of greeting. He was borne to a chair; was made to sit down in state, and still laughing and talking in the general hubbub was introduced to my mother and sister. "My cousin, Mr. Stevenson," said Bob, and there ensued a grave inclination of heads, while I wriggled on my chair very much overcome and shyly stole peeps at the stranger. He was tall, straight, and well-formed, with a fine ruddy complexion, clustering light-brown hair, a small tawny moustache and extraordinarily brilliant brown eyes. But these details convey nothing of the peculiar sense of power that seemed to radiate from him – of a peculiar intensity of character that while not exactly dominating had in its quality something

infinitely more subtle and winning; and he was besides, so gay, so
sparkling, so easily the master in all exchange of talk and raillery that I
gazed at him in spell-bound admiration.

. . . after the meal when we all trooped down to the riverside to see the
"Cigarette" and the "Arethusa" – the two canoes that had just finished
the "Inland Voyage" – the stranger allowed me to sit in his, and even
went to the trouble of setting up the little masts and sails for my
amusement. I was very flattered to be treated so seriously – R.L.S.
always paid children the compliment of being serious, no matter what
mocking light might dance in his brilliant brown eyes – and I instantly
elected him to a high place in my esteem.

While the others talked I appraised him silently . . . Stevenson's
peculiar clothes and long unkempt hair have often been regarded as
affectations. The truth, however, throws a rather pathetic light on these
supposed idiosyncrasies. It must be recalled that his literary earnings at
the start were so scanty that he was forced, much against his will, to live
with his family in Edinburgh; and that his rare cheques represented just
so much freedom from the deadening life at home. The longer he could
spin out his money, the longer he could remain away from Edinburgh.
Like many another poor young man he wore flannel shirts to save
washing and economised on his clothes till they were wretchedly
shabby. Such a reduced wardrobe was saving, too, in tips and cabs, for
he could carry all he had in the world in a small valise; and there was the
added advantage that he could lodge in the cheapest quarters without
exciting remark. It can be imagined what a singular figure he cut in
conventional London drawing-rooms and clubs, and how naturally and
smilingly he made a virtue of necessity and hid the humiliating truth . . .

[At Grez] he was gay and buoyant and kept everyone in fits of laughter.
He wore a funny-looking little round cap such as schoolboys used to
have in England; a white flannel shirt, dark trousers, and very neat
shoes. Stevenson had very shapely feet; they were long and narrow with
a high arch and instep, and he was proud of them. However shabbily he
might be dressed, he was always smartly shod . . .

It is strange how many of Stevenson's strongest opinions failed to find
any expression in his books. He was emphatically what we could call
today a "feminist". Women seemed to him the victims alike of man and
nature. He often spoke of the chastity enforced on them under pain of
starvation; he often said there would be no children had men been
destined to bear them and that marriage itself would disappear. What
man, he asked besides, would ever have the courage of a woman of the
streets? In those days of large families the accepted right of men to breed
their wives till they died filled him with loathing. He spoke of instances
amongst his own Edinburgh acquaintance – one of them an important
judge and a pillar of the church – and said that "his gorge rose" at sitting
at the same table with him. "He killed his first wife, and is now killing

his second, damn him!" The obligation for women to be attractive at any age and in any circumstances appeared to him also as not the least of their many disabilities. I remember him saying: "My God, Lloyd, think of all those poor old slab-sided, broken-backed frumps having to stick flowers in their hats and go through with the horrible affectation of pretending to be desirable" . . . It was the same with social reform. Both on this subject and his views about women, Stevenson was far ahead of his times – so far ahead, indeed, that I imagine he thought there was no audience for such opinions. The Victorian era, superficially at least, appeared set in an unalterable mould; nothing seemed ever destined to change . . . Of course, he was no saint. One would do his memory a poor service by endowing him with all the perfections. His early life had been tempestuously intermixed with those of many women, and I have never heard him express a wish that it might have been otherwise; on occasions he could swear vociferously, and when roused he had a most violent temper; he loved good wine and the good things of life; he often championed people who were not worth championing, impulsively believing in them, and getting himself, in consequence, in a false position . . . [But] no human being was ever freer from pettiness, meanness, or self-seeking; none ever more high-minded or sincere; and none surely ever possessed of a greater indulgence towards the erring and fallen. In this, indeed, one does see a saintly quality. There were no irreparable sins to Stevenson; nothing that man or woman might do that was not redeemable; he had an immeasurable tolerance, an immeasureable tenderness for those who had been cast by the world outside the pale . . .

Young as I was, I could not help noticing that R.L.S. and my mother were greatly attracted to each other; or rather how they would sit and talk interminably on either side of the dining-room stove while everybody else was out and busy, under vast white umbrellas, in the fields and woods. I grew to associate them as always together, and in a queer, childish way I think it made me very happy. I had grown to love Luly Stevenson as I called him; he used to read the *Pilgrim's Progress* and the *Tales of a Grandfather* to me, and tell me stories "out of his head": he gave me a sense of protection and warmth, and though I was far too shy ever to have said it aloud, he seemed so much like Greatheart in the book that this was my secret name for him. When autumn merged into early winter, and it was time for us to return to Paris, I was overjoyed when my mother said to me: "Luly is coming, too".

*Stevenson at Twenty-Eight*: I was ten when my mother left Paris and came to London to spend several months before sailing for New York on the way to California . . . Our lodgings at 3 Radnor Street, Chelsea . . . was a mean little house in a mean little street, and was as dingy and depressing as cheap London lodgings usually are . . . When R.L.S.

finally came I was conscious of a subtle change in him; even to childish eyes he was more assured, more mature and responsible. I was quite awed by his beautiful blue suit with its double-breasted coat, and the new stiff felt hat he threw on one side; and there was much in his eager talk about "going to press" and "closing the formes" and Henley "wanting a middle" about such and such a subject. He was now connected with new weekly, called *London*, and evidently found the work very congenial and amusing. He was constantly dashing up in cabs, and dashing away again with the impressive prodigality that apparently journalism required. Indeed, he seemed extraordinarily happy in his new occupation and was full of zest and high spirits.

I was greatly fascinated by the cane he carried. In appearance it was just an ordinary and rather slender walking-stick, but on lifting it one discovered that it was a steel bludgeon of considerable weight. R.L.S. said it was the finest weapon a man could carry, for it could not go off of itself like a pistol, nor was it so hard to get into action as a sword-cane. He said that in a tight place there was nothing to equal it, and somehow the impression was conveyed that journalism often took a man into very dangerous places. When he forgot it, as he often did, I was always worried until he returned . . .

. . . Meanwhile the hour of parting was drawing near. I had not the slightest perception of the quandary my mother and R.L.S. were in, nor what agonies of mind their approaching separation was bringing; and doubtless I prattled endlessly about "going home" and enjoyed our preparations, while to them that imminent August spelled the knell of everything that made life worth living. But when the time came I had my own tragedy of parting, and the picture lives with me as clearly as though it were yesterday. We were standing in front of our compartment, and the moment to say goodbye had come. It was terribly short and sudden and final, and before I could almost realise it R.L.S. was walking away down the long length of the platform, a diminishing figure in a brown ulster. My eyes followed him hoping that he would look back. But he never turned, and finally disappeared in the crowd. Words cannot express the sense of bereavement, of desolation that suddenly struck at my heart. I knew I would never see him again.

*Stevenson at Twenty-Nine* (Plate 13): Monterey in 1879 was a sleepy old Mexican town, with most of its buildings of sun-dried bricks called *adobe*. Fashionable people could be told by the amount of silver embellishments on their saddles, bridles and spurs, and how richly they jingled as they passed . . . Our home was a small, two-storeyed, rose-embowered *adobe* cottage fronting on Alvarado Street . . . it was here one morning in our sitting-room that my mother looked down at me rather oddly, and with a curious brightness in her eyes, said: "I have news for you. Luly's coming." I think R.L.S. must have arrived the next day. I remember his walking into the room, and the outcry of delight that greeted him; the incoherence, the laughter, the tears; the heart-welling joy of reunion. Until that moment I had never thought of him as being in ill-health. On the contrary, in vigour and vitality he had always seemed amongst the foremost of those young men at Grez; and though he did not excel in any of the sports he had shared in them exuberantly. Now he looked ill even to my childish gaze; the brilliancy of his eyes emphasised the thinness and pallor of his face; his clothes, no longer picturesque but merely shabby, hung loosely on his shrunken body, and there was about him an indescribable lessening of his alertness and self-confidence. This fleeting impression passed away as I grew more familiar with him in our new surroundings. Certainly he had never seemed gayer or more light-hearted, and he radiated laughter and good spirits . . . my father came down for a short stay, his handsome smiling face just a little clouded and with a curious new intonation in his voice during his long closeted talks with my mother . . . shortly afterwards I was taking a walk with Stevenson. He was silent and absorbed; I might not have been there at all for any attention he paid me. Ordinarily a walk with him was a great treat . . . a richly imaginative affair . . . But this walk had been thoroughly dull . . . not a breath of romance had touched us; and Luly's pace had been so fast besides, that my little legs were tired.

All at once he spoke, and here again was this strange, new intonation, so colourless, and yet so troubling, that had recently affected the speech of all my elders.

"I want to tell you something," he said. 'You may not like it, but I hope you will. I am going to marry your mother." I could not have uttered a word to save my life. I was stricken dumb. The question of whether I were pleased or not did not enter my mind at all. I walked on in a kind of stupefaction, with an uncontrollable impulse to cry – yet I did not cry – and was possessed of an agonising feeling that I ought to speak, but I did not know how, nor what.

But all I know is that at last my hand crept into Luly's, and in that mutual pressure a rapturous sense of tenderness and contentment came flooding over me. It was thus we returned, still silent, still hand in hand, still giving each other little squeezes, and passed under the roses into the house.

*Stevenson at Thirty-One*: Davos in 1881 consisted of a small straggling town where nearly all the shops were kept by consumptives. It possessed a charity sanitorium and three large hotels, widely separated from one another, in which one could die quite comfortably . . . The dead were whisked away very unobtrusively. You might meet Miss Smith coming out of room 46, say – and then suddenly realise that this had been Mrs. Robinson's room, and that you had not seen her for some time. People you had not seen for some time could usually be found in the cemetery, though their intervening travels had been marvellously screened from notice. The only note of tragedy that was ever apparent was at the weekly weighing of patients . . . R.L.S. stood the weekly ordeal very creditably. Davos agreed with him; he steadily gained weight and was unquestionably better. My mother and he kept themselves somewhat aloof from the others and though friendly and approachable, they were never drawn into the passionate enmities and intimacies of the place. Stevenson was never much at ease with ordinary, commonplace English people, possibly because they always regarded him with suspicion. He had untidy hair, untidy clothes, unconventional convictions, no settled place – at that time – in the scheme of things; and was, moreover, married to a divorcée. The Hotel Belvedere thought very little of him, one way or the other . . . One of the inmates of the hotel was a gaunt, ill-dressed, sallow young woman, the wife of a dying clergyman, who used to waylay me, and ask in the most frightening way whether I loved Jesus . . . Later she made a point of descending to the dining-room at the very early and unfrequented hour that Stevenson breakfasted and started the habit of passing him little notes – all about his soul, and the sleepless nights his spiritual danger was causing her.

Stevenson was as polite and considerate as he was to everyone; too polite and considerate, for one morning . . . a young man who habitually sat near us – detected the transfer of one of these little notes, and that night, swelling with self-righteousness, pointedly ignored Stevenson, and made a stage-play of speaking only to my mother.

This led to an explanation in our bedroom. The young man was sent for, the notes were shown him in the presence of my mother, I gave my childish evidence and R.L.S. was exonerated. But my principal recollection was his zest in the whole little drama – the unjust accusation, the conspicuous public affront borne in silence, the thumping vindication with its resultant apologies and expressions of regret, and finally the stinging little sermon on scandal and scandal-mongers.

*Stevenson at Thirty-Two:* . . . It was about this time [in Davos 1882] I noticed how much darker R.L.S.'s hair was becoming. It had turned to a dark brown and was so lank that at a little distance it appeared almost black. The hair has a curious way of reflecting one's physical condition; and judging by this criterion R.L.S. must have been very ill. He no longer tobogganned with me, and seldom walked as far as the town – about a mile distant. Usually he contented himself with pacing up and down his verandah, or descending to the foot of our hill to drop in on John Addington Symonds.

*Stevenson at Thirty-Four:* When I came out to Hyères in 1884, I had been absent a year from my mother and R.L.S. A year is an immense period in a growing boy's life, and I was now almost sixteen . . . I was aware of a curious change in my family . . . I had expected to take up things where I had left off, and felt a little baffled and lonely as I readjusted myself to altered conditions. It is not that R.L.S. was not extremely kind, or that anything was lacking in the warmth of his welcome. But somehow he had receded from me; and though my mother stuffed me with delicacies, and overflowed with confidences about the new life and new interests, she had receded, too. Woggs, the Skye terrier, alone met me on the old basis. That year was nothing to Woggs; there was no recession about him; he jumped all over me and smelled the same boy.

This first impression of aloofness gradually disappeared, but on marshalling my recollections it does seem strange that I strolled so seldom with R.L.S. and talked with him so little . . . the only time in my life when Stevenson and I were not delightfully intimate. My own idea is that the routine of his days was so pleasantly filled that I was hardly more than a supernumerary; too old for any childish appeal, and too immature for any other. I was in the nature of an interruption, to be borne with amiably but exciting no special interest.

R.L.S. looked very well, and much better than I last remembered him. His hair was cut short; he wore presentable clothes; and at a little distance, in a straw hat, he might have been mistaken for an ordinary member of society. The short black cape, or *pélérine*, that he always preferred to an overcoat was a typically French garment, and in France, of course, aroused no comment. In fact I found he had become very much of a Frenchman, even to the little "Imperial" on his chin. Speaking French fluently as his own language, as familiar with French literature and French politics as with English, nowhere more at home than in his adopted country, he had shed nearly everything English about him . . .

It is easy to understand what R.L.S. wrote afterwards that the time he spent in Hyères was the happiest of his life. He was working hard and well, was gaining recognition and making a fair income; had many irons in the fire, or coming out of it . . . The routine of his existence suited him to perfection – at his desk all the morning; then luncheon with an excellent *vin du pays*, and never lacking a salad; a stroll afterwards in the sunshine, to drop in and talk politics with old Le Roux, the wine merchant, . . . or his friend, Powell, the English chemist. Then home to look over his correspondence and write a few letters, with an excellent little dinner to follow and a conversation . . . Although R.L.S. always wrote so feelingly about his friends it was remarkable how well he could do without them. Few men had so little need of intimacies as he. Human intercourse of some kind was essential; . . . but anyone with any originality of mind and power of expression would suffice . . . who loved talk and argument and discussion; it refreshed him, exhilarated him, brought him home with brightened eyes and a good appetite . . . he

was one of the most prepossessed men that ever lived . . . his work
always came first . . . was the consuming joy and passion of his life.
Unconsciously I think he graded his friends by their interest in it;
regarded them as helpful satellites who could assist and cheer him on his
way . . .
*Stevenson at Thirty-Five*: "Wensleydale" was one of a tall row of lodging-
houses on the West Cliff of Bournemouth, overlooking the sands below,
and with a gloriously sparkling view of the Needles and the Isle of
Wight . . . It was lovely autumn weather when R.L.S. and my mother
arrived. They were in the highest spirits; everything pleased them; and
although they were carrying all they possessed with them, and had
neither home nor plans – and ought to have been rather forlorn, one
should think – they were as happy as grigs, and seemed not to have a care
in the world. They were supposed to come for a few weeks to see a little
of me before I left my tutor's to enter Edinburgh University; nothing
was further from their minds than to remain in England; it was taken for
granted that they would finally return to the Continent to seek another
and a more hygienic Hyères. Little could they foresee that their visit to
Bournemouth was destined to last almost three years, and was then to
lead, not to France or Italy, but to America and the South Sea Islands. I
am dwelling on the gaiety of those months at "Wensleydale" because it
marked what might be called the end of an epoch in Stevenson's life. He
was never afterwards so boyish or so light-hearted; it was the final flare-
up of his departing youth. The years that followed, however full they
were of interest and achievement, were greyer; it was a soberer and a
more preoccupied man that lived them. The happy-go-lucky Bohemian,
who had been rich if he could jingle ten pounds in his pocket and who
talked so cheerfully of touring France in a caravan . . . was soon to
discover that success had its penalties as well as its sweets. It was all
inevitable, of course; such hard work could not escape its reward, and
none of us can keep back the clock. Stevenson is to be envied that he
retained his youth as long as he did.
But he left it at "Wensleydale".
Henley came – a great, glowing, massive-shouldered fellow with a big
red beard and a crutch; jovial, astoundingly clever, and with a laugh that
rolled out like music . . . And he had come to make us all rich! . . .
R.L.S. was no longer to plod along as he had been doing; Henley was to
abandon his grinding and ill-paid editorship; together they would
combine to write plays – marvellous plays that would run for hundreds
of nights and bring in thousands of pounds . . . *Beau Austin* was written in
four days, and I shall never forget Henley reading it aloud – so
movingly, so tenderly, that my eyes were wet with tears. But deep
down within me was a disappointment I tried hard to stifle . . . But
disillusion was slow in coming, even though the succeeding plays
pleased me as little as the first. The gorgeous dream was not so easily

wafted away . . . But Stevenson, I think, came soonest out of the spell;
was the first to rub his eyes and recover his common sense. His ardour
certainly declined; in the interval of Henley's absences he very gladly
returned to his own work, and had, as a playwright, to be resuscitated by
his unshaken collaborator, who was as confident and eager as ever.
R.L.S. lost not only the last flicker of his youth in "Wensleydale", but I
believe also any conviction that he might become a popular dramatist.

*Stevenson at Thirty-Seven:* "Skerryvore" was an unusually attractive
suburban house, set in an acre and a half of ground, and its previous
owner – a retired naval captain – had been at no little expense to
improve and add to it . . . The house and five hundred pounds towards
furnishing it were a wedding present to my mother from R.L.S.'s
parents. The wanderers were now anchored; over their heads was their
own roof-tree; they paid rates and taxes and were called on by the vicar.
Stevenson, in the word he hated most of all, had become the "burgess"
of his former jeers. Respectability, dullness and similar villas
encompassed him for miles in every direction . . . of all men he was the
least fitted for ordinary English suburban life. Not that he saw much of
it; he was virtually a prisoner in that house the whole time he lived in it;
for him those years in "Skerryvore" were grey indeed.
His health throughout was at its lowest ebb; never was he so spectral, so
emaciated, so unkempt and tragic a figure. His long hair, his eyes so
abnormally brilliant in his wasted face, his sick-room garb, which he
picked up at random and to which he gave no thought – all are
ineffaceably pictured in my mind; and with the picture is an ineffable
pity. Once at sunset I remember him entering the dining-room, and,
with his cloak already about him, mutely interrogating my mother for
permission to stroll in the garden. It had rained for several days, and this
was his first opportunity for a breath of outside air.
"Oh, Louis, you mustn't get your feet wet", she said in an imploring
voice.
He made no protest; he was prepared for the denial; but such a look of
despair crossed his face that it remains with me yet. Then, still silent, he
glanced again towards the lawn with an inexpressible longing.
Afterwards in Samoa, I reminded him of that little scene at a moment
when his exile was weighing most heavily on him. We were both on
horseback and had stopped for a cigarette; the palms were rustling in the
breeze and the lovely shores of Upolu far below were spread out before
us in the setting sun. He gave a little shudder at the recollection I had
evoked, and after a moody pause exclaimed: "And all for five minutes in
a damned back-yard! No, no, no; I would be a fool ever to leave Samoa!"
And, as though to emphasise the contrast, dug the spurs into his horse
and started off at a headlong gallop.
Of course his health varied. There were periods when he was

comparatively well; when he would go to London to spend a few days. Once he even got as far as Paris; once he went to Dorchester to see Thomas Hardy and, continuing on to Exeter, was overtaken by an illness that lasted three weeks, and brought him to death's door. But in general he was a prisoner in his own house and saw nothing of Bournemouth save his own little garden. There could be no pretence that he was not an invalid and a very sick man. He had horrifying haemorrhages; long spells when he was doomed to lie motionless on his bed lest the slightest movement should re-start the flow; when he would speak in whispers, and one sat beside him and tried to be entertaining – in the room he was only too likely to leave in his coffin. How, thus handicapped, he wrote his books is one of the marvels of literature – books so robustly and aboundingly alive that it is incredible they came out of a sick-room; and such well-sustained books with no slowing down of their original impetus, nor the least suggestion of those intermissions when their author lay at the point of death . . . One day he came down to luncheon in a very preoccupied frame of mind – hurried through his meal – an un-heard of thing for him to do – and on leaving said he was working with extraordinary success on a new story that had come to him in a dream, and that he was not to be interrupted or disturbed even if the house caught fire.

For three days a sort of hush descended on "Skerryvore"; we all went about, servants and everybody, in a tiptoeing silence; passing Stevenson's door I would see him sitting up in bed, filling page after page, and apparently never pausing for a moment. At the end of three days the mysterious task was finished, and he read aloud to my mother and myself the first draft of *The Strange Case of Dr. Jekyll and Mr. Hyde*. . . . Then R.L.S.'s father died suddenly and we had all to go to Edinburgh to attend the funeral. I returned soon after . . . In the course of time two letters arrived, the first from my mother – such a heart-broken letter – saying that the doctors had ordered R.L.S. to leave England at once . . . as the only means of prolonging his life. England was ended for him; he was never to set foot in it again. She wrote of her "little nest" and the unendurable wrench it would be to leave it. "Life has been too happy in Skerryvore – the envying gods have struck it down."

*Stevenson at Thirty-Eight*: Saranac [New York] suited R.L.S. extremely well. He gained in weight; his spectral aspect disappeared; in a buffalo-coat and astrakhan cap he would pace the veranda for hours, inhaling that piercing air which was so noticeably benefiting him. He worked hard; hard and well . . . R.L.S. had set his heart on the Pacific, but as there seemed no likelihood whatever of finding a suitable yacht in San Francisco, it looked as though he would have to content himself with the Indian Ocean . . . When mother left us in the spring to visit her sister in

California, our plans were so definitely leading towards the Indian
Ocean, that it was only in a joking spirit that R.L.S. had said at parting:
"If you *should* find a yacht out there, mind you take it."
Six weeks later came the telegram that was to have such a far-reaching
effect on our lives . . . [*Casco*] . . . can be ready for sea in ten days. Reply
immediately – Fanny."
Stevenson answered: "Blessed girl, take the yacht and expect us in ten
days – Louis."

*Stevenson at Thirty-Nine*: [Hawaii] . . . The seven months' cruise [to
Hawaii on *Casco*] had just concluded. It had had a marvellous effect on
R.L.S. He had become almost well; could ride, take long walks, dine
out, and in general lead the life of a man in ordinary health . . . His fine
complexion had regained its ruddy tint; his hair, now cut short, was no
longer lank, but glossy and of a lighter brown; his eyes, always his most
salient feature and always brilliant, had no longer that strange fire of
disease; he walked with a firm, light step; and though to others he must
have appeared thin and fragile, to us the transformation in him was
astounding. In his soft white shirt, blue serge coat, white flannel
trousers, white shoes and white yachting cap (such caps were his
favourites till his death) he looked to perfection the famous author who
has arrived in a yacht, and who 'dressed the rôle' as actors say, in a
manner worthy of his dashing schooner.
It was typical of Stevenson that instead of choosing the best room in the
house for his own he should seek out a dilapidated, cobwebby little
shack, thirty or forty yards away, and papered with mildewed
newspapers, in which to install himself. Here in complete contentment,
with his cot, flageolet, and ink-bottle, he set himself to the task of
finishing *The Master of Ballantrae* – while centipedes wriggled unnoticed
on his floor, lizards darted after flies, and the undisturbed spiders
peacefully continued the weaving of their webs. Here King Kalakaua
would occasionally drop in on him for a long and confidential talk, while
the horses of the royal equipage flicked their tails under a neighbouring
tree, and the imposing coachman and footman dozed on their box . . .
Kalakaua . . . grave, earnest, rather careworn man, dressed usually in
the most faultless of white flannels, who seldom came to see us without
his chamberlain carrying books and who was always urging Stevenson
to "stay and make your home with us – Hawaii needs you" . . . But most
compelling of all . . . was R.L.S.'s desire to stroll into the Savile Club
and electrify all his old friends as the returned seafarer from the South
Sea Islands. At least he was constantly dwelling on this phase of his
return, and choosing the exact hour when he could make the most
dramatic entrance. But as the conviction grew that he never could be so
well as in the Pacific, and with the vague and romantic idea of finding an
island of his own, he began to talk of another cruise and look about for

the means. The means, alas, were strictly limited to one ship, the missionary vessel *Morning Star* . . . on her annual tour of the mission stations . . . there ensued a laughable daily discipline in which we tried to prepare ourselves for the ordeal. R.L.S. determined to cure himself of swearing, but whenever he was brought up short in the middle of conversation he was apt to lose his temper and swear roundly at the interrupter – usually myself . . . recovering his equanimity, would send us off afresh by saying with absolute seriousness: "I am sorry, Lloyd; you are perfectly right; and for God's sake keep it up".

In ordinary society Stevenson never swore; he was as conventional in this respect as any other man of his position and breeding; but when he felt the need of emphasis, especially when he was excited, and in the midst of his family and intimates, the oaths came ripping out in startling profusion . . . One noonday R.L.S. came driving in from Honolulu, his horses in a lather, and it needed but a single look at his face to see that he was wildly excited!

"Have chartered a schooner!" he shouted out before he even jumped down; and as we all crowded about him he breathlessly continued: "The *Equator*, sixty-eight tons and due back from San Francisco in a month to pick us up for the Gilbert Islands. Finest little craft you ever saw in your life, and I have the right to take her anywhere at so much a day!"

A hectic luncheon followed; champagne was opened in honour of the occasion . . . "And we can smoke on that blessed ship!" cried Stevenson with uplifted glass.

"And drink!" cried I . . . "And swear!" exclaimed my mother delightedly – she who had never said 'damn' in her life . . .

*Stevenson at Forty*: It was exhilarating to work with Stevenson [in Apemama]; he was so appreciative, so humorous – brought such gaiety, *camaraderie* and goodwill to our joint task. We never had a single disagreement as the book [*The Wrecker*, which was written in collaboration with Lloyd Osbourne] ran its course; it was a pastime, not a task, and I am sure no reader ever enjoyed it as much as we did. Well do I remember him saying: "It's glorious to have the ground ploughed, and to sit back in luxury for the real fun of writing – which is rewriting."

*Stevenson at Forty-Three* (Plate 23): Stevenson made a very large income and spent it all on Vailima. His letters often show much anxiety about money and some of his intimate correspondents lectured him severely on his extravagance. Often he lectured himself, as the assiduous Stevensonian well knows; often in moments of depression he called Vailima his Abbotsford, and said he was ruining himself like Scott . . . Much of the money spent on Vailima was in the nature of capital investment; and once completed – had he never written another line – he could have lived there comfortably, and in no lessened state, on his income from royalties. Moreover, at his mother's death, he was to come into a very considerable inheritance from his father. While Vailima was undoubtedly a fantastic extravagance, it was at least within his means, and he had nothing to fear from the future had he lived.

In recent years people have surprised me by asking, usually in a lowered voice: "Wasn't Stevenson very morose? Did he not have violent outbreaks of temper when it was unendurable to live with him? Was there the least truth in that idyllic life in Vailima?" . . . There were times when Stevenson was terribly on edge with nerves; when he would fly into a passion over nothing; when jaded and weary he would give way to fits of irritation that were hard, indeed, to bear. But it must be remembered that he was one of the most unselfish, lofty-minded and generous of men; there was no pettiness in him, nothing ignoble or mean. He was no petulant sick man raging at his family because one of his comforts had been overlooked. Rather was it the other way. He cared nothing for risk or danger, and went into it with an appalling unconcern. Of all things he hated most were anxious efforts to guard his health or make him comfortable. Once I tried to put a mattress on the almost bare boards he slept on. It was like disturbing a tiger! The mattress nearly went out of the window in a fury of oaths. Such passions were not without their humour, and afterwards Stevenson was often as ready to laugh over them as we.

How could anyone hold the least resentment against such a sorely tried and heroic man whose repentances were as impulsive as his outbreaks? No, the sad part of life in Vailima was the consciousness of that physical martyrdom; of that great, striving heart in so frail a body; the sight of that wistful face, watching us at tennis, which after but a single game had ended – for him – in a haemorrhage; the anguish which underlay that invincible optimisim and which at rare moments would become tragically apparent; the sense of a terrible and unequal struggle; the ineffable pity swelling in one's breast until it became almost insupportable . . .

That Stevenson sometimes chafed against his enforced exile is only too true. There are passages in his letters that read very pathetically. But had his health improved and had he returned to Europe, would he really have been content in some pretentious "Skerryvore" or "La Solitude?" I cannot think so. His life of feudal splendour in Samoa would have seemed twice as resplendent in the retrospect and in some French or Italian villa I believe he would have broken his heart to return. Samoa filled his need for the dramatic and the grandiose; he expanded on its teeming stage, where he could hold warriors in leash and play Richelieu to half-naked kings . . .

On his day-time visits to Apia, Stevenson usually wore a coat and riding-breeches of what were called "Bedford cord", with high-laced tan boots and spurs. This "cord" was very fine, light-weight whipcord, and suits of it were made for Stevenson by one of the best Sydney tailors. He was very particular too, about his boots,which were also made to order in Australia, and fitted his long, slender aristocratic feet to perfection. At home he ordinarily dressed in white trousers, white shirt, and low shoes to match, though like everybody else in that hot, sticky climate, he went barefooted about the house. Even our highest European dignitaries were apt to scurry for their shoes and socks when callers were unexpectedly announced. It was all part of that delightful *"fa'a samoa"* which meant following the custom of the country, and condoned in one disarming word almost everything – from lack of shoes to lack of marriage certificates . . .

Stevenson may not have been always happy in Vailima, but of one thing I am sure, he was happier there than he could have been in any place in the world.

*The Death of Stevenson*: Stevenson had never appeared so well as during the months preceding his death, and there was about him a strange serenity which it is hard to describe, for in quoting from his talks I might easily convey a sense of depression and disillusionment that would read like a contradiction. I think he must have had some premonition of his end; at least, he spoke often of his past as though he were reviewing it, and with a curious detachment as though it no longer greatly concerned him.

"I am the last of Scotland's three Robbies," he said once. "Robbie Burns, Robbie Fergusson, and Robbie Stevenson – and how hardly life treated them all, poor devils! If ever I go back I shall put up a stone to poor Fergusson on that forgotten grave of his." Then he repeated the words in broad Scots as though their cadence pleased him: "Scotland's three Robbies!"

On another occasion he said to me: "I am not a man of any unusual talent, Lloyd; I started out with very moderate abilities; my success has been due to my really remarkable industry – to developing what I had in me to the extreme limit. When a man begins to sharpen one faculty, and keeps on sharpening it with tireless perseverance, he can achieve wonders. Everybody knows it; it's a commonplace; and yet how rare it is to find anybody doing it – I mean to the uttermost as I did. What genius I had was for *work!*"

Another observation of his comes back to me: "A writer who amounts to anything is constantly dying and being re-born. I was reading *Virginibus* the other day, and it seemed to me extraordinarily good, but in a vein I could no more do now than I could fly. My work is profounder than it was; I can touch emotions that I then scarcely knew existed; but the Stevenson who wrote *Virginibus* is dead and buried, and has been for many a year..."

Several times he referred to his wish to be buried on the peak of Mount Vaea. Although it was on our property and was always conspicuously in our view, Stevenson was the only one of us who had ever scaled its precipitous slopes. But in spite of his request I never could bring myself to cut a path to the summit . . . I shrank . . . from the association with his death that it involved. What was it but the path to his grave? And to work on it was unutterably repugnant to me . . . I always contrived to evade his request. In the late afternoon, as some of us played tennis in front of the house, he would walk up and down the veranda, and I began to notice how often he stopped to gaze at the peak.It was specially beautiful at dusk with the evening star shining above it, and it was then he would pause the longest in an abstraction that disturbed me. I always tried to interrupt such reveries; would call to him; ask him the score; would often drop out of a game in order to join him and distract his attention. It is a curious thing that his previous illnesses, which might so easily have concluded in his death, caused me less anguish than the look on his face as he now stared up at Vaea. I think it was the realisation that he meant to fight no longer; that his unconquerable spirit was breaking; that he was not unwilling to lie on the spot he had chosen and close his eyes for ever . . . He was working hard on *Weir of Hermiston*, and was more than pleased with his progress. He was well. Why then, should his glance linger so persistently on the peak of Vaea and always in that musing way? It troubled me . . .

. . . I had some business in Apia, and did not return until late in the afternoon . . . R.L.S. was dictating some of *Weir* to my sister and they both seemed glad to stop and listen to the budget of news I had brought up . . . Then after a little talk, which looking back on it I recall as even gayer than usual, I went over to the cottage to change and have a plunge in the pool. I was away perhaps an hour or more, when I heard a curious stir in the house and a voice calling my name. Tragedy always has its own note. The intonation was sufficient to send me in startled haste across the way.

Stevenson was lying back in an arm-chair, unconscious, breathing stertorously and with his unseeing eyes wide open; and on either side of him were my mother and sister, pale and apprehensive. They told me in whispers that he had suddenly cried out: "My head – oh, my head!" and then had fallen insensible. For a while we fanned him; put brandy to his lips, strove in vain to rouse him by speaking. We could not bring ourselves to believe he was dying. Then we had a cot brought down, and taking him in my arms – it was pitiable how light he was – I carried him to it and extended him at length. By this time the truth was evident to us – that he had had an apoplectic stroke. His reddened face and that terrible breathing were only too conclusive . . . I went at breakneck speed for the doctor in Apia . . . At my urging – I simply would not tolerate any denial – he timidly mounted my horse, giving me the little black bag he dared not carry himself. With this in my hand I ran after him through the town hoping to find a tethered horse on the way. Sure enough there was one and in an instant I was on it and galloping off, while its astonished owner, emerging from a bar, gazed after me with amazement...

Stevenson, where I left him on the cot, was still breathing in that dreadful way. The doctor looked down at him long and earnestly and then almost imperceptibly shook his head.

"A blood-clot on the brain," he said, "He is dying."

In half an hour, at about eight in the evening, Stevenson was dead . . .

Among the hundreds of letters which arrived after his sudden death were moving tributes from his close friends; Henry James wrote to Fanny, ' . . . To have lived in the light of that splendid life, that beautiful, bountiful being – only to see it, from one moment to the other, converted into a fable as strange and romantic as one of his own, a thing that *has* been and has ended, is an anguish into which no one can enter with you fully and of which no one can drain the cup for you. You are nearest to the pain, because you were nearest the joy and the pride . . . He lighted up one whole side of the globe, and was in himself a whole province of one's imagination . . . He has gone in time not to be old, early enough to be generously young and late enough to have drunk deep of the cup . . . I hope that you are feeling your way in feeling all sorts of encompassing arms – all sorts of outstretched hands of friendship. Don't, my dear Fanny Stevenson, be unconscious of *mine*, and believe me more than ever faithfully yours – Henry James.'

Fanny treasured this memorial along with one other. Pencilled on a scrap of paper, from Hawaii, it came unsigned, 'Mrs. Stevenson, Dear Madam: All over the world people will be sorry for the death of Robert Louis Stevenson, but none will mourn him more than the blind white leper of Molokai.'

For further aspects of Stevenson's character *see* **Christianity of Stevenson; Children; Marriage; Morals; 'On Falling in Love'; Social Conscience of Stevenson.**

Books and articles about Stevenson, the titles of which commence with his name in some form, are so numerous that for ease of reference they have been brought together and are arranged in alphabetical order of the cross-reference. For a list of Stevenson's works see pages 349–356.

CROSS-REFERENCE

'R.L. Stevenson'                                          *Academy, The*
*Robert Louis Stevenson: His Work
    and Personality*                                      Adcock, A.St.J.
'Stevenson's "Lost" Home'                                 Angus, D.
'R.L.S. at Skerryvore'                                    Archer, William
'R.L.S.: His Style and Thought                            ,,          ,,

'Stevenson's Catholic Leaning'
'Mr. Robert Louis Stevenson'
'Stevenson Unwhitewashed'
Robert Louis Stevenson: A Life
   Study in Criticism
Stevenson: Homes and Haunts of
   Famous Authors
'Robert Louis Stevenson: By
   Two of his Cousins'
Stevenson Study, A: Treasure Island
Robert Louis Stevenson at Buckstone
'Robert Louis Stevenson in an
   English Home: Skerryvore
Robert Louis Stevenson
Robert Louis Stevenson and
   Jules Simoneau
'Stevenson's California'
'R.L.S.'
R.L.S. and His Sine Qua Non
'Some Stevenson Pictures'
'Stevensonia: The Trudeau
   Dedications'
'Robert Louis Stevenson'
Robert Louis Stevenson
Robert Louis Stevenson
'R.L.S.: 1850–1950'
Robert Louis Stevenson
'Robert Louis Stevenson and
   "Henderson's Weekly"'
Robert Louis Stevenson
R.L.S.: A Life Study
Robert Louis Stevenson Companion, The
Stevenson and Victorian Scotland
'Robert Louis Stevenson:
   The Hills of Home'
'Stevenson and Monterey: Thirty
   Years After'
Robert Louis Stevenson
'Stevenson in the South Seas'
'Robert Louis Stevenson in Samoa'
'Stevenson Library of H.A.
   Colgate, NY City'
'Robert Louis Stevenson at
   Hampstead'

Ashe, Rev. Matthew
Athenaeum Club
Atlantic Monthly

Baildon, H. Bellyse

,,        ,,

Balfour, Mr. and Mrs. J. Craig
Barnett, David
Bennet, James

Black and White Magazine
Black, Margaret Moyes

Blanch, Josephine Mildred
Bland, Henry Mead
Bohemian, The
Boodle, Adelaide
Book Buyer, The

,,        ,,
Bookman
Bowman, John
Brill, Barbara
British Broadcasting Corporation
Brown, Alice

Bushnell, G.H.
Butts, Denis
Calder, Jenni
,,        ,,
,,        ,,

Chambers Journal

Chase, J.S.
Chesterton, G.K.
Churchill, William
Clarke, Rev. W.E.

Colgate, H.A.

Colvin, Sir Sidney

**Stevenson's Baby Book,** the record of the sayings and doings of Robert Louis Balfour Stevenson, printed for John Howell by John Henry Nash, San Francisco, 1922

**'Stevenson's Companion to the Cook Book, Adorned with a Century of Authentic Anecdotes',** first published in Tusitala Edition 5, 1924.

'Authentic Anecdotes' on Fielding and Richardson, Laurence Sterne, Robert Burns, Judge Jeffries [sic], St. Athanasius, John Knox and the Almoner of the Galley. It was begun during the cruise of the *Casco* and continued throughout his time in the South Seas. 'It really is a cookery book, and he' [McClure] 'has published the plums and left out the cookery.' (McClure did not however publish.) The Stevensons had other cookery book projects but none materialised

**Stevenson, Thomas,** (1818–1887) an eminent member of a famous family of lighthouse builders. He married Margaret Balfour and Stevenson was their only child. *Christianity Confirmed by Jewish and Heathen Testimony*, Adam & Charles Black, Edinburgh, 1884

The suggestion of stern Victorian father, rigid, harsh and bigoted, is conveyed in granite-faced photographs (Plate 2). Thomas Stevenson did, however, have humour and had a deep love for his strange son whom he nicknamed 'Smout' ( Scots word for a young salmon). When Smout was feverish, his father would sit outside his bedroom door and converse with imaginary persons for the invalid's entertainment. Thomas Stevenson obviously had a certain charm, since Stevenson wrote in a note to *Kidnapped* in 1880, 'I have rarely been well received among strangers, never if they were womenfolk . . . it pleased and amused me to be a sharer in my father's popularity, and in the public sitting-rooms to be the centre of delighted groups of girls; the stormy and tender old man with the noble mouth and great luminous eyes, had, almost to the end, so great a gift of pleasing.' On his daily walks he made friends with dogs, maintaining that dogs had souls; he also stopped schoolboys and asked what they were learning out of the load of books they carried. Shaking his head he would then advise them to drop the whole thing, learn only what seemed good to them or , if it pleased them better, nothing.

When during student days, the relationship between Stevenson and his parents became rather strained, he wrote to Mrs. Sitwell (*Letters*, Tusitala Edition *31*, p.187), 'I have discovered why I get on always so ill, am always so nasty, so much worse than myself, with my parents; it is because they always take me at my worst, seek out my faults, and never give me any credit . . . I am always bad with them because they always seem to expect me to be not very good; and I am never good because they never seem to see when I am good.'

Stevenson thought it a good idea that his father and Fanny should meet in Paris in 1878. However, perhaps Thomas Stevenson was too innocent to see the situation between the two which was being spelled out for him as he seemed quite unprepared for his son's dash to America to persuade Fanny to leave her husband and marry him. 'Divorce' was an ugly word and Thomas Stevenson wrote to Colvin, 'For God's sake use your influence. It it fair that we should be half murdered by his conduct? I am unable to write more about this sinful mad business . . . I see nothing but destruction to himself as well as to all of us. I lay all this at the door of Herbert Spencer. Unsettling a man's faith is indeed a very serious matter.'

Doutbless their son's outrageous behaviour caused them considerable unhappiness as well as the social stigma of having a divorcée in the family. Stevenson wrote to Baxter from San Francisco, ' . . . with my parents all looks black', and to Henley, 'I am glad they mean to disinherit me . . . I always had moral doubts about inherited money and this clears me of that forever'. However, love conquered bitterness and when they thought he might die, a cable came, 'Count on £250 a year'. And just before his marriage to Fanny, Stevenson wrote to her brother Jake Vandegrift, ' . . . if I can keep well next winter, I have every reason to hope the best; but on the other hand, I may very well never see next spring. In view of this, I am all the more anxious she should see my father and mother; they are well off, thank God, and even suppose that I die, Fanny will be better off than she had much chance of being otherwise. . . ' But Fanny soon had the elder Stevensons eating out of her small determined brown hands. She wooed them with letters first and then, when they met, by her great personal charm. Whenever she and Stevenson were in financial distress, which was constant, Stevenson would groan that they had better write to his father. And Thomas Stevenson never failed them; as Stevenson wryly put it, 'I always fall on my feet, but the legs are my father's'.

In 1884 when Thomas was sixty-six, it was obvious that he was 'failing'; he was suffering from a series of cerebral haemorrhages (perhaps something of the same affliction which had so tragically and prematurely destroyed his brilliant brother Alan). As the condition grew worse he clung more than ever to his only son, now completely reconciled, and his dependence too grew on Fanny, whom he loved and treated as a beloved daughter. Sometimes in Bournemouth and elsewhere the father and son were observed together, the son a pathetic nurse for his father.

Margaret Stevenson patiently endured her husband's erratic behaviour, his sudden changes from joviality to abject melancholia. When he could not sleep he kept her awake to keep pace with his restlessness. One night exhausted, they both fell asleep. A short while afterwards Margaret was aroused by her husband's announcement, 'My dear, the end is now come; I have lost the power of speech'. In May 1887, a telegram arrived at Skerryvore. Immediately they left for Edinburgh. 'My father-in-law was fighting death inch by inch,' wrote Fanny. 'His memory gone, his reason shattered, nothing remained but his determined will. It was a terrible figure we found sitting grimly in the drawing room of the house at Heriot Row . . . Mr. Stevenson had always vowed that he wanted to die on his feet, so he was sedately clad in a broadcloth suit and cravat, smoking his pipe in an armchair.' He did not recognise Fanny or his son, which was a great shock. ' . . . it was not until an hour or two before his death that he could be persuaded to lie upon his bed and then only after a narcotic had been administered.' At midday on 8 May, he fell gently asleep. He had always considered life ' "as a shambling sort of omnibus which is taking him to his hotel," ' wrote Stevenson to Mrs. Sitwell (*Letters*, Tusitala Edition *31*, p. 184). His funeral was the largest private occasion Edinburgh had seen. Stevenson caught cold and was forbidden to attend by his uncle. Dr. George Balfour. To Colvin he remembered his 'dear, wild noble father, as a man of fifty, lying on a hillside and carving mottoes on a stick, strong and well; and as a younger man running down the sands into the sea near North Berwick.'

Before his death, his achievements had been recognised in his appointment as President of the Royal Society of Edinburgh. He supported privately a 'Magdalen Institution for. fallen women', and, despite his feeling when divorce came to his own doorstep, maintained that Victorian womanhood was ill-treated by the law and that any woman should have divorce for the asking while no man be allowed divorce.

(*See also* **Christianity of Stevenson; Stevenson, Bob; Stevenson, Margaret, Isabella Balfour; Stevenson, Robert; L.J.R. Club;** Dedication to **Familiar Studies of Men and Books;** 'Thomas Stevenson' in **Memories and Portraits;** Part 2 (Thomas Stevenson); Part 4 (Letters))

**'Stevensonia; The Trudeau Dedications'** (*see* **Book Buyer, The**)

**Stevensonian, The,** journal of the Robert Louis Stevenson Club, London (ed.), Ernest J. Mehew

**Stevensoniana: An Anecdotal Life and Appreciation of Robert Louis Stevenson** (*see* **Hammerton, J.A.**)

**Stewart, George R.,** 'The Real Treasure Island'. Speculation as to the island's location, *University of California Chronicle*, April 1926

**'Stimulation of the Alps, The'**, an essay, first published in *Pall Mall Gazette*, 5 March 1881; in book form in *Essays and Criticisms*, Herbert B. Turner, Edinburgh, 1903; 'Swiss Notes', *Further Memories*, Tusitala Edition *30*

**Stobo Manse** (*see* **Peebles**)

**Stoddard, Charles Warren,** 'Stevenson's Monterey', National Magazine, December 1906 (*See also* Part 4 (Letters))

**'Story of a Lie, The'**, a story, first published in *New Quarterly Magazine*,

October 1879; Tusitala Edition *14*; Stevenson received £50 for this story

Misunderstanding concerning a prodigal artist father, Van Tromp, who has not seen his daughter Esther since she was a child, and a young friend of his, Dick Naseby, who becomes her suitor, and has then to set matters right between them.

**'Story of a Recluse, The'**, an unfinished story, first published in *Hitherto Unpublished Prose Writings*, 1921; Tusitala Edition *16*

*Story of Robert Louis Stevenson, The (Tusitala the Tale-Teller)*, (*see* **Vulcan, Jenny**)

**Strange Case of Dr. Jekyll and Mr. Hyde, The**, (*see* **Dr. Jekyll and Mr. Hyde**)

*Strange Case of Robert Louis Stevenson, The*, (*see* **Elwin, Malcolm; Schultz, Myron G.**)

**Strathdee, R.B.**, '*R.L.S.-nomad*', *Aberdeen University Review*, autumn 1954. Stevenson's delight in the gipsy life; his early wanderings at home and abroad

**Stringer, Raymond**, 'A Davos Printing-Press: R.L.S. and his Stepson's Publishing Firm', *Chambers Journal*, February 1950

**Strong, Austin**, 'His Oceanic Majesty's Goldfish', *The Atlantic Monthly*, Boston, May 1944; 'The Most Unforgettable Character I've Met', *The Reader's Digest*, New York, March 1943. Childhood reminiscences of his step-grandfather Robert Louis Stevenson in Samoa.

Fanny had been married to Stevenson for less than a year when she became a grandmother, the result of her daughter Belle's elopement with the artist Joe Strong in California. Austin joined the Vailima household when he was ten years old and, after his parents divorced, was sent to school in Monterey, so that he could vacation in Samoa. 'Not very forward in his schooling, not very brilliant at understanding,' was Stevenson's comment on his step-grandson. However, he showed symptoms of his 'Fanny-Gran's' green fingers by fulfilling an early ambition to be a landscape architect. Later he took to playwriting: *The Toymaker of Nuremburg* and, after World War I, *Three Wise Fools* and *Seventh Heaven* (which was made into a film). All his life he loved Fanny-Gran and when she died he said, 'To say that I miss her means nothing. Why, it is as if an Era had passed into oblivion. She was so much the Chief of us all, the Ruling Power. God rest her soul!'
(*See also* Part 4 (Letters))

**Strong, Isobel (Belle) (Isobel Osbourne)** (1858-1953) Daughter of Sam and Fanny Osbourne, stepdaughter of Stevenson. Married (1) Joseph

Stevenson dictating to Belle Strong in Vailima. *Mansell Collection*

Dwight Strong (one son, Austin) and (2) Edward Salisbury Field (no children)

Belle was seventeen when her mother met Stevenson, 'a bewitching young girl, with eyes so large as to be out of drawing'. She did not at first approve of her mother divorcing her darling papa, and her husband Joe Strong resembled him in character. He too had a way with women, but as he was not always scrupulously honest about money, Belle and he parted in Vailima and she became part of the Stevenson household, invaluable to her stepfather as amanuensis. One of the early island scandals, occasioned by Belle's rather swarthy beauty, was that she was Stevenson's illegitimate daughter by a native woman. Stevenson, far from being shocked, was delighted by the story – he was only eight years her senior – and he proceeded to build up a yarn that the story was true. His lost love, Belle's mother, had been a 'Moroccan, black but a damned fine woman', and when Fanny chided him before guests for not wearing his cape one rainy night, he said reproachfully, 'Moroccy never spoke to me like that!'

It was on his second visit to Sydney that he persuaded Belle to remain at Vailima. 'He gave me his side. It is the only time I ever knew him to be despondent in any way. He described the despair he felt when told he could never go back to London, to his home in Bournemouth; he would never see his native city Edinburgh again. Sentenced to exile for the rest of his life, what he wanted now was to make that exile bearable. "You and Lloyd are all the family I have," he said, "I want a home and a family, *my* family, round me." He told me too, that Lloyd's great ambition had been to go to Oxford, but that he had given it up to stay with Louis and our mother in Samoa. We talked till late, going back over old scores, clearing up old misunderstandings. Though I admired Louis and respected him, there had always been a hidden antagonism between us. Perhaps because I had adored my father, I was unconsciously critical of him. Even if he was the head of our family, I saw no reason why he should plan my life. But now all was changed. He talked with such kindness, such understanding, that every bit of resentment I had held towards him melted away, and I felt myself to be truly his loving daughter.'

Stevenson returned to the hotel with three topaz rings (his birthstone) one for each of them. Inside his own were engraved the initials F and B, and in theirs, R.L.S. With them a poem:

> 'These rings, O my beloved pair,
> For me on your brown fingers wear:
> Each, a perpetual caress
> To tell you of my tenderness . . .'

Divorced from Joe, she fell in love with Stevenson's cousin Graham Balfour, visiting the islands. The household at Vailima, particularly her mother, would have been delighted by the match, but Graham departed without proposing. After Stevenson's death Belle lived mostly with her mother in Santa Barbara, California, where Fanny died in 1914. Belle was then aged fifty-six and she married Edward (Ned) Salisbury Field, who had been one of her mother's protégés and secretary since 1902. Ned was contemporary to her son Austin and he too had drifted into playwriting. Belle died in 1953, aged ninety-four, surviving her brother Lloyd and son Austin.

(*See also* **Field, Edward; Field, Isobel (Belle) Strong** (for list of publications); *Catalogue (2);* Part 4 (Letters))

### Strong, Joseph Dwight

Young artist with whom Belle Osbourne eloped at Monterey in 1879. It was their enthusiasm for Hawaii, where Joe had gone to paint and had been córdially received into the Royal Hawaiian Court circle (as official artist) that encouraged the Stevensons to visit them in Honolulu and voyage to Samoa. Joe became part of the Vailima ménage but his continued instability, irritability (and alternate conviviality), were too much for Belle. They parted, then divorced, while Belle remained at Vailima as Stevenson's amanuensis.

**Stubbs, Laura,** *Stevenson's Shrine: The Record of a Pilgrimage,* Alexander

Moring, London, 1903. Interesting account with photographs of author's visit to Apia in Samoa.

***Studies of a Biographer,*** (*see* **Stephen, Sir Leslie**)

***Style of Robert Louis Stevenson, The,*** (*see* **Leatham, James**)

**'Suicide Club, The'**, a collection of three stories, first published (with 'The Rajah's Diamond') as 'Latter-Day Arabian Nights', 17 weekly instalments, *London*, 8 June-26 October 1878 (for which Stevenson received £44. 12s. 0d.); *New Arabian Nights*, 1882; Tusitala Edition *1*

First adventures of Prince Florizel of Bohemia and Colonel Geraldine in the Suicide Club, whose unlikely members have one bond in common – weary, dissolute men, they have had enough of life and are determined to die.

(*See also* **Stevenson, Bob**; Part 6 (Media)

**Sullivan, Thomas Russell,** *Passages from the Journal of T.R. Sullivan, 1891-93,* Houghton Mifflin, Boston, n.d. Contains an account of Sullivan's stage version of *Jekyll and Hyde* which had taken Boston by storm and was due to open in New York soon after Stevenson's arrival in August 1887

***Supernatural Short Stories of Robert Louis Stevenson, The,*** (*see* **Hayes, Michael**)

**Swanston Cottage**

In the summer of 1867, Thomas Stevenson took on the lease of Swanston Cottage, which was grander than the name implies – not a country holiday home but an imposing two-storey country residence on the slopes of the Pentland Hills. For the next seven years it was occupied at various times by young Stevenson, in sickness and in health, and it played a considerable part in his life at that time, part-refuge and part-inspiration. He could read, walk and dream in isolation, yet it was near enough to Edinburgh if he felt like a convivial evening with his friends. He remembered it fondly in exile, where it conjured up 'the hills of home'. (*See* Plate 9)

**Swanston Edition,** *The Works of Robert Louis Stevenson*, with an Introduction by Andrew Lang, 25 volumes, Chatto & Windus, London, 1911

**Swearingen, Roger C.,** *The Prose Writings of Robert Louis Stevenson: A Guide,* Macmillan, London, 1980. Highly-recommended, authoritative guide, containing much new material
(*See also* **Bibliographies**; **'Old Song, An'**)

**Swinnerton, Frank,** *R.L. Stevenson: A Critical Study,* Martin Secker, London, 1914. 'Only in boys' books has Stevenson's work been first rate, his other works seem nowadays to be consumptive.' 'R.L. Stevenson, Master-swordsman', *John o'London's Weekly*, 26 September 1952

**Swiss Notes,** four essays, forming part of *Further Memories*, Tusitala Edition *30*; (*see* **'Health and Mountains'**; **'Davos in Winter'**; **'Alpine Diversions'**; **'Stimulation of the Alps, The'**)

**Sydney, Australia**

The Stevensons arranged to meet Belle in Sydney, leaving the newly-cleared site for Vailima, February 1890. They appeared in the elegant Victoria Hotel, brown as gipsies, with a weird assortment of baskets. They were ill-received in reception and Belle arrived in time to see her stepfather leaving the lift and heading towards the desk in a tight-lipped fury. He had asked for a suite on the first floor and had been taken up to the fourth. He wanted two or three large rooms and was shown into one small one. And his luggage had not been sent up. He pointed at the shabby cedarwood chests tied with rope and the native baskets with their rolls of tapa cloth, coconut shells and calabashes. There were also fine mats and some dangerous looking weapons. The Stevensons were as odd-looking as their possessions: among the wasp-waisted elegant ladies, Fanny, small and sturdy, brown as a native, was wearing a flowing grey silk *holoku*, while Stevenson's suit had just emerged from six months in a cedarwood chest in the hold.

Belle suggested they go to a less grand hotel – the Oxford. They were courteously received and given a suite of comfortable rooms. When next day the manager and clerk of the Victoria read of the arrival of Mr. R.L. Stevenson, complete with interviews and stories about his books, they came to apologise abjectly and beg him to return – at half-rate. Stevenson refused and took a 'mildly malicious pleasure in the fact that the big hotel must send his letters over to the less fashionable Oxford in markets baskets'.

He visited Sydney again in 1890, and in 1891 and 1893. (*See* Plate 17)

**Symonds, John Addington,** (1840-93), *Letters and Papers,* (ed.) Horatio F. Brown, Murray, London, 1923; *Our Life in the Swiss Highlands*, Black, London, 1907; *Recollections of a Happy Life*, Black, London, 1892; *Some Further Recollections of a Happy Life*, Black, London, 1893

At Davos, Stevenson and the English critic and poet had consumption and literary matters in common. Symonds wrote of 'the beautiful companionship of the Shelley-like man, the eager gifted wife and the boy, for whom they both thought in all their ways and hours'. Despite an accompanying wife and four daughters to whom he was devoted, Symonds was one of the few homosexuals among his friends and

Stevenson described their friendship as 'an adventure in a thornbush, but his mind is interesting'.
(*See also* Part 4 (Letters))

# T

**Taalolo,** cook at Vailima and minor Samoan chief in his own right
Stevenson took him to see Honolulu (the equivalent of taking a
European boy to Paris). Taalolo developed measles before landing, but
fortunately was out of quarantine in time to take care of his master, who
was taken ill in the boarding-house at Waikiki. In gratitude, Stevenson
arranged that Taalolo should fulfil his great ambition – to ride on the
narrow-gauge railway from Honolulu to Pearl Harbor

**'Tadpole and the Frog, The',** a fable, Tusitala Edition 5 (*see also* **Fables**)

**Tahiti,** (*see* **Papeete; Moë, 'Princess'**)

**'Talk and Talkers',** an essay, first published in *Cornhill Magazine*, April
1882, a sequel in August 1882; in book form in *Memories and Portraits*,
1887; Tusitala Edition 29

**Tamasese, 'King',** one of the rival Samoan chiefs supported by the
Germans; rumour was rife that he sought to capture the Stevensons
and hold them as hostages against Mataafa and Malietoa
(*See also* **'Footnote to History, A'; Malietoa Laupepa, 'King';
Mataafa, 'King'; Samoan War**)

**Tamatai,** Fanny Stevenson's Samoan name, 'Madam'

**Tauchnitz,** German publishers prosecuted and fined for reprinting the
anti-German 'A Footnote to History'. Stevenson was so appreciative
of their gesture that he offered to pay half the fine and costs

**Tautira,** (*see* **Papeete; Moë, 'Princess'**)

**Taylor, A.P.,** *Under Hawaian Skies*. Stevenson's visit to Honolulu.
Advertiser Publishing Co., Honolulu, 1926

**Taylor, Sir Henry,** (1800–1886) and **Lady**
Part of Bournemouth society, 'that nest of British invalidism and British
Philistinism', as Stevenson described it. The Taylors were an exception.
He was a retired Colonial Office official and a poet; his wife befriended
Stevenson and gave him the famous South American red poncho which,
ink-spotted and shabby, became a permanent feature in his wardrobe to
the extent of his being photographed/sculpted in it. The Taylors also
introduced him to their psychical-researcher friend, F.W.H. Myers.

(*See* Dedication to *The Merry Men and Other Tales;* **Myers, Frederick W.H.: Taylor, Una;** Part 4 (Letters))

**Taylor, Una,** daughter of the above. *Guests and Memories: Annals of a Seaside Villa,* Oxford University Press, 1924. More about Bournemouth and Skerryvore
(*See also* Part 4 (Letters))

## Tembinok, 'King'

The shrewd and ruthless tyrant who earned the title 'Napoleon of the Gilberts', reigning over Apemama with an armed bodyguard of wives of all ages, a rule of terror supported by effective marksmanship. 'Whites' were unwelcome, the one missionary was tolerated only until he had served his purpose of teaching Tembinok English. Personally boarding all trading vessels, calmly appropriating whatever took his fancy, Tembinok's thatched palace abounded with rusted weapons and clocks. 'A beaked profile like Dante's in the mask, a mane of long black hair, the eye brilliant, imperious and inquiring. His voice matched it well, being shrill, powerful, and uncanny, with a note like a sea-bird's,' was Stevenson's description. Among the curios King Tembinok collected were fancy garments which he wore without regard to fashion. Frock coats with ladies'. evening gowns, top hats together with sunbonnets, flowered cravats and red flannel drawers. Yet he wore these incongruous garments with such dignity that it would have taken a very courageous man (or a very foolish one) to express amusement at the sight.

Boarding the *Equator* when it landed in Apemama in 1889, he decided that he liked Fanny Stevenson's dressing-case. As it had sentimental (and useful) associations for her, she refused his offer to buy it. However, when he became dangerously aggressive, she smiled sweetly and presented it to him as a gift. For once Tembinok was nonplussed. 'I shamed,' he said. By forcing him to accept something he had coveted, the Stevensons dinted his prestige. There was a photograph of Queen Victoria in the cabin. When informed that they were subjects of the British Queen, Tembinok presumed that Mr. Stevenson was a close relative of the Royal Family and hospitality was accordingly lavished upon them. They were persuaded to stay in a portable thatched house, carried on the shoulders of a dozen men to a place chosen by the King. With outhouses for servants, it was christened 'Equator Town' and protected from light-fingered inhabitants by a taboo placed by Tembinok walking in a circle around it. However, this 'magic' was made more effective by the constant threat of receiving a bullet in the back, should any of his subjects feel tempted to a little larceny.

The Stevensons settled in Apemama while the *Equator* continued her voyage, planning to collect them on the return journey. An unlikely

friendship ensued between the King and the author and soon the monarch was confessing shyly that he, too, wrote poetry. He 'knew it good' and was eager for Stevenson to read and praise it. Expecting a high proportion of blood and violence, Stevenson was amazed and delighted to encounter a passion for romance. As defined by Tembinok himself, it was, 'About sweethearts, and trees and the sea – and no true, allee same lie'. The King had never encountered a woman like Fanny Stevenson in his harem; she designed a royal standard for him (with a black shark in its centre in acknowledgement of his legendary descent from a woman-chief impregnated by the shark-god). Tembinok was delighted because this white woman was also an excellent shot with a rifle and a ruler in her own household. He shed genuine tears when the Stevensons departed on the next stage of their travels and, of Fanny, told her husband admiringly, 'She good; look pretty, plenty sense.'
(*See* **Apemama**)

**Tennant, Kylie,** *Long John Silver*, the story of the film adapted by Kylie Tennant from the motion picture screenplay by Martin Rackin, Sydney, 1954

**Tennyson, Alfred Lord,** (1809-1892), admired *The Merry Men* greatly and on hearing his son read it aloud pronounced, 'Hallam, remember we must have this book in the house'

**Teriitera,** (*see* **Ori à Ori**)

**Teuila,** Belle Strong's Samoan name, 'Adorner of the ugly', in gratitude for her habit of making the servants unexpected small gifts of trinkets and pieces of cloth

*This Life I've Loved,* (*see* **Field, Isobel Osbourne Strong**)

**Thistle Edition,** *The Works of Robert Louis Stevenson*, 26 vols., Scribner's New York, 1902

**Thomas, Dylan,** *The Beach of Falesá: Based on a Story by R.L. Stevenson*, 1964

**'Thomas Stevenson',** an obituary, in *Contemporary Review*, June 1887; in book form in *Memories and Portraits*, 1887; Tusitala Edition 29

**Thompson, Francis,** *The Real Robert Louis Stevenson and Other Critical Essays*, (ed.) Terence L. Connolly, University Publishers Inc., New York, 1959

**'Thrawn Janet',** a short story, first published in *Cornhill Magazine*, October 1881; in book form in *The Merry Men and Other Tales*, 1887; Tusitala Edition 8
A classic ghost story of a departed servant, Janet M'Clour, haunting her

employer, the Reverend Murdoch Soulis, in a Scottish Highland manse.
(*See also* **Pitlochry**; Part 6 (Radio))

**'Three David Balfours of Powis and their Friends, The',** (*see* **Morrison, Alexander**)

**Three Plays,** by W.E. Henley and R.L. Stevenson, David Nutt, London, 1892. Contains *Admiral Guinea, Beau Austin* and *Deacon Brodie.* With other plays in Tusitala Edition 24

**Through the Magic Door,** (*see* **Doyle, Arthur Conan**)

**Thurston, Sir John,** British High Commissioner of the Western Pacific during Stevenson's Vailima days

His 'Regulations for the Maintenance of Peace and Good Order in Samoa' prescribed imprisonment or fine for any British subject guilty of sedition towards the Samoan government; 'all practices, whether by word, deed, or writing, having for their object to bring about in Samoa, discontent or dissatisfaction, public disturbance, civil war, hatred or contempt towards the King or Government of Samoa or the laws or constitution of the country, and generally to promote public disorder in Samoa.' This document so worried Stevenson, who had been busily supporting the rebel chiefs, that he sought aid from Sidney Colvin in London, with the result that Thurston was reprimanded; 'No steps were to be taken about Mr. Stevenson and he was to amend his Regulation in accordance with British notions of law.'

(*See also* **'Footnote to History, A'**; **Mataafa, 'King'**; **Samoan War**)

**Thyne, C.A.M.,** 'A Footnote to History of R.L. Stevenson and the German Dictatorship,' *Scots Magazine*, December 1939

**'Time',** an essay, first published in *Vailima Edition* 1923; Tusitala Edition 25

**Today,** contained an article entitled 'A Chat with Mr. Robert Louis Stevenson' by an unnamed San Francisco journalist, 2 December 1893

**Todd, John,** shepherd, and friend of the young Stevenson at Swanston (*See also* **Waugh, J.L.**)

**Todd, Rev. William,** 'Robert Louis Stevenson in Braemar'. *Deeside Field*, No. 21, 1925. The writing of *Treasure Island*

**Too Many Birthdays,** Fanny Stevenson's first publication, a fairy story for an American periodical for children, *St. Nicholas Magazine*, 1878

**'To Prospero at Samoa'** (*see* **'Y.Y.'**)

**'To R.L.S.',** (*see* **Drinkwater, John**)

**Torquay,** Stevenson spent part of 1864 and 1865 in Torquay with his mother for his health's sake – and hers. His education at this time was by private tutor

*'To Tusitala in Vailima',* (*see* **Gosse, Sir Edmund William**)

**'Touchstone, The',** a fable, Tusitala Edition 5 (*see also* **Fables**)

*'Tragic End of Stevenson's Yacht "Casco", The',* (*see* **Dickie, Francis**)

**Travelling Companion, The,** a novel of Stevenson written at Hyères which has not survived. It was turned down by one publisher as 'a work of genius but indecent'. Stevenson decided it had 'no urbanity and glee and no tragedy'. It was destroyed but there is confusion among biographers whether he did so voluntarily or whether Fanny burned it, adding to the legend that *The Travelling Companion* may have been his autobiographical novel about Edinburgh associations with a street-walker.
(*See* **'Claire'; Drummond, Kate**)

*Travels in Hawaii* (*See* **Day, A. Grove**)

**Travels with a Donkey in the Cévennes,** first published by C. Kegan Paul, London, 1879; frontispiece by Walter Crane; Tusitala Edition 17 (*See also* **Skinner, R.T.**; Part 6 (TV))

Written at an unhappy time time in Stevenson's life; Fanny had returned to America – to her husband Sam Osbourne. 'For the present all idea of a union was impossible . . . the pain of parting without prospect of return, and he who was afterwards so long an exile from his friends, now suffered separation from his dearest by the breadth of a continent and an ocean', so wrote Graham Balfour in his *Life.*

Stevenson hints at his troubles in the Dedication letter to Sydney Colvin. 'The journey which this little book is to describe was very agreeable and fortunate for me. After an uncouth beginning, I had the best of luck to the end. But we are all travellers in what John Bunyan calls the wilderness of this world – all, too, travellers with a donkey; and the best that we can find in our travels is an honest friend. He is a fortunate voyager who finds many. We travel, indeed, to find them. They are the end and the reward of life. They keep us worthy of ourselves; and, when we are alone, we are only nearer to the absent. Every book is, in an intimate sense, a circular letter to the friends of him who writes it. They alone take his meaning; they find private messages, assurances of love, and expressions of gratitude dropped for them in every corner. The public is but a generous patron who defrays the postage. Yet though the letter is directed to all, we have an old and kindly custom of addressing it on the outside to one. Of what shall a man

be proud, if he is not proud of his friends? And so, my dear Sidney
Colvin, it is with pride that I sign myself?

Affectionately yours,

R.L.S.'

**Treasure Hunter, The: The Story of Robert Louis Stevenson,** (*see* **Proudfit, Isabel**)

**Treasure Island,** originally entitled *The Sea Cook*, it was first published
as *Treasure Island or The Mutiny of the Hispaniola* by 'Captain George
North', in *Young Folks*, 1 October 1881 to 28 January 1882 (for which
Stevenson received £30); in book form by Cassell, London, 1883;
Tusitala Edition 2.

Stevenson's best-known story for young readers tells how Jim Hawkins,
whose mother keeps the Admiral Benbow Inn, encounters an old
buccaneer who has in his possession a map showing the whereabouts of
Captain Flint's treasure. Jim outwits the old pirate's confederates, takes
the map to Squire Trelawney and thereupon sets out with the Squire and
Dr. Livesey in search of the treasure. Unfortunately the crew of the
*Hispaniola* are recruited by the sinister Long John Silver who plans to
dispose of the Squire and his party. Warned by Jim, a series of flights and
adventures follow which culminate in a meeting with a marooned
pirate, Ben Gunn, who leads them to where the treasure is hidden.

*Dedication:* 'To Lloyd Osbourne, an American gentleman in accordance
with whose classic taste the following narrative has been designed. It is
now, in return for numerous delightful hours and with the kindest
wishes, dedicated by his affectionate friend, THE AUTHOR.)

The Stevensons had fled from a family holiday in Pitlochry, hoping for a
milder climate in Braemar, in Deeside. Imprisoned by torrential rain
and chill winds, Fanny's son Lloyd Osbourne, 'a schoolboy . . . home for
the holidays, and much in want of "something craggy to break his mind
upon"', took to drawing. One day Lloyd was drawing a map of an island
when Stevenson offered help in colouring and naming it, 'the shape of it
took my fancy beyond expression; it contained harbours that pleased me
like sonnets; and with the unconsciousness of the predestined, I ticketed
my performance *Treasure Island* . . . The next thing I knew, I had some
paper before me and was writing out a list of chapters. How often have I
done so, and the thing gone no farther! But there seemed elements of
success about this enterprise. It was to be a story for boys; no need of
psychology or fine writing; and I had a boy at hand to be a
touchstone . . . On a chill September morning, by the cheek of a brisk
fire, and the rain drumming on the window I began *The Sea Cook*, for
that was the original title . . . And now, who should come dropping in,
*ex machina*, but Doctor Japp . . . charged by my old friend, Mr.
Henderson, to unearth new writers for *Young Folks*. Even the

ruthlessness of a united family recoiled before the extreme measure of inflicting on our guest the mutilated members of *The Sea Cook*; at the same time we would by no means stop our readings . . . the tale was . . . solemnly redelivered for the benefit of Doctor Japp . . . when he left us, he carried away the manuscript in his portmanteau . . . a set of lucky accidents: had not Doctor Japp come on his visit, had not the tale flowed from me with singular ease, it must have been laid aside like its predecessors, and found a circuitous and unlamented way to the fire.' The story of TREASURE ISLAND was not quite over: 'The proofs came,' [from Cassell] 'they were corrected, but I heard nothing of the map. I wrote and asked; was told it had never been received, and sat aghast. It is one thing to draw a map at random . . . and write up a story to the measurements. It is quite another to have to . . . design a map to suit the data. I did it, and the map was drawn again in my father's office, with embellishments of blowing whales and sailing ships . . . But somehow it was never *Treasure Island* to me.'

(*See also* **Admiral Guinea; Barnett, David; Braemar; Calahan, Harold Augustin; Connell, John; England, G.A.; 'My First Book'; Skinner, R.T.; Winterich, J.T.;** Part 6 (Media))

**'Treasure Island'** (*see* **Fagan, J.B.**)

**'Treasure of Franchard, The'**, a story, first published in *Longman's Magazine*, April and May 1883; in book form in *The Merry Men and Other Tales*, 1887; Tusitala Edition 8
Doctor Desprez and his wife Anastasie adopt a stable-lad, Jean-Marie, who helps in the search for the treasure of Franchard. It disappears and in the resumed search Doctor Desprez learns much about himself and Jean-Marie.
(*See also* Part 6 (Media))

**'Treasure of Robert Louis Stevenson, The'**, (*see* **Peattie, Donald and Louise**)

**Tree, Sir Herbert Beerbohm,** (1853–1917) English actor-manager who was invited to Bournemouth to consider Stevenson's and Henley's plays. He politely turned down a suggestion that he play in *Macaire*, but took the lead in *Beau Austin*

**Triggs, W.H.,** 'R.L. Stevenson as a Samoan Chief', *Cassell's Family Magazine*, February 1895; 'Stevenson's Life in Samoa', *Bookman*, New York April 1931. Articles on Vailima

**Trinity Academy, Edinburgh,** *William Fowler Stevenson Collection* compiled by A.S. Cowper, privately printed, Edinburgh, 1965. A catalogue of Stevensoniana in the the school library, bequeathed by William Fowler

**Trudeau, Dr. E.L.**, famous tuberculosis specialist of Saranac Lake. *An Autobiography*, Doubleday, Page & Co., New York, 1916
He found no active disease in Stevenson, only that it had been present and might recur. Stevenson inscribed the doctor's copy of *Prince Otto*, 'This is my only love tale, this Prince Otto, which some folks like to read and others *not* to.' The presentation copy of *Kidnapped* which followed in due course was inscribed, 'Here is the one sound page of all my writing, the one I'm proud of and that I delight in.'

***True Stevenson, The: A Study in Clarification,*** (*see* **Hellman, George S.**)

**'Truth of Intercourse'**, a essay, first published in *Cornhill Magazine*, May 1879; in book form in *Virginibus Puerisque*, 1881; Tusitala Edition 25

***Tuberculosis and Genius,*** (*see* **Moorman, Lewis J.**)

**Tusitala,** Stevenson's Samoan name, 'Teller of tales'

**Tusitala Edition,** *The Works of Robert Louis Stevenson*, 35 volumes, Heinemann, London, 1924

***Tusitala of the South Seas: The Story of Robert Louis Stevenson's Life in the South Pacific,*** (*see* **Ellison, Joseph W.**)

Tusitala – Teller of Tales. *Mansell Collection*

*Tusitala (Teller of Tales)* (*see* **Hines, L.J.** and **King, Frank**)

'**Tutuila**', an essay, first published in *Hitherto Unpublished Prose Writings*, by Bibliophile Society of America, 1921; Tusitala Edition *21*

**Twain, Mark,** (1835–1910), the American novelist and humorist met Stevenson on his second visit to America in 1887 and they spent an afternoon talking together in Washington Square, the prelude to a sporadic correspondence

*Twelfth Night,* in May 1875, as a student at Edinburgh University, Stevenson made one of his rare stage appearances in Edinburgh, as Orsino in Shakespeare's play, directed and produced by Professor and Mrs. Fleeming Jenkin

'**Two Falconers of Cairnstone, The**', projected tale for a volume which did not materialise but which eventually became the basis for 'An Old Song'.

'**Two Matches, The**', a fable, Tusitala Edition *5* (*see also* **Fables**)

'**Two Tahitian Legends**', I. Of the Making of Pai's Spear. II. Honoura and the Weird Women, essays, first published in *Longman's Magazine*, March 1892

# U

'**Uma**', original title of *The Beach of Falesá*

*Under Hawaiian Skies,* (*see* **Taylor, A.P.**)

*'Under Sentence of the Law',* (*see* **Stevenson, Fanny**)

'**Underwoods**', a collection of poems, first published in *Scribner's Magazine,* 26 August 1887; in book form by Chatto & Windus, London, 1887; Tusitala Edition *22*

*'Unique Bit of Stevensonia, An',* (*see* **Lee, Albert**)

*'Unique Collection of Stevenson, A',* (*see* **Gregg, Frederick James**)

*Unpossessed, The,* (*see* **McLaren, Moray**)

*Unpublished Manuscripts of Robert Louis Stevenson's Record of a Family of Engineers,* (*see* **Bay, J. Christian**)

*'Unveiling Ceremony at 17 Heriot Row Edinburgh, 5th March 1947'* privately-printed pamphlet describing the unveiling of a memorial tablet at Stevenson's home. Available for reference in Edinburgh Room, Edinburgh Central Library

**Upolu, Samoa,** island on which Vailima was built, first visited by Stevensons 7 December 1889. Apia was its chief town. (*See* **Apia; Equator; Vaea, Mount; Vailima**)

# V

**Vaea, Mount,** 1,300 ft. above sea level, its conical shape dominates
the Apia landscape and it was clearly visible from the Vailima house

After Stevenson's death on 4 December 1894, the Samoan servants
cleared a path through dense jungle growth to its summit and carried
'Tusitala's' coffin, draped with the Union Jack, up its steep side to the
flattened top, the size of a small room, where Stevenson prophesied that
he would be buried. In a letter to Colvin dated 23 August 1893, he wrote
(*Letters*, Tusitala Edition *35*, p.80), 'I *would* like you to [see Vailima], for
it's beautiful and my home and tomb that is to be; though it's a wrench
not to be planted in Scotland – that I never can deny – if I could only be
buried in the hills, under the heather and a table tombstone like the
martyrs . . . "Where about the graves of the martyrs the whaups are
crying. *His* heart remembers how!" Ah, by God, it does! Singular that I
should fulfil the Scots destiny throughout, and live a voluntary exile,
and have my head filled with the blessed, beastly place all the time!'
(*See also* **Apia**; Plates 24, 25)

**Vaekehu, 'Queen'**

During their six-week stay in the Marquesas, the Stevensons were
invited to a ceremonial visit to be received by the ex-cannibal queen,
whose tattoo from head to foot was 'perhaps the greatest masterpiece of
that art'. In recent years she had been converted by missionaries to the
Catholic Church, and now hid her 'masterpiece' under a *holoku* from
which only hands and wrists protruded. At first glance, 'Maggie'
Stevenson presumed she was wearing blue lace mittens, then she realised
they were of dye and not of material and had been 'paid for in the cooked
flesh of men'. 'Once her leg was one of the sights of Taiohae' wrote
Stevenson, impressed by her life of love and adventure. Beautiful in her
youth, men had fought over her, died for her, and she had been passed
from husband to husband, captor to captor, with the varying fortunes of
war. One of the few women privileged by her station to take part in the
cannibal orgies that were the triumphant end of all victories, she now
lived in a neat wooden house built in European style, and received
visitors with European grace. Although her manners were exquisite,
Stevenson remembered those other days and 'found it a little strange to
sit at table with a lady who was well-known to have kept cold
missionary on the sideboard'.

(*See also* **Kooamua, Chief; Moanatini, 'Prince' Stanislas**)

*Above* '. . . two Burmese gods flanked the great staircase . . .' *Mansell Collection*

**Vailima, Apia, Samoa,** pronounced 'Vye-LEE-ma', meaning 'five waters'

In February 1890 Stevenson wrote to Baxter (*Letters*, Tusitala Edition *33*, p.285) 'I have bought 314½ acres of beautiful land in the bush behind Apia; when we get the house built, the garden laid, and cattle in the place, it will be something to fall back on for shelter and food; and if the island could stumble into political quiet, it is conceivable it might even bring a little income . . . We range from 600 to 1,500 feet, have five streams, waterfalls, precipices, profound ravines, rich tablelands . . . a great view of forest, sea, mountains, the warships in the haven . . .' and in August (*Letters*, Tusitala Edition *33*, p.303) 'If I die, it will be an endowment for the survivors, at least my wife and Lloyd . . . There is my livelihood, all but books and wine . . .'

He did not add that Vailima had a bad reputation locally as a great haunt of *aitu*, demon-ghosts of both sexes. Once a cannibal chief had lived just where the house of Vailima was sited – he used to stretch a rope across the ground and claim all who crossed it for his table. Not surprisingly, he was haunted by the ghosts of his victims, and servants were ready with the tale of a man and woman who were murdered where the house was being built and claimed that their spirits often appeared. Although Fanny supported Stevenson in the Vailima venture, she wrote, 'Because

I make my sacrifice with flowers on my head and point out the fine views on the way, do not think that it is no sacrifice and only for my own pleasure. The Samoan people are picturesque but I do not like them . . . I shall be able to get no servants but cannibal black boys . . . I do want Louis, and I do want everybody to think I like going to Samoa – and in some ways I do like it; I don't want people to think I am making a sacrifice for Louis. In fact I *can't* make a sacrifice for him; the very fact that I can do the thing in a way makes it a pleasure to do it, and it is no longer a sacrifice, though if I did it for another person it would be.' In January 1891 the house was begun. Money was short and it could not be completed according to the original plan; extensions would have to be added later. The Sydney architect's design would cost $20,000 and they could afford only $7,500. Refusing to be defeated, they consulted the local carpenter and insisted on a chimney – mostly for drying Stevenson's bed-sheets. Chimneys in Samoa were a rare sight and this one cost a thousand dollars for the bricks and haulage. The temporary cottage cost the same as every piece of wood, glass, nails and paint had to be imported from the United States, Australia or New Zealand. Eventually the main house was complete. Made of wood, large and airy, it conformed strongly to British tropical architecture and was painted peacock blue with a red iron roof. There were shutters to keep out the winds and gauze-screened windows to keep the insects at bay. Hanging mats or curtains sufficed for doors and the verandahs extended along the whole north side both up and downstairs. Bathroom and kitchen had

*Below* Stevenson's house in Samoa. *Mansell Collection*

piped water from storage tanks filled when the rain obligingly poured down the corrugated roof. The cookhouse was separate, in the South Seas manner, but joined to the main house by a covered way. The main room was the dining-room (until such time as the Stevensons could afford a drawing-room). Furnished according to Fanny's taste it was 'papered with yellowish tapa, the woodwork of dull blue, the window and door hung with curious Indian fabrics of yellow silk and silver, a real fireplace in the wide corner, a source of never-ending wonder to our people . . . old leather-covered chairs, the Chippendale sideboard and corner cupboard [from Heriot Row, via Bournemouth and Skerryvore], the latter containing the most precious of the old china. Some chairs . . . and pictures, including one of Bob's. The painting of Louis with a conceited smile and a dislocated leg is by Sargent.'

After December 1892 the downstairs accommodation consisted of three rooms, a bath, a storeroom and cellars below, with five bedrooms and the library upstairs. On the ground floor, a verandah, twelve feet deep, ran in front of the whole house and along one side of it. The chief feature within was the large hall that occupied the whole of the ground floor of the newer portion of the house – a room about sixty feet long and perhaps forty wide, lined and ceilinged with varnished redwood from California. Local society was impressed by the imposing display of mahogany and rosewood, silver, crystal, china, family portraits. Two Burmese gods flanked the great staircase and, as well as a bust of Grandfather Robert Stevenson, there were carved cabinets dated 1642. The islanders were awed by the pomp and style, as well as the many possessions of the Vailima household, where even important whites lived in meagre style, 'making-do', and whenever a family left the island there were others ready to rush to the auction sale which normally followed and snap up a few bargains and necessities of civilised life. Visitors were impressed not only by the surroundings but by the delicious food and wines, for dinner at Vailima became an event of island life. The fine cooking was supervised by Fanny, with artichokes, aubergines, sweet corn, melons, tomatoes and beans from her unique vegetable garden, served in the elegance of silver covers, with crystal goblets of red wine and under shaded lights which reflected the redwood panelling of the 'great hall'. Samoans with flowers in their hair were in attendance, keeping watch too on the braziers under the table which smoked away the mosquitoes. On special occasions, such as birthdays, Thanksgiving, Christmas and the like, the servants wore the Stevenson Clan uniform, invented by their master and consisting of striped blazers and *lavalavas* (loin-cloths) of Royal Stewart tartan, carefully chosen to compliment their light brown skins. Samoans who neither wanted nor needed to work, thanks to a life-giving and preserving climate where food could be obtained from the trees, were delighted to swarm upon Vailima and in due course, with appropriate sad stories ingeniously invented, produce an abundance of cousins and kin-by-marriage. Such a household was a considerable drain upon Stevenson, who soon found that he had to write to keep Vailima's roof above his head – and the numerous heads of his ever-growing dependants. In addition he was haunted by nostalgia for the native land to which he could never return. On 6 June 1893, he wrote to Colvin (*Letters*, Tusitala Edition *35*, p.35), 'I was standing out on the little verandah in front of my room this morning, and there went through me or over me a wave of extraordinary and apparently baseless emotion. I literally staggered. And then the explanation came, and I knew I had found a frame of mind and body that belonged to Scotland, and particularly to the neighbourhood of Callander. Very odd these identities of sensation, and the world of connotations implied; highland huts, and peat smoke, and the brown swirling rivers, and wet clothes, and whisky, and the romance of the past, and that indescribable bite of the whole thing at a man's heart, which is – or rather lies at the bottom of – a story.' In addition he relished the chieftain image but remarked drily, 'We call them our marble halls, because they cost so much to keep up.' He was acutely conscious of the fate of his hero Sir Walter Scott, who had found himself similarly trapped by the glories of Abbotsford, which destroyed him as surely as the demands of Vailima were to destroy Stevenson. (*See also* **Scott, Sir Walter**)

Vailima is now the official residence of the head of state of Western Samoa

(*See* Plates 19, 20, 21, 22, 23)

**Vailima Edition,** *The Works of Robert Louis Stevenson,* (ed.) Lloyd Osbourne and Fanny Stevenson, 26 vols., Wm. Heinemann, London, 1922-23

**'Vailima Letters of Robert Louis Stevenson, The',** (*see* **Booth, Bradford A.**)

**'Valiant in Velvet',** (*see* **Brill, Barbara**)

**Vallandigham, Edward N.,** 'Robert Louis Stevenson', *Book Buyer*, April 1895

**Vallings, Harold,** 'Stevenson Among the Philistines', *Temple Bar,* February 1901

**Vandegrift family,** family of Fanny Stevenson. Her father Jacob was a farmer, lumberjack-merchant, real-estate businessmen, who made and lost money with fearsome regularity. Her mother, Esther Keen, was a women of considerable fortitude, whom Fanny resembled both in appearance and character. There was one son, Jake, and four younger daughters, Cora, Elizabeth, Josephine and Nellie (*see* **Sanchez, Nellie Vandegrift; Stevenson, Fanny**)

**Van Renssalear, Mrs. M.G.,** 'Robert Louis Stevenson and His Writing', *Century*, November 1895

**Vendetta in the West, A,** Soon after landing in America for the first time, Stevenson planned a novel the central character of which was named 'Arizona Breckenridge'; later he abandoned the idea

**'Victor Hugo's Romances',** a essay, first published in *Cornhill Magazine*, August 1874; in book form in *Familiar Studies of Men and Books*, 1882; Tusitala Edition 27

*Victorians All,* (*see* **Masson, Flora**)

**Vince, C.A.,** 'Stevenson and Scott', *Century Literary Magazine*, 1927

*Violent Friend, The: The Story of Mrs. Robert Louis Stevenson,* (*see* **Mackay, Margaret**)

**'Virginibus Puerisque',** an essay, first published in *Cornhill Magazine*, August 1876, became the title of Stevenson's earliest volume of collected papers, published by C. Kegan Paul, London, 1881; Tusitala Edition 25

*'Visit to the Library of R.L. Stevenson at Vailima, Samoa',* (*see* **Mahaffy, A.W.**)

*Voyage to Windward,* (*see* **Furnas, J.C.**)

**Vulcan, Jenny,** *The Story of Robert Louis Stevenson (Tusitala the Tale-Teller),* Stead's Publishing House, London, 1896

# W

'**Waif Woman, The**', a short story, a folk tale of Iceland in the style of the great sagas, first published in *Scribner's Magazine*, December 1914; in book form by Chatto & Windus, London, 1916; Tusitala Edition 5. When it first appeared suggestions were that its publication had been suppressed by Fanny during her lifetime

**Waingrow, Marshall,** (*see* **Ferguson, De Lancey**)

**Wakefield, Sir Charles,** 'My Meeting with Stevenson', an essay in *A Cadger's Creel* (*see* **Douglas, Sir George**)

'**Walking Tours**', an essay, first published in *Cornhill Magazine*, June 1876; in book form in *Virginibus Puerisque*, 1881; Tusitala Edition 25

**Wallace, William,** 'The Life and Limitations of Stevenson', *Scottish Review*, January 1900; 'Scotland, Stevenson and Mr. Henley', *New Liberal Review*, February 1902

'**Wallace's Russia: Book of the Week**', a review, first published in *London*, 24 February 1877

**Walpole, Hugh:** 'A Letter to R.L.S.', an essay in *A Cadger's Creel* (*see* **Douglas, Sir George**)

'**Walt Whitman**', a essay, first published in *New Quarterly Magazine*, October 1878; in book form in *Familiar Studies of Men and Books*, 1882; Tusitala Edition 27

**Watson, William,** 'Written in a Copy of Stevenson's "Catriona" ', an essay in *Bookman* Extra Number, London 1913

**Watt, Francis,** *R.L.S.,* Methuen, London, 1913. Particular emphasis on Stevenson's early life and how it influenced his writing; *Edinburgh and the Lothians*, Methuen, London, 1912. Connections with Stevenson

**Watt, L.M.,** *Hills of Home,*T.A. Foulis, London and Edinburgh, 1913. Swanston and the Pentland Hills, their influence upon Stevenson as man and writer; 'R.L.S.', a poem in *A Cadger's Creel* (*see* **Douglas, Sir George**)

**Waugh, J.L.,** 'Honest John, the Shepherd Friend of R.L. Stevenson', *Chambers Journal*, 1914; 'My Stevenson Find', an essay in *A Cadger's Creel* (*see* **Douglas, Sir George**)

**Webster, Alexander,** *R.L. Stevenson and Henry Drummond*, Essex Hall, London, 1923

**Weir, Major,** Edinburgh warlock whose grisly history fascinated the young Stevenson

**Weir of Hermiston: An Unfinished Romance,** first published in four instalments in *Cosmopolis*, January–April 1896; in book form by Chatto & Windus, London and Scribner's, New York, 1896; Tusitala Edition *16*

Archie Weir despises and fears his father, Lord Hermiston, a 'hanging judge', for his cruelty. Hermiston derides his son and banishes him to the remote village where he meets and falls in love with Christina Elliott, who is seduced by Archie's friend, Frank Innes. In the ensuing quarrel Archie kills Frank. He is tried by his own father and sentenced to death. Christina's brothers avenge Archie who escapes to America with Christina while Lord Hermiston dies, his end brought about by shock and remorse.

This was Stevenson's last novel, unfinished at his death. The fragment which exists promised to have been his finest work and it is regarded, even incomplete, as a masterpiece. At work on it, he had dictated a strong beginning to Chapter IX on the morning of his death, 3 December 1894. Its last words are, 'There arose from before him the curtains of boyhood, and he saw for the first time the ambiguous face of woman as she is. In vain he looked back over the interview; he saw nowhere he had offended. *It seemed unprovoked, a wilful convulsion of brute nature . . .*'

(*See also* **Braxfield, Lord**)

**'Wellington',** an essay, first published in Vailima Edition, 1923; Tusitala Edition *28*

***Westminster Gazette,*** contained anonymous articles entitled 'A Reminiscence by One who Knew R.L.S.', 'Some Stevenson Gleanings', 'The Late Mr. R.L. Stevenson', 18 December 1894; 'With Stevenson in Samoa: Personal Recollections of a Writer's Life', 18–19 December 1894; 'The Dynasty of the Shark: A Personal Reminscence of Robert Louis Stevenson', 22 February 1895

**'When the Devil was Well',** a short story first published by Boston Bibliophile Society, 1921; Vailima Edition 1923; Tusitala Edition *5*

A tale of passion set in Italy. A cruel husband, Duke Orsino, and his young unhappy wife, Ippolita, have their lives altered by the arrival of the sculptor, Sanazarro.

Believed to be the earliest extant piece of prose fiction written by R.L.S.
He mentions it in letters to Mrs. Sitwell in 1874

**Whitmee, Rev. S.J.**, of the London Missionary Society in Apia, gave
Stevenson lessons in the Samoan language
(*See also* Part 2 (Eatuina))

**'Who Shot the Red Fox?'**, (*see* **MacGregor, A.A.**)

**Widener, H.E.**, (*see* **Catalogue**)

**Williams, Alan**, 'So this is Ballantrae', *Scotland's S.M.T. Magazine*,
November 1939

**Williams, Virgil and Dora**, San Francisco friends of Fanny Osbourne.
Dora was witness at Fanny's marriage to Stevenson.
(*See also* **Oakland; Silverado Squatters, The**)

**'Will o' the Mill'**, a short story, a rustic tale of life, love and
death, first published in *Cornhill Magazine*, January 1878; in book form
in *The Merry Men and Other Tales*, 1887; Tusitala Edition *8*

**Winterich, J.T.**, 'The Romantic Stories of Books: Treasure Island',
*Publishers' Weekly*, 16 August 1930

**'Winter's Walk in Carrick and Galloway, A'**, an essay, first published
in *Illustrated London News* and *The Chap-Book*, Chicago, 1896; Tusitala
Edition *30*

**'With Stevenson at Grez'**, (*see* **Harrison, Birge**)

**'With Stevenson in Old Samoa'**, (*see* **Safroni-Middleton, A.**)

**'With Stevenson in Samoa'**, (*see* **Cornhill Magazine; Moors, H.J.;
Westminster Gazette**)

**'With Stevenson Last May'**, (*see* **Roberts, M.**)

**'Witness in Danger'**, (*see* **Orr, Christine**)

**Wogg** (also **Woggs** and **Bogue**), Stevenson's beloved Skye terrier, a
gift of Walter Simpson
He was devoted to his master and, when he suffered from canker of the
ear, only Stevenson's bony hand could soothe his moans. A fighter to the
end, he died at Skerryvore, still in bandages, following injuries sustained
in an earlier battle. When Stevenson and Fanny were apart, Wogg had a
special place in the letters, 'Kiss my Wogg; I like him to be bad'.(*Letters*,
Tusitala Edition *32*). Also: 'And all things seem uncanny, When separate
from Fanny. Where is my wife? Where is my Wogg? I am alone, and
life's a bog.'

'Your Bogue is oppressive, affectionate and expository; he lets me alone till I sit in the armchair, but then (says he) my hour is come. By windmilling, anatomical gesture, cat-mewing, pig-grunting and trembling, not forgetting rabbit-digging in his pantaloons, I shall constrain this man to conversation . . .'

**Woman and Home,** contained an anonymous article entitled 'Mr. Robert Louis Stevenson at Home, by One who Knows Him', February 1894

**Woolf, Leonard,** (1880-1969) 'The Fall of Stevenson', *Nation* and *The Athenaeum*, 5 January 1924. Attacks the reputation of Stevenson as a writer, 'A consumptive Scotsman was just the man to captivate the taste of the romantic 90s . . . he appeals to the child or the primitively childish in grown men and women . . .' (Woolf's wife, Virginia, was a daughter of Leslie Stephen, Stevenson's old friend.)

**Wordsworth, William,** (1770-1850). Stevenson wrote of the celebrated Lakeland poet, 'He wasnae sound in the faith, sir, and a milk-blooded, blue-spectacled bitch forbye. But his po'mes are grand – there's no denying that'

**'Work of R.L.S., About The',** (*see* **Clouston, J. Storer**)

**'Works of Edgar Allan Poe, The',** a essay, first published in *The Academy*, 2 January 1875; Tusitala Edition *28*

**Works of Robert Louis Stevenson, The,** (*see* **Beeching, J.; Bibliographies**; *see also* **Edinburgh, Pentlands, Skerryvore, South Seas, Swanston, Thistle, Tusitala** and **Vailima Editions**)

**World Magazine,** New York, offered Stevenson $10,000 a year for a weekly contribution on his second and triumphant arrival in New York. Stevenson was nervous about accepting such a vast sum, conditioned by his years of poverty.

**'Wreath of Immortelles, The',** a essay, first published in *Edinburgh Edition* 1896; Tusitala Edition *30*

**Wrecker, The,** a novel, written in collaboration with Lloyd Osbourne, first published as a serial in *Scribner's Magazine*, August 1891 to July 1892; in book form by Cassell, London and Scribner's, New York, 1892; Tusitala Edition *12*

It tells of Loudon Dodd's adventures in Paris art circles, his shady finances in California and his involvment in piracy.
The idea occurred aboard the trading schooner *Equator* shortly after leaving Honolulu, '. . . on a moonlit night when it was a joy to be alive, the authors were amused with several stories of the sale of wrecks. The

subject tempted them,' [wrote Stevenson in his Epilogue] 'and they sat apart . . . to discuss its possibilities. . . . Before we turned in, the scaffolding of the tale had been put together. But the question of treatment was as usual more obscure . . .' Lloyd would write a chapter, Stevenson would rewrite it and the two would then discuss the next chapter. 'We never had a single disagreement as the book ran its course; [wrote Lloyd] it was a pastime, not a task, and I am sure no reader ever enjoyed it as much as we did. Well do I remember Stevenson saying: ' "It's glorious to have the ground ploughed, and to sit back in luxury for the real fun of writing – which is rewriting." ' (*An Intimate Portrait of Robert Louis Stevenson*)
(*See also* Part 6 (Radio))

**'Writer's Dilemma, The: A Case History and Critique of R.L.S.'**, (*see* **Rosenblatt, L.M.**)

**'Written in a Copy of Stevenson's "Catriona" '**, (*see* **Watson, William**)

**Wrong Box, The,** a novel written in collaboration with Lloyd Osbourne, Longmans Green, London and Scribner's, New York, 1889; Tusitala Edition *11*

A farcical black comedy in which cousins Michael and Morris Finsbury, heirs to two old men, are survivors of a tontine. A corpse, wrongly identified as one of the deceased uncles, leads to numerous complications, as the coffin has a habit of disappearing. All ends well and decorously.
' "Nothing like a little judicious levity," says Michael Finsbury in the text: nor can any better excuse be found for the volume in the reader's hand. The authors can but add that one of them is old enough to be ashamed of himself, and the other young enough to learn better.' (Preface by R.L.S. and L.O.) The first draft, titled *The Finsbury Tontine*, was completed in December 1887. It had taken two months to write and in a letter to J.A. Symonds (Tusitala Edition *33*, p.161) Stevenson wrote: 'Lloyd has learned to use the typewriter, and has most gallantly completed upon that the draft of a tale, which seems to me not without merit and promise, it is so silly, so gay, so absurd, in spots (to my practical eyes) so genuinely humorous.'
(*See also* Part 6 (Media)

**Wurmbrand, Count,** Austrian gaoler of the rebel Samoan chiefs in Apia Wurmbrand lost his job thanks to ignoring Fanny Stevenson's intervention when one of the chiefs was taken ill. Stevenson invited him to live at Vailima until the matter was sorted out satisfactorily and he personally stood bond for the sick chief's return to gaol.
(*See also* **'Footnote to History, A'; Mataafa, 'King'; Samoan War**)

# Y

**Yeats, William Butler,** (1865–1939)

In 1890 the Irish poet wrote an admiring letter to Stevenson, assuring him that *Treasure Island* was the only book that his seafaring grandfather ever found satisfaction in reading. He even read it on his deathbed 'with infinite satisfaction'.

(*See also* Part 4 (Letters))

**'Yellow Paint, The'**, a fable, Tusitala Edition *5* (*see also* **Fables**)

**'Yoshida-Torajiro'**, an essay, first published in *Cornhill Magazine*, March 1880; in book form in *Familiar Studies of Men and Books*, 1882; Tusitala Edition *27*

**'Young Chevalier, The'**, an unfinished story, first published in Edinburgh Edition, 1897; Tusitala Edition *16*

*Young Folks,* English boys' paper which published *Treasure Island* (under the pseudonym of 'Captain George North') as a serial from 1 October 1881 to 28 January 1882

For this commission, the editor James Henderson paid Stevenson £34.7s.6d. He also serialised *The Black Arrow* and *Kidnapped*, swashbuckling tales referred to by Stevenson as 'tushery', yet it was from such works that he gained both fame and money for the first time in his life.

*Young Robert Louis Stevenson, The,* (*see* **Finlay, Ian**)

**'Y.Y.'** 'Genius of Robert Louis Stevenson' and 'To Prospero at Samoa', *Bookman* Extra Number, London, 1913

# Z

**Zassetsky, Madame,** (*see* **Garschine, Mme**)

**Zassetsky, Neletchka,** daughter of above (*see* **Children**)

# Part 2
# UNPUBLISHED MANUSCRIPTS

MS Field — Consigned by Belle Strong to Anderson Auction Company in 1914 (*See* Part 1, **Catalogue (2)**)
MS Huntington — Henry E. Huntington Library, San Marino, California
MS NLS — National Library of Scotland, Edinburgh
MS Silverado — Silverado Museum, St. Helena, California
MS Yale — The Edwin J. Beinecke Collection at Yale University

**Adventures of John Carson in Several quarters of the world: dictated by himself: including the exploits of Diamond Charlie;** spring 1880, MS Yale. Based on reminiscences of Stevenson's landlord at 608 Bush Street, San Francisco.
Stevenson wrote to Colvin, 'most promising. real life throughout.'
*Note:* Did the tragic death of John's son Robbie and Stevenson's illness, aggravated by nursing the sick child, put an end to this promising project? Afterwards Stevenson moved to Oakland across the Bay to be taken care of by Fanny.

**Advocate's Thesis;** early summer 1875, MS NLS. Discusses distinction between 'Pro Dote' and 'Pro Suo' applied to before and after marriage. (*See* Part I, **Edinburgh University**)

**American Travellers, The;** 1857, MS Field. An adventure tale dictated to his 'dearest of aunts', Jane Whyte Balfour, during a visit to Colinton Manse.

**Antiquities of Midlothian, The;** dictated to his mother 1861, MS Yale. Concerns excursions to Craigmillar Castle and Corstorphine Church, Edinburgh.

**April Day, or Autolycus in Service, An;** Feb. 1879, MS Folger Library, Washington. Two drafts of a 3-act farce begun as a short story then revived as a play project with Henley (*Letters,* Tusitala Edition *31*, p.213).

**Archibald Usher;** n.d., MS Yale. 6 lines from notebook.

**Art of Literature, On the;** Feb. 1880, MS Silverado. Pages from a notebook, incomplete.

**Assassinat par amour;** c. 1884, MS Yale. 4 pages of essay based on sensational murder case in popular press.

**Authors and Publishers;** *c.* 1889-90, MS Yale. Stevenson's views on the controversy between publishers and their authors seem curiously contemporary in tone.

**Benjamin Franklin and the Art of Virtue;** MS notes, Princeton University Library. In 1880 and 1881 Stevenson planned to write on Franklin, but only the notes and his annotated copy of *The Life of Benjamin Franklin* (in Beinecke Collection) survive.

**Catspaw, The;** n.d., MS Yale. 12 chapter outlines.

**Civilisation, Law, Public Sentiment;** n.d., MS Yale. Draft of material dealing with Fenian outrages in 1884.

**Colonel Jean Cavalier;** June 1881, MS Yale. Notes, etc. begun during *Travels with a Donkey* when he became interested in the commander of the Camisards. Only first paragraph written.

**Cosmo;** 1868-9, MS Yale. Outline of chapters and characters for novel in Edinburgh University notebooks.

**Covenanting Profiles;** summer 1878, MS Yale. Mention of outline in notebook for *An Inland Voyage.*

**Covenanting Story Books;** 1868-9, MS Yale, Haverford College Library, Haverford, PA. Two lists (one in Yale, one in Haverford) of titles for short stories set in Scotland in the seventeenth century. Set of seven planned, including 'Curate of Anstruther's Bottle' and 'Devil on Cramond Sands'. MSS have vanished although these two were mentioned in *Letters,* Tusitala Edition *31,* pp.213-14, Tusitala Edition *32,* pp.89, 150-1. Only 'Thrawn Janet' was published.

**Death in the Pot;** early 1893, MS Yale. Outline, reference to 'a narrative of Californian Coasts ten years ago'.

**Definition of Good Literature;** autumn 1892, MS NLS. 1-page outline of planned essay.

**Desiderata;** 5-6 July 1873, MS Lloyd Osbourne. Facsimiles in sale catalogue (MS Yale); mentioned in *Letters,* Tusitala Edition *31,* pp. 185-6.

**Dialogue on Men, Women and Clarissa Harlowe, A;** late 1877/8, MS Field. Imaginary dialogue between husband and wife about Richardson's novel (*Letters,* Tusitala Edition *32,* p.37).

**Differences of Country;** winter 1874/5, MS Yale. First draft on Théophile Gautier's comparison of Spain and France.

**Early Memories;** Oct.-Nov. 1894, MS Field. Reminiscences of childish days. Possibly intended for *Scribner's Magazine* series.

**Eatuina;** summer 1892, MS Yale. 4 pages written in Samoan language; a story exercise (Stevenson took lessons from Rev. S.J. Whitmee of London Missionary Society in Apia).

**Enchantress, The;** n.d., MS Field. 27 pages of unfinished story.

**Essays planned at Davos;** winter 1880-1, MS Yale. List of 5 essays unpublished with titles and brief outlines. 'The Beginning of a Soul'; 'Health Resorts'; 'Simoneau's Inn'; 'Relations of Children'; 'My Russians'.

**Fighting the Ring;** spring 1888, MS photostats Yale, Silverado. Projected work in collaboration with Lloyd Osbourne for *New York Ledger,* on one firm's heroic resistance to monopolies in the copper industry.

**Four Seasons;** 1878, MS outline Yale. Notes written on pages of notebook for *An Inland Voyage.*

**Frances and Fred Archerfield:** *see* **Go-Between, The**

**Go-Between, The: a Boy's Romance;** late 1892, MS Yale. First two chapters, twelve chapter headings.

**Goldenson Mystery, The;** n.d., MS photostats Yale, Silverado. 6 pages of first chapter of detective novel set in San Francisco.

**Hair Trunk, The, or the Ideal Commonwealth;** *c.* May 1877, MS Huntington. Comments on unfinished comedy extravaganza (*Letters,* Tusitala Edition *32,* p.28)

**Hester Noble;** 1879, MS Princeton University Library. Outline describes it as 'Hester Noble's Mistake; or a word from Cromwell'. Drama in 4 acts, with alternative title 'The Tragedy of Hester Noble'. Projected play in collaboration with Henley (*Letters,* Tusitala Edition *32,* p.98).

**History of Scotland;** Nov. 1891, MS Huntington. 1 page outlining treatment.

**House Divided, A, Fate of the House;** Feb.-June 1880, MS Yale. List of characters of projected play with Henley which Stevenson worked on in San Francisco. Henley did not care for the result and the plan was abandoned.

**Imaginary Conversations;** winter 1871-2, MS Yale. Written in notebook

of Professor James Muirhead's course in public law at Edinburgh
University.

**Imaginary Dispatches;** n.d., MS Yale. 7 pages containing 5 imaginary
and satirical news reports.

**Intellectual Powers;** winter 1871-2, MS Yale. First page of essay in same
notebook as **Imaginary Conversations.**

**In the Windbound Arethusa;** *c.* May 1877, MS Field. Part 2, chapters
2-9, 7 chapters of unfinished novel.

**Last of the Yeomen;** n.d., MS photostats Yale, Silverado. 9 pages
outlining 3 chapters of comic novel.

**Law and Free Will. Notes on the Duke of Argyll;** winter 1872-3, MS
Field. Criticism of G.D. Campbell's 'Reign of Law 1866', delivered
before Speculative Society, 11 February 1873 (*Letters,* Tusitala Edition
*31,* p.78).

**Malaga in Samoa, A;** Dec. 1889-Jan. 1890, MS Yale. Contains Stevenson's
earliest impressions of Samoa.

**Matthew Daventry;** n.d., MS Yale. First-person narrative of Captain
Daventry in 1721-2. Beginning of novel *c.* 1890.

**Murder of Red Colin, The;** notes, fragments, source books in Yale and
Huntington. Wrote to father from Davos in 1881 that he intended an
essay on Colin Campbell of Glenure; idea was abandoned and later
developed in *Kidnapped.*

**Music for the Flageolet;** n.d., photostat of Stevenson's autographed MS
in Library of Congress, Washington.

**New Light-house at Dhu Heartach Rock, Argyllshire;** summer
1872, MS Huntington. Essay on building of the lighthouse with
corrections by Thomas Stevenson.

**Night Outside the Wick Mail;** before mid-Nov., 1868, MS Yale. Essay
included in unpublished letter to cousin Bob describing journey Oct.
1868.

**Obermann;** 1870, MS Yale. Beginning of essay.

**Onlooker in Hell, An;** 1890-1, MS NLS, typescript Silverado. Personal
reminiscences of a gambling casino at Hamburg, plus list of chapter
titles.

**Painting and Words;** 1868-9, MS Yale. Draft in pencil in Stevenson's

'Modern Geometry Notebook' on relative merits of painting in words and in colour.

**Plague Cellar, The;** *c.* 1864, MS Princeton. Stevenson opposed vehemently his cousin Henrietta Traquair's wish to publish this early work which she rediscovered among her papers in July 1893. Mention by James Milne in Rosaline Masson's *I Can Remember.*

**Plain John Wiltshire on the Situation;** *c.* 1892, MS Huntington. 10 pages of typescript written in the first person of main character in 'The Beach of Falesá' (noted 'by R.L.S.' in Lloyd Osbourne's writing).

**Popular Press and Crimes Passionelles, The;** n.d., MS Yale. Fragment.

**Prologue: At Monte Carlo;** n.d., MS Yale. 10 pages of story of John Carton, 'a young man (as they call it) of some promise'.

**Prose Poems:** 'The Lighthouse: No. 1; On the Roof', 29 May 1875, 'The Lightroom', 30 May 1875, MS Huntington; 'The Quiet Waters By', 25 May 1875 (dedicated to Mrs. Sitwell), MS Field.

**Roux Illustrations for 'Treasure Island', The;** n.d., MS Yale. Fragment.

**Royal Fortune, The;** 1881-2, MS Yale. List of 17 chapter titles.

**Samoan Scrapbook, A;** spring 1889, MS Yale. Intended as text for photographs taken by Belle Strong's husband Joe during Hawaiian Expedition 1887-8.

**School Boys Magazine, The;** Oct. 1863, MS Pierpoint Morgan Library, New York. Mentioned in Balfour's *Life.* Stevenson wrote 4 stories during his autumn term at Burlington Lodge Academy, Isleworth, Middlesex, 1863.

**School for the Sons of Gentlemen;** summer 1877, typescript by Lloyd Osbourne, Yale. Outlines plan for the Barbizon Free-Trading Company, Unlimited. They hoped to outfit a barge and finance their travels by teaching art with the assistance of Will H. Low.

**Scotland and the Union, the Transformation of the Scottish Highlands;** 1880-1, MS Yale. Source books, materials sent to Stevenson by parents; his father was eager that he should write this work.

**Simoneau's at Monterey;** winter 1880-1, MS Yale. Outline and draft of article published in James Hart's *From Scotland to Silverado.*

**Sophia Scarlett;** Jan. 1892, MS Free Library of Philadelphia. 15 pages dictated to Belle Strong with detailed summary of the first ten chapters entitled 'The Plantation'.

**Springtime 1875;** MS Yale. Fragment of essay mentioned to Colvin (*Letters,* Tusitala Edition *32,* pp.14-16). Probably sent to Colvin and lost.

**Squaw Man, The;** Sept. 1881, MS Field. Abandoned while writing *Treasure Island.* First chapter and part of second indicate a novel of the American West with Indians.

**Students' Meeting and Class Excursion;** April 1871, MS Field. Stevenson's narrative on class supper and Glasgow outing with Fleeming Jenkin's engineering class.

**Sleeper Awakened, The;** June 1893, MS Field. 4 pages begin as a play, followed by chapter headings for a novel.

**Sunbeam Magazine, The;** Jan.-March 1866, MS Yale. Contains original of 'The Banker's Ward' and fragment of 'The Pentland Rising'.

**Talofa, Togawera;** *c.* 1891, MS Yale. 4 pages prepared for printers, 1900, signed by Rev. Arthur E. Claxton of London Missionary Society, expressing Stevenson's concern regarding lepers.

**Thomas Stevenson;** *c.* 1885, MS Huntington. 12 pages containing projected account of his father's childhood.

**Travels in Perthshire;** summer 1859, MS Field. A family holiday to Bridge of Allan with drawings by Stevenson June-July 1859; also excursions to Dundee, Crieff and Perth. Dictated to his mother in July.

**Trial Magazine, The;** 5 June 1865, MS Yale. Boyhood collaboration with H.B. Baildon; 2 serials by Stevenson. 'The Count's Secret' and 'The Convicts'.

**Two St. Michael's Mounts, The;** *c.* Aug. 1877, MS Yale. Notes for essay mentioned to Mrs Sitwell (*Letters,* Tusitala Edition *32,* p.32).

**Value of Books and Reading, On the;** n.d., MS Field. Perhaps intended as part of 'The Morality of the Profession of Letters'.

**Water of Leith;** 1890-1, MS Yale. Perhaps intended as essay for *Scribner's Magazine* series.

**White Nigger, The;** spring 1888, MS photostat Yale. 3-page summary of plot and main characters of novel dealing with the Indian Mutiny, by Stevenson and Lloyd Osbourne.

**William Hazlitt;** 1881-2, MS Yale. List of books to consult for this projected work, also miscellaneous notes.

**Weak and the Strong, The;** n.d., MS Yale. 12 pages of notes and chapter headings.

## Part 3
# FICTIONAL CHARACTERS AND PLACES

**Admiral Benbow Inn;** home of Jim Hawkins     *Treasure Island*
also setting of Act II     *Admiral Guinea*
**Ainslie, Andrew;** robber in Brodie's gang     *Deacon Brodie*
**Alain;** young man     *The Owl*
**Alan;** honest seaman on the *Hispaniola*     *Treasure Island*
**Aline;** maidservant }     *Macaire*
    *The Treasure of Franchard*
**Allonby Shaw;** home of John Fenwick     *Beau Austin*
**Amalia Seraphina;** wife of Prince Otto     *Prince Otto*
**Amersham Place;** home of the Comte de Kéroual de
Saint-Yves     *St. Ives*
**Anderson, Job;** crew-member of the *Hispaniola*     *Treasure Island*
**Appleyard, Nick;** archer     *The Black Arrow*
**Arblaster;** captain of the *Good Hope*     *The Black Arrow*
**Archer, Mr.;** introduced by Lord Windermoor     *The Great North Road*
*Arethusa;* ship     *Admiral Guinea*
**Ariane;** young woman     *The Owl*
**Arrow, Mr.;** crew-member of the *Hispaniola*     *Treasure Island*
**Asdis;** daughter of Aud the Light-minded     *The Waif Woman*
**Asenath;** Destroying Angel     *The Dynamiter*
**Attwater, William John;** character     *The Ebb-Tide*
**Auberge des Adrets;** setting     *Macaire*
**Austin, George Frederick ('Beau');** central character     *Beau Austin*
**Aud the Light-minded;** wife of Finnward Keelfarer     *The Waif Woman*

**Balfour of Pilrig;** cousin of David Balfour     *Catriona*
**Balfour of Shaws, David;** central character and narrator,
*m.* Catriona Drummond     *Kidnapped* and *Catriona*
  **Alan and Barbara;** their children     *Catriona*
  **Alexander;** David's father }     *Kidnapped* and *Catriona*
  **Ebenezer;** his rascally uncle }
**Ballantrae, Master of:** *See* **Durie, James**
**Ballantrae, Mr.**     *The Young Chevalier*
**Bally, Mr.;** *See* **Durie, James**
**Balmile, Lord Gladsmuir;** Ballantrae's friend     *The Young Chevalier*
**Baskerville, Mr.**     *Mr Baskerville and his Ward*
**Bazin's Inn, Dunkirk**     *Catriona*
**Beamish;** a Bow Street runner     *The Hanging Judge*

**Beaulieu, Denis de;** central character ⎫    *The Sire de Malétroit's Door*
   **Guichard;** his brother          ⎭

**Bell, Mr.;** clerk to Mr. Bloomfield          *The Wrong Box*

**Bellairs, Harry D.;** attorney-at-law         *The Wrecker*

**Bellamy, Mr.;** suitor to Dorothy Greensleeves      *St. Ives*

**Bertrand;** friend of Robert Macaire           *Macaire*

**Berthelini, Léon;** strolling player ⎫    *Providence and the Guitar*
   **Elvira;** his wife              ⎭

**Black Dog;** pirate                  *Treasure Island*

**Bloomfield, Edward Hugh (Uncle Ned);**
  uncle of Gideon Forsyth            *The Wrong Box*

**Bohemian Cigar Divan, Rupert Street, Soho;**
  setting                       *The Dynamiter*

**Bones, Captain Billy;** former pirate       *Treasure Island*

**Box Court;** London headquarters        *The Suicide Club*

**Bostock;** captain of the *Currency Lass*       *The Wrecker*

**Bourron;** hamlet near Fontainebleau   *The Treasure of Franchard*

**Brackley, Sir Daniel;** guardian of Dick Shelton   *The Black Arrow*

**Breck, Alan;** *See* **Stewart, Alan Breck**

**Brigadier of Gendarmerie**                *Macaire*

**Brisetout;** home of Enguerrand de la Feuillée   *A Lodging for the Night*

**British Linen Bank;** David Balfour's exit from
  *Kidnapped* and entrance to *Catriona*    *Kidnapped* and *Catriona*

**Brodie, William;** Deacon, Master carpenter ⎫
  and housebreaker                 ⎬  *Deacon Brodie*
    **Mary;** his sister                ⎪
    **'Old' Brodie;** his father           ⎭

**Broun, Jessie;** ex-mistress of James Durie   *The Master of Ballantrae*

**Brown of Colstoun, Sheriff;** James Stewart's counsel   *Catriona*

**Bryant, Dr.;** parson ⎫
**Bryce, Mr.;** master of Long Dumbleton ⎪
  Green School          ⎬  *Adventures of Henry Shovel*
    **Mrs.;** his wife            ⎭

**Bullier Ball Rooms;** Paris meeting-place     *The Suicide Club*

**Burke, Francis, Chevalier de;** Irish colonel
  in the service of the Pretender    *The Master of Ballantrae*

**Butler, Charles;** friend of William Rutherford   *Edifying Letters of the
                                 Rutherford Family*

**Byfield;** balloonist                     *St. Ives*

**Campbell, Colin, of Glenure (Red Fox);** King's factor, ⎫
  Appin                         ⎬  *Kidnapped*
**Campbell, Mungo;** witness to Red Fox's murder   ⎪
**Campbell, Reverend Mr.;** minister of Kirk Essendean ⎭

**Candlish;** a drover                   *St. Ives*

**Capper, John;** an outlaw                                    *The Black Arrow*
**Captain Kidd's Anchorage;** destination of the *Hispaniola*
                                                              *Treasure Island*
**Carew, Sir Danvers;** murdered by Edward Hyde
                                                    *Dr. Jekyll and Mr. Hyde*
**Carlyle, Mr.;** lawyer                           *The Master of Ballantrae*
**Carnegie, David Keith (Lord Glenalmond);**
   friend of Archie Weir                               *Weir of Hermiston*
**Carthew, Norris**                                        *The Wrecker*
**Case;** villainous trader                        *The Beach of Falesá*
**Casimir;** brother of Anastasie Desprez     *The Treasure of Franchard*
**Cassilis, Frank;** central character and narrator *The Pavilion on the Links*
**Castel-le-Gâchis,**
   **Commissary of Police of;** character     *Providence and the Guitar*
   **Maire of;** character
**Caulder, Mr.;** character in 'The Fair Cuban'
**Challoner, Edward;** central character of            *The Dynamiter*
   'The Squire of Dames'
**Champdivers;** *See* **Saint-Yves**
**Champdivers, Florimond de**                  *The Sire de Malétroit's Door*
**Chandler;** a carrier                               *The Wrong Box*
**Charles, Gendarme;** supposed son of Dumont            *Macaire*
**Château Landon;** de Beaulieu's
   destination                                 *The Sire de Malétroit's Door*
**Cherté de la Médoc, Marquis de la;** father of Charles    *Macaire*
**Chevenix, Major**                                          *St. Ives*
**Christ-Anna;** wrecked ship                          *The Merry Men*
**Clarges, Samuel;** benefactor of Henry Shovel *Adventures of Henry Shovel*
**Clouston, Jennet;** enemy of Ebenezer Balfour
**Cluny's Cage;** secret hiding place on Ben Alder    *Kidnapped*
**Colenso, Captain;** of the *Lady Nepean*
   **Reuben;** his son, mate of the *Lady Nepean*         *St. Ives*
**Collette's;** unlicensed inn    *The Misadventures of John Nicholson*
**Cook;** crew-member of the *Farallone*              *The Ebb-Tide*
*Covenant*; ship                                          *Kidnapped*
**Crail, Captain**                                 *The Master of Ballantrae*
**Crabtree, Sir John;** English traveller              *Prince Otto*
**Craven Hotel, Craven Street, London;** setting    *The Suicide Club*
**Croqueloup, Baron de**                                  *The Owl*
**Crozer, Jock**                                          *Heathercat*
*Currency Lass*; ship and public house                  *The Wrecker*


**Dale, Andrew (Black Andie);** Prefect of Bass Rock
   **Tam;** his father ('Tale of Tod Lapraik')             *Catriona*

| | |
|---|---|
| **Dance, Supervisor;** law officer | *Treasure Island* |
| **Darnaway, Charles;** central character<br>**Gordon;** his uncle<br>**Mary Ellen;** his cousin | *The Merry Men* |
| **Dass, Secundra;** Indian friend of James Durie | *The Master of Ballantrae* |
| **Davis, Captain John;** of the *Sea Ranger* | *The Ebb-Tide* |
| **Dawson;** servant at Amersham Place | *St. Ives* |
| **Denman;** the Carthew butler | *The Wrecker* |
| **Desborough, Harry;** central character in 'The Brown Box' | *The Dynamiter* |
| **Desprez, Dr.;** central character<br>**Anastasie;** his wife | *The Treasure of Franchard* |
| **Dick,** cabin boy on the *Hispaniola* | *Treasure Island* |
| **Diogenes;** central character | *Diogenes* |
| **Dodd, Loudon;** central character | *The Wrecker* |
| **Dogger;** Supervisor Dance's assistant | *Treasure Island* |
| **Doig;** servant of Lord Prestongrange | *Catriona* |
| **Drake, Mrs;** landlady of Admiral Benbow Inn | *Admiral Guinea* |
| **Drummond, Catriona;** central character<br>**James More Macgregor** (also known as **Drummond**); her father, son of Rob Roy Macgregor<br>**Drummond-Ogilivie of Allardyce, Mrs.;** kinswoman of Catriona | *Catriona* |
| **Ducie;** *See* **Saint-Yves** | *St. Ives* |
| **Duckworth, Ellis;** leader of the company of the Black Arrow | *The Black Arrow* |
| **Dudgeon, Thomas;** clerk to Daniel Romaine | *St. Ives* |
| **Dumont;** landlord of Auberge des Adrets | *Macaire* |
| **Duncansby, Lieutenant Hector;** King's officer<br>**Duncanson, Neil;** servant to Drummond | *Catriona* |
| **Dungaree;** crew-member of the *Farallone* | *The Ebb-Tide* |
| **Durie, James;** Master of Ballantrae (presumed killed at Culloden; alias Mr. Bally)<br>**Henry, Lord Durrisdeer;** his brother<br>**Alison, Lady Durrisdeer;** (*née* Graeme)<br>**Alexander** and **Katharine;** their children<br>**Durrisdeer;** setting<br>**Dutton;** pirate on the *Sarah* | *The Master of Ballantrae* |
| **Eilean Aros;** island setting | *The Merry Men* |
| **Elliott, Kirstie;** housekeeper to Lord Weir<br>**Gilbert;** her brother<br>**Hob**<br>**Gib** Gilbert's sons: The | *Weir of Hermiston* |

Clem ⌐Four Black Brothers                               ⌐          Weir of Hermiston
Dand ⌐                                                  |
**Christina (Kirstie the younger);** Gilbert's          |
daughter, beloved of Archie Weir                        ⌐
**Enfield, Richard;** kinsman and friend
of Utterson                                          *Dr. Jekyll and Mr. Hyde*
**Erskine;** Sheriff of Perth                                 *Catriona*
**Escherolles, Comte Clané des;** kinsman of Baron
de Croqueloup                                               *The Owl*
*Espirito Santo*; Armada ship                            *The Merry Men*
**Essendean;** home of David Balfour in the Forest of Ettrick   *Kidnapped*


**Falconer, Colonel John,**                            ⌐
  **John and Malcolm,** his nephews                     |
  **Miss Rebecca,** his aunt                            ⌐         *An Old Song*
  **Mary,** Malcolm's wife                              ⌐
*Farallone*; schooner                                    *The Ebb-Tide*
**Felipe;** Olalla's brother                                  *Olalla*
**Fenn, Burchell;** friend to escaping French prisoners       *St. Ives*
**Fenwick, John;** of Allonby Shaw                          *Beau Austin*
**Fettes;** drunken Scots medical student, later ('Doctor')*The Body-Snatcher*
**Feuillée, Enguerrand de la;** Seigneur
de Brisetout                                       *A Lodging for the Night*
**Finsbury, Morris and John;** brothers, sons of          ⌐
Jacob (decd.), adopted by Joseph; central characters     |
    **Joseph;** their uncle                              ⌐        *The Wrong Box*
    **Masterman;** their uncle, popular writer           |
    **Michael;** Masterman's son                         ⌐
**Fisher, Professor Daubeny;** friend of
James Rutherford          *Edifying Letters of the Rutherford Family*
**Flint, Captain;** Long John Silver's parrot             *Treasure Island*
**Florizel, Prince of Bohemia;** (alias Theophilus Godall)
central character                                        *The Suicide Club*
*Flying Scud*; ship                                        *The Wrecker*
**Forsyth, Gideon;** lover of Julia Hazeltine              *The Wrong Box*
**Foster, Evelina;** aunt of Anthony and
Dorothy Musgrave                                         *Beau Austin*
**Fowler;** a smuggler                                     *The Wrecker*
**Foxham, Lord;** guardian of Joanna Sedley              *The Black Arrow*
**Fraser, Simon;** forfeited clan chief, Lord Lovat          *Catriona*
**French, Kit;** suitor of Arethusa Gaunt                 *Admiral Guinea*
**Frodis Water;** setting                              *The Waif Woman*
**Fritz;** lover of Ottilia Gottesheim                      *Prince Otto*

**Garroway, Sergeant**                                *The Hanging Judge*

**Gaunt, Captain John;** (alias Admiral Guinea) ⎫
  of the *Arethusa*                                      *Admiral Guinea*
**Arethusa,** his daughter ⎭
**Gebbie, Mr. and Mrs.;** Catriona placed in their charge on
  journey to Holland                                      *Catriona*
**George, The, at Debenham;** meeting-place        *The Body-Snatcher*
**Geraldine, Colonel;** (alias Major Alfred ⎫
  Hammersmith and Mr. Morris)
  Master of the Horse to Prince Florizel ⎬       *The Suicide Club*
**Mr.;** the Colonel's younger brother ⎭
**Gerolstein;** state bordering Grünewald              *Prince Otto*
**Gilchrist, Flora;** heroine ⎫
  **Miss;** her aunt                                          *St. Ives*
  **Ronald;** her brother ⎭
**Gillespie, Will;** alias Jack Johnson ⎫
  **Eleanor;** known as Harlowe ⎭                *The Hanging Judge*
**Gladsmuir;** *See* **Balmile**
**Glenalmond;** *See* **Carnegie**
**Glencorse Kirkyard;** setting                     *The Body-Snatcher*
**Glenkindie, Lord**                                 *Weir of Hermiston*
**Glenure;** *See* **Campbell, Colin**
**Goat and Bagpipes, The;** alehouse                 *The Black Arrow*
**Godall, Theophilus;** alias of Prince Florizel
  of Bohemia                                         *The Suicide Club*
**Goddedaal, Elias;** mate of the *Flying Scud*         *The Wrecker*
**Goguelat, Philippe;** French prisoner of war killed
  in duel with Saint-Yves                                 *Saint Ives*
**Gondremark, Baron Heinrich von,** chief conspirator    *Prince Otto*
*Good Hope;* ship from Dartmouth                    *The Black Arrow*
**Goriot;** character ⎫
  **Ernestine;** his daughter ⎭                          *Macaire*
**Gottesheim, Killian;** of the River Farm ⎫
  **Ottilia;** his daughter ⎭                          *Prince Otto*
*Grace Darling;* ship                                   *The Wrecker*
**Graden Easter;** site of the Pavilion ⎫
  on the Links                                  *The Pavilion on the Links*
**Graden Floe;** quicksands ⎭
**Grady;** pirate on the *Sarah*                 *The Master of Ballantrae*
**Graeme, Alison;** *See* **Durie**
**Grafinski;** treasurer                                *Prince Otto*
**Grant, William, of Prestongrange;** ⎫
  Lord Advocate of Scotland                             *Catriona*
  **Miss Barbara;** his daughter ⎭
**Gray;** disreputable fellow-conspirator of
  Wolfe Macfarlane                                 *The Body-Snatcher*

**Gray, Abraham;** carpenter's mate on the *Hispaniola*     *Treasure Island*
**Green Dragon;** inn                                              *St. Ives*
**Greensheve;** outlaw ⎱                                   *The Young Chevalier*
                                                              *The Black Arrow*
**Greensleeves, Dorothy;** character ⎱
   **Mr.;** father of Dorothy          ⎰                          *St. Ives*
**Gregg;** lawyer                                              *The Wrecker*
**Gregory, Dr.;** celebrated physician                    *Weir of Hermiston*
**Greisengesang, von;** Chancellor of Grünewald                *Prince Otto*
**Grierson, Dr.;** (Destroying Angel)                       *The Dynamiter*
**Grünewald;** setting                                          *Prince Otto*
**Guest;** head clerk to Utterson                       *Dr. Jekyll and Mr. Hyde*
**Guest, Dr.;** physician                                 *The Hanging Judge*
**Gunn, Ben;** castaway, marooned by Flint                  *Treasure Island*

**Hadden, Tommy;** Australian sailor                         *The Wrecker*
**Haddo;** curate                                              *Heathercat*
**Hammersmith, Major Alfred;** alias of
   Colonel Geraldine                                       *The Suicide Club*
**Hammond;** mate of the *Sarah*                     *The Master of Ballantrae*
**Hands, Israel;** coxswain of the *Hispaniola*             *Treasure Island*
**Hargreave, Bernard**                                ⎫
   **Old;** his father                                ⎪
**Harlowe, Mr. Justice;** 'The Hanging Judge'         ⎬    *The Hanging Judge*
   **Annie;** his wife                                ⎪
   **Eleanor (Gillespie);** his stepdaughter          ⎪
**Harne;** parson                                     ⎭
**Harris, Captain;** Indian trader                   *The Master of Ballantrae*
**Harry;** crew of the *Hispaniola*                        *Treasure Island*
**Hartley, Harry;** secretary to Sir
   Thomas Vandeleur                                     *The Rajah's Diamond*
**Hastie, Alison;** girl in Limekilns who assisted
   David and Alan's escape                         *Kidnapped* and *Catriona*
**Hatch, Bennet;** bailiff                                 *The Black Arrow*
**Haulbowline Head;** South-west of
   Treasure Island                                        *Treasure Island*
**Hawes Inn at Queensferry;** scene of David
   Balfour's kidnapping                                      *Kidnapped*
**Hawkins, Jim;** central character ⎱
   **Mrs.;** his mother             ⎰                       *Treasure Island*
**Hazeltine, Julia;** niece adopted by Joseph Finsbury    *The Wrong Box*
**Henderland, Mr.;** evangelist                              *Kidnapped*
**Hermiston;** *See* **Weir**
**Herrick, Robert;** central character                      *The Ebb-Tide*
**Higgs, Mr. and Mrs.;** servants of Carthew                *The Wrecker*

**Hispaniola**; ship chartered to search for
buried treasure                                                *Treasure Island*
**Hohenstockwitz, Dr. Gotthold**; cousin and librarian of
Prince Otto                                                         *Prince Otto*
**Holdaway, Jonathan**; central character ⎫                *The Great North Road*
**Nance**, his niece ⎭
**Holywood Abbey**; setting                                    *The Black Arrow*
**Hoseason, Elias**; Captain of the *Covenant*                    *Kidnapped*
**Hotel of the Black Head**; setting            *Providence and the Guitar*
**House of Shaws, nr Cramond**; home of Ebenezer
Balfour                                                            *Kidnapped*
**Houston, Alan**; John's childhood friend
                              *The Misadventures of John Nicholson*
**Huddlestone, Bernard**; defaulting banker ⎫     *The Pavilion on the Links*
**Clara**; his daughter ⎭
**Huish**; a villainous Cockney                               *The Ebb-Tide*
**Hunt**; a Bow Street runner                                 *Deacon Brodie*
**Hunter, John**; servant of Squire Trelawney         *Treasure Island*
**Hyde, Edward**; Dr. Jekyll's evil *alter ego*        *Dr. Jekyll and Mr. Hyde*

**Innes, Frank**; false friend of Archie Weir          *Weir of Hermiston*
**Ippolita, Duchess of Orsino**                    *When the Devil Was Well*

**Jean-Marie**; boy                              *The Treasure of Franchard*
**Jekyll, Dr. Henry**; distinguished doctor;
alias Mr. Hyde                                       *Dr. Jekyll and Mr. Hyde*
**Johnny**; crew of the *Hispaniola*                        *Treasure Island*
**Johnson**; of the *Norh Creina*                             *The Wrecker*
**Johnson, Jack**; *See* **Gillespie, Will**
**Johnson, Sir William**; diplomat            *The Master of Ballantrae*
**Jopp, Duncan**; executed criminal                      *Weir of Hermiston*
**Joyce, Richard**; servant of Squire Trelawney        *Treasure Island*
**Judkin**; clerk                                              *The Wrong Box*

**Kalamake**; father of Lehua                           *The Isle of Voices*
**Keawe**; central character and purchaser of bottle       *The Bottle Imp*
**Keelfarer, Finnward**; goodman of Frodis Water         *The Waif Woman*
**Kentish, Mr.**; officer on the *Nemorosa*                *The Dynamiter*
**Keola**; husband of Lehua                            *The Isle of Voices*
**Kettley**; hamlet                                        *The Black Arrow*
**Kiano**; father of Kokua                                 *The Bottle Imp*
**Kirkup**; *See* **Wicks**
**Kokua**; wife of Keawe                                   *The Bottle Imp*
**Kuno**; huntsman                                           *Prince Otto*

**Lady Nepean**; ship                                                 *St. Ives*
**Lanyon, Dr. Hastie;** eminent physician and
  friend of Utterson                             *Dr. Jekyll and Mr. Hyde*
**Lapraik, Tod;** central character of Andie Dale's story        *Catriona*
**Lawless, Will;** an outlaw                             *The Black Arrow*
**Lawson, William;** Procurator-Fiscal, uncle of Brodie    *Deacon Brodie*
**Lehua;** daughter of Kalamake                         *The Isle of Voices*
**Leslie, Walter;** suitor of Mary Brodie                  *Deacon Brodie*
**Livesey, Dr.;** friend of Squire Trelawney              *Treasure Island*
**Longhurst, Douglas B.;** speculator             ⎫
**Loudon, Adam;** uncle of Loudon Dodd            ⎬          *The Wrecker*
  **Alexander;** Dodd's grandfather              ⎭
**Lovat;** *See* **Fraser**


**Macaire, Robert;** central character in                       *Macaire*
**M'Brair;** elder                                            *Heathercat*
**M'Clour, Janet;** witch-wife housekeeper
  to Rev. Mr. Soulis                                        *Thrawn Janet*
**M'Clour, Janet;** character                                 *Heathercat*
**Macconochie;** drunken serving-man              *The Master of Ballantrae*
**Macfarlane, Dr. Wolfe (Toddy);**
  celebrated London doctor                           *The Body-Snatcher*
**M'Glashan, Miss;** Esther's aunt                       *The Story of a Lie*
**M'Guire, Patrick;** carpenter                           *The Dynamiter*
**Macgregor;** *See* **Drummond**
**Macgregor of Bohardie;** kinsman of Catriona,
  resident in Paris                                            *Catriona*
**Macgregor, Robin Oig (or Drummond);** ⎫
  son of Rob Roy MacGregor                  ⎬              *Kidnapped*
**MacKeigh, Duncan**                          ⎭
**Macintosh, Robert:** James Stewart's counsel                *Catriona*
**Mackellar, Ephraim;** family steward and
  narrator                                        *The Master of Ballantrae*
**Mackenzie, Miss Flora;** beloved of
  John Nicholson               *The Misadventures of John Nicholson*
**M'Killop;** butler to Lord Weir                      *Weir of Hermiston*
**Maclaren, Duncan Dhu (of Balquhidder)**    *Kidnapped* and *Catriona*
**Maclean, Hector;** clansman                               *Kidnapped*
**Macmorland, Patey and Tam;** Jacobite   ⎫
  supporters                               ⎬       *The Master of Ballantrae*
**McMurtrie;** captain of the *Nonesuch*     ⎭
**Macpherson, Cluny;** chief of Clan Vourich  ⎫
**Macrob, Neil Roy;** skipper of ferryboat    ⎬          *Kidnapped*
**Malétroit, Alain, Sire de** ⎫
  **Blanche de;** his niece   ⎬          *The Sire de Malétroit's Door*

**Malthus, Bartholomew;** honorary member     *The Suicide Club*
**Mamie, Miss;** marries Jim Pinkerton     *The Wrecker*
**Marjory, Miss;** heroine     *Will o' the Mill*
**Markheim;** villainous central character     *Markheim*
**Matcham, John;** alias of Joanna Sedley     *The Black Arrow*
**Mendizabal, Madam;** character     *The Dynamiter*
**Menteith;** Beau Austin's valet     *Beau Austin*
**Merren, Auld;** spaewife (fortune-teller)     *Catriona*
**Merry, George;** one of Long John Silver's men     *Treasure Island*
**Miller, Sheriff;** James Stewart's counsel     *Catriona*
**Mittwalden;** town of Grünewald     *Prince Otto*
**Mizzenmast Hill;** south-west of Treasure Island     *Treasure Island*
**Montigny;** thief     *A Lodging for the Night*
**Montroymont, Ninian Traquair of** ⎫     *Heathercat*
    **Francis;** his son, 'Heathercat' ⎭
**Moore, Humphrey;** robber in Brodie's gang     *Deacon Brodie*
**Morgan, Tom;** crew of *Hispaniola*     *Treasure Island*
**Morris, Mr.;** alias of Colonel Geraldine     *The Suicide Club*
**Mountain;** trader     *The Master of Ballantrae*
**Musgrave, Anthony** ⎫     *Beau Austin*
    **Dorothy,** his sister ⎭
**Myner;** artist     *The Wrecker*


**Nance;** old nurse of Dick Naseby     *The Story of a Lie*
**Nares,** Captain of the *Norah Creina*     *The Wrecker*
**Naseby, Richard (Dick);** central character ⎫     *The Story of a Lie*
**Naseby House;** setting ⎭
*Nemorosa*; yacht     *The Dynamiter*
**Nicholson, John Varey;** ⎫
    central character        ⎬    *The Misadventures of John Nicholson*
    **Alexander;** his brother ⎪
    **Maria;** his sister ⎭
**Nicolas, Dom;** Picardy monk     *A Lodging for the Night*
**Noel, Dr.;** English physician     *The Suicide Club*
*Nonesuch*; ship     *The Master of Ballantrae*
*Norah Creina*; ship     *The Wrecker*
**Northmour, R. of Graden Easter;** one-time student
    friend of Frank Cassilis     *The Pavilion on the Links*
**Notary, The**     *Macaire*


**O'Brien;** seaman on the *Hispaniola*     *Treasure Island*
**Oglethorpe, Tom;** guard of North Mail     *The Young Chevalier*
**Olalla;** central character     *Olalla*
**O'Rooke, Major;** character     *The Suicide Club*
**Orsino, Duke of;** husband of Ippolita     *When the Devil was Well*

**Otto, Prince;** Prince of Grünewald (alias Transome)          *Prince Otto*

**Padre, The;** character                                                *Olalla*
**Palliser;** Captain of the *Seahorse*                                  *Catriona*
**Paradou, M;** wine-seller ⎱
  **Marie-Madeleine;** his wife ⎰                            *The Young Chevalier*
**Paul, John;** solemn serving-man                      *The Master of Ballantrae*
**Pendragon, Charles;** brother of Lady Vandeleur   *The Rajah's Diamond*
**Penny, Mr;** tradesman ⎱
  **Little Peter**          ⎰                                  *The Hanging Judge*
**Pensete, Thevenin;** thief                            *A Lodging for the Night*
**Pew, David, 'Blind';** once boatswain of the *Arethusa* ⎱ *Admiral Guinea*
                                                            ⎰ *Treasure Island*
**Pinkerton, Jim;** journalist                                *The Wrecker*
**Pitman, William Dent;** artist and ne'er-do-well       *The Wrong Box*
**Poole;** servant of Dr. Jekyll                    *Dr. Jekyll and Mr. Hyde*
**Porter, Dr.;** Archdeacon of Singleton Abbas
                                           *Mr Baskerville and his Ward*
**President, The;** character                              *The Suicide Club*
**Prestongrange, Lord;** *See* **Grant, William**

**Raeburn, Mr.;** nurseryman                          *The Rajah's Diamond*
**Ramsay, Miss Tibbie;** friend of Miss Grant                  *Catriona*
**Randall, Captain William T.;** drunkard           *The Beach of Falesá*
**Rankeillor, Mr.;** lawyer
**Ransome;** cabin boy of the *Covenant,*                      *Kidnapped*
  murdered by Shuan
**Red Fox;** *See* **Campbell, Colin**
**Redruth, Tom;** Squire Trelawney's gamekeeper          *Treasure Island*
**Riach, Mr.;** second officer of the *Covenant*               *Kidnapped*
**Rich, Lieutenant Brackenbury;** Indian army officer   *The Suicide Club*
**Ridley, Barbara;** maid to Evelina Foster                  *Beau Austin*
**Risingham, Earl** ⎱
  **Alicia;** his niece ⎰                                   *The Black Arrow*
**River Farm**                                               *Prince Otto*
**Rivers, Captain;** English highwayman                     *Deacon Brodie*
**Robbie, Mr;** lawyer (in charge of Miss Gilchrist)            *St. Ives*
**Roederer;** 'licentiate' and author                       *Prince Otto*
**Rolles, Rev. Simon;** young man in holy orders   *The Rajah's Diamond*
**Romaine, Daniel;** solicitor to Vicomte de Saint-Yves         *St. Ives*
**Rorie;** Darnaway's servant                              *The Merry Men*
*Rose*; ship which carried David and Catriona to Holland       *Catriona*
**Rosen, Countess Anna von;** mistress of Gondremark      *Prince Otto*
**Rowley, George;** valet to Vicomte de Saint-Yves              *St. Ives*
**Rupert Street, Soho;** (*see* **Bohemian Cigar Divan**)    *The Dynamiter*

**Rutherford, William;** chief correspondent ⎫     *Edifying Letters of the*
  **James;** his father                 ⎭        *Rutherford Family*
**Rutledge, Robin;** ward of Mr. Baskerville   *Mr. Baskerville and his Ward*
**Rutter;** a spy                               *The Black Arrow*

**St. Bride's Cross;** crossroads               *The Black Arrow*
**Saint-Yves, Vicomte Anne de Kéroual de;** ⎫
  (alias Champdivers and Edward Ducie) French prisoner- ⎪
  of-war, central character and narrator ⎬      *St. Ives*
  **Alain;** his rascally cousin and spy ⎪
  **Comte de Kéroual de;** his great-uncle ⎭
**'Sally Day',** crew of the *Farallone*            *The Ebb-Tide*
**Sam;** hostler of Green Dragon Inn        *The Young Chevalier*
**Sanazarro;** sculptor          *When the Devil Was Well*
**Sang;** Captain of the *Rose*                *Catriona*
**Sarah;** ship             *The Master of Ballantrae*
**'Saxpence',** Catriona's nickname for David      *Catriona*
**Scala, Bartolomeo della;** enemy of
  Duke Orsino         *When the Devil Was Well*
**Scougal, Andie;** of the *Thistle*             *Catriona*
**Scrymgeour, Francis;** Edinburgh bank-clerk   *The Rajah's Diamond*
**Scuddamore, Silas Q.;** wealthy American     *The Suicide Club*
**Seahorse;** ship                     *Catriona*
**Sea Ranger;** ship                *The Ebb-Tide*
**Sebright, Lieut. J. Lascelles;** of the *Tempest*    *The Wrecker*
**Sedley, Joanna;** alias John Matcham      *The Black Arrow*
**Señora, The**                     *Olalla*
**Sharpe;** smuggler                 *The Wrecker*
**Shelton, Richard (Dick);** central character ⎫
  **Sir Harry;** his father ⎪
**Shoreby, Lord;** protagonist ⎬     *The Black Arrow*
**Shoreby Abbey Church** ⎪
**Shoreby-on-the-Till;** town ⎭
**Shovel, Henry;** central character ⎫   *The Adventures of Henry Shovel*
  **Rev. Diggory;** his kinsman ⎭
**Shuan, Mr.;** brutal mate of the *Covenant*        *Kidnapped*
**Silver, Long John;** sea-cook on the *Hispaniola*   *Treasure Island*
**Sim;** a drover                     *St. Ives*
**Skalaholt;** burial place of Thorgunna      *The Waif Woman*
**Skeleton Island;** location on map ⎫        *Treasure Island*
**Smollett;** Captain of the *Hispaniola* ⎭
**Smith, George;** robber in Brodie's gang      *Deacon Brodie*
**Somerset, Paul;** character           *The Dynamiter*
                                 *Edifying Letters of the*
  also correspondent in                   *Rutherford Family*

**Soulis, Reverend Murdoch;** minister                     *Thrawn Janet*
**Speedy and Sons;** creditors                             *The Wrecker*
**Spy-glass Inn (Sign of the), Bristol;** ⎫
   Long John Silver's inn                   ⎬    *Treasure Island*
**Spy-glass Hill;** location on map        ⎭
**Sprott, Sandie;** Scots merchant in Helvoetsluys           *Catriona*
**Stennis;** friend of Loudon Dodd                         *The Wrecker*
**Stewart, Alan Breck;** alias Thomson, Jamieson, ⎫ *Kidnapped* and *Catriona*
   Chevalier Stewart (also known as Breck) ⎭
**Stewart, James (Duror), 'James of the Glen'** ⎫
   **Charles;** lawyer                      ⎬
   **Yr. of Stewart Hall;** James Stewart's counsel ⎬  *Catriona*
**Stobo, Tam;** sea-captain                 ⎭
**Stubbs, Mr.;** undergraduate in Paris       *Providence and The Guitar*
**Swanston Cottage;** below Pentland Hills, near Edinburgh,
   used as fictitious setting                    *St. Ives*

**Tabary, Guy;** thief                          *A Lodging for the Night*
**Tarleton, Mr;** missionary                     *The Beach of Falesá*
**Teach;** pirate captain of *Sarah*          *The Master of Ballantrae*
**Teena;** servant                                 *The Wrong Box*
***Tempest*;** ship                                  *The Wrecker*
**Tentaillon, Madame;** innkeeper's wife    *The Treasure of Franchard*
***Thistle*;** ship                                    *Catriona*
**Thomson Mr;** alias of Alan Breck Stewart              *Kidnapped*
**Thorgunna;** central character                 *The Waif Woman*
**Thymebury;** town                             *The Story of a Lie*
**Tom;** honest seaman in the *Hispaniola*,
   killed by Silver                          *Treasure Island*
**Torrance;** clerk to Mr Rankeillor                     *Kidnapped*
**Torrance, Rev. Mr.;** minister of Glencorse      *Weir of Hermiston*
**Traquair;** *See* **Montroymont**
**Transome;** alias of Prince Otto                    *Prince Otto*
**Tregonwell Arms;** inn                            *The Wrong Box*
**Trelawney, Squire**                             *Treasure Island*
**Trent;** Captain of the *Flying Scud*              *The Wrecker*
***Trinity Hall*;** schooner                         *The Ebb-Tide*
**Tunstall Forest;** setting                    ⎫
**Tunstall Moat House;** home of Sir Daniel Brackley ⎬  *Black Arrow*

**Uma;** wife of Wiltshire                       *The Beach of Falesá*
**Uncle Ned;** crew of the *Farallone*               *The Ebb-Tide*
**Urquhart;** doctor                               *The Wrecker*
**Utterson;** lawyer and friend of Dr. Jekyll    *Dr. Jekyll and Mr. Hyde*

| | |
|---|---|
| **Valdevia, Señor**<br>  **Teresa;** his daughter | *The Dynamiter* |
| **Vandeleur, Major-General Sir Thomas;**<br>  employer of Harry Hartley<br>  **Clara;** his wife (née Pendragon)<br>  **John;** his brother | *The Rajah's Diamond* |
| **Van Tromp, Admiral**<br>  **Esther;** his daughter | *The Story of a Lie* |
| **Villon, Francis;** used as central character | *A Lodging for the Night* |
| | |
| *Walrus*; Flint's old ship | *Treasure Island* |
| **Watt, Jean;** mistress of Deacon Brodie | *Deacon Brodie* |
| **Watts, Mr;** innkeeper | *The Wrong Box* |
| **Weir, Adam; Lord Hermiston**<br>  **Jean;** his wife<br>  **Archibald (Archie);** their son | *Weir of Hermiston* |
| **'White Man';** crew of the *Farallone* | *The Ebb-Tide* |
| **Wickham;** Michael Finsbury's friend | *The Wrong Box* |
| **Wicks, Captain;** of the *Grace Darling*<br>  (alias Captain Kirkup) | *The Wrecker* |
| **Will o' the Mill;** central character | *Will o' the Mill* |
| **Wiltshire, John;** central character | *The Beach of Falesá* |
| **Windermoor, Lord** | *The Great North Road* |
| | |
| **Zéphyrine, Madame;** neighbour of Scuddamore | *The Suicide Club* |
| **Zero;** character | *The Dynamiter* |

## Part 4
# INDEX OF LETTERS FROM STEVENSON

This section contains a list of letters from Stevenson, most of which appear in the Tusitala Edition. The name of the recipient is followed by a brief description of the contents of the letter which, if read in conjunction with the Chronology (p.xix), will provide a background and lend a greater significance to each letter.

*Academy, The:* 7 May 1881, 'The Morality of the Profession of Letters'. Replies to criticism of his essay of the same title, Paris, 27 April 1881. 20 March 1886, 'American Rights and Wrongs'. US copyright explained for the benefit of English authors, Skerryvore, Bournemouth, 15 March 1886

**Angus, W. Craibe:** 'Scotland's three "Robins" ' (Burns, Fergusson and Stevenson): re. Burns exhibition; 'I have gone into far lands to die, not stayed like Burns to mingle in the end with Scottish soil', Vailima, April 1891
Suggestions for monuments to Fergusson and Burns, Vailima, Summer, 1891.
Reply to request for preface to *Jolly Beggars,* asking for ample time: 'I am still "a slow study" and sit a long while silent on my eggs', Vailima, Nov. 1891

**Anonymous Correspondent:** Allegory of *Dr. Jekyll and Mr. Hyde* and reviewers, Skerryvore, Bournemouth, 25 Feb. 1886

**Archer, Thomas 'Tomarcher':** Son of William (below): Regarding South Sea Islands children, Tahiti, 17 Oct. 1888
Tahiti children at play and other topics, Tautira, Nov. 1888

**Archer, William:** Introduction letter: 'Best criticism I have ever had' (*Child's Garden of Verses*), Bournemouth, 29 March 1885
'Every gay, every bright word or picture', Skerryvore, 28 Oct. 1885
'To suffer, sets a keen edge on what remains of the agreeable', Skerryvore, 30 Oct. 1885
'The rich fox-hunting squire speaks with one voice, the sick man of letters with another', Skerryvore, 1 Nov. 1885
'I am now a salaried party; I am a bourgeois now', Saranac, NY, 1 Oct. 1887
In praise of G.B. Shaw's *Cashel Byron's Profession,* Saranac, Winter 1887-8

279

'One thing in which my stories fail: I am always cutting the flesh off the bones', Saranac, Feb. 1888

Regarding unchivalrous scene in Dumas' *le Demi-Monde*, Saranac, Feb. 1888

Re Tomarcher's delight in *The Black Arrow*, Vailima, 27 March 1894

**Athenaeum, The:** 21 Oct. 1882. 'Plagiarism'. Refutes claim that James Payn was indicated in 'borrowing gist of a story' from *New Arabian Nights*; same letter to *New York Tribune*, Marseilles, 16 Oct. 1882. 11 and 25 Oct. 1884, 'The Bell Rock Lighthouse'. Questions authenticity of book by Frederick Whymper; especially and vehemently denies that credit for its design and building should go to David Rennie (consultant engineer) instead of his grandfather, Robert Stevenson, Bournemouth, 3 and 20 Oct. 1884.

24 Jan. 1885, 'A Warning'. Denounces Augustin Filon's 'Histoire de la littérature anglaise' as imposture, Bournemouth, 10 Jan. 1885.

(*See also* Part 1 (**Athenaeum, The**))

**Babington, Mrs. Churchill** (cousin **Maud**, *née* **Balfour**): Description of Swanston summer; invitation to visit, Swanston, Summer 1871

**Baildon, H. Bellyse:** 'Sick and well, I have had a splendid life . . . grudge nothing, regret very little', Vailima, Spring 1891

Thanks for dedication: Edinburgh nostalgia, Vailima, 15 Jan. 1894

'Begins to look as if I should survive to see myself impotent and forgotten', Vailima, 30 Jan. 1894

**Baker, Mrs. A:** Giving permission for Braille versions of *Kidnapped* and *Catriona* with poem: 'I was a barren tree before', Vailima, Dec. 1893

'When the night falls you need ask no blessing on your work', Vailima, 16 July 1894

**Bakewell, Dr. W:** Reply to physician in Australia, Vailima, 7 Aug. 1894

**Balfour, Jane:** (Stevenson's aunt) On her receiving *Travels with a Donkey*, Swanston, June 1879

**Bamford, Doctor:** Letter about *Travels with a Donkey*, San Francisco, April 1880

**Barrie, Sir James Matthew:** Introduction letter, Vailima, Feb. 1892

Re 'The Young Chevalier' and *Weir of Hermiston*, Vailima, 1 Nov 1892

'Edinburgh Eleven': nostalgia for Scotland, Vailima, Dec. 1892

Thanks for *A Window in Thrums*, Vailima, 7 Dec. 1893

Poem: 'There was racing and chasing in Vailele Plantation'; invitation to visit, Vailima, 13 July 1894

**Bates, J.H:** Honoured to be associated with society; founder of R.L.S. Society, Cincinnati, Vailima, 25 March 1894.

**Baxter, Charles:** Description of country, Dunblane, 5 March 1872
    Election to the Speculative Society, Edinburgh, Dunblane, 9 April 1873
    Poem: 'Blame me not that this epistle', Boulogne-sur-Mer, 3/4 Sept. 1872
    Gum-boil; philosophy on fools, 17 Heriot Row, Edinburgh, Oct. 1872
    Troubles with father, 17 Heriot Row, Edinburgh, 2 Feb. 1873
    Description of Menton countryside, Menton, Dec. 1873
    Poem: 'Noo lyart leaves blaw', Edinburgh, Oct. 1875
    Acquisition of donkey 'Modestine', Le Monastier, Sept. 1878
    Hard times, poverty in San Francisco, 608 Bush Street, 26 Jan. 1880
    Description of Strathpeffer, Ben Wyvis Hotel, July 1880
    Ill, bored and sad in Davos, Chalet-am-Stein, 5 Dec. 1881
    Delight at coming to Scotland, Chalet-am-Stein, 22 Feb. 1882
    Letter in Scots from Nice, Grand Hotel, 12 June 1883
    In style of Edinburgh ex-elder Thomson, Bonallie Towers, Bournemouth, 11 Nov. 1884
    In style of Edinburgh ex-elder Johnstone, Bournemouth, 13 Nov. 1884
    Proposed August visit, Skerryvore, Bournemouth, July 1886
    'Times are changed since the Lothian Road', Saranac, NY, Nov. 1887
    Christmas letter sending money gifts to friends, Saranac, NY, 12 Dec. 1887
    Permission to include Baxter and Edinburgh office in *Master of Ballantrae*, Saranac, NY, Jan. 1888
    Hire of *Casco* bound for South Seas, Manasquan, NJ, 11 May 1888
    Vision of Drummond Street, Edinburgh, *Casco*, 6 Sept. 1888
    Sending photos and copy of journal, Tahiti, 6 Oct. 1888
    Delight of Tautira 'garden of world', Tautira, Nov. 1888
    Poem: 'Home no more home to me', Tautira, 10 Nov. 1888
    Success of cruise, Honolulu, 8 Feb. 1889
    *The Wrong Box*, part of *The Master of Ballantrae* to rewrite, Honolulu, 8 March 1889
    Acquisition of *Equator*, bound for Gilberts, Honolulu, April 1889
    'God's sweetest works — Polynesia', Honolulu, 10 May 1889
    Landing in Samoa, Samoa, Dec. 1889
    Poem: 'To my old comrades', S.S. *Lübeck* en route Sydney, Feb 1890
    Ill in Sydney, Union Club, 7 March 1890
    Decision to stay in Samoa, Hotel Sebastopol, Noumea, Aug. 1890
    Neglect of parents by offspring, S.S. *Lübeck* en route Samoa, Feb. 1891

Novel idea from 'Henry Shovel', Vailima, 19 May 1891
*The Wrecker* project, Vailima, Nov. 1891
Dedication of *David Balfour* (*Catriona*), Vailima, 28 April 1892
Edinburgh reminiscences; W.E. Henley, Vailima, 18 July 1892
Writing difficulties with *Weir of Hermiston*, Vailima, 1 Dec. 1892
Poem: 'O Sovereign of my Cedercrantz', Vailima, 28 Dec. 1892
*Ebb-Tide* (original title *The Pearl Fisher*); influenza at Vailima, Feb.
1893
Stevenson: name adopted by proscribed Macgregors, Vailima, April
1893
Samoan war; health, Vailima, 19 July 1892
Genealogical search for Stevenson family, Vailima, Sept. 1893
'Heathercat', Vailima, 6 Dec. 1893
Plans for Edinburgh Edition of works, Vailima, 1 Jan. 1894
Progress of *St. Ives*, Vailima, 17 April 1894
Edinburgh Edition; suggestions for monument to Robert
Fergusson, Vailima, May 1894
Death of Baxter's father, Vailima, Sept. 1894
*Robert Louis Stevenson's Letters to Charles Baxter* (*see* Part I (**Ferguson,
De Lancey and Waingrow, Marshall**)) contains many hitherto
unpublished letters. (*See also* **Whitefriars Journal**)

**Boodle, Adelaide:** (friend of Skerryvore household)
Thanks for paper-knife farewell gift, Bournemouth, 19 Aug. 1887
Arrival and report from Saranac Lake, Saranac, NY, Dec. 1887
Christmas letter, mentioning 'new story which has bewitched me':
*Master of Ballantrae*, Saranac, Christmas 1887
Begins 'My dear Gamekeeper' and ends 'Your indulgent but
intemperate Squire', c/o Charles Scribner's Sons, New York, April
1888
Written in character of paper-cutter gift, Tahiti, 10 Oct 1888
Life in Honolulu, Honolulu, 6 April 1889
Reverie about Skerryvore; various writing projects, Union Club,
Sydney, 1 Sept. 1890
Naming road from house 'Adelaide Road', Vailima, May 1891
Samoan life and children (signed 'Tusitala'), Vailima, 4 Jan. 1892
Samoan life (calling himself 'The Lean Man'), Vailima, 14 Aug. 1892
Postscript to letter to the Children in the (Kilburn) Cellar, Vailima,
4 Sept. 1892
Reactions to her going into mission work, Vailima, 14 July 1894

**Brown, Horatio F.:** Stevenson sent him Penn's *Fruits of Solitude,* Hotel
Belvedere, Davos, Feb. 1881
Praise of Penn, Hotel Belvedere, Feb. 1881
Poem: 'Brave lads in olden musical centuries', Hotel Belvedere,
April 1881

**Browne, Gordon:** (artist who illustrated 'Uma' ('The Beach of Falesá')
Thanks for care and talent shown, Vailima, Autumn 1892

**Burlingame, Ed. Livermore:** (editor of *Scribner's Magazine*)
First letter, enclosing proof of 'Beggars' with apologies for
accidental breach of agreement, Saranac Lake, NY, Nov. 1887
Acceptance of 'The Lantern Bearers', Saranac Lake, Nov. 1887
Delays on *Master of Ballantrae*, Saranac Lake, Winter 1887/8
Requesting copies of G.P.R. James's works, Saranac Lake, Feb. 1888
Returning corrected proof: 'Pulvis et Umbra', Saranac Lake, Feb.
1888
Enclosing parts of *Master of Ballantrae*; hoping to finish 'Game of
Bluff' (*The Wrong Box*), Honolulu, Jan. 1889
Requesting Scott's Waverley novels and others, Honolulu, April
1889
Work on *The Wrecker*, prospective serial? *Equator* at sea, 4 Dec. 1889
Progress on *The Wrecker*; prospective travel book, S.S. *Lübeck* en route
Sydney, Feb. 1890
Discussing future work for Scribner's, *Janet Nicholl*, off Peru Island,
Kingsmills Group, 13 July 1890
Proposed volume of verse: *Ballads*, etc., Union Club, Sydney, Aug.
1890
*The Wrecker*; description of Vailima, Vailima, 7 Nov. 1890
*The Wrecker*; talk of 'farming', Vailima, Dec. 1890
Grandfather's reminiscences for publication, Vailima, Summer 1891
Promised 'Tales of a Grandfather', Vailima, 8 Oct. 1891
*The Wrecker* complete; request various books, Vailima, Oct. 1891
Announcing 'A Footnote to History', Vailima, Dec. 1891
Pleased by reception of *The Wrecker*, Vailima, 2 Jan. 1892
Regarding 'Footnote to History', Vailima, March 1892
Corrections to *The Wrecker*, Vailima, Summer 1892
Enclosing 'Tales of Grandfather'; progress on *David Balfour*, Vailima,
1 Aug. 1892
'Footnote to History' not arrived, anxious, Vailima, 10 Oct. 1892
Acknowledging cheque $350; still no 'Footnote', Vailima, 2 Nov.
1892

**Campbell, Rev. Prof. Lewis:** Thanks for books; incl. translation of
Sophocles, Wensleydale, Bournemouth, Nov. 1884

**Carrington, C. Howard:** Reply to correspondent not personally known
who had heard of 'Great North Road' project, Skerryvore,
Bournemouth,9 June 1885

**Charteris, Evan:** (close friend of Stevenson's father)
Asking for memories in writing paper on Thomas Stevenson,

RLST – K

Saranac, NY, Winter, 1887/8
'[My father] was a tragic thinker', Saranac, Spring 1888

**Chatto, Andrew:** (of Chatto and Windus)
Mentioning offer of £25 for *Prince Otto* from US, Wensleydale,
Bournemouth, 3 Oct. 1884

**Chatto and Windus:** Enclosing 'Underwoods' and *Memories and Portraits,*
Bournemouth, Aug. 1887

**Children in the (Kilburn) Cellar (*see* Boodle)**
Life of Samoan boy, Arick, Vailima, 4 Sept. 1892

**Church of Scotland Home and Missionary Record:** 1 May 1871,
'Parochial Work and Organisation'. (Published anonymously but
referred to in his mother's Diary, Vailima Edition, 1923.)

**Colvin, Sidney:** To Inns of Court for admission as student, Edinburgh,
15/16 Oct. 1873
Regarding Bob Stevenson's proposed Paris visit, Menton, Jan. 1874
Commission to buy him a cloak in Paris, Menton, Jan. 1874
Re 'The Curate of Anstruther's Bottle', subsequently abandoned,
Menton, Jan. 1874
Poor health; work on 'Victor Hugo', Hotel St Romain, Paris, April
1874
Lytton's *Fables* for *Fortnightly Review,* Swanston, Edinburgh, May 1874
Acceptance of first contract from *Cornhill Magazine,* Edinburgh,
May 1874
Poor health; away to Greenock, Edinburgh, June 1874
Progress on volume of essays, later abandoned, Swanston, Summer
1874
Cannot guarantee one essay per month, 'must fall . . . as they ripen',
Swanston, Summer 1874
Thanks for Japanese prints, Edinburgh, Nov. 1874
Cannot afford to visit, 17 Heriot Row, Edinburgh, Jan. 1875
Enclosing list of 12 projected stories, Edinburgh, Jan. 1875
Proof of 'John Knox' essay, Edinburgh, 8 Feb. 1875
Re Ruysdael landscape painting, Edinburgh, Spring 1875
Effects of beautiful spring days at, Swanston, Spring 1875
Enclosing Henley's 'hospital work', Edinburgh, July 1875
Work on Burns for *Encyclopaedia Britannica,* Edinburgh, Autumn 1875
Enquiry about essay 'On the Spirit of Spring' (subsequently lost by
Colvin), Swanston, Autumn 1875
Accepting Colvin's apologies on above, Edinburgh, Autumn 1875
Leslie Stephen (*Cornhill Magazine*) does not like 'Fontainebleau';
work on 'Winter's Walk', Edinburgh, Feb. 1876

Cottage, Pitlochry, June 1881

Intention to apply for Chair of History at Edinburgh University, Kinnaird Cottage, Pitlochry, June 1881

Report on 'Thrawn Janet', 'The Body-Snatcher' and 'The Merry Men', Kinnaird Cottage, Pitlochry, July 1881

Ill; moving to Braemar; Fenian outrages, Kinnaird Cottage, Pitlochry, Aug. 1881

About Keats volume proposed by Colvin, Chalet-am-Stein, Davos, Feb. 1882

Enclosing 'Moral Emblems'; report on *Silverado* progress, Chalet-am-Stein, Davos, March 1882

Left Campagne Defli; signed 'Brabazon Drum', Hotel du Petit Louvre, Marseilles, 15 Feb. 1883

Reproaches at non-replies: 'Father of Unanswered Correspondence', La Solitude, Hyères, May 1883

Re *Child's Garden of Verses* ('Penny Whistles' original title), La Solitude, Oct. 1883

'The Travelling Companion's progress, subsequently abandoned, La Solitude, Nov. 1883

Death of Walter Ferrier; beauty of La Solitude, Nov. 1883

Progress of *Prince Otto* and other topics, La Solitude, 9 Mar. 1884

Supplementary verses for *Child's Garden,* Marseilles, June 1884

*Deacon Brodie* to be performed in London, Hotel Chabassière, Royat, July 1884

Defoe and *Treasure Island,* Hotel Chabassière, Royat, July 1884

Request for books for work on Wellington, Bonallie Towers, Bournemouth, 4 Jan. 1885

Has written Gladstone re Wellington, Bonallie Towers, Jan. 1885

Disgusted at Britain's betrayal of Gordon at Khartoum, Bonallie Towers, Feb. 1885

On reading *The Aeneid,* Skerryvore, March 1886

Poem: 'He may have been this and that', Skerryvore, April 1886

Ill; depressed by 'Travelling Companion': 'foul, gross, bitter, ugly daub', Skerryvore, June 1886

Hopes of knighthood for sick father, Skerryvore, 14 Dec. 1886

Reading Huxley and Cotter Morison, Skerryvore, Spring 1887

Father's death; 'He will begin to return to us in the course of time, as he was and as we loved him', Edinburgh, June 1887

Departure for America, off Havre de Grace, MD, 22 Aug. 1887

Desc. of voyage among cargo of animals, Newport, RI, Sept. 1887

Illness; arrival of St. Gaudens, sculptor, New York, Sept. 1887

Description of Saranac, Saranac Lake, NY, Dec. 1887

Beginning of *Master of Ballantrae,* Saranac Lake, NY, 24 Dec. 1887

Fanny ill; bitter climate; progress of work, Saranac Lake, NY, March 1888

Projected Mutiny novel, never materialised, Saranac Lake, NY, 9 April 1888

Desc. of pleasant watering-place at Manasquan, Union House, NJ, May 1888

Climate delightful, 'one of loveliest spots', Casco, Marquesas, July 1888

Desc. of island, signed 'The Old Man Virulent' (reference to violent temper in youth), Fakarava, 21 Sept. 1888

Enclosing 'Ballads'; poem: 'O, how my spirit languishes', Tahiti, 16 Oct. 1888

Desc. of two months in Tautira, Casco at sea, 14 Jan. 1889

Encl. drawing of Honolulu house; work on 'Song of Rahero' in progress, Honolulu, March 1889

Cruise plans; not coming home for another year, Honolulu, 2 April 1889

Visit to Molokai leper colony, Honolulu, June 1889

Meeting with murderer and family, Equator, Apaiang Lagoon, 22 Aug. 1889

Desc. of King Tembinok, Apemama, Oct. 1889

'I am minded to stay not very long in Samoa', Equator, 190 miles off Samoa, 2 Dec. 1889

Fire on ship; history of Samoan wars, S.S. Janet Nicholl, off Upolu, Spring 1890

Clearing jungle for Vailima; writing The Wrecker (diary-letter, 14 pp.), In the mountain, Apia, 2 Nov. 1890

Description of life in Vailima (diary-letter), Vailima, 25 Nov. 1890

'Jack' an island horse; life in Vailima, Vailima, Dec. 1890

Arrival of Cedarcrantz; a marriage party; Poem: 'We're quarrelling, the villages', S.S. Lübeck, en route for Sydney, 17 Jan. 1891

Ill in Sydney; proofs of In the South Seas, en route for Apia, Feb. 1891

Diary-letter of daily life in Vailima, Vailima, 19 March, 1891

Diary-letter of daily life in Vailima, Vailima, 18 April, 1891

Arrival of mother from Edinburgh; disappointed South Seas — not well received by friends, Vailima, 29 April, 1891

Received Colvin's portrait; various writings, Vailima, June 1891

Desc. of servants; plan of extending Vailima, Vailima, June/July 1891

Distressed by politics in Samoa; work in progress, Vailima, 5 Sept. 1891

Rewriting 'Beach of Falesá'; Samoan politics, Vailima, 28 Sept 1891

The Wrecker; island politics, Vailima, 24 Oct. 1891

Four chapters of Samoan history finished, Vailima, 25 Nov. 1891

Exploration of Mt. Vaea; diary-letter, Vailima, Dec. 1891

South Sea novel Sophia Scarlet, never materialised, Vailima, 31 Jan. 1892

Native servant troubles; progress with *David Balfour,* Vailima, Feb. 1892

15 chapters, 100 pages *David Balfour;* diary-letter, Vailima, 9 March 1892

Diary-letter; Vailima desc.; writing progress, Vailima, 1 May 1892

Family expedition to visit Mataafa in exile, Vailima, 29 May 1892

Writer's cramp; Vailima matters, Vailima, 2 July 1892

*David Balfour;* cousin Graham Balfour's visit, Vailima, Aug. 1892

Family expedition to Malie; writing progress, Vailima, Aug. 1892

Departure of Belle Strong's son for school in Calif.; Vailima matters; work in progress, Vailima, 15 Sept. 1892

Plan announced to write *Weir of Hermiston,* Vailima, 28 Oct. 1892

Stories: 'Bottle Imp', 'Isle of Voices', 'Waif Woman', Vailima, 30 Nov, 1892

Asking proofs of *David Balfour;* influenza among servants, Vailima, Jan. 1893

Recuperative holiday in Sydney, at sea, S.S. *Mariposa,* 19 Feb. 1893

Disastrous holiday; all ill, (Apia due), S.S. *Mariposa,* 1 March 1893

*David Balfour* published in *Atalanta,* now to be changed to *Catriona,* Vailima, April 1893

Outbreak of Samoan hostilities, Vailima, April 1893

Completion of *Ebb-Tide,* beginning *History of a Family of Engineers,* account of grandfather, Vailima, 29 May 1893

Worst headache ever; diary-letter, Vailima, 24 June 1893

Slight haemorrhage; family also ill, Vailima, Aug. 1893

Colvin's reception of *The Ebb-Tide;* work on *St. Ives,* Vailima, 23 Aug. 1893

Recovering from fever; Fanny's arrival; success of *The Wrecker* over *Ballantrae,* Waikiki, 23 Oct. 1893

Gratitude of imprisoned island chiefs, Vailima, Dec. 1893

Trials of rebelling chiefs, Vailima, 29 Jan. 1894

Pleased with *Ebb-Tide;* sensitive about reviews, Vailima, Feb. 1894

Another rising in Samoa, Vailima, April 1894

Proposals for Edinburgh Edition; cuts to *Emigrant,* Vailima, May 1894

More about Edinburgh edition; attack by local press on Stevenson's support of rebel chiefs, Vailima, 8 June 1894

Work in progress; visitors to Vailima, Vailima, July 1894

Sunday paper-chase offended missionaries, Vailima, 7 Aug. 1894

Work on *St. Ives,* Vailima, Sept. 1894

'Road of Gratitude' built by chiefs for Tusitala, Vailima, 6 Oct. 1894

Last letter; social activities at Vailima, Vailima, Nov. 1894

**Court and Society Review:** 29 July 1886, 'Honour and Chastity'. Comments on the conduct of Sir Charles Dilke in the Crawford divorce case; Dilke 'chose to save his own reputation and heartlessly destroy that of a woman who had trusted him', 22 July 1886; reproduced in *The Stevensonian*, Aug. 1967

**Crockett, Samuel Rutherford:** Addressed 'Dear Minister of the Free Kirk at Penicuik', thanking him for charming letter, Saranac Lake, NY, Spring 1888
'Do you know where the road crosses the burn under Glencorse Church? Go there, and say a prayer for me . . . shut your eyes . . . and if I don't appear to you!', Vailima, 17 May 1893

**Cunningham, Alison:** (his nurse Cummy)
'You have made much that there is in me, just as surely as if you had conceived me . . . ', 1871 ?
Concern at her illness, Chalet-am-Stein, Davos, Feb. 1882
Informing her of dedication to *Child's Garden,* Nice, Feb. 1883
Adding some more verses; sorry she has been ill, France, Summer 1883
Thinking of her on New Year's Day, Skerryvore, Bournemouth, 1 Jan. 1886
With copy of *Kidnapped,* Skerryvore, July 1886
Concern for her and dog 'Hecky', Skerryvore, July 1886
Thanking her for gift of cupboard on way, Skerryvore, July/Aug. 1886
Appreciation of cupboard 'most beautiful', Skerryvore, Sept. 1886
Talk of dogs and other family matters, Skerryvore, 16 April 1887
Christmas letter, signed 'With much love, I am your laddie', Vailima, 5 Dec. 1893
Sorry she's ailing; telling her about chief's 'Road', Vailima, 8 Oct. 1894

**Daily Chronicle:** 18 Mar. 1895. 'Robert Louis Stevenson's Swan Song; His Dying Appeal for Mataafa' (the Samoan chief) (letter to J.F. Hogan, Esq., M.P.), Vailima, 7 Oct. 1894; collected in *Vailima Papers*, Tusitala Edition *21*

**de Mattos, Mrs. Katharine:** Depression and illness: 'To think that the sun is still shining in some happy places . . .', Edinburgh, Jan. 1876
'You never answer . . .', Skerryvore, Bournemouth, Summer 1885
Dedication of *Jekyll and Hyde*; Poem: 'Bells upon the city', Skerryvore, 1 Jan. 1886

**Dew-Smith, A.G.:** Thanks for gift of cigarettes; poem. 'Figure me to yourself, I pray —', Hotel Belvedere, Davos, Nov. 1880

**Dick, Mr.** (Head clerk in family firm at Edinburgh):

Friendly letter, regarding work and family, La Solitude, Hyères, 12 March 1884

**Dobson, Austin:** Thanks for gift of a desk, Bonallie Towers, Bournemouth, Dec. 1884

**Dover, T.W.:** Acknowledging letter on reading 'Beggars', Vailima, 20 June 1892

**Doyle, Arthur Conan:** Congratulations on Sherlock Holmes, Vailima, 5 April, 1893
Directions for visit to Vailima, Vailima, 12 July 1893
Reactions of Samoans to 'Bottle Imp'; re Doyle's *Engineer's Thumb*, Vailima, 23 Aug. 1893
Pleasure in contributions to *The Idler*, Vailima, 9 Sept. 1894

**Droppers, Garrett, Professor:** Delighted by article on 'influence of Stevenson' in *Harvard Monthly*, Skerryvore, Bournemouth, 5 April 1887

**Eeles, Lieutenant, R.N. (the *Curaçoa*):** Friend and visitor to Vailima; interested in Fiji legend, Vailima, 15 Nov. 1892
Advice re London visit, Vailima, 21 Nov. 1894

**Fairchild, Charles:** Could he send some grapes; no fruit, Saranac Lake, NY, Oct. 1887

**Fairchild, Mrs. Charles:** Regretting letter to Dr. Hyde re Damien, Union Club, Sydney, Sept. 1890
Daily work schedule: Vailima, Aug. 1892
Thoughts on youth and life, Vailima, Aug. 1892

**Ferrier, 'Coggie':** On death of her brother Walter, La Solitude, Hyères, Sept. 1883
On old friendship with Walter, La Solitude, 30 Sept. 1883
Thanks for photograph of Walter, La Solitude, 22 Nov. 1883
Persuading her to visit, La Solitude, 22 March 1884
Thanks for photo Bell Rock; ref. to 'Wild Woman of the West has been much amiss and complaining sorely...', Bonallie Towers, Bournemouth, 12 Nov. 1884
Death of her kinsman Sir Alexander Grant, Bonallie Towers, Dec. 1884
'Cogia Hassan was cast for the part of passenger' (on their projected cruise), Saranac Lake, NY, April 1888

**Ferrier, James Walter:** Thanks for *Forester*, autobiographical paper on Ferrier's boyhood, P.O. San Francisco, 8 April 1880

**Gosse, Sir Edmund William:** Plan to write a book of murder stories together, Edinburgh, 16 April 1879

Working on book on morals, 17 Heriot Row, Edinburgh, Spring 1879

Discussing Meredith and Burns: 'Something in him of the vulgar, bagmanlike, professional seducer', Swanston, 24 July 1879

'Weg' is your name: W E G', 17 Heriot Row, Edinburgh, 29 July 1879

Report from the angora goat-ranch, Monterey, 8 Oct. 1879

Thanks for letter; writing *Vendetta in the West,* Monterey, 15 Nov. 1879

Acknowledging Gosse's *New Poems,* Monterey, 8 Dec. 1879

Engaged to 'the woman whom I have loved for three years and a half', 608 Bush Street, San Francisco, 23 Jan. 1880

Serious illness, nursed by Fanny, San Francisco, 16 April, 1880

Gosse's collecting odes, Hotel Belvedere, Davos, 6 Dec. 1880

Regarding *Duke of Wellington,* Hotel Belvedere, Davos, 19 Dec. 1880

Requesting information about Jean Cavalier, Kinnaird Cottage, Pitlochry, 6 June, 1881

Applying for Chair in History, Edinburgh; asking for testimonial, Kinnaird Cottage, 24 June 1881

Thanks for testimonial, Kinnaird Cottage, July 1881

Invitation to Braemar, Castleton of Braemar, 10 Aug. 1881

'If you had an uncle who was a sea captain and went to the North Pole, you had better bring his outfit...', Castleton of Braemer, 19 Aug. 1881

Further to matters concerning clothes, Castleton of Braemar, 19 Aug. 1881

Regarding *Young Folks* readers' objections to early instalments of *Treasure Island,* Chalet-am-Stein, Davos, 9 Nov. 1881

Collaboration on murder papers, Hotel Buol, Davos, 26 Dec. 1881

As above, Chalet-am-Stein, 23 March 1882

Return to Stobo Manse, Peeblesshire, Edinburgh, June 1882

Poem: 'I would shoot you, but I have no bow', Stobo Manse, July 1882

Writing matters; *Silverado Squatters,* La Solitude, Hyères, April 1883

'The £40 was a heavenly thing', La Solitude, 20 May 1883

*Century Magazine* to keep *Silverado,* La Solitude, 21 May 1883

Praise of Gosse's *Seventeeth Century Studies,* Hyères or Royat, Summer 1883

'For the first time, I shall pass £300' (per annum), La Solitude, 26 Sept 1883

Praise of Gosse's office, La Solitude, 17 March 1884

Congratulations on appointment as Clark Reader in Eng. Lit. at Trinity College, Cambridge; Stevenson very ill ('From my bed'), La Solitude, 29 May 1884

Poem: 'My Stockton if I failed to like', Bonallie Towers, Bournemouth, 15 Nov. 1884

Proposed edition of Gray, Bonallie Towers, 12 March 1885

Bad reviews of *Prince Otto*, Skerryvore, Bournemouth, 2 Jan. 1886

Thanks for £5 from American magazine which published verses to Will Low, Skerryvore, 17 Feb. 1886

Review of 'Underwoods' by Gosse; amused, Saranac Lake, NY, 8 Oct. 1887

Cannot write for *Fortnightly,* under 'pledge to Scribner's, Saranac Lake, NY, 31 March 1888

Thanking him for *Life* of Gosse's father, Vailima, April 1891

Surprised at two-year silence; letter sent never received, Vailima, 10 June 1893

Acknowledging dedication 'To Tusitala' of *In Russet and Silver* just received. Stevenson's last letter written two days before his death, Vailima, Dec. 1894

**Gosse, Mrs:** Thanks for miniature Bible, illustrated, Chalet-am-Stein, Davos, 16 March 1882

**Guthrie, Charles:** Announcing intention of applying for Chair of History, Edinburgh. Asking for help in making candidature known, Kinnaird Cottage, Pitlochry, 30 June 1881

Thanks for support and advice, Kinnaird Cottage, 2 July 1881

Lloyd Osbourne, student at Edinburgh University, has got into Spec. Soc., Skerryvore, Bournemouth, 18 Jan. 1886

**Haddon, Trevor:** Student who had read essay on Walt Whitman asking for further counsel and comment, 17 Heriot Row, Edinburgh, June 1882

'You remind me of myself...', 17 Heriot Row, Edinburgh, June 1882

'Let me have a note from time to time, until we shall have another chance to meet', Campagne Defli, 29 Dec. 1882

Congratulations on winning scholarship to Slade School, La Solitude, Hyères (from Clermont-Ferrand), 5 July 1883

Re Skelt's *Juvenile Dramas*, La Solitude, 23 Apr. 1884

**Hamerton, Philip Gilbert:** Read 'Essays on Art' with great interest, Monterey, Nov. 1879

'It was not my bliss that I was interested in when I was married; it was a sort of marriage *in extremis*...', Kinnaird Cottage, Pitlochry, July 1881

Thanks for testimony (for Chair of History), Chalet-am-Stein, Davos, Dec. 1881

Greatly interested in Hamerton's sheets in *Landscape,* Bournemouth, 16 March 1885

**Henley, William Ernest:** Bad weather on travels for *Inland Voyage*, Chauny, Aisne, Sept. 1876
'Travels with a Donkey in the French Highlands'; with details of a Gargantuan feast, Le Monastier, Sept. 1878
'Living like a fighting-cock, and have not spoken to a real person for about sixty hours', Trinity College, Cambridge, Autumn 1878
'Please yourself as to the name. Only spell it rightly please: Robert LOUIS; mind, not Lewis), 17 Heriot Row, Edinburgh, Autumn 1878
Re 'Our Lady of the Snows', published 'Underwoods';
Poem: 'O Henley, in my hours of ease', Edinburgh, April 1879
Letter from emigrant train, Crossing Nebraska, 23 Aug. 1879
Enclosing 'Pavilion on the Links', 'grand carpentry story in nine chapters', Monterey, Oct. 1879
Re story, *A Vendetta in the West*, Monterey, Oct. 1879
Concerning changes in 'Story of a Lie' and *Travels with a Donkey,* Monterey, 11 Dec. 1879
'Do not damp me about my work...You know the wolf is at the door...', 608 Bush Street, San Francisco, Jan. 1880
*Cornhill's* acceptance of 'Pavilion on Links'; poem: 'Here's breid an' wine an' kebbuck', 608 Bush Street, San Francisco, 23 Jan. 1880
Re *Forest State* (to be written three years later as *Prince Otto*), 608 Bush Street, San Francisco, Feb. 1880
Hoping for visit, Kinnaird Cottage, Pitlochry, July 1881
Re criticisms of *The Merry Men*, Kinnaird Cottage, Aug. 1881
The beginning of *The Sea-Cook or Treasure Island: A Story for Boys:* 'If this don't fetch the kids, why, they have gone rotten since my day...', Braemar, 25 Aug. 1881
Progress on *Treasure Island*, Braemar, Sept. 1881
'Dear Henley, with a pig's snout on...' Illness and bad weather, sent him south with a respirator for inhalation, Braemar, Sept. 1881
Contributions to *Magazine of Art*, edited by Henley, Davos, Nov. 1881
Injured knee, dog with canker of ear; finished 'Gossip on Romance', Chalet-am-Stein, Davos, Feb. 1882
Regarding publishers, Chalet-am-Stein, Davos, March 1882
Henley acting as agent, Chalet-am-Stein, Davos, April 1882
Depressed by bad news of Symond's consumption, Stobo Manse, Peeblesshire, July 1882
*Child's Garden of Verses* and Poem: 'Nor you, O Penny Whistler, grudge', Nice, March 1883
Rapid progress on *Prince Otto*, La Solitude, Hyères, April 1883
*Black Arrow*; requesting proofs of *Treasure Island*; progress on *Otto*, La Solitude, May 1883
Poem: 'The pleasant river gushes...', La Solitude, May 1883

'£100 is a sight more than *Treasure Island* is worth ...', La Solitude, May/June 1883

'A kind of prose Herrick, divested of the gift of verse', La Solitude, June 1883

'I sleep upon my art for a pillow', La Solitude, June 1883

Sadness at Walter Ferrier's death, La Solitude, 19 Sept. 1883

Re Lippincott's request for sailing trip to Greek isles made subject of book, La Solitude, Oct. 1883

Contributions to *Magazine of Art,* La Solitude, Autumn 1883

Re faulty seamanship in *Treasure Island,* La Solitude, Nov. 1883

Refusal of 'Salvini' article (signed 'The Prosy Preacher'), La Solitude, Autumn 1883

Poem: 'I counted miseries by the heap', La Solitude, Feb./March 1884

Ill with sciatica, haemorrhage, etc. (signed 'The Sciaticated Bard'), La Solitude, 20 April 1884

'Old Mortality', essay suggested by Ferrier's death, La Solitude, May 1884

Excellent news of *Deacon Brodie,* Hôtel Chabassière, Royat, July 1884

Illness and depression, Wensleydale, Bournemouth, Oct. 1884

'All to pieces in health'; working on *The Dynamiter; More New Arabian Nights,* Wensleydale, Bournemouth, Nov. 1884

Offer of £40 for ghost story for *Pall Mall*; handicapped by illness, Bonallie Towers, Bournemouth, 11 Nov. 1884

Thanks for Molière; birthday a great success, Bonallie Towers, 13 Nov. 1884

Re publishers for various works, Bonallie Towers, Dec. 1884

More re publishers (signed 'The Roaring R.L.S.'), Bonallie Towers, Dec. 1884

Ill with haemorrhage 'by too sedulous attentions to my dear Bogue' (their dog), Bonallie Towers, Bournemouth, Winter 1884

Play-writing in collaboration with Henley, Bournemouth, March 1885

'I must go on and drudge at *Kidnapped,* which I hate, and am unfit to do . . .', Bournemouth, March 1885

Reviews of *Prince Otto,* Skerryvore, Bournemouth, Autumn 1885

Depressed by father's death: 'My spirits are rising after three months of black depression: I almost begin to feel as if I should care to live . . .', Skerryvore, July/Aug. 1887

'I am now a salaried person, £600 a year to write twelve articles in *Scribner's Magazine',* New York, Sept. 1887

Congratulations on Ballades, Rondeaus, etc. by Henley dedicated to Stevenson, Saranac, NY, Oct. 1887

Volume on elder Dumas, Henley preparing, Saranac, Dec. 1887

Congratulations on new volume of poetry, Vailima, 1 Aug. 1892

**Hogan, J.F.:** *see* **Daily Chronicle**

**Ide, Annie:** Thanks for birthday photographs (she was his 'name-daughter' Louisa), Vailima, Nov. 1891

**Ide, H.C:** Transferring his own birthday 13 Nov. to Ide's daughter, born on Christmas Day, Vailima, 19 June 1891

**Ireland, Alexander:** Reply to the biographer and critic's query on Stevenson's proposed life of Hazlitt, Chalet-am-Stein, Davos, March 1882

**James, Henry:** Re *A Humble Remonstrance* and a continuance of their friendly controversy on the aims and quality of fiction, Bonallie Towers, Bournemouth, 8 Dec. 1884
Re James' *Princess Casamassima* and his 'chair' at Skerryvore, Bournemouth, 28 Oct. 1885
Written on set of *Memories and Portraits* proofs, hints at quarrels with Fanny and ends: 'Here are the kindest recollections from the canary-bird and from King Lear, from the Tragic Woman and the Flimsy Man', Skerryvore, Jan. 1887
Recent illness; writing matters ('The Merry Men' etc.), Skerryvore, Feb. 1887
Description of animal cargo on *Ludgate Hill,* Newport, US, Sept. 1887
The voyage; visit to Newport; desc. of, Saranac Lake, NY, Oct. 1887
James' *Roderick Hudson*; dislike of *Portrait of a Lady,* Saranac Lake, NY, Winter 1887/88
Announcement of work on *Master of Ballantrae,* Saranac Lake, NY, March 1888
Announcing departure for cruise on *Casco,* Manasquan, NJ, 28 May 1888
In praise of James' *Solution,* Union Club, Sydney, 19 Feb. 1890
Not coming home 'for another year'; desc. of, Honolulu, March 1889
Ill in Sydney: 'I must tell you plainly — I do not think I shall come to England more than once, and then it'll be to die . . .', Union Club, Sydney, Aug. 1890
Henry Adams and La Farge visitors to Vailima; more praise of Kipling as writer, Vailima, 29 Dec. 1890
Poems: 'Adela Chart'; 'Though oft I've been touched by the volatile dart', Vailima, Oct. 1891
Pleased with Bourget's *Sensations d'Italie*; praise of James' *Tragic Muse,* Vailima, 7 Dec. 1891
Have had no letter since June, Vailima, 5 Dec. 1892
Fanny's illness; Bourget's ignoring of dedication mention of *Ebb-Tide,* Vailima, 17 June 1893

Reading *Fountainhall's Decisions*, Apia, July 1893
Delighted James likes *Catriona*, Apia, Dec. 1893
Description of visit of war-ship *Curaçoa*, Vailima, 7 July 1894

**Japp, Alexander H.:** (biographer, also known as H.A. Page)
Reply to criticism of 'Essay on Thoreau'; invitation to, Braemar, Aug. 1881
Thanks for help with publication of *The Sea Cook* (*Treasure Island*) in *Young Folks*, Braemar, Sept. 1881
Enclosing 'Davos Press' cuts, Chalet-am-Stein, Davos, March 1882
Re *Familiar Studies of Men and Books*, Chalet-am-Stein, Davos, 1 April, 1882

**Jenkin, Mrs. Fleeming:** Written on death of his friend and professor at Edinburgh University, Skerryvore, Bournemouth, June 1885
Notice in *Academy*; invitation to visit, Skerryvore, June 1885
Progress of *Memoir of Fleeming Jenkin*; music, etc., Skerryvore, March 1886
Scheme of going to Ireland as personal protest against boycott of Curtin family by Fenians, Skerryvore, 15 April 1887
*Memoir of Fleeming Jenkin*; more about Ireland, Skerryvore, April 1887
Re *Memoir* and other matters at home, Saranac Lake, NY, Dec. 1887
Invitation to Vailima, Vailima, 5 Dec. 1892

**Jersey, Countess of:** (wife of Governor of New South Wales, visitor to Vailima with brother, Captain Leigh). Adopted by Stevenson as 'cousin', addressed as 'Miss Amelia Balfour' and his letter to her dated 'August 14, 1745', Vailima
Invitation to ride at Vailima, from Tusitala, Vailima, n.d.

**Jones, Henry Arthur:** Thanks for paper (no details), Bonallie Towers, Bournemouth, 30 Dec. 1884

**Kingero, Mr.:** (Japanese gentleman Stevenson met in France)
Reply to questions on European politics, with family news, 17 Heriot Row, Edinburgh, 25 July, 1877
More about politics, 17 Heriot Row, Edinburgh, 6 Dec. 1877

**Kipling, Rudyard:** Letter written in character of Alan Breck, Vailima, 1891

**Lang, Andrew:** Re Samoan religious customs, Union Club, Sydney, Aug. 1890
Thanks for material for 'Young Chevalier', Vailima, Aug. 1892
Re *Weir of Hermiston*; written two days before death, Vailima, 1 Dec. 1894

**Le Gallienne, Richard:** Admiration of writings, Vailima, 28 Dec. 1893

**Locker-Lampson, Frederick:** (friend of Tennyson, met through Andrew
   Lang) Poem: 'Not roses to the rose', Skerryvore, Bournemouth, 4
   Sept. 1886
   Asking for nomination of friend's son to Blue-Coat School,
   Skerryvore, Sept. 1886
   Did not wish to receive cheque in response, Skerryvore, Sept. 1886
   Thanks for generosity, cheque to boy's mother, Skerryvore, 24 Sept.
   1886
   Ill; regret declining invitation to visit Rowfant, Skerryvore, 5 Feb.
   1887

**Low, Will H.:** Re *Manhattan,* short-lived New York magazine; desc. of
   house and garden, 'Angels I know frequent it . . .', La Solitude,
   Hyères, Oct. 1883
   'I now draw near to the Middle Ages; nearly three years ago, that
   Fatal Thirty struck; and yet the great work is not yet done — not yet
   even conceived . . .', La Solitude, 23 Oct. 1883
   *Prince Otto* almost complete: 'I do not know if I have made a spoon, or
   only spoiled a horn', La Solitude, 13 Dec. 1883
   Suffering from ophthalmia, letter written by Fanny re 'The Canoe
   Speaks', later published in 'Underwoods', La Solitude, April 1884
   Re *Child's Garden of Verses,* Bonallie Towers, Bournemouth, Nov.
   1884
   Re publishers and writing matters, Bonallie Towers, 13 March 1885
   Illness; Sargent's painting: 'excellent, but is too eccentric to be
   exhibited', Skerryvore, Bournemouth, 22 Oct. 1885
   Re fetishes; illness, writing matters, Skerryvore, 26 Dec. 1885
   Accepting dedication of Low's illustrated edition of Keats' *Lamia,*
   sending him newly published *Jekyll and Hyde* and set of verses,
   Skerryvore, 2 Jan. 1886
   Enclosing photographs by Sir Percy Shelley, Skerryvore, Jan. 1886
   Gilder's (of *Century Magazine*) suggestion that he should collaborate
   with Low on French travel book, Skerryvore, March 1886
   Proposed visit by Low en route to United States from Paris;
   Directions re travel, Skerryvore, April 1887
   Announcing departure for New York on S.S. *Ludgate Hill,*
   Skerryvore, 6 Aug. 1887
   Arrival at Saranac. Visit when settled, Saranac, NY, Oct. 1887
   'I love the Polynesian', Honolulu, 20 May 1889
   Re Chicago art exhibition and other matters, Vailima, 15 Jan. 1894

**Mackay, Professor Aeneas:** On hearing he was retiring from Chair of
   History at Edinburgh University, interested in applying. What

prospects?, Kinnaird Cottage, Pitlochry, 21 June 1881
Thanks for kind letter and good opinion, Kinnaird Cottage, June 1881

**MacMorland, Mrs.** (no details). Regarding his conscience, La Solitude, Hyères, Summer 1884

**Martin, A. Patchett:** Thanks to this admirer for a book of poems. Edinburgh, Autumn 1877
Delayed reply to second letter: 'Are you not my first, my only, admirer?', 17 Heriot Row, Dec. 1877

**Maxwell, Sir Herbert:** On reading Rhind Lecture, asks about origin of Stevenson name, Vailima, 10 Sept. 1894
Thanks for advice to consult Lyon King, Vailima, 1 Dec. 1894

**Meiklejohn, Professor John** (of St. Andrew's University, met at Savile Club): Re Burns, Thoreau and Yoshida Torajiro, 608 Bush Street, San Francisco, Feb 1880
Congratulations on sailor son, officer on *Curaçoa*, Vailima, 6 Nov. 1894

**Meredith, George:** Description of Vailima; writing matters, Vailima, 5 Sept. 1893
Looking forward to receiving *Amazing Marriage*, Vailima, 17 April 1894

**Middleton, Miss:** (Edinburgh friend of Stevenson family)
Recalling memories of their Skye terrier, Jura, Vailima, 9 Sept. 1894

**Milne, Mrs. Henrietta** (cousin and a favourite childhood playmate):
Reply to her recognising 'A Pirate Story' in *Child's Garden of Verses*, La Solitude, Hyères, Nov. 1883

**Monkhouse, Cosmo** (art critic, poet, friend of Savile Club days)
Re British weather/Dover, La Solitude, Hyères, 16 March 1884
Ill; cannot read, speak; offer to exchange places, La Solitude, 24 April 1884

**Monroe, Miss:** (lady in Chicago who wrote criticising *Prince Otto*)
Reply to criticism, Skerryvore, Bournemouth, 25 May 1886
Re poor health; *Kidnapped* soon to appear, Skerryvore, June 1886
*Deacon Brodie* on stage in Chicago, Saranac, NY, 19 Dec. 1887

**Morris, William:** Admiration for poetry, Vailima, Feb. 1892

**Morse, Miss:** (American lady who derived help and encouragement from his writings) Reply, Vailima, 7 Oct. 1892

**Myers, Frederick W.H.:** Criticisms and questions re *Jekyll and Hyde*; reply. Skerryvore, Bournemouth, 1 March 1886

**Nature:** 12 Apr. 1888. 'Life of Fleeming Jenkin'. Stevenson defends his 'Memoir of Fleeming Jenkin', 28 Mar. 1888

**New York Sun:** 1, 8, 15 Feb.; 15, 22, 29 Mar.; 5, 12, 19, 26 Apr.; 3, 10, 17, 24, 31 May; 7 14, 21, 28 June; 5, 12 July; 6, 13, 20, 27 Sept.; 4, 11,18, 25 Oct.; 1, 8, 15, 22 Nov.; 13 Dec. 1891. 'Life under the Equator: Letters from a Leisurely Traveller'. A record of three cruises.
24 May 1891. 'Letters from the South Seas'. A Pearl Island: Penrhyn, Upolu, Dec. 1890.
21 June-12 July 1891. 'The Lazaretto', 'The Lazaretto Today', 'The Free Island', Upolu, Jan. 1891.
These four letters express Stevenson's concern for island conditions and leprosy in particular.
Both series were also published in *Black and White*, London; collected in *Vailima Papers*, Tusitala Edition *21*

**New York Tribune:** *see* **Athenaeum, The**

**Niles, Mr.:** (no details); re publication of *Silverado Squatters,* Skerryvore, Bournemouth, 6 Jan. 1885

**Orr, Fred:** (Request for autograph from young American); 'Who can spell Stevenson with a "v" at sixteen, should have a show for President before fifty', Vailima, 28 Nov. 1891

**Pacific Commercial Advertiser:** 6 Oct. 1893. In defence of the Sans Souci Seaside Resort, Honolulu, Stevenson claims that the nickname of 'A Disorderly House' is inappropriate. 'The only thing disorderly was the telephone which was bleating like a deserted infant from the dining room.'

**Pall Mall Gazette:** Sept. 1893. 'War in Samoa'. Vailima, 4 Sept. 1893; collected in *Vailima Papers*, Tusitala Edition *21.*

**P-n, John:** (brother below, two small boys whose mother desired anonymity when the letters were published); Stevenson writes on own childhood writings, Vailima, 3 Dec. 1893

**P-n, Russell:** 'When you grow up and write stories like me . . .', Vailima, 3 Dec. 1893

**Payn, James:** (friend of *Cornhill Magazine* days); his daughter recognises features of own town house in *The Dynamiter,* Skerryvore, Bournemouth, 2 June 1886
Sorry about ill health; describes visit to lepers, Honolulu, 13 June 1889
Friendly letter written at sea, S.S. *Lübeck,* 4 Feb. 1890
In thick of Samoan war, Vailima, 11 Aug. 1894
On reading 'Gleams of Memory', Vailima, 4 Nov. 1894

**Pennell, Mr. and Mrs. Joseph:** Acknowledging dedication of *Canterbury Pilgrimage,* Skerryvore, Bournemouth, June 1885

**Pilsach, Baron Senftt von,** *see* **von Pilsach**

**Proof Reader for 'Young Folks':** Amendments to *Black Arrow* signed 'alias Captain George North', La Solitude, Hyères, n.d.

**Rawlinson, May:** Poem: 'Of the many flowers you brought me', Skerryvore, Bournemouth, April 1887
Congratulations on her engagement to Mr. A. Spender, Vailima, April 1891

**Rodin, Auguste:** (In French). Regarding arrival of 'Le Printemps', Skerryvore, Bournemouth, Nov./Dec. 1886
(In French.) Too ill to write regarding portrait Skerryvore, Feb. 1887

**St. Gaudens, Augustus:** Re copies of medallion, Vailima, 29 May 1893
Awaiting medallion's arrival, Vailima, Sept. 1893
Arrival: placed on smoking-room mantelpiece, Vailima, 8 July 1894

**St. Gaudens, Homer:** (son of sculptor); Letter at father's request to keep until grown up, Manasquan, NJ, 27 May 1888

**Saintsbury, George:** His opinion of Lockhart; donating umbrella to Kipling, Kinnaird Cottage, Pitlochry, June 1881

**Schwob, Marcel:** (distinguished French scholar and critic):
Thanks for letters. Hope to be in Paris in summer, Honolulu, 8 Feb. 1889
Reply to request to translate *Black Arrow,* Union Club, Sydney, 19 Aug. 1890
Suggested translations of various writings, Sydney, 19 Jan. 1891
Thanks for remembering in exile, Vailima, 7 July 1894

*Scots Observer:* 25 Feb. 1890. 'Father Damien: An Open Letter to the Reverend Dr. Hyde of Honolulu from Robert Louis Stevenson'. Sydney; collected in *Vailima Papers,* Tusitala Edition *21*

**Scott, Dr. Thomas Bodley** (Bournemouth physician): Health in South Seas, Apia, Samoa, 20 Jan. 1890

**Scribner, Charles:** Apologies for publishing/contract mix-up, Saranac, NY, 20/21 Nov. 1887

**Simoneau, Jules:** (friend of Monterey days)
Friendly letter (in indifferent French), La Solitude, Hyères, May/June 1883

In English; congratulations on marriage, Hyères or Royat, Summer
1883

**Simpson, Sir Walter Grindley:** 'Home of our own, in a most lovely
situation', Bonallie Towers, Bournemouth, Nov. 1884
Delay on acknowledging *Art of Golf*; ill, British Museum, July 1887
Some financial calculations, Saranac, NY, Oct. 1887

**Sitwell, Fanny:** (afterwards Lady Colvin) (*see* Part 1)
Desc. train journey to Edinburgh via Newcastle, 17 Heriot Row,
Edinburgh, 1 Sept. 1873
'I hate the place now to the backbone . . . they were glad to see me
and in a kind of way so was I', 17 Heriot Row, Edinburgh, Sept. 1873
Diary-letter: 'You would require to know . . . many grim and
maudlin passages out of my past life to feel how great a change has
been made for me by this past summer . . .', 17 Heriot Row,
Edinburgh, 6 Sept. 1873
Cousin Bob's altercation with Thomas Stevenson, etc., Edinburgh, 9
Sept. 1873
Diary-letter; writing matters, 'Roads', 'John Knox', 17 Heriot Row,
Edinburgh, 12 Sept. 1873
Diary-letter: excursion with father to Dumfries, Edinburgh, 16 Sept.
1873
'I am killing my father — he told me tonight . . . that I alienated
utterly my mother . . .', Edinburgh, 22 Sept. 1873
Favourite coast between Granton and Queensferry, Edinburgh, 24
Sept. 1873
Diary-letter: church with mother; encounter with 'poor woman' in
Portobello, Edinburgh, 4 Oct. 1873
'My head and eyes both gave in this morning and I had to take a day of
complete idleness', Edinburgh, 14 Oct. 1873
Visit to Sir Andrew Clark in London, advised to go to Menton
immediately for his health, London, 4 Nov. 1873
Arrival in Dover, travel to Paris; lodgings, (Dover), 5 Nov. 1873
Desc. of travels in French countryside, Avignon, Nov. 1873
Arrived Menton, no letter (birthday), Menton, 13 Nov. 1873
Idea for the essay 'Ordered South'; 'O Medea, kill me, or make me
young again', Menton, 23 Nov. 1873
Scruples re money (later in 'Lay Morals'), Menton, 30 Nov. 1873
'The first violet'; ill, effects of opium, Menton, Dec. 1873
With Colvin in Monaco, Monaco, Dec. 1873
Desc. of dreams; meeting with Mme Garschine and Mme Zassetsky,
Menton, 13 Jan. 1874
Puzzled by Mme Garschine's (flirtatious) behaviour, Menton, Jan.
1874
Cold weather; working on 'Walt Whitman', Menton, Jan. 1874

The Russian ladies 'are two of the splendidest people in the world', Menton, Jan. 1874

'If I am like what she [Mme Garschine] says, I must be a very nice person', Menton, Feb. 1874

Desc. of Mediterranean, Menton, Jan. 1874

Quarrel with American; 'Four Great Scotsman' project, Menton, 26 Jan. 1874

Masquerade at Villa Marina; 'Ordered South' finished, Menton, 6 Feb. 1874

Work on 'Walt Whitman'; arrival of Prince Galitzin, friend of the Russian ladies, Menton, Feb. 1874

Last night in Menton; considering Göttingen for lectures arranged by Prince Galitzin, Menton, April 1874

Too ill to travel; violent cold, bronchial, Paris, April 1874

First letter from Swanston: 'I have made an arrangement with my people: I am to have £84 a year . . .' Swanston, May 1874

Cold weather; 'I find I must write to you pretty often for dear life. I am not so strong as I thought I was . . .', Swanston, May 1874

'Struggling away at *Fables in Song*', Swanston, May 1874

'A blackbird executed one long flourish . . . as if a spring has been touched or a sluice-gate opened, the whole garden just brimmed and ran over with bird-songs', Swanston, May 1874

Return to Edinburgh; cousin Bob seriously ill with diphtheria; ordered *Consuelo* by George Sand, June 1874

Bob much improved; back to Swanston; early summer description, June 1874

Announcing a yachting tour with Sir Walter Simpson, in the Inner Hebrides, for his health's sake, Edinburgh, June 1874

'My health is better. I work like a common sailor when it is needful, in rain and wind, without hurt . . .', Yacht *Heron,* Oban, 1874

'Back again here, as brown as a berry with sun, and in good form.' Lost portmanteau with Whitman notes, Swanston, Summer 1874

Expedition to Wales with parents, Train between Edinburgh and Chester, 8 Aug. 1874

Diary-letter: Llandudno: 'Cold bleak place of stucco villas with wide streets to let the wind in at you', Barmouth, Sept. 1874

Hard at work on 'John Knox and his Relations With Women', Swanston, Autumn 1874

'On the Enjoyment of Unpleasant Places' for *Portfolio,* Swanston, Autumn 1874

'I shall never be a great man, I may set myself peacefully on a smaller journey; not without hope of coming to the inn before nightfall', Edinburgh, Autumn 1874

'. . . why I get on always so ill, am always so nasty, so much worse than myself, with my parents; it is because they always take me at my

Afternoons pleasantly occupied, taking Henley for drives, Edinburgh, April 1875

'I read some pages over, and found them bad . . . This is harder than I thought; but I'll make it right or die', Edinburgh, Spring 1875

'I cannot write letters — that is all', Swanston, Spring 1875

Interest in Scotch ecclesiastical politics, Swanston, Spring 1875

'I have been in town, and had a fine time with toothache', Swanston, Spring 1875

'Sunday — I don't know why the recurrence of this day always depresses me; but it does', Swanston, Spring 1875

Commission to write article on *Burns* for *Encyclopaedia Britannica*, Edinburgh, Spring 1875

'I am much better here in the forest . . .', Barbizon, Spring 1875

'I shall be in London . . . tomorrow at six', Paris, Spring 1875

'Your son must be better than the sons of other people, madonna', Edinburgh, Spring 1875

'I was at that beautiful church [Glencorse] my *petit poème en prose* was about', Swanston, end June 1875

'I can make no plans for the summer. I do not think I shall get my thousand pounds' (Promised by parents if he qualified as an advocate), Swanston, Summer 1875

'Passed. Ever your R.L.S.', Edinburgh, 15 July 1875

'I could not write for a thousand reasons', Chez Siron, Barbizon, Summer 1875

Poem: 'Far have you come, my lady', Château Renard, Loiret, Aug. 1875

'I feel like a person in a novel of George Sand's', Swanston, late Summer 1875

'Yesterday I was twenty-five', Edinburgh, 14 Nov. 1875

Concert: heard Hallé and Norman Neruda play 'that Sonata of Beethoven's you remember', Edinburgh, Dec. 1875

Disgusted by visit to Leith, Edinburgh, Jan. 1876

'I am in capital health . . . in a state of wonderful mental activity', Edinburgh, early Spring 1876

'Three days in the house with sore throat, very painful but not serious', Edinburgh, early Spring 1876

'There are times when people's lives stand still', Swanston, July/Aug. 1876

'A letter frightens me worse than the devil', 17 Heriot Row, Edinburgh, May 1877

Work on 'Sire de Malétroit's Mousetrap' (changed to 'Door') also 'Will o' the Mill' with *Cornhill*, Penzance, Aug. 1877

Ill in Paris; Father's visit, Barbizon or Paris, Spring 1878

'I am in a somewhat curious humour', Café Palais Royal, Paris, early Spring 1878

'I have begun several letters to you . . . My book [*An Inland Voyage*] is through the press, Gairloch [Gareloch, Dunbartonshire], Easter and Patmos, Ash Wednesday, 1878

'[Fanny's] letter to me was mostly about you . . . no surprise if you have made a very enthusiastic friend of her', 17 Heriot Row, Edinburgh, Summer 1878

'I suppose you heard of our ghost stories', Castleton of Braemar, Aug. 1881

'I write out of a dark cloud', Hotel Buol, Davos, 1882

'Like old times to be writing you from the Riviera . . . how fortune tumbles men about!', La Solitude, Hyères, April 1883

'Nothing like a good correspondent . . . it's like living in the same house', Hyères, Autumn 1883

'I have no taste for old age, and my nose is to be rubbed in it in spite of my face. I was meant to die young, and the gods do not love me', Vailima, April 1894

**Stevenson, David A.:** (his cousin)
'A look from Aunt Elizabeth was like sunshine', La Solitude, Hyères, 31 Dec. 1883
Re David's preparation of map for *Kidnapped,* Skerryvore, Bournemouth, 1886

**Stevenson, James S.:** (remote cousin). Requesting information about origins of the Stevenson family, Vailima, 19 June 1893
Connection with Nether Carsewell, Neilston?, Vailima, 4 Sept. 1893

**Stevenson, J. Horne:** Specialist in genealogical research:
Information for 'A Family of Engineers', Vailima, 5 Nov. 1893

**Stevenson, R.A.M.:** (cousin Bob, his close friend)
Enclosing woodcuts which Lloyd prints on Davos Press: 'I doat on them.' Intending to settle in Britanny: 'Intending visitors . . . must not look for nightingales' tongues', Chalet-am-Stein, Davos, April 1882
House at Campagne Defli: £48 per annum, Terminus Hotel, Marseilles, Oct. 1882
'Toothache; fever; Ferrier's death; lung . . . Poor Ferrier, it bust me horrid. He was, after you, the oldest of my friends', La Solitude, Hyères, Oct. 1883
Bob's reactions to experiment in music composition, Skerryvore, Bournemouth, July 1886
Another piece: 'Looks like a piece of real music from a distance', Skerryvore, July 1886
Arrival in America; desc. of sea voyage, Saranac, NY, Oct. 1887
Voyage to Honolulu, Honolulu, Feb. 1889

Information in tracing genealogy of Stevensons, Vailima, 17 June 1894

Family tracing; other matters: 'If I had to begin again . . . I believe I should try to honour Sex more religiously. The worst of our education is that Christianity does not recognise and hallow Sex', Vailima, Sept. 1894

### Stevenson, Mrs. R.L. (Fanny)

'If you think I don't want to see you, you are a great baby; kiss my Wogg; I like him to be bad . . . Marriage does soften a person . . . I have wearied awful for you . . . I don't want you when I am ill', Montpellier, Oct. 1882

'A person who has been a good while married (to an angel) chafes at this position [absence]', Montpellier, Oct. 1882

'My dear Fellow: Send the thing to Jones and answer our questions', Bournemouth (?), 1886

'I should never look forward or backward now; having come to a fine plateau of life . . . busy with letters and *Jenkin* and the seraphic spurt at the piano', Bournemouth, 1887

'My dear Old Girl —.' Refers to picture of Beau (Brummel) and arrival of writing table, sans keys, Bournemouth, 1887

'My dearest Fellow': Writing, financial and domestic, Saranac, NY, Winter 1877/8

'My dearest Girlie.' Reference to quarrel with Henley: 'I have not had time to miss you; when I am alone I think of nothing but the one affair. Say nothing of it to anyone, please', Manasquan, NJ, Spring 1888

Anniversary letter; referring to first time he saw her in Paris, or day after first absence, Manasquan, May 1888

Visit to the leper colony, Kalawao, Molokai, May 1889

Referring to a sick child, for whom they are providing comforts, Vailima, 1893

### Stevenson, Mrs. Thomas:

'Ma chère Maman' letter written partly in French. 'I do not feel well and I wish to get home. Do take me with you' (to Menton), Spring Grove School, nr. London, 12 Nov. 1863

'We had parlour croquet . . . some Old Maid and an amusing game called "Fright", Rostrevor House, Spring Grove, Nov./Dec. 1863

'I am utterly sick of this grey, grim, sea-beaten hole. I have a little cold in my head', Kenzie House, Anstruther, July 1868

Train journey with eccentric old man, Anchor House (undated)

'Tell Papa that his boat-builders are the most illiterate writers', Anstruther, July 1868

'I shall want some more money soon', Kenzie House, July 1868

Arrival in Hampstead; Savile Club, Hampstead, June 1874
Visits to Oxford, Buckinghamshire, and Savile Club, Euston and
Victoria Hotels, 16 Oct. 1874
Description of arrival in Grez, Chez Siron, Barbizon, Aug. 1875
Staying for week in Paris, Hôtel du Grand Cerf, Pontoise, 16 Sept.
1876
'Weather . . . enchanting; like Spring.' Bob and picture of Thos.
Stevenson, 5 Rue Douay, Paris, 10 Jan. 1877
Writing *An Inland Voyage,* Paris, 17 Feb. 1878
Re newspaper criticisms of *An Inland Voyage,* Hotel du Val de Grâce,
Rue St. Jacques, Paris, June 1878
Requesting 'coins for this little banishment', Chez Morel, Monastier,
n.d.
'I shall buy a donkey and set forth upon my travels to the south;
another book ought to come of it', Le Monastier, 8 Sept. 1878
'The country is beautiful, rather too like the Highlands, but not so
grand', Chez Morel, Sept. 1878
Progress on *Portfolio* papers. *Edinburgh: Picturesque Notes:* 'A kind of
book nobody would ever care to read; but none of the young men
could have done it better than I have, which is always a consolation',
Le Monastier, Sept. 1878
'I am one of the most weary people in the world', Chez Morel, 1878
Re praise of *An Inland Voyage,* Paris, Oct. 1878
Publication of *Travels with a Donkey,* Box Hill, Dorking, 12 May 1879
'I am having such up-hill work. I sit and sit, and scribe and scribe, but
cannot get my back into it', Paris, 19 June 1879
'Desperate struggle . . . possessor of 4 shillings', Savile Club, July
1879
Re Christian life and conduct, Davos, 26 Dec. 1880
Journey in an open sleigh: 'The cold was beyond belief. I have often
suffered less at a dentist's', Chalet Buol, Davos, 26 Dec. 1881
Enclosing birthday present: *Cornhill* containing 'Talk and Talkers',
Chalet-am-Stein, Davos, 9 April 1882
'Unfit to do any work whatever . . . I have my home and my garden,
and my hills and my table wine, and my wife— and my dog',
Campagne Defli, San Marcel, 11 Nov. 1882
Fanny ill; 'I can do no work', Campagne Defli, San Marcel, 13 Nov.
1882
'*Deacon Brodie* . . . hissed off the board . . . at Bradford', San Marcel, 23
Dec. 1882
Changes in Nice: 'I stay mostly in bed', Nice, 5 Jan. 1883
Regarding health and acquisition of La Solitude, Hôtel des Iles d'Or,
Hyères, 2 March 1883
'As for my wife, that was the best investment ever made by man; but
"in our branch of the family" we seem to marry well. I, considering

Plans for article on the Appin murder, Chalet am Stein, Davos, Oct. 1881.

Writing matters, re Knox and Pepys, 'Davos Printing Office', Nov. 1881

Delighted with Campagne Defli, Terminus Hotel, Marseille, 17 Oct. 1882

Re translation of treatise on Marine Works, San Marcel/Hyères, n.d.

Re Dickens' *Great Expectations,* Hotel des Iles d'Or, 17 March 1883

'I did not like your getting thin', La Solitude, Hyères, 15 June 1883

'A little decent resignation is not only becoming a Christian, but it is likely to be excellent for the health of a Stevenson', La Solitude, 12 Oct. 1883

Advising him not to read Lockhart's *Scott,* La Solitude, 20 Dec. 1883

Arrival of *Cornhill's* with 'Thrawn Janet'; 'The love of the slap-dash and the shoddy grew upon Scott with success', La Solitude, 19 April 1884

Approving father's letting himself be proposed for President of Royal Society of Edinburgh, Bonallie Towers, Bournemouth, Nov. 1884

Reply to protest against Pew in *Admiral Guinea,* Bonallie Towers, Bournemouth, 5 Nov. 1884

Father's 'On the Principal Causes of Silting in Estuaries', Bonallie Towers, Bournemouth, 15 Jan. 1885

Review in November *Time*; illustrated *Treasure Island* due December, Skerryvore, Bournemouth, 28 Oct. 1885

*Kidnapped* and the Appin Murder, Skerryvore, 25 Jan. 1886

More about *Kidnapped,* Skerryvore, April 1886

'We have decided not to come to Scotland', Skerryvore, 28 July 1886

**Stevenson, Mr. and Mrs. Thomas:** Threatened failure of harbour works on which family firm engaged at Anstruther, Wick, Sept. 1868

Thanks for '25 quid'; 'snowing in Edinburgh . . . here, it is so warm we drive about at night-in open cabs', Paris, 15 Oct. 1877

'My favourite author just now? . . . Anthony Trollope!', 44 Bd. Haussmann, Paris, 21 Feb. 1878

En route for Paris with P.S. by Fanny S., Grosvenor Hotel, Victoria Stn., late Oct. 1880

En route for Davos, Landquart, 5 Nov. 1880

Re Highland history plans and poem to Dr. Brown, Hotel Belvedere, Davos, 21 Dec. 1880

'If we are to come to Scotland, I *will* have fir-trees, and I want a burn, the firs for my physical, the water for my moral health', Hôtel du Pavillon Henry IV, St. Germain, 1 May 1881

'There has been offered for *Treasure Island* . . . A hundred jingling, tingling, golden, minted quid. Is not this wonderful?', La Solitude, Hyères, 5 May, 1883

'Our lovely garden is a prey to snails . . . not having the heart to slay, I steal forth and deposit near my neighbour's garden wall', La Solitude, 8 May 1883

Christmas letter, La Solitude, 25 Dec. 1883

'£50 in the bank, owing no man nothing . . .', 'I can look back on . . . £465.0.6d for the last 12 months.' La Solitude, 1 Jan. 1884

Remembrance of Edinburgh of childhood, Hôtel Chabassière, Royat, July 1884

'My dear People: I keep better and am to-day downstairs for the first time. I find the lockers entirely empty; not a cent to the front. Will you pray send us some?', Wensleydale, Bournemouth, 28 Sept. 1884

About writing: 'I am afloat and no more . . . unless I have great luck, I shall have to fall upon you at the New Year like a hundredweight of bricks. Doctor, rent, chemist, all are threatening . . .', Bonallie Towers, Bournemouth, 9 Dec. 1884

'The drawing-room will soon be lovely, and we bankrupt', Skerryvore, Bournemouth, 31 July 1885

'Many happy returns of the day to you all', Skerryvore, 1 Jan. 1886

'We are all on the mend, and mean soon to be quite well', Skerryvore, April 1886

Regarding parents' winter visit to Bournemouth; Father's health deteriorating, Skerryvore, 7 July 1886

'Dear Young Folks': Re London travels, British Museum, June 1886

**Stoddard, Charles Warren:** Author of *Summer Cruising in the South Seas,* Stevenson had made friends with him and was later to describe their meeting in *The Wrecker.*

Stoddard's writing, East Oakland, California, May 1880

' "Blessed is he that expecteth little", in one of the truest, and in a sense, the most Christlike things in literature', Hotel Belvedere, Davos, Dec. 1880

'Any story can be made *true* in its own key; [or] *false* by the choice of a wrong key of detail or style', Skerryvore, 13 Feb. 1886

**Strong, Austin:** (Belle's son) Re Samoan boy Arick; also Donald the pack-horse. Signed 'Your respected Uncle, O Tusitala', Vailima, 2 Nov. 1892

Description of the new house and native workmen, Vailima, 15 Nov. 1892

Domestic matters; native with influenza attack, Vailima, 27 Jan. 1893

Adventures of the Jersey cow and new calf, Vailima, 18 June 1893

Tales of Vailima servants, Vailima, n.d.

'I am kept away in a cupboard because everybody has the influenza;' more about the packhorse and the cow, Vailima, n.d.

Native 'medicine', Vailima, n.d.

**Strong (Belle), Isobel:** Reply to her enquiry two days after arrival: 'May coins fall into your coffee and the finest wines and wittles lie smilingly about your path . . .' Signed 'Your dear papa, R.L.S.', Hotel Belvedere, Davos, Nov. 1880

**Symonds, John Addington:** (Friend of Davos days, also a consumptive writer) 'Why should I blame Gladstone, when I too am a Bourgeois . . .We believe in nothing, Symonds: you don't, and I don't . . .', Bonallie Towers, Bournemouth, Feb. 1885
Dostoevsky's *Crime and Punishment,* Skerryvore, Bournemouth, Spring 1886
'My wife again suffers in high and cold places; I again profit', Saranac, NY, 21 Nov. 1887
Proposed dedication to South Seas Travel book, Tautira, 11 Nov. 1888

**Taylor, Miss Ida:** (daughter of Lady Taylor) Re character by handwriting, Vailima, 7 Oct. 1892

**Taylor, Lady:** Dedication of *The Merry Men,* Skerryvore, New Year 1887
Re 'Thrawn Janet', 'Olalla', Skerryvore, Bournemouth, Jan. 1887
Announcing departure from San Francisco on S.S. *Casco,* Manasquan, May 1888
Preparations to leave Honolulu on *Equator,* Honolulu, 19 June 1889
'I am now the owner of an estate upon Upolu', Apia, Samoa, 20 Jan. 1890

**Thompson, Rev. H. Wardlaw:** Missionary movement and the political situation in Samoa, Vailima, 12 July 1892

*Times, The* **(London):** 6 Sept. 1886, 'Rodin and Zola'. Objects to correspondent calling Rodin 'The Zola of sculpture', Skerryvore, Bournemouth, undated
31 March 1886, 'International Copyright'. Enclosing copies of correspondence with Harper & Brothers, New York, who published several of his works without permission. (*See also* **Academy, The** 'American Rights and Wrongs')
The following letters deal with Stevenson's concern with British, German and American behaviour in Samoan affairs and were collected in *Vailima Papers,* Tusitala Edition *21:*
11 March 1889, 'Recent German Doings in Samoa'. Vailima, 10 Feb. 1889
17 Nov. 1891, 'Samoa'. Vailima, 12 and 14 Oct. 1891
4 June 1892, 'The Latest Difficulty in Samoa'. Vailima, 9 and 12 Apr. 1892
23 July 1892, 'Samoa'. Vailima, 22 June 1892

19 Aug. 1892, 'Mr. Stevenson and Samoa'. Vailima, 19 July 1892
17 Oct. 1892, 'Mr. Stevenson and Samoa'. Vailima, 14 Sept. 1892
2 June 1894, 'The Deadlock in Samoa'. Vailima, 23 Apr. 1894
30 June 1894, 'Mr. Stevenson in Samoa'. Vailima, 22 May 1894

**von Pilsach, Baron Senfft:** 'Correspondence between residents of Apia' (Stevenson and E.W. Gurr) 'and the Baron'. Concerns the bad treatment by Germans of Samoan chiefs in prison, Apia, 28 Sept. 1891; collected (with von Pilsach's replies) in *Vailima Papers*, Tusitala Edition *21*
Misunderstanding of complimentary copy sent by Stevenson's publishers, Vailima, 16 Dec. 1892

**Watts-Dunton, T:** Critic of *Athenaeum*; review of *Kidnapped,* Skerryvore, Sept. 1886

***Whitefriars Journal:*** Vol. 4, Nos. 4-6, Dec. 1914, June 1915, Jan. 1916. Contain a number of previously unpublished letters of Stevenson, formerly in the possession of Clement Shorter.

**Whitmee, Rev. S.J.:** Missionary who suggested Samoan troubles could be settled by one-man power: Outline of Stevenson's own policy for Samoa, Vailima, 24 April 1892

**Yeats, William Butler:** Letter in admiration of the poet's 'Lake Isle of Innisfree', Vailima, 14 April 1894

# Part 5

# INDEX OF POEMS AND MUSICAL SETTINGS

## Poems

Poems are listed below both under first line and under title (the latter in italic type) with a reference to the collection in which they appeared: *A Child's Garden of Verses* (CGV), *Underwoods* (U), *Songs of Travel* (ST), *Moral Emblems* (ME), *Ballads* (B), *New Poems* (NP). Volume and page numbers of the Tusitala Edition are also given: I = Tusitala Edition Vol. 22, II = Vol. 23. Where relevant, reference is made to the letters, Tusitala Edition, Vols. 31 to 35, and to Part 4.

Musical settings follow at the end under the name of the composer.


A birdie with a yellow bill, CGV, I, 17
About my fields, in the broad sun, NP, II, 209
About the sheltered garden ground, NP, II, 103
About us lies the summer night, NP, II, 83
A child should always say what's true, CGV, I, 2
Adela, Adela, Adela Chart (See also Part 4 (Letters): James), NP, II, 234
*Ad Magistrum Ludi,* NP, II, 252
*Ad Martialem,* NP, II, 225
*Ad Nepotem,* NP, II, 247
*Ad Olum,* NP, II, 250
*Ad Piscatorem,* NP, II, 250
*Ad Quintilianum,* NP, II, 248
*Ad se ipsum,* NP, II, 134
*After reading 'Anthony and Cleopatra',* NP, II, 102
Again I hear you piping, for I know the tune so well, NP, II, 165
A golden service, most loveworthy yoke, NP, II, 201
*Air of Diabelli's,* NP, II 214
A lover of the moorland bare, U, I, 73
All influences were in vain, NP, II, 95
All night long, and every night, CGV, I, 2
All night through, raves or broods, NP, II, 146
All on a day of gold and blue, NP, II, 255
All round the house in the jet-black night, CGV, I, 22
All the names I know from nurse, CGV, I, 39
All things on earth and sea, NP, II, 230
Alone above the stream it stands, ME, I, 217
A mile an' a bittock, a mile or two, U, I, 105
A naked house, a naked moor, U, I, 70

## Musical Settings

Those marked * are available in the Music Library, Edinburgh Central Library

**Adam, James:** A mile an' a bittock; words from 'Underwoods', baritone solos, 1933.

**Byron, May:** Four children's songs, 1904; including The cow; The wind.

***Carmichael, Mary:** *Child's Garden of Verses*; Twelve songs for children, n.d.; Kindergarten series No. 1; Bed in summer; Singing; Where go the boats?; Marching song; The swing; The cow; My bed is like a little boat; Farewell to the farm; The sun's travels; Fairy bread; Foreign lands; Looking-glass river.

***Clarke, R.C:** I will make you brooches, bass solo, 1903.

***Coleridge-Taylor, Samuel:** She rested by the broken brook, bass or baritone solo, 1906.

***Gibbs, C.A:** In the Highlands (Op.9), soprano or tenor solo, 1928.

**Hathaway, J.W.G:** Two songs (1), Block city (2), Windy nights, contralto or baritone solo, 1913.

**Hoddinott, Alun:** *The Beach of Falesá*, a three-act opera based on the short story, 1974. (*See also* Part 6 (Radio and TV) The Beach of Falesá); *The Rajah's Diamond*, an opera based on the short story, 1979. (See also Part 6 (Radio and TV) The Rajah's Diamond).

***Homer, Sidney:** Requiem (Under the wide and starry sky, Op.15, No.2), bass baritone solo, 1904; Sing me a song of a lad that is gone (Op.15); words from 'Underwoods', tenor solo, 1904.

***Johnson, P.M.B:** Six songs from *A Child's Garden of Verses*, 1915; Bed in summer; Pirate story; Where go the boats?; The land of counterpane; My shadow; The swing.

**Lehmann, Liza:** The swing (How do you like to go up in a swing?), mezzo-soprano solo, 1900.

**Orr, Robin:** *Hermiston*, an opera in three acts, based on *Weir of Hermiston*, 1975. (*See also* Part 6 (Radio), Weir of Hermiston)

***Peel, Graham:** Bright is the ring of words, bass solo; Requiem, 1907; Where go the boats? (Dark brown is the river), contralto solo, 1910.

***Quilter, Roger.** Over the land is April, tenor solo, 1922.

***Ramsay, K.M:** Song flowers from *A Child's Garden of Verses*, 61 pp., 1897.

***Riego, Teresa del:** Shadow March (All round the house), contralto solo, 1910.

***Smith, G.H:** A chaplet of airs from *A Child's Garden of Verses*, 18 pp., 1907.

**\*Stanford, C.V:** A child's garland of songs; gathered from *A Child's Garden of Verses,* 35 pp., 1892.

**\*Swepstone, Edith:** Songs for children, 1897.

**\*Williams, R.Vaughan:** Songs of travel, for low and medium voice, 1905–7. The vagabond; Bright is the ring of words; The roadside fire; Let beauty awake; Youth and love; In dreams; The infinite shining heavens.

# Part 6
# FILMS, TELEVISION AND RADIO

All broadcasting networks in the English-speaking world were approached for information on Stevenson programmes, but only some responded, so the list below is necessarily incomplete. Most of the material is from the British Broadcasting Corporation (BBC) except those identified as from the Canadian Broadcasting Corporation or New Zealand Television. No repeats or details of the numerous showings of films on television are given.

**Across the Plains** (from *The Amateur Emigrant*)
1980 Radio 4. Dramatised account of Robert Louis Stevenson's journey across America from New York to San Francisco in 1879. Written by Alanna Knight. Producer Pat Trueman

**Admiral Guinea**
1932 Radio. National (no details)
1956 Radio. Home Service. Arranged by Cyril Wood

**The Beach of Falesá**
1950 Radio. Scotland (no details)
1974 Radio 3. Three-act opera by Alun Hoddinott, based on the short story. First broadcast performance. Welsh National Opera Company production

**The Black Arrow**
FILM
1948 (British title: *The Black Arrow Strikes*) Columbia Pictures. Director Gordon Douglas. With Louis Hayward, Janet Blair and George Macready
RADIO
1958 Radio. Home Service. 'The Arrow Strikes'. Serial

**The Body-Snatcher**
FILM
1945 Film. RKO. Director Robert Wise. With Henry Daniell, Boris Karloff, Bela Lugosi, Edith Atwater and Russell Wade
RADIO
1970 Radio. Scotland. *Six Stories*
1977 Radio 4. Script adapted by David Pinner

## The Bottle Imp

1933 Radio. National (no details)
1950 Radio. Light Programme. Adapted by James MacGregor
1954 TV. Canadian Broadcasting Corporation. *On Camera.* Adapted by Richard Denis
1959 Radio. Scotland. *This is my Country*
1966 Radio. Scotland. *Schools Programme*
1966 Radio. All regions. *Story Time: Two Island Tales.* No. 1

## Catriona (*see* Kidnapped)

## The Celestial Surgeon (poem)

1957 Radio. Home Service. *Lighten our Darkness*
1967 Radio. Light Programme. *Ten to Eight: By Request.* Poems of Today, First series

## A Child's Garden of Verses

1955 Radio. Scotland. *Poetry Reading*
1957 Radio. Scotland. *Scottish Heritage:* 'Smout' — Stevenson's childhood linked with reflections on his early life. Script by Derek Walker
1959 Radio. Home Service. Poem: *My Kingdom*
1959 Radio. Home Service. Extracts. *Children's Hour*
1966 Radio. Scotland. *Fireside Sunday School.* Seven poems
1960 Radio. Home Service. *Home this Afternoon.* Talk by Elizabeth Seager
1975 Radio 3. *Night hath no Wings.* Thoughts on insomnia and some suggestions for its cure

## Christmas at Sea (poem)

1957 Radio. Home Service. *Senior English 1*
1975 Radio 4. *Poetry Prom*

## The Counterblast (poem)

1956 Radio. Scotland. *Annals of Scotland*

## The Cow (poem)

1957 Radio. Light Programme. *Listen with Mother*
1966 Radio. All regions. *Fireside Sunday School.* Read by James Crampsey.
1980 Radio 3. Interval Reading by Jon Curle: *An anthology of Animals*

## The Dumb Soldier (poem)

1969 Radio 4. *Stories and rhymes*

## Dr. Jekyll and Mr. Hyde

FILMS
1908 Selig (no details available)

1910 Nordisk (no details available)
1913 Universal Pictures, Director James Cruze. With King Baggott, Jane Gail, Mark Snyder and William Sorrell
1920 Famous Players-Lasky Corporation. Director John S. Robertson. With John Barrymore, Brandon Hurse, Martha Mansfield and Nita Naldi
1920 (Germany): Director F. W. Murnau. With Conrad Veidt
1920 (USA): With Sheldon Lewis
1932 Paramount Pictures. Director Rouben Mamoulian. With Fredric March, Miriam Hopkins, Edgar Norton, Rose Hobart and Holmes Herbert
1941 Metro-Goldwyn-Mayer. Director Victor Fleming. With Spencer Tracy, Ingrid Bergman, Lana Turner, Ian Hunter, C. Aubrey Smith, Donald Crisp and Sara Allgood
1960 *The Two Faces of Dr. Jekyll* (US title: *House of Fright*), Hammer Film Productions. Director Terence Fisher. With Paul Massie, Dawn Addams, Christopher Lee, David Kossoff, Francis de Wolff and Norma Marla
1961 *Le Testament du Docteur Cordelier* (Dr. Jekyll and Mr. Hyde). (US title: *Experiment in Evil*). Director Jean Renoir. With Jean-Louis Barrault
1973 Timex-NBC-TV. Musical directed by David Winters. With Kirk Douglas, Susan George, Susan Hampshire, Stanley Holloway and Donald Pleasance

## RADIO and TV

1938 Radio. National. Schools Broadcast. *Senior English VI.* Book Talk
1950 TV. *The Strange Case of Dr. Jekyll and Mr. Hyde.* Adapted by John Keir Cross. Produced by Fred O'Donovan
1950 Radio. Home Service. Adapted by Barbara Burnham
1956 Radio. Light Programme. *Curtain Up!*
1959 Radio. Home and Scotland. *This is my Country*
1966 Radio. Light Programme. *Mid-Week Theatre*
1968 TV. Canadian Broadcasting Corporation. *Series Festival.* Teleplay by Ian McLellan Hunter
1968 Radio. Scotland. *Scottish Studies.* Schools Programme
1971 Radio 3. *Further Education.* Classics of psycho-horror. J. G. Ballard, a modern writer of science fiction, talks to Dr. Christopher Evans
1972 TV. BBC1. Teleplay
1977 Radio 4. *Story Time.* Read in 5 parts by Leonard Maguire
1978 Radio 4. *Bestseller No. 4.* Producer Stanley Williamson
1980 TV. BBC2. With David Hemmings. Written by Gerald Savory and produced by Jonathan Powell

## The Ebb-Tide

FILMS

1922 Famous Players-Lasky Corporation. Director George Melford. With Lila Lee, James Kirkwood, George Fawcett and Jacqueline Logan

1937 Paramount Pictures Corporation. Director James Hogan. With Oscar Homolka, Frances Farmer, Ray Milland, Lloyd Nolan and Barry Fitzgerald

1947 (Title: *Adventure Island*). Paramount Pictures. With Rory Calhoun, Rhonda Fleming and Paul Kelly

TV

1952 BBC. (No details)

## Edinburgh: Picturesque Notes

1954. Radio. Home Service. Quotations read by Richard Baker

## Escape at Bedtime (poem)

1967 Radio. Home Service. Read by John Betjeman

## Foreign Children (poem)

1971 Radio 4. *Schools Programme*

## From a Railway Carriage (poem)

1966 Radio. All regions. *Springboard:* Trains

## Good and Bad Children (poem)

1979 Radio 3. Read by Peter Barker. Producer Cormac Rigby

## An Inland Voyage

1978 Radio 3. *Interval Programme*. Extracts

1980 Radio 3. Extracts read by Donald Price. Producer Cormac Rigby

## In the South Seas

1954 Radio. Third Programme. Prose reading (no details)

## Island Nights' Entertainments

1954 Radio. Third Programme. Prose reading (no details)

## The Isle of Voices

1966 Radio. All regions. *Story Time*

## Kidnapped (and Catriona)

FILMS

1938 Twentieth-Century Fox. Director Alfred Werker. With Warner Baxter, Freddie Bartholomew, Aileen Whelan, John Carradine, C. Aubrey Smith, Nigel Bruce and Reginald Owen

1948 Monogram Picture Corporation. Director William Beaudine.

With Roddy McDowall, Sue England and Dan O'Herlihy
1960 Walt Disney Productions. Director Robert Stevenson. With
Peter Finch, James McArthur, Bernard Lee, Peter O'Toole and John
Laurie
1972 Omnibus Productions. Director Delbert Mann. With Michael
Caine, Lawrence Douglas, Trevor Howard, Jack Hawkins, Donald
Pleasance, Gordon Jackson and Vivien Heilbron
RADIO and TV
1937 Radio. National (no details)
1949 TV. Canadian Broadcasting Corporation. Adapted by Andrew
Allan
1950 Radio. Scotland. *Scottish Heritage*
1950 Radio. Scotland. *This is my Country*. Reading from *Tod Lapraik*
(*Catriona*)
1951 TV. Canadian Broadcasting Corporation. *Fun with Books*
1952 TV. Canadian Broadcasting Corporation. Serial
1953 Radio Scotland. *May we Recommend?* Children's Hour
1956 TV. Canadian Broadcasting Corporation. Six-part serial *For the
Children*
1956 Radio. Scotland. *This is my Country*. Extract from *Catriona*
1957 Radio. Scotland. *Enjoying Literature* Fifth and Sixth Forms.
Extract from *Kidnapped*
1961 Radio. Home Service. *In the Steps of David Balfour*. A tramp over
the route taken by David Balfour and Alan Breck from Mull to
Edinburgh. Producer Ian Nimmo
1963 Radio. Scotland. *Scottish Heritage*. Alan Breck, friend of David
Balfour and joint hero of *Kidnapped*. Script by Barbara Kerr
1963 TV. Canadian Broadcasting Corporation. 'House of Shaws'
from *Kidnapped* (series)
1968 Radio. Scotland. *Story Time*. Children's Hour. The adventures of
David Balfour. Abridged by Gordon Emslie, with Bryden Murdoch
and Calum Mill
1975 TV. New Zealand Television. Cartoon version.
1977 TV. New Zealand Television. *Around Scotland*. Extract from
*Kidnapped*
1980 TV. BBC Scotland. *Kidnapped* film adaptation. Produced by Tom
Cotter
1980 TV. BBC Scotland. *Kidnapped* Serial
1981 Radio 4. *Woman's Hour*. Reading from *Catriona* by June Knox-
Mawer

**A Lodging for the Night**
1966 Radio. Third Programme. The Art of the Short Story

**A Lowden Sabbath Morn** (poem)
1954 Radio. Scotland. *The Autumn Garden*

**Markheim**
 1928 Radio. Daventry experimental (no details)
 1932 Radio. London Region. Adapted by Ursula Branston
 1938 Radio. National. Adapted by Francis Dillon
 1952 TV (no details)
 1957 TV. Canadian Broadcasting Corporation. *On Camera Series.*
 Adapted by Alfred Harris
 1963 Radio. Scotland. *Late Night Bookshelf*
 1970 TV. BBC 1. Adapted by Tom Wright
 1971 Radio 4. Adapted by Tom Wright

**The Master of Ballantrae**
FILM
 1953 Film. Warner-First National Productions. Director William
 Keighley. With Errol Flynn, Beatrice Campbell, Roger Livesey,
 Anthony Steel, Felix Aylmer, Mervyn Johns, Jacques Berthier,
 Yvonne Furneaux and Roger Trueman. Narrated by Robert Beatty
RADIO and TV
 1950 Radio. Adapted by R. J. B. Sellar. Produced by James
 Crampsey. Serial
 1950 TV. Canadian broadcasting Corporation. Adapted by Andrew
 Allan
 1954 Radio. Scotland. *Arts Review*
 1954 Radio. All regions. *May we Recommend?* Children's Hour
 1954 Radio. Third Programme. Prose reading
 1962 TV. Scotland. Telerecording
 1970 Radio 4. *Story Time.* Children's Programmes
 1975 Radio 4. Adapted by D. Bancroft. Serial. Read by Ian
 Cuthbertson

**The Merry Men**
 1959 Radio. Scotland. *This is my Country*

**The Misadventures of John Nicholson**
 1964 Radio. Scotland. *Late Night Bookshelf*
 1974 Radio 4. *Story Time*

**My Shadow** (poem)
 1966 Radio. All regions. *Things I have Done*

**Nurses** (essay)
 1976 Radio 3. Interval Reading

**The Pavilion on the Links**
FILM
 1920 (Title: *The White Circle.*) Paramount Pictures. Director

Maurice Tourneur. With Spottiswoode Aiken, Harry S. Northrup, Jack Gilbert and Jack McDonald
RADIO
1975 Radio 4. Abridged by Neville Teller. Read by Ian Cuthbertson

**The Philosophy of Nomenclature** (essay)
1975 Radio 3. Interval Reading by Patricia Hughes

**Poems** (Miscellaneous)
1950 Radio. Scotland. *This is my Country.* Poems and Songs
1953 TV. BBC 1. *More Stories in Verse*
1957 Radio. All regions. *Adventures in English*
1957 Radio. Scotland and Northern Ireland. *Poets and Poetry.* No. 6: Robert Louis Stevenson
1975. Radio 3. Interval Reading by Jon Curle of five poems

**Rain** (poem)
1957 Radio. Light Programme. Reading

**The Rajah's Diamond**
1979 TV. BBC 2 and Radio 3. An opera commissioned by the BBC in association with the Welsh Arts Council. Music by Alun Hoddinott; libretto by Myfanwy Piper. Introduced by Humphrey Burton. Produced by J. Mervyn Williams

**St. Ives**
FILM
1949 Film. (Title: *The Secret of St Ives.*) Columbia Pictures. Director Philip Rosen. With Richard Ney, Vanessa Brown, Henry Daniell and Aubrey Mather
RADIO and TV
1938 Radio. Regional. Adapted by Sybil Clarke and broadcast in four parts
1954 Radio. All regions. Eight-part dramatisation
1955 TV. BBC 1. Serial in six parts
1957 Radio. Scotland. *Scottish Heritage*
1960 TV. BBC1. Telerecording
1967 TV. BBC 1. Telerecording

**The Silverado Squatters**
1977 TV. BBC 1 Scotland. *The Silverado Episode*

**The Sire de Malétroit's Door**
FILM
1951 (Title: *The Strange Door.*) Universal International. Director Joseph Pevney. With Charles Laughton, Boris Karloff, Michael Pate, Sally Forrest, Richard Stapley and Alan Napier

RADIO and TV
   1951 TV. BBC 1 (no details)
   1965 Radio. All regions (no details)

**Sleep beneath the Stars** (extracts from several works)
   1979 Radio 3. *Interval Programme.* Reading by Jon Curle

**Stevenson, Robert Louis:** His life at home and abroad
   1924 Radio. 2LO. A talk about R.L.S.
   1924 Radio. 2LO. *Workshops of Famous Men.* Stevenson at Samoa, by
Caroline Buchan
   1925 Radio. 2LO. *Schools Programme.* Modern English Poetry:
Stevenson and Henley, by J. C. Stobart and Mary Somerville
   1926 Radio. 2LO. Anniversary programme arranged by C. A. Lewis
   1944 Radio. Scotland. *Children's Hour.* The Childhood of R. L.
Stevenson
   1950 Radio. Home Service. Robert Louis Stevenson by Richard
Hughes
   1950 Radio. Home Service. A biographical study by John Keir Cross.
Produced by Robin Richardson
   1950 Radio. Scotland. *This is my Country.* Biography — Part 1
   1953 TV. BBC 1. *An American Gentleman.* A Play about R.L.S.
   1954 Radio 3. *Prose Readings* Extracts from works
   1954 Radio 3. *Prose Readings* Extracts from letters to Sidney Colvin
   1955 Radio. Home Service. *Life and Letters.* Extracts
   1956 Radio. Home Service. *Life and Letters.* The Unforgotten. Extracts
   1956 Radio. Scotland. *This is my Country.* Biography — Part 2
   1956 Radio 3. *The Ivory Lighthouse* by Eric Evans. R. L. Stevenson and
the Samoan Imbroglio, 1890-94
   1956 Radio. All regions. *Adventures in English.* Teller of Tales: a short
biography
   1958 Radio. Home Service. *Today.* 'Life as a cook-houseboy for
R.L.S.', by Charles Howard
   1958 TV. BBC 1. *Focus.* 'Stamp Collection, Stevenson'
   1959 Radio. Home Service. *I Remember.* Charles Howard interviewed
   1959 Radio. Home Service. *To Travel Hopefully.* Extracts
   1960 Radio. Home Service. *The Eye Witness.* 17th-century village of
Swanston. Cottages famous for Stevenson associations being
restored by Edinburgh Corporation
   1961 Radio. Home Service. *Two of a Kind.* On the Road of the Loving
Heart. A visit to Samoa and how the islanders felt about R.L.S. Talk
by Elizabeth Bryson
   1963 Radio. Scotland. *Scottish Life and Letters.* Jorge Luis Borges talks
to George Bruce
   1963 Radio. Home Service. *Today.* 'I was cook-houseboy to R.L.S.'
Charles Howard interviewed

1963 Radio. Scotland. *Scottish Heritage.* Samoa Days. Stevenson's love of the islanders, who called him Tusitala. Script by Derek Walker
1964 Radio. Home Service. *The Eye Witness.* Stevenson's house in Edinburgh to be auctioned (3 March). Geoffrey Cameron interviews Mrs M. Merrilees
1964 Radio. Home Service. *Indian Summer.* Requiem. Charles Howard now 86, talked to Jack Singleton about Stevenson
1964 Radio. Scotland. *Scottish Life and Letters.* Memories of R.L.S. Helen Barclay and Ethel Blair-Wilson interviewed by George Bruce
1964 TV. BBC 1. Film of relics of R.L.S. housed in Lady Stair's House in Lawnmarket, Edinburgh
1965 Radio. Home Service. *R.L.S. in Bournemouth.* Interval talk by Vincent Waite
1965 Radio. All regions. *Home this Afternoon.* A shipmate of R.L.S. Talk by George Nash. (From Northern Ireland)
1965 Radio. Scotland. *The Living Voice.* Memories of R.L.S. Bella Lunan recalls J. M. Barrie, her sister Ethel Blair-Wilson recollects Stevenson, John Ruskin and others
1966 Radio. Scotland. *Town and Country.* R.L.S. in Orkney. Talk by Ernest Marwick
1966 Radio. All regions. *Ten to Eight.* By Request. Prayers written at Vailima. Read by Peter Barker
1967 Radio. Scotland. *Scottish Studies.* Life of Stevenson. In two parts. Script by Phillipa Pierce
1968 TV. Canadian Broadcasting Corporation. *The Day it Is.* Interview with Argentinian poet and philosopher, Jorge Luis Borges, about Stevenson's life and achievements
1968 Radio. Canadian Broadcasting Corporation. *Shape of Childhood Series.* The adventure of faraway places. Extracts
1970 Radio 4. *Home this Afternoon.* Anthea Cameron talks to Charles Howard, servant at Vailima
1970 Radio 4. *Woman's Hour.* The Ingenious Traveller — To travel hopefully is better than to arrive (R.L.S.) — discussed by Cicely Williams and Keith Brace. (From Birmingham)
1971 Radio 4. *Story Time* Strange Tales from Scotland. Excerpts
1972 Radio 4. Scotland. *The Adventures of Robert Louis Stevenson and Marcel Schwob.* Michael Sadler tells strange story of relationship between R.L.S. and this 19th-century French writer
1973 Radio 4. Scotland. *Scottish News.* Alanna Knight talks to Allan Rogers about her play *The Private Life of Robert Louis Stevenson*
1974 Radio 4. *Kaleidescope. R. L. Stevenson* by James Pope Hennessy. David Daiches talks to Nigel Nicholson about the author and reviews the book
1975 Radio 4. Scotland. *Memories of R. L. Stevenson.* Recalled by Helen Barclay and Ethel Blair-Wilson to George Bruce

1976 Radio 3. *Interval Programmes.* Patricia Hughes reads extracts
1977 TV. BBC Scotland. *Schools Programme: Around Scotland. A Scottish Writer: R.L.S.* A biographical study written and produced by Tom Cotter
1977 Radio 4. *Kaleidescope. The Illustrated Robert Louis Stevenson* by Roy Gasson. Reviewed by Antonia Byatt
1977 Radio 4. *P.M. Reports. Penny Whistles* — a musical based on life of Stevenson. Interview by Rosalind Morris
1978 Radio 4. *Tusitala and Swift Cloud.* Portrait of Stevenson and his wife. Written and presented by June Knox-Mawer
1978 TV. BBC Scotland. *Spectrum. Another Child, Far, Far Away.* Autobiographical programme (also on *Schools Programme*)
1979 TV. BBC 2. *Penny Whistles of Robert Louis Stevenson.* A musical Evening with Mike Maran as Stevenson and David Sheppard as Thomas Stevenson, his father. Produced by David Rose (from Birmingham)
1979 TV. BBC Scotland. *Around Scotland. Read All about It.* David Daiches presents a literary quiz on R.L.S.
1979 Radio 4. *Round Midnight.* Richard Garrett writes and presents programme on Stevenson, born 129 years ago today (13 November)
1980 Radio 4. *Kaleidescope. R.L.S.: A Life Study* by Jenni Calder. Reviewed by Christopher Stace
1980 Radio 4. *Stevenson and Victorian Edinburgh.* Report by Jack Reagan who interviews Jenni Calder
1980 TV. BBC 2. *Great Railway Journeys of the World.* Part 1 of series. Ludovic Kennedy retraces journey of fellow-Scot R.L.S., on emigrant train from New Jersey to California in 1879. Director Gerry Troyna
1981 Radio 4. *Late Night Bookshelf.* Robert Louis Stevenson

## The Suicide Club

FILMS

1909 American Mutoscope Biograph Company (no details available)
1914 British and Colonial Kinematograph Company. Director Maurice Elvey. With Montagu Love, Fred Groves and Elizabeth Risdon
1933 (Title: *The Living Death.*) Germany. Director Richard Oswald. With Paul Wegener
1936 (US title: *Trouble for Two.*) Metro-Goldwyn-Mayer. Director J. Walter Ruben. With Robert Montgomery, Rosalind Russell, Reginald Owen, Frank Morgan, Louis Hayward, E.E. Clive and Walter Kingsford
1973 Universal Productions. With Joseph Haskell, Margot Kidder and Joseph Wiseman

RADIO
1937 Radio. National. Adapted by Ursula Branston
1966 Radio. Scotland. *The Young Man with the Cream Tarts*

**Thrawn Janet**
1950 Radio. Scotland. Read by Harold Wightman

**To S. R. Crockett** (letter)
1955 Radio. Light Programme. *Woman's Hour.* Quotation Club

**Travels With a Donkey in the Cévennes**
1954 Radio. Scotland and Northern Ireland. Prose and Verse
1955 Radio. Home Service. *May we Recommend?* Children's Hour
1957 Radio. Light Programme. *Before we Sleep*
1963 Radio. Scotland. *Late Night Bookshelf*
1964 Radio. Wales. Michael Vickers talks to Clive Critchley, leader of 5 Bristol students who intend to walk through the Cévennes with two donkeys following Stevenson's route
1966 Radio. All regions. *Home this Afternoon.* Travels with a Bicycle. Michael Gilliam interviews Fred Ablethorpe who followed the tracks of Stevenson and Modestine (the donkey)
1968 Radio. Scotland. Two-part drama
1969 Radio 4. *Story Time*
1978 TV. BBC 1. *Robert Louis Stevenson Pilgrimage* G. Touzeau walks with a donkey through Europe towards homeland of Stevenson
1979 TV. BBC 1 Scotland. *The Donkey that Walked into History.* Documentary tracing Stevenson's 1878 travels

**Treasure Island**
FILMS
1920 Paramount-Artcraft. Director Maurice Tourneur. With Charles Ogle, Shirley Mason and Josie Melville
1934 Metro-Golwyn-Mayer. Director Victor Fleming. With Wallace Beery, Jackie Cooper, Lionel Barrymore, Otto Kruger, Douglas Dumbrille, Nigel Bruce and Chic Sale
1950 RKO-Walt Disney. Director Byron Haskin. With Robert Newton, Bobby Driscoll, Basil Sydney, Denis O'Dea, Geoffrey Williamson and Ralph Truman
1971 Towes Production. Director John Hough. With Orson Welles, Kim Burfield, Walter Slezak, Lionel Standen, Paul Muller and Rik Battaglia
1971 Cartoon entitled *Dobutsu Takarajima* (Japan) Toei Company. Director Hiroshi Ikeda.
RADIO and TV
1936 Radio. National. Adapted by E. M. Delafield
1936 Radio. Regional. Adapted by Olive Dehn

1947 TV. Canadian Broadcasting Corporation. Adapted by Fletcher Markle
1950 Radio. Light Programme. Produced by Thurston Holland
1950 Radio. Scotland. *How Treasure Island came to be Written*. Script by E. J. B. Mace. Produced by James Crampsey
1951 TV. BBC 1. *For the Children*
1951 TV. BBC 1. Seven-part serial
1954 Radio. All regions. *Senior English I*. The Old Buccaneer and Treasure Island
1955 Radio. Scotland. *Scottish Heritage*. Serial
1956 Radio. Home Service. *May we Recommend?* Children's Hour
1956 Radio. All regions. *Senior English II*. Quotations
1957 Radio. All regions. *Out of Term*. Account of writing of *Treasure Island* in 1881
1957 TV. BBC 1. *For the Children*: The Old Buccaneer
1965 Radio. All regions. *Ideas in Education*. No.4. A Second Start: Children and Fiction. Extracts
1967 Radio. All regions. *Story Time*. Adapted by Aileen Mills. Serial in seven parts
1968 TV. BBC 1. *Billy Bones*. Telerecording film series
1969 TV. Canadian Broadcasting Corporation. Thirteen-week serial. Produced by Franco London Films in collaboration with CBC
1972 Radio 4. *Serial Reading for Children*. The Old Sea Dog at Admiral Benbow Inn
1972 Radio 4. *Readings for Children*. Treasure Trove
1972 Radio 4. *Christmas Afternoon Theatre*
1974 TV. New Zealand Television. Film
1976 Radio 4. *Kaleidoscope*
1977 TV. BBC 1. Four-part serial by John Lucarotti. With Alfred Lynch, Anthony Bate, Patrick Troughton, Jack Watson. Produced by Barry Letts
1981 TV. New Zealand Television. Serial
1981 Radio 4. Alanna Knight interviewed by Ken Bruce on the centenary of the writing of *Treasure Island* at Braemar

## The Treasure of Franchard
FILM
1952 Film. (Title: *Treasure of Lost Canyon*.) United Artists. Director Ted Tetzlaff. With William Powell, Julia Adams, Charles Drake, Rosemary de Camp, Henry Hull, Tommy Iva
RADIO
1972 Radio 4. *Sunday Theatre Series*. Dramatised by Ronald Hambleton

## The Vagabond (poem)
1955 Radio. Scotland. *St Andrew's Children*
1956 Radio. Scotland. *Party Pieces*

**Virginibus Puerisque**
1974 Radio 3. *For Better for Worse*. Richard Hurndall reads extracts, selected by April Cantelo

**Walking Tours** (essay)
1957 Radio. North and Northern Ireland. *In Praise of Walking*. Extracts from *Walking Tours*

**A Winter's Walk in Carrick and Galloway**
1978 Radio 3. *Interval Programmes*. Malcolm Ruthven reads during music interval from Pebble Mill

**Weir of Hermiston**
1935 Radio. Scottish Regional. Adapted by Halbert Talbot
1943 Radio. Scotland. Adapted by Moultrie Kelsall
1956 Radio. Scotland. *Arts Review — Theatre*
1957 Radio. Scotland. Adapted by R. J. B. Sellar
1957 Radio. Scotland. *Repertory in Britain*
1972 Radio 3. Music-Opera. Based on *Weir of Hermiston*. *Orbit*: Penny Craig interviews Robin Orr regarding preparation of his new opera
1973 TV. BBC 2. Serial. Adapted by Tom Wright
1975 Radio 3. *Hermiston*: An opera in three acts. Music by Robin Orr. Libretto by William Bryden
1977 TV. BBC 1 Scotland. Compilation of *Weir of Hermiston*

**The Wrecker**
1930 Radio. Daventry Experimental. Adapted by Michael Talbot

**The Wrong Box**
FILMS
1913 Solax (no details available)
1966 Salamander. Director Bryan Forbes. With John Mills, Sir Ralph Richardson, Michael Caine, Wilfred Lawson, Nanette Newman, Peter Cook, Dudley Moore, Tony Hancock, Peter Sellers, Thorley Walters, Cecily Courtneidge, Irene Handl, John le Mesurier, Gerald Sim, Norman Bird and Tutte Lemkov
RADIO
1959 Radio. Home Service. Play
1972 Radio 4. *Saturday Night Theatre*

## Part 7

# CLASSIFIED LIST OF STEVENSON'S PUBLISHED WORK

This list gives, in the case of books, the date of first publication only (with first magazine publication in brackets) but in the case of essays, short stories, etc., the date of first publication and the name of a collection or volume of the Tusitala Edition in which they subsequently appeared.

At the end is a list of volume numbers and titles of the Tusitala Edition, to which reference is made in Part 1.

NOVELS
   *Black Arrow, The*, 1888 (1883)
   *Catriona*, 1893 (1892–3)
   *Dr. Jekyll and Mr. Hyde, The Strange Case of*, 1886
   *Ebb-Tide, The* (in collaboration with Lloyd Osbourne), 1894 (1893–4)
   *Kidnapped*, 1886
   *Master of Ballantrae, The*, 1889 (1888–9)
   *Prince Otto*, 1885
   *St. Ives*, 1897 (1896–7)
   *Treasure Island*, 1883 (1881–2)
   *Weir of Hermiston*, 1896
   *Wrecker, The* (in collaboration with Lloyd Osbourne), 1892 (1891–2)
   *Wrong Box, The* (in collaboration with Lloyd Osbourne), 1889

SHORT STORY COLLECTIONS
   *Island Nights' Entertainments*, 1893
   *Merry Men and Other Tales, The*, 1887
   *More New Arabian Nights: The Dynamiter* (in collaboration with Mrs. R. L. Stevenson), 1885
   *New Arabian Nights*, 1882

SHORT STORIES
   Banker's Ward, The, 1866
   Beach of Falesá, The, 1892
   Body-Snatcher, The, 1884
   Bottle Imp, The, 1891
   Edifying Letters of the Rutherford Family, 1982
   Isle of Voices, The, 1893
   Lodging for the Night, A, 1877
   Markheim, 1886
   Merry Men, The, 1882
   Misadventures of John Nicholson, The, 1887

Object of Pity, An; or, The Man Haggard, 1900
Olalla, 1885
Old Song, An, 1877 (published anonymously: republished 1982)
Pavilion on the Links, The, 1880
Providence and the Guitar, 1878
Rajah's Diamond, The, 1878
Sire de Malétroit's Door, The, 1878
Story of a Lie, The, 1879
Suicide Club, The, 1878
Thrawn Janet, 1881
Treasure of Franchard, The, 1883
Waif Woman, The, 1914
When the Devil Was Well, 1921
Will o' the Mill, 1878

FABLES (1895–6)
Cart-Horses and the Saddle-Horse, The
Citizen and the Traveller, The
Devil and the Innkeeper, The
Distinguished Traveller, The
Faith, Half-Faith and No Faith at All
Four Reformers, The
House of Eld, The
Man and his Friend, The
Penitent, The
Persons of the Tale, The (published with *Treasure Island*)
Poor Thing, The
Reader, The
Sick Man and the Fireman, The
Sinking Ship, The
Something in It
Song of the Morrow, The
Tadpole and the Frog, The
Touchstone, The
Two Matches, The
Yellow Paint, The

FRAGMENTS (*Tusitala Edition 5 and 16*)
Adventures of Henry Shovel (1923)
Cannonmills (1923)
Diogenes at the Savile Club (1923)
Diogenes in London (1923)
Great North Road, The (1895)
Heathercat (1897)
Mr. Baskerville and His Ward (1923)

Owl, The (1923)
Story of a Recluse, The (1921)
Young Chevalier, The (1897)

## PLAYS

*Admiral Guinea* (in collaboration with W. E. Henley), 1892
*Beau Austin* (in collaboration with W. E. Henley), 1892
*Charity Bazaar, The* (an allegorical dialogue), 1898
*Deacon Brodie* (in collaboration with W. E. Henley), 1892
*Hanging Judge, The* (in collaboration with Mrs. R. L. Stevenson), 1922
*Macaire* (in collaboration with W. E. Henley), 1895
*Monmouth: A Tragedy* (incomplete: in collaboration with R. A. M. Stevenson), 1928

## COLLECTIONS OF POEMS (for individual poems, see Part 5)

*Ballads*, 1890
*Child's Garden of Verses, A*, 1885
*Moral Emblems*, 1898
*New Poems*, 1924
*Songs of Travel*, 1896
*Underwoods*, 1887

## TRAVEL

*Amateur Emigrant, The*, 1895
*Cèvennes Journal*, 1978
*Edinburgh: Picturesque Notes*, 1879
*Inland Voyage, An*, 1878
*In the South Seas*, 1890
*Our Samoan Adventure* (with Mrs. R. L. Stevenson), 1956
*Silverado Squatters, The*, 1883
*Travels with a Donkey in the Cèvennes*, 1879

## BIOGRAPHY

*Memoir of Fleeming Jenkin*, 1887
*Records of a Family of Engineers*, 1896

## LETTERS (see Part 4)

## COLLECTIONS OF ESSAYS

*Familiar Studies of Men and Books*, 1882
*Memories and Portraits*, 1887
*Virginibus Puerisque*, 1881

## ESSAYS AND BELLES-LETTRES

Address to the Samoan Chiefs, 1895
Address to the Samoan Students at Malua, 1901
Address to the Speculative Society, 1898

Aes Triplex, 1878 (*Virginibus Puerisque*)

Alpine Diversions, 1881 (*Tusitala Edition* 30)

Apology for Idlers, An, 1877 (*Virginibus Puerisque*)

Appeal to the Clergy of Scotland, An, 1875 (*Tusitala Edition 26*)

Autumn Effect, An, 1875 (*Tusitala Edition 30*)

Bagster's Pilgrim's Progress, 1882 (*Tusitala Edition 28*)

Ballads and Songs of Scotland, The, 1874 (*Tusitala Edition 28*)

Beggars, 1888 (*Tusitala Edition* 25)

Béranger, 1875 (*Tusitala Edition 28*)

Book of Joseph, The, 1923 (*Tusitala Edition 28*)

Books which have Influenced Me, 1887 (*Tusitala Edition 28*)

Byways of Book Illustration, 1882 (*Tusitala Edition 28*)

Chapter on Dreams, A, 1888 (*Tusitala Edition* 30)

Character, A, 1896. (*Tusitala Edition* 30)

Character of Dogs, The, 1884 (*Memories and Portraits*)

Charles of Orléans, 1876 (*Familiar Studies of Men and Books*)

Child's Play, 1878 (*Virginibus Puerisque*)

Christmas Sermon, A, 1888 (*Tusitala Edition 26*)

Coast of Fife, The, 1888 (*Tusitala Edition 30*)

Cockermouth and Keswick, 1896 (*Tusitala Edition 30*)

College for Men and Women, 1874 (*Tusitala Edition 28*)

College Magazine, A, 1887 (*Memories and Portraits*)

Crabbed Age and Youth, 1878 (*Virginibus Puerisque*)

Davos in Winter, 1881 (*Essays and Criticisms*)

Day after Tomorrow, The, 1887 (*Tusitala Edition 26*)

Debating Societies, 1871 (*Tusitala Edition* 25)

Edinburgh Students in 1824, 1871 (*Tusitala Edition* 25)

Education of an Engineer, The, 1888 (*Tusitala Edition 30*)

El Dorado, 1878 (*Virginibus Puerisque*)

English Admirals, The, 1878 (*Virginibus Puerisque*)

Ethics of Crime, The, 1923 (*Tusitala Edition 26*)

Father Damien, An Open Letter to the Rev. Dr. Hyde of Honolulu,
   1890 (*Tusitala Edition 21*)

Fielding and Richardson, 1924 (*Tusitala Edition 5*)

Fontainebleau, 1884 (*Tusitala Edition 30*)

Footnote to History, A: Eight Years of Trouble in Samoa, 1892
   (*Tusitala Edition 21*)

Foreigner at Home, The, 1882 (*Memories and Portraits*)

Forest Notes, 1876 (*Tusitala Edition 30*)

François Villon: Student, Poet and Housebreaker, 1877 (*Familiar
   Studies of Men and Books*)

French Legend, A, 1921 (*Tusitala Edition 25*)

Gentlemen, 1888 (*Tusitala Edition 26*)

Gossip on a Novel of Dumas's, A, 1887 (*Memories and Portraits*)

Gossip on Romance, A, 1882 (*Memories and Portraits*)

Grand Hotel Godam, 1928
Health and Mountains, 1881 (*Essays and Criticisms*)
Henry David Thoreau, 1880 (*Familiar Studies of Men and Books*)
History of Moses, 1923 (*Tusitala Edition 28*)
Humble Remonstrance, A, 1884 (*Memories and Portraits*)
Ideal House, The, 1898 (*Tusitala Edition 25*)
In the Latin Quarter. No. I — A Ball at Mr. Elsinare's, 1877
In the Latin Quarter. No. II — A Studio of Ladies, 1877
John Knox and his Relations to Women, 1875 (*Familiar Studies of Men and Books*)
John Knox and the Almoner of the Galley, 1924 (*Tusitala Edition 5*)
Journal written aboard the *Pharos*, 1899
Judge Jeffries, 1924 (*Tusitala Edition 5*)
Jules Verne's Stories, 1876 (*Tusitala Edition 28*)
Lantern Bearers, The, 1888 (*Tusitala Edition 30*)
Late Sam Bough, The, 1878 (*Tusitala Edition 28*)
Laurence Sterne, 1924 (*Tusitala Edition 5*)
Lay Morals, 1896 (*Tusitala Edition 26*)
Letter to a Young Gentleman who Proposes to Embrace a Career of Art, 1888 (*Tusitala Edition 28*)
Letters to *The Times, The Athenaeum, Pall Mall Gazette*, etc. 1889–94 (*Tusitala Edition 21*)
Local Conditions Influencing Climate, 1873
Manse, The, 1887 (*Memories and Portraits*)
Measure of a Marquis, 1875
Memoirs of an Islet, 1887 (*Memories and Portraits*)
Memoirs of Himself, 1914 (*Tusitala Edition 29*)
Misgivings of Convalescence, 1881
Missions in the South Seas, 1893
Mr. Browning Again!, 1875
Mr. Tennyson's 'Harold', 1877
Mock Trial, A, 1968
Modern Student Considered Generally, The, 1871 (*Tusitala Edition 25*)
Monterey, 1880 (*The Old and New Pacific Capitals*)
Morality of the Profession of Letters, The, 1881 (*Tusitala Edition 28*)
Mountain Town in France, A, 1896–7 (*Travels with a Donkey*)
My First Book. Preface to *Treasure Island*, 1894
Night in France, A, 1921 (*Tusitala Edition 30*)
Noctes Ambrosianae, 1876 (*Tusitala Edition 28*)
Note at Sea, A, 1921 (*Tusitala Edition 30*)
Note on Realism, A, 1883 (*Tusitala Edition 28*)
Notes on the Movements of Young Children, 1874 (*Tusitala Edition 25*)
Nuits Blanches, 1896 (*Tusitala Edition 30*)
Nurses, 1896 (*Tusitala Edition 30*)
Old Mortality, 1884 (*Memories and Portraits*)

Old Scots Gardener, An, 1871 (*Memories and Portraits*)
On a New Form of Intermittent Light for Lighthouses, 1871 (*Tusitala Edition 28*)
On Falling in Love, 1877 (*Virginibus Puerisque*)
On Lord Lytton's *Fables in Song*, 1874 (*Tusitala Edition 28*)
On Morality, 1923 (*Tusitala Edition 26*)
On Some Technical Elements of Style in Literature, 1885 (*Tusitala Edition 28*)
On the Choice of a Profession, 1915 (*Tusitala Edition 28*)
On the Enjoyment of Unpleasant Places, 1874 (*Tusitala Edition 25*)
On the Thermal Influence of Forests, 1875 (*Tusitala Edition 28*)
Ordered South, 1874 (*Virginibus Puerisque*)
Our City Men. No. I — A Salt-Water Financier, 1877
Pan's Pipes, 1878 (*Virginibus Puerisque*)
Paris Bourse, The, 1877
Pastoral, 1887 (*Memories and Portraits*)
Penny Plain and Twopence Coloured, A, 1884 (*Memories and Portraits*)
Pentland Rising, The, 1924 (*Tusitala Edition 28*)
Philosophy of Nomenclature, The, 1871 (*Tusitala Edition 25*)
Philosophy of Umbrellas, The, 1871 (*Tusitala Edition 25*)
Plea for Gas Lamps, A, 1878 (*Virginibus Puerisque*)
Poets and Poetry of Scotland, The, 1876 (*Tusitala Edition 28*)
Popular Authors, 1888 (*Tusitala Edition 28*)
Prayers written for Family Use at Vailima, 1896 (*Tusitala Edition 21*)
Protest on behalf of Boer Independence, 1921 (*Tusitala Edition 28*)
Pulvis et Umbra, 1888 (*Tusitala Edition 26*)
Quiet Corner of England, A, 1874 (*Tusitala Edition 28*)
Reflections and Remarks on Human Life, 1898 (*Tusitala Edition 26*)
Reminiscences of Colinton Manse, 1901
Retrospect, A, 1896 (*Tusitala Edition 30*)
Reviews of 'Shamrock and Rose,' 'Kilcorran', 'Mottiscliffe', 'Against Her Will', 1877 (*Tusitala Edition 28*)
Roads, 1873 (*Tusitala Edition 25*)
Robert Burns, 1924 (*Tusitala Edition 5*)
Rosa Quo Locorum, 1896 (*Tusitala Edition 30*)
St. Athanasius, 1924 (*Tusitala Edition 5*)
Salvini's *Macbeth*, 1876 (*Tusitala Edition 28*)
Samuel Pepys, 1881 (*Familiar Studies of Men and Books*)
San Carlos Day, 1879
San Francisco, 1883 (*The Old and New Pacific Capitals*)
Satirist, The, 1896 (*Tusitala Edition 30*)
Scott's Voyage on the Lighthouse Yacht, 1893
Scottish Rivers, 1874 (*Tusitala Edition 28*)
Selections from his Notebook, 1923 (*Tusitala Edition 29*)
Some Aspects of Robert Burns, 1879 (*Familiar Studies of Men and Books*)

Some College Memories, 1887 (*Memories and Portraits*)
Some Gentlemen in Fiction, 1888 (*Tusitala Edition 26*)
Some Portraits by Raeburn, 1881 (*Virginibus Puerisque*)
Stevenson at Play — War Correspondence from Stevenson's
   Notebook, 1898 (*Tusitala Edition 30*)
Stimulation of the Alps, The, 1881 (*Essays and Criticisms*)
Talk and Talkers, 1882 (*Memories and Portraits*)
Thomas Stevenson, 1887 (*Memories and Portraits*)
Time, 1923 (*Tusitala Edition 25*)
Truth of Intercourse, The, 1879 (*Virginibus Puerisque*)
Tutuila, 1921 (*Tusitala Edition 21*)
Two Tahitian Legends, 1892
Victor Hugo's Romances, 1874 (*Familiar Studies of Men and Books*)
Virginibus Puerisque, 1876 (*Virginibus Puerisque*)
Walking Tours, 1876 (*Virginibus Puerisque*)
Wallace's Russia, 1877
Walt Whitman, 1878 (*Familiar Studies of Men and Books*)
Wellington, 1923 (*Tusitala Edition 28*)
Winter's Walk in Carrick and Galloway, A, 1896 (*Tusitala Edition 30*)
Works of Edgar Allan Poe, The, 1875 (*Tusitala Edition 28*)
Wreath of Immortelles, The, 1896 (*Tusitala Edition 30*)
Yoshida-Torajiro, 1880 (*Familiar Studies of Men and Books*)


## TUSITALA EDITION

Volume numbers and titles of the most popular collection of Stevenson's works, published in 1924:

Vol. No.  1.  New Arabian Nights
          2.  Treasure Island
          3.  The Dynamiter
          4.  Prince Otto
          5.  Dr. Jekyll & Mr. Hyde
              Fables & other Stories & Fragments
          6.  Kidnapped
          7.  Catriona
          8.  The Merry Men & other Tales
          9.  The Black Arrow
         10.  The Master of Ballantrae
         11.  The Wrong Box
              The Body-Snatcher
         12.  The Wrecker
         13.  Island Nights' Entertainments
              The Misadventures of John Nicholson

14. The Ebb-Tide
    The Story of a Lie
15. St. Ives
16. Weir of Hermiston
    Some Unfinished Stories
17. An Inland Voyage
    Travels with a Donkey
18. The Amateur Emigrant
    The Silverado Squatters
19. Memoir of Fleeming Jenkin
    Records of a Family of Engineers
20. In the South Seas
21. Vailima Papers
22. Poems Vol. I
23. Poems Vol. II
24. Plays
25. Virginibus Puerisque & other Essays in Belles Lettres
26. Ethical Studies
    Edinburgh: Picturesque Notes
27. Familiar Studies of Men & Books
28. Essays Literary and Critical
29. Memories and Portraits & other Fragments
30. Further Memories
31. Letters Vol. I (November 1863-July 1875)
32. Letters Vol. II (July 1875-July 1884)
33. Letters Vol. III (September 1884-September 1890)
34. Letters Vol. IV (November 1890-December 1892)
35. Letters Vol. V (January 1893-December 1894)

# Part 8
# FURTHER READING

The books and articles set out in Part 1 constitute a substantial reading list; for further study of Stevenson, the following bibliographic works would be particularly helpful:

Prideaux, W.F. *A Bibliography of the Works of Robert Louis Stevenson*, Hollings, London and Scribner's, New York 1917.
McKay, George L. *The Stevenson Library of the Edwin J. Beinecke Collection*, 6 vols., Yale University Press, New Haven, CT, 1964.
Swearingen, Roger C. *The Prose Writings of Robert Louis Stevenson: A Guide*, Macmillan, London 1980.
Maixner, Paul (ed.) *Robert Louis Stevenson: The Critical Heritage*, Routledge & Kegan Paul, London 1981.

The following is a personal selection of biographies and general works recommended to the reader. Most of these titles and many of the works mentioned in Part 1 are available for reference in the Edinburgh Room of the Edinburgh Central Library. Its collection of Stevensoniana is outstanding and includes historical photographs, transparencies, and translations. Other large collections of material, including unpublished manuscripts, are to be found in the National Library of Scotland, George IV Bridge, and in the Lady Stair's House Museum, Lawnmarket, Edinburgh.

Balfour, Graham *The Life of Robert Louis Stevenson* (official first biography) 2 vols, Methuen, London 1901
Booth, Bradford A. *Selected Poetry and Prose of Robert Louis Stevenson*, HM Press, New York 1968
Calder, Jenni (ed.) *The Robert Louis Stevenson Companion*, Paul Harris, Edinburgh 1980; *R.L.S.: A Life Study*, Hamish Hamilton, London 1980; (ed.) *Stevenson and Victorian Edinburgh*, Edinburgh University Press 1981.
Campbell, Ian (ed.) *Selected Short Stories of R.L. Stevenson*, Ramsay Head Press, Edinburgh 1980.
Chesterton, Gilbert Keith *Robert Louis Stevenson*, Hodder & Stoughton, London 1927.
Colvin, Sidney *Memories and Notes of Persons and Places, 1852–1914*, Arnold, London 1921.

Daiches, David *Robert Louis Stevenson*, William MacLellan, Glasgow 1947; *Stevenson and the Art of Fiction*, Folcroft, New York 1951; *Robert Louis Stevenson and His World*, Thames & Hudson, London 1973.

Day, A. Grove (ed.) *Travels in Hawaii*, University Press of Hawaii, Honolulu 1973.

Eaton, Charlotte *Stevenson at Manasquan, Queen's Quarterly*, 1931.

Elwin, Malcolm *The Strange Case of Robert Louis Stevenson*, Macdonald, London 1950

Field, Isobel Osbourne Strong *This Life I've Loved*, Michael Joseph, London 1937.

Fletcher, C. Brunsdon *Stevenson's Germany: The Case against Germany in the Pacific*, Heinemann, London 1920.

Furnas, J.C. *Voyage to Windward*, Faber & Faber, London 1952.

Genung, John F. *Stevenson's Attitude to Life*, Thomas Y. Crowell, New York 1901.

Gibson, John S. *Deacon Brodie: Father to Jekyll & Hyde*, Paul Harris, Edinburgh 1977.

Hammerton, J.A. *Stevensoniana, An Anecdotal Life and Appreciation of Robert Louis Stevenson*, John Grant, Edinburgh 1910.

Hellman, George S. *The True Stevenson, A Study in Clarification*, Little, Brown & Co., Boston 1925.

Issler, Anne Roller *Stevenson in Silverado*, Caxton Printers, Caldwell, ID 1939.

Knight, Alanna *The Passionate Kindness, The Love Story of Robert Louis Stevenson and Fanny Osbourne*, Milton House Books, Aylesbury, 1974.

Low, Will H. *A Chronicle of Friendships, 1873–1900*, Hodder & Stoughton, London 1908.

McGaw, Sister Martha Mary *Stevenson in Hawaii*, University of Hawaii Press, Honolulu 1950.

Mackay, Margaret *The Violent Friend: The Story of Mrs. Robert Louis Stevenson*, Doubleday, New York 1968; Dent, London 1969.

McLaren, Moray *Stevenson and Edinburgh*, Chapman & Hall, London and Folcroft, New York 1950.

Mair, Craig *A Star for Seamen: The Stevenson Family of Engineers*, John Murray, London 1978.

Masson, Rosaline (ed.) *I Can Remember Robert Louis Stevenson*, Chambers, London and Edinburgh 1922.

Mrantz, Maxine *R.L. Stevenson: Poet in Paradise*, Aloha Graphics, Honolulu 1977.

Osbourne, Lloyd *An Intimate Portrait of Robert Louis Stevenson*, Scribner's, New York 1924.

Rice, Richard Ashley *Robert Louis Stevenson: How to Know Him*, Bobbs-Merrill, Indianapolis, n.d.

Ricklefs, Roger *The Mind of Robert Louis Stevenson*, Arno Press, New York 1962.

Smith, Janet Adam (ed.) *Henry James and Robert Louis Stevenson: A Record of Friendship and Criticism*, Hart-Davis, London 1948.

Stern, G.B. *Robert Louis Stevenson: Writers and their Work*, Longmans, London, n.d.

Stevenson, Fanny Van de Grift and Robert Louis *Our Samoan Adventure*, Weidenfeld and Nicolson, London 1956.

Stevenson, Margaret Isabella Balfour *From Saranac to the Marquesas and Beyond*, Methuen, London 1903.

Stubbs, Laura *Stevenson's Shrine: The Record of a Pilgrimage*, Alexander Moring, London 1903.

# Across the Plains

Calistoga
Napa
Reno
Elko
Ogden

*Wyoming*

*Nebraska*

Sacramento
Oakland
*Nevada*
Salt Lake City
Laramie
Cheyenne

San Francisco
Monterey
*Utah*
Denver •

*California*

• Los Angeles

The first South Seas voyage
started from San Francisco
— in June, 1888 —

• O

PACIFIC
OCEAN

Hou

M E X I C O